WOMEN
IN THE
CLASSICAL
WORLD

WOMEN IN THE CLASSICAL WORLD

Image and Text

Elaine Fantham
Helene Peet Foley
Natalie Boymel Kampen
Sarah B. Pomeroy
H. A. Shapiro

New York   Oxford
OXFORD UNIVERSITY PRESS
1994

Oxford University Press

Oxford   New York   Toronto
Delhi   Bombay   Calcutta   Madras   Karachi
Kuala Lumpur   Singapore   Hong Kong   Tokyo
Nairobi   Dar es Salaam   Cape Town
Melbourne   Auckland   Madrid

and associated companies in
Berlin   Ibadan

Published by Oxford University Press, Inc.
200 Madison Avenue, New York, New York 10016

Oxford is a registered trademark of Oxford University Press

Library of Congress Cataloging-in-Publication Data
Women in the classical world : image and text /
Elaine Fantham . . . et al.
p. cm.
Includes bibliographical references and index.
ISBN 0-19-506727-4
1. Women—History—To 500—Sources.
2. Women—Greece—History—Sources.
3. Women—Rome—History—Sources.
I. Fantham, Elaine.
HQ1127.W652   1994   305.4'09—dc20   92-47284

2 4 6 8 9 7 5 3 1

Printed in the United States of America
on acid-free paper

ACKNOWLEDGMENTS

For permission to reprint copyrighted material, grateful acknowledgment is made to the following sources:

Bantam Books: From *The Aeneid of Virgil* by Allen Mandelbaum. Translation copyright © 1971 by Allen Mandelbaum.

Cambridge University Press: From *The Hellenistic Age from the Battle of Ipsos to the Death of Kleopatra VII* (1985), edited and translated by Stanley Burstein. From *Theocritus*, vol. 1 (1965), translated by A. S. F. Gow. From *Herodas: The Mimes and Fragments* (1966), edited by Walter Headlam and A. D. Knox. From *Herophilus: The Art of Medicine in Early Alexandria* (1989), edited and translated by Heinrich von Staden.

Cornell University Press: From *Galen: On the Usefulness of the Parts of the Body*, vol. 2, translated from the Greek with an introduction and commentary by Margaret Tallmadge May. Copyright © 1968 by Cornell University.

Gerald Duckworth and Co.: From *Women's Life in Greece and Rome* (1982) by M. R. Lefkowitz and M. B. Fant. Published in the United States by Johns Hopkins University Press.

HarperCollins Publishers: From *The Odyssey of Homer*, translated by Richmond Lattimore. Copyright © 1965, 1967 by Richmond Lattimore.

Harvard University Press and the Loeb Classical Library: From *Xenophon*, vol. 7 (1925, 1968), translated by G. W. Bowersock. From *Athenaeus*, vol. 6 (1917, 1955), translated by C. B. Gulick. From *Select Papyri*, vol. 1 (1932, 1970), vol. 2 (1934, 1963), translated by A. S. Hunt, and vol. 3 (1941, 1970), translated by D. L. Page. From *Hippocrates*, vol. 1 (1923, 1972), vol. 4 (1931, 1967), translated by W. H. S. Jones. From *Lysias* (1930, 1960), translated by W. R. M. Lamb. From *Aristotle: Generation of Animals*, vol. 13 (1942, 1979), translated by A. L. Peck. From *Plutarch's Lives*, vol. 1 (1914, 1967), vol. 3 (1916, 1967), vol. 9 (1920, 1968), translated by B. Perrin.

Indiana University Press: From *The Poems of Propertius* (1963), translated by Constance Carrier.

Johns Hopkins University Press: From *Women's Life in Greece and Rome* (1982) by M. R. Lefkowitz and M. B. Fant. From *Callimachus: Hymns*,

Epigrams, Selected Fragments (1988), translated by Stanley Lombardo and Diane Rayor. From *The Poems of Catullus* (1990), translated by Charles Martin. From *Soranus' Gynecology* (1956), translated by Owsei Temkin.

Macmillan Publishing Company: From *The Poems of Propertius*, translated by John Warden. Copyright © 1972 by Macmillan Publishing Company.

Penguin Books: From *The Erotic Poems* by Ovid (Penguin Classics 1982), translated by Peter Green. Copyright © Peter Green, 1982. From *The Republic* by Plato (Penguin Classics, second revised edition 1987), translated by Desmond Lee. Copyright © H. D. P. Lee, 1953, 1974, 1987. From *The Rise and Fall of the Roman Empire* by Polybius (Penguin Classics 1979), translated by Ian Scott-Kilvert. Copyright © Ian Scott-Kilvert, 1979. From *The Politics* by Aristotle (Penguin Classics 1962, revised edition 1981), translated by T. A. Sinclair, revised by Trevor J. Saunders. 1962 translation copyright © the Estate of T. A. Sinclair. Revised translation copyright © Trevor J. Saunders, 1981. From *The Early History of Rome* by Livy (Penguin Classics 1960), translated by Aubrey de Sélincourt. Copyright © the Estate of Aubrey de Sélincourt. From *Plutarch on Sparta* (Penguin Classics 1988), translated by Richard J. A. Talbert. Copyright © Richard J. A. Talbert, 1988.

Princeton University Press: From *The Complete Works of Aristotle* (1984), edited by Jonathan Barnes.

Ennis Rees: From *The Iliad of Homer*, translated by Ennis Rees. Copyright © 1963, 1991 by Ennis Rees.

Routledge: From *The Games of Venus* (1991), translated by P. Bing and R. Cohen.

Scholars Press: From *Greek Historical Documents: The Hellenistic Period* (1981), translated by Roger S. Bagnal and Peter Derow.

Southern Illinois University Press: From *The Woman and the Lyre: Women Writers in Classical Greece and Rome* (1989), translated by Jane McIntosh Snyder.

University of California Press: From *Sappho's Lyre: Archaic Lyric and Women Poets of Ancient Greece*, translated by Diane Rayor. Copyright © 1991 by Diane Rayor.

University of Chicago Press: From *Greek Lyrics*, translated by Richmond Lattimore. Copyright © 1949, 1960 by the University of Chicago.

University of North Carolina Press: From *The Poems of Theocritus*, translated and edited by Anna Rist. Copyright © The University of North Carolina Press, 1978.

University of Oklahoma Press: From *The Poems of Hesiod*, translated by R. M. Frazer. Copyright © 1983 by the University of Oklahoma Press.

PREFACE

The purpose of this book is to gather the most important primary sources, both written and visual, for the lives of ancient women, and to present them within their historical and cultural context. This is the first sourcebook organized in a chronological framework that allows the changing roles of women to unfold in their proper historical sequence. It is also the first sourcebook in classical studies to give equal weight to artistic representations and to written texts, and not to use photographs as mere illustrations of what is already known from the written texts. This book is not intended to serve as a comprehensive introduction to the subject of women in classical antiquity, but should be used in conjunction with a social history text such as Sarah B. Pomeroy's *Goddesses, Whores, Wives, and Slaves: Women in Classical Antiquity* (New York, 1975).

The arrangement of the book is both diachronic and synchronic. We have organized the chapters to provide a sense of the development of ancient societies and the changing social conditions that relate to the roles, status, and images of women. The chapters follow the usual chronological divisions of ancient history (see the introductions to "Women in the Greek World" and "Women in the Roman World"). Although much interesting work is now being done on religion and society in the Minoan-Mycenaean Age (ca. 1500–1200 b.c.e.), we have decided to begin with the historical period in Greece, in the late eighth century b.c.e., the first period for which both written texts and archaeological evidence are available. Similarly, we have chosen to end with the later Roman Empire and not to deal with the Early Christian period, when many new issues relating to the role of women arose.

The excursuses are devised to present special or "deviant" aspects of women in the ancient world: for example, the "deviant" aspects of Spartan women, Amazons, and Etruscans, products of male fear and fantasy and distorted perceptions of "the other;" the changing views of the female body presented in male-authored gynecological treatises; the "new woman" represented by the love poetry of the late Republic and Augustan Age, emancipated and outside respectable society; and upper- and lower-class life in Pompeii, everyday and ordinary, but unique in historical preservation.

Bits of information about women are scattered throughout the fragmented mosaic of ancient history. Our intention was not to include a welter of unrelated, fragmentary sources in each chapter and excursus, but rather to highlight particular themes such as women's creativity, sexuality, and experience in marriage, and to select documents and images relevant to these themes. We thought it important to include such famous women as Aspasia, Cleopatra VII, and Lucretia, who have captured the imaginations of later audiences, but we have declined to discuss goddesses and purely mythical females, except insofar as mortal women were involved in their cults or were affected by their imagery. We have also endeavored to discuss contradictions generated by the presentation of material from different genres that were produced over a thousand-year period, and the historiographic and methodological problems that the various pieces of evidence pose. We have tried to create an independent narrative in which the texts are allowed to speak for themselves, but within a setting that guides the reader and frames the most important issues.

The book was written in a collaborative mode; we thought that this was the best way to approach the different types of evidence relating to women in antiquity. The first draft of each chapter in the Greek section was written by at least two of the authors. The other authors commented on each draft of the entire manuscript. In some cases, a third author took responsibility for writing a subsequent draft. Alan Shapiro, Sarah B. Pomeroy, and Helene P. Foley were the principal authors of the chapters and excursuses on Greek women; Natalie B. Kampen and Elaine Fantham were responsible for most of the Roman material.

Historically, this book evolved from a much larger collaborative effort. Four of the five authors directed or participated in the National Endowment for the Humanities Summer Institute on "Women in Classical Antiquity" at Hunter College in 1983. Together with other participants, we wrote "Women in Classical Antiquity: Four Curricular Modules." We distributed more than two thousand copies of that pamphlet to scholars and teachers in North America, Australia, and Europe who requested it. This document was, in large part, the basis for the organization and content of the present book, and the book responds to a need expressed by many readers of the modules. We would like to thank the participants in the institute and the readers of the curriculum modules for their help.

We are grateful to David Castriota and Barbara McManus for their comments on the manuscript, to Lesley Dean-Jones for writing the excursus on Greek medicine, and to Larissa Bonfante for writing the excursus on Etruscan women.

We thank our editors at Oxford University Press, Rachel Toor who initiated the project, Angela Blackburn and Robert Dilworth who kindly saw it to completion, and Susan Hannan, whose help throughout was invaluable; Hedda Garza did the index in good time and with admirable thoroughness.

We are also grateful to Ingrid Muan of the Department of Art History and Archaeology at Columbia University, who checked references and credits with a patience and enduring good humor that boggles the mind; she also provided some of the photography.

To our kin and friends, as always, we owe our thanks, and to one another for being wonderful to work with. We dedicate this book to the fine women who pioneered in the fields of ancient history, classics, art history, and archaeology without whom our work, and our participation in these fields, would be unlikely at best!

New York   E. F.
Princeton   H. P. F.
January 1993   N. B. K.
                                                                              S. B. P.
                                                                              H. A. S.

CONTENTS

I
WOMEN IN
THE GREEK WORLD

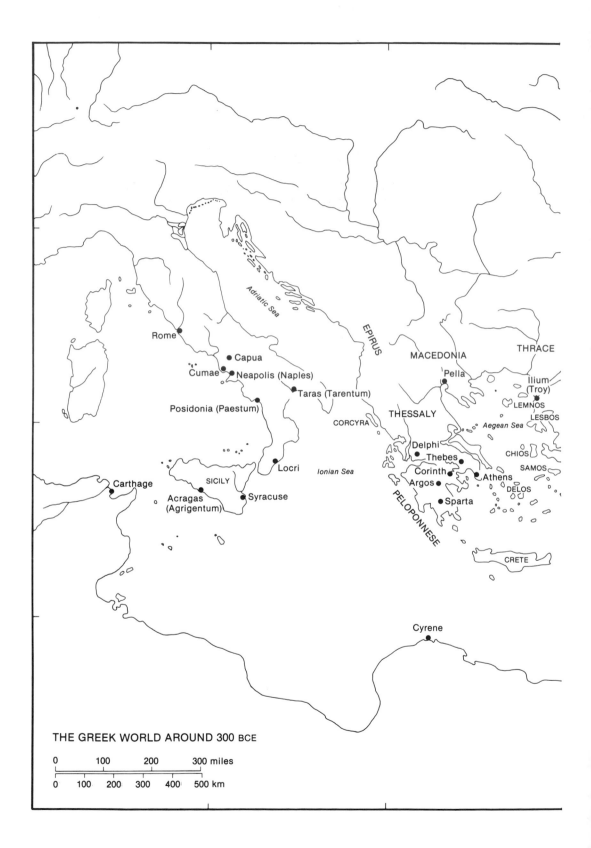

Rome

Capua

Cumae

Neapolis (Naples)

Taras (Tarentum)

Posidonia (Paestum)

Adriatic Sea

EPIRUS

MACEDONIA

THRACE

Pella

Ilium
(Troy)

LEMNOS

LESBOS

Aegean Sea

THESSALY

CORCYRA

Delphi

Thebes

CHIOS

Corinth

Athens

SAMOS

Argos

DELOS

Sparta

Ionian Sea

Locri

Carthage

SICILY

Syracuse

Acragas
(Agrigentum)

PELOPONNESE

CRETE

Cyrene

THE GREEK WORLD AROUND 300 BCE

| 0 | 100 | 200 | 300 miles |

| 0 | 100 | 200 | 300 | 400 | 500 km |

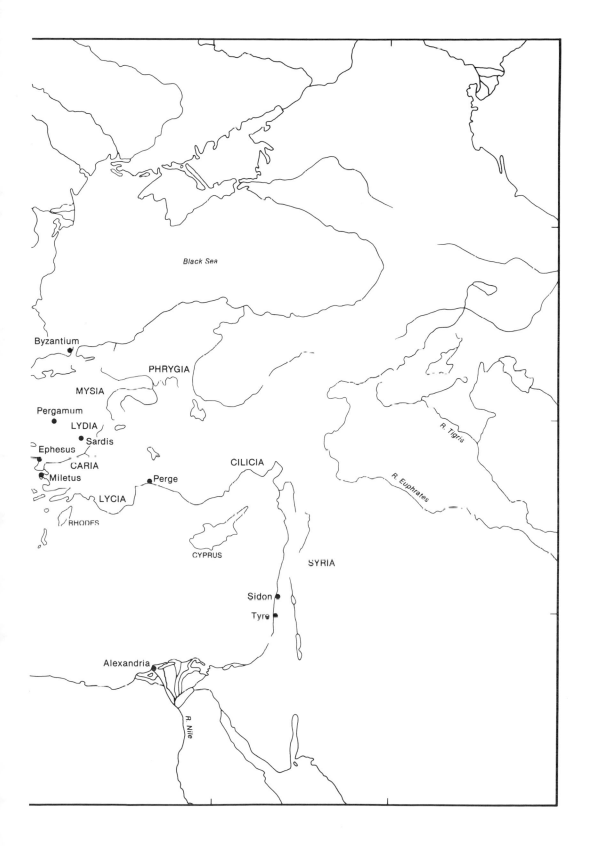

Black Sea

Byzantium

PHRYGIA

MYSIA

Pergamum

LYDIA

Sardis

Ephesus

CARIA

Miletus

Perge

CILICIA

R. Tigris

R. Euphrates

LYCIA

RHODES

CYPRUS

SYRIA

Sidon

Tyre

Alexandria

R. Nile

Mnesarete, daughter of Socrates.

This woman left a husband and siblings, and grief to her mother,
and a child and an ageless renown for great virtue *(aretê)*.

Here the chamber of Persephone holds Mnesarete,
who has arrived at the goal of all virtue *(aretê)*.

Inscriptiones Graecae II/III[2]
[(Ed. J. Kirchner, 1916–1935, Berlin) = W. Peek,
Griechische Vers-Inschriften 1962 (Berlin, 1955)]

This epigram celebrates the life of an early fourth-century
B.C.E. Athenian woman, Mnesarete, who has lived up to the
promise of her name, which means "remembering *(mnes-)* virtue
or excellence *(aretê)*." The poem balances the sorrow that she
has left to her husband, siblings (the word *adelphoi*, which ordi-
narily means brothers, includes sisters in some cases), and above
all to her mother against her imperishable reputation for great
virtue. In the presence of the goddess of the underworld Persephone, Mnesarete will continue to receive divine honor in the
world of death. The marble grave stele on which this epigram
appears (Fig. 1) shows the dead Mnesarete seated on the right,
her head bowed in mourning and her left arm wrapped in her
mantle. On the left she is observed by a standing (and probably
still living) young woman dressed in a thin chiton with long
sleeves. The identity of this second woman is uncertain; various
scholars have suggested that she is the daughter, younger sister,
or less probably the slave of Mnesarete, who apparently contem-
plates and absorbs this example of deathless womanly achievement. Both the poem and the physical beauty of the monument,
with its graceful curved and vertical lines and its moving composition, aim to create a permanent testimony to the excellence of
a woman who still links her natal and marital family in grief and
admiration.

    This stele is one of the best preserved of its type: many are
fragmentary, inscriptions lost or obliterated. It preserves not only
the full epigram, but also two names neatly carved on a ledge
above the epigram, that of Mnesarete herself and of her father,

Figure 1. Marble stele of Mnesarete. Attic (Early 4th century B.C.E.).

Socrates. The use of the patronymic, long after Mnesarete's marriage and the death of her father (he is not mentioned as alive in
the epigram), suggests that a woman was thought to belong to
her natal family, and especially to her father, throughout her life.

Socrates was a common name in Athens (Mnesarete's father must have been a close contemporary of the famous philosopher), and this man is not known from other sources, but sometimes such inscriptions help us to reconstruct the family tree of a woman who would otherwise be unknown to us. This was obviously an affluent family, judging from the large size of the monument (about five feet in height) and the high quality of the carving. The stele is said to have been found in the Attic countryside, in an area where several prominent Athenian families are known to have owned property. Such rural cemeteries have yielded some of the most impressive archaic and classical grave monuments (see Chapter 1).

Although this book aims to bring together visual, written, and archaeological evidence for the lives of ancient women, history rarely provides us, as in this case, with all three in conjunction. Normally we are left with even less substantial fragments, mute unnamed images without precise historical provenance, tantalizing passing references in works that do not make the lives and concerns of women their central area of investigation, or named women who play a role in the imaginary creations of artists and poets that may bear only an oblique or distorted relation to the lives of actual women in Archaic, Classical, or Hellenistic Greece. Even a relatively undamaged grave monument such as this one may be deceptive and leave us with difficult questions that go far beyond the identity of the standing woman and her function on the monument.

To read it properly we would need to know, for example, what virtues brought a woman renown in Classical Athens. Paradoxically, our other sources suggest that the virtues for which Mnesarete receives eternal public recognition in death would in life have been known only to her family and probably to some women friends, and that her name would not have been publicly announced while she was alive. Ideally, every man in the Classical period spent his life aiming to establish a permanent honorable reputation for himself and his city. But his relatively secluded wife avoided a public reputation and turned her energies above all to familial concerns, to producing children and to caring for her household. Yet the same monument, if it were dated to another time or place in the Greek world, might hint at greater public recognition of a living wife's virtues. We know that a girl who died a virgin was often said to become a symbolic "bride of Hades," lord of the underworld, and thus to acquire in death the marriage that would have given full meaning to her life. It is more difficult to interpret Persephone's welcoming reception of the virtuous, married mother Mnesarete. Was Mnesarete to be recognized for her excellence by Persephone, who in one myth at least, was said to have sent the noble queen Alcestis back to the upperworld in admiration for her courage in dying for her husband? Or was she, perhaps, guaranteed this reception through her initiation into the Eleusinian Mysteries, which promised the initiate a better life in the world below? The grief that Mnesarete bequeathes to her mother in particular reflects the generic sorrow felt by parents who live to mourn a child and perhaps in addition the special role that Greek women had in mourning the dead.

Women were often represented on grave monuments with the child (above all, the male child—here the word *teknon* does not allow us to specify the child's sex) who signified a fulfilled life; if the young woman on this monument, however, is not Mnesarete's daughter or sister or a female slave, we have no way of knowing why she is there. Perhaps the family chose a ready-made design that does not accurately reflect this particular woman's case (the scheme of seated woman and standing attendant occurs often on gravestones [see Fig. 3.1], and this particular design reappears elsewhere). Nevertheless, it seems possible that image and epigram were designed to complement each other, and that Mnesarete is indeed meant to serve as a model for a younger, unmarried woman (such as a sister or daughter) who has not yet reached the goal of a woman's life.

The monument suggests how visual and written evidence can reinforce each other (if we had found the offerings and grave goods in her tomb, or, as is less likely, the physical remains of Mnesarete herself, yet another piece could have been added to the puzzle) and how carefully we must use our nevertheless fragmentary knowledge from other sources to interpret its possible meaning. By contextualizing as much as possible the visual, physical, and written evidence for women in the Greek world from the eighth through the first centuries B.C.E., and by considering what problems and questions our sources present, we aim to provide the groundwork for a study of women in this period. We are concerned as much with the poet's, prose writer's, or artist's image of women as with reconstructing "reality," and we have tried to present our material in the context of a narrative that stresses what we believe are the issues concerning women that are central to each of three shorter periods within this larger time-span.

In Chapter 1 (the Archaic period, late eighth–early fifth centuries B.C.E.), for example, we have little more than poetry, sculpture, and vase painting scattered over the whole Greek world to examine. Hence we chose to emphasize what sources throughout the Greek world aimed to praise or blame all women, and to examine how these texts and monuments represented the major phases of a generic (and above all aristocratic) woman's passage through life. All the Greek excurses (Chapters 2, 4, and 6) present material from all three of our historical periods. Chapter 2 uses evidence that begins in the Archaic period in order to offer a more detailed picture of women in the changing context of a particular, important Greek city-state, Sparta, which differs considerably from our next focus of concern, Classical Athens.

In the Classical period (early fifth–late fourth centuries B.C.E.) we have concentrated on Athens, in large part because it is the city-state about which we know the most. Legislation that began to be passed in the Archaic period and continued into the Classical period apparently aimed to control family life and the relation of public to private life in Athens far more precisely than before. We have organized our often highly tendentious and contradictory evidence on women's lives in the light of the historical transition to democracy and the social and ideological changes that accompanied it. Chapter 4 explores the way that representations of the mythical Amazons served in part to define by inversion the proper role of Athenian women. Whereas Athenian women took no part in war and politics and served to reproduce children of their husbands' lineage, Amazons rejected marriage and domesticity, perpetuated their line through female children, engaged in war, and ruled their own societies.

Chapter 5 concentrates above all on the lives of women in Hellenistic Egypt. From after the death of Alexander the Great in 323 B.C.E. and until the defeat of the Ptolemaic queen Cleopatra by Roman forces under Octavian in 31 B.C.E., Greek culture was imposed on Egypt (as well as on other parts of the Eastern Mediterranean) by ruling Macedonian kings. This international context contributed to changes in the role of women in all social classes. The preservation in the dry climate of Egypt of written documents on papyrus enables us to study more closely the lives and transactions of ordinary citizens as well as queens; the art and literature of the period also expresses interest in the experiences of a greater range of social classes. Chapter 6 stresses the important gynecological discoveries of Herophilus, who, under the patronage of the Ptolemies, dissected human cadavers for the first time, and examines the ways that Greek medical and biological theories in both the Greek and Greco-Roman worlds shaped attitudes to female biology and to childbirth practices (and vice versa). Thus Chapters 5 and 6 also serve as a bridge to the study of women in the Roman world.

1

WOMEN IN ARCHAIC GREECE: TALK IN PRAISE AND BLAME

Sources and Their Limitations

From the time of the Homeric poems in the eighth century through the close of the sixth century B.C.E., aristocratic women in most parts of Greece seem to have passed through a similar life cycle. The visual arts and poetry, which, along with fragmentary archaeological remains, constitute our entire contemporary evidence for the Archaic period, marked for public attention rites of initiation and marriage, wifely fidelity, and death. Accordingly, this chapter reflects the limitations of our historical evidence in emphasizing the representation of important roles and social transitions in the lives of aristocratic (and where possible middle- to upper-middle-class) women: in particular, the transition from maidenhood to marriage, conflicting representations of the wife in Archaic literature, and finally, the important role of women in death rituals.

Art and poetry in the Archaic period were largely made by and for the ruling classes; to the degree possible, however, we include a discussion of the lives of slaves and lower-class women. Occasionally we catch glimpses of historical women in, for example, religious dedications (some of which were made by nonaristocratic women), or in Sappho's reference to her period of exile from Lesbos during one of the frequent political struggles among competing aristocrats that punctuated this often unsettled period. But Archaic art and literature generally aimed to immortalize the praise or blame of individuals and to hold up behavior to be imitated or avoided in a timeless and ahistorical fashion by its audience. Yet although the wives and maidens of the Archaic period are largely fictional and measured according to received paradigms of deportment, the important moments of their life cycle and the constraints under which they lived in many ways remained characteristic of

Greek women in the Classical and later periods as well. The evidence does not permit us to contextualize the lives of Archaic women, but we can offer vivid fragments of the cultural conceptions that aimed, through praise and blame, to shape their experience.

In this chapter we draw on evidence from Ionia and the islands near the coast of Asia Minor, the cultural center of the early Archaic period, as well as from the Greek mainland. To the degree that we can reconstruct it, the environment in which a work of art or literature was created clearly affects the vision of social roles represented by that work. On the one hand, the societies that produced the epic poems attributed to Homer and the lyric poetry composed by Sappho were aristocratic. The wealth of the ruling aristocrats was based on land, and much of the labor was performed by slaves. The exchange of women among the aristocrats was an important part of foreign policy among Greek city-states, since it established, along with the exchange of gifts, a panhellenic network of social obligations and a complex group of kin relations. In some cases, women brought dowries to their marriages, but it seems they rarely owned property or controlled inheritance (Dorian Crete and, possibly, Archaic Sparta, are exceptions). Yet, as we shall see, they performed important functions in the household. On the other hand, Archaic poets like Hesiod speak for a lower stratum of society than the Homeric hero. Hesiod in his *Works and Days* portrays himself as a free farmer who must struggle to farm with abundance and to retain his property. He speaks of having one female slave to do the work, and a wife who performs few if any functions in the household beyond producing children.

Reconstructing the social life of this period is highly problematic. For example, the Homeric epics may reflect an actual historical context at any time from the tenth to eighth centuries B.C.E., possibly even earlier, or an imaginary social world, a tapestry that includes historical detail from a number of different periods and social contexts woven together over a period of centuries by an oral poetic tradition. To give just one example, some scholars have argued that the Homeric epics show a puzzling mixture of practices involving the exchange of gifts at marriage (see further, Lacey 1968, Snodgrass 1974, Donlan 1981–82, Morris 1986, Leduc 1992). As the city-state emerged in Greece, husbands no longer offered gifts to the bride's family at marriage; rather, dowries were often given with the bride. This shift may have occurred because husbands no longer acquired the same political and social advantages from aristocratic marriages, and families wished to maintain their own interests in the bride and to insure her welfare. The largely idealized picture of both sexes in the Homeric poems and much Archaic art and lyric may well reflect the demands of a tradition that aimed to praise and blame rather than to reflect contemporary attitudes at any historical period. Certainly the epic tradition is known to have suppressed negative details in its poetic inheritance in order to succeed in this aim. Similarly, Sappho's poetry is conditioned by the need to fulfill the demands of her social role as an aristocrat, as an initiator of young women, and as a poet who is operating within the expectations of such a tradition. We cannot even be certain whether or when the Archaic poets who speak in the first person in Archaic lyric are persons or personae.

Factors relating to genre (epic, lyric, or iambic poetry) may condition the portrait of the social world represented in all Archaic poetry as much as the constraints of social and economic reality. Such differences may help to explain the conflicting views of women presented by Homer and some of the lyric poets on the one hand (who aimed largely to praise) and by Hesiod, Semonides, and other poets of the Archaic period on the other (who aimed largely to blame). Epic poets apparently addressed a broad panhellenic audience, whereas some lyric poets aimed at local audiences or at a combination of more- and less-restricted groups. The breadth of the audience conditions the degree to which the views presented may have been familiar and acceptable to Greeks of the Archaic period as a whole. Finally, our literary sources, especially in the case of the lyrics of Sappho and Alcman that have been recovered from damaged papyri, are full of gaps and distorting errors in transmission.

Like the literary record, the corpus of Archaic Greek art is fragmentary, and most objects are found removed from their original contexts. We do not know, for example, just how the korai (statues of maidens) were displayed in public places, nor is any Archaic tomb building preserved in its entirety. Many important sites, like the Acropolis of Athens, were excavated before the era of scientific archaeology, and much valuable information has been lost. Finally, some parts of the Greek world are much better represented in the archaeological record than others, creating a skewed picture for certain periods or artistic genres. Thus we have virtually no depictions of Spartan women (see Chapter 2), while women from Athens and East Greece are especially well represented. For depictions of women mourners, our evidence is almost exclusively Athenian.

Maidens

Initiation into Adulthood

Some fragmentary seventh-century B.C.E. poems of the poet Sappho of Lesbos and the closely contemporary *Partheneia* or Maiden Songs of the Spartan poet Alcman constitute our most important sources for interpreting the social and emotional significance of Archaic rites of women's initiation into adulthood (we have virtually no evidence until the Classical period for the nature of these rites; for more discussion, see Chapters 2 and 3). In these two Archaic societies at least, the poets show a close association between young women on the verge of marriage and more mature women who served as mentors and, it appears, often as lovers to the initiates. In this sense the initiatory stage for women resembled to some extent that of young men of the period, although the goals were different; while young men were prepared for war, leadership, and diplomacy, young women were prepared through dancing, singing, and other religious events for marriage and motherhood (see Chapter 2). Alcman's *Partheneia* emphasize the striking beauty and desirability of the women, and especially the attractions of the choral leaders (in this poem, Agido and Hagesichora):

Frag. 1.39–101

But I sing   40
the light of Agido. I see
her like the sun, which
Agido asks to shine
as our witness. But I can't praise
or blame her. Our glorious leader
won't let us, who clearly stands out
herself, as if you put
among the herds a racehorse,
sturdy, thundering, a champion
from soaring dreams.   50

Don't you see?—That's a
Venetic steed. But the tresses
Of my cousin
Hagesichora blossom
like pure gold;
and her silvery face—
why do I say what's obvious?
There's Hagesichora herself.
But the girl who's next to Agido in beauty
shall race but as a Kolaxeian horse behind an Ibenian: 60
for while we bear the torch to the dawn
the Pleiàdes, rising like the dog-star
through the ambrosial night,
strive against us.

For all the purple dye we have
won't help at all,
nor a dazzling serpent
all of gold, nor Lydian cap, the pride
of tender-glancing girls,   70
nor even the locks of Nanno,
nor god-like Areta,
nor Thylakis, nor Kleesithera,
and no longer coming to Ainesimbrota's house will you say:
"if only Astaphis were mine,
or Philylla would look my way,
or Demareta, or lovely Vianthemis—
but Hagesichora wears me out with desire."

For Hagesichora of the lovely
ankles is not here: 80
she waits with Agido,
applauding our festival.
Hear their prayers,
you gods; to gods belong the outcome
and the end. My chorus leader,
maiden as I am, I say
I have only shrilled in vain from the rafter
like an owl; yet I too wish to please
the Dawn; she's the one who
cures us of our labors.   90
And thanks to Hagesichora, maidens
find their way to lovely peace.

For you have to heed
the trace horse and
whoever's at the helm.
We (can't) sing better
than the Sirens—
they are goddesses, and we're just a bunch
of children—ten, in place of eleven—singing,
our tone like a swan's on Xanthos'   100
streams. But she, with her gorgeous golden hair
. . .

(Bing and Cohen 1991)

The nature of this fragmentary papyrus, in which the beginning and
end of the poem are lost, and the rest is permeated with gaps and mutila-
tions, makes it particularly difficult to interpret the text. The relationship between the leaders and followers in Alcman's *Partheneia* is uncertain—whether the leaders are those about to depart the circle of less
mature maiden contemporaries (the ten in place of eleven) for marriage,
or whether they are simply young women of particularly high birth.[1] We
are not sure whether the maidens in the chorus are competing with another chorus of girls or with Agido and Hagesichora (described as stars
in a constellation, the Pleiades); or whether the chorus is about to bring
a torch (an emendation: in the original text the girls mysteriously dedicate a plough or perhaps a robe) to the dawn goddess. Nevertheless, both
lines 73ff., and the fragmentary *Partheneion* below particularly stress the
erotic appeal of the choral leader to her probably less mature followers.
In the first case the girls imagine no longer going to the house of Anesimbrota, who is probably a woman who can work magic spells to reward a
girl's unrequited desires with success, and stress the powerful effects of
the desire engendered by their leader Hagesichora. The second fragment
dwells on the effects of being touched by the beautiful Astymeloisa:

. . . and the desire that looses the limbs, but she looks glances more melting
than sleep and death; nor in vain she . . . sweet.
But Astymeloisa makes me no answer; but like a star that falls through the

radiant sky or a branch of gold or soft plume, holding the garland . . . she passed
on slender feet; and on the tresses of the girls sits the lovely-haired dewy grace
of Cinyras. Astymeloisa (moves) among the gathering, an object of care to the
people . . . If she should come near and take me by the soft hand, at once I
would become her suppliant.
But now . . . a girl of deep [?] thought . . .

(Frag. 3.61–64, 79–82 Segal 1985)

Some poems of Sappho show groups of women involved in religious
rites and festivals or engaging in private relationships with each other.
Alcman's choral songs were composed for girls to perform in a public,
festal contest. Sappho also wrote such poetry, but most of her extant
fragments apparently involve women engaging in private or smaller
group experiences. These poems have in a sense two audiences, the
women of Sappho's circle and the wider public who eventually made
Sappho the most famous woman poet of antiquity. Sappho's poems highlight not only the desirability of the women and the pleasures and erotic
sufferings of the time spent in their company, but the pain of separation
felt over the departure of a member of the circle. Why women joined
or departed from Sappho's circle remains unknown. Later commentators
imagined that Sappho ran a school for girls, or that she was a priestess
of Aphrodite who was joined for a period of time by young acolytes or
initiates in the cult of the goddess. The most likely explanation is that
the girls were departing for marriage. Sappho's fragmentary poems 94
and 96 are notable for the elegance and beauty of the consolation offered
on or after the painful separation from the circle of women.

94

. . . .
"Honestly, I wish I were dead!"
Weeping many tears she left me,

Saying this as well:
"Oh, what dreadful things have happened to us,
Sappho! I don't want to leave you!"

I answered her:
"Go with my blessings and remember me,
for you know how we cherished you.

"But if you have [forgotten], I want
to remind you . . .
of the beautiful things that happened to us:

"Close by my side you put around yourself
[many wreaths] of violets and roses and saffron . . .

"And many woven garlands
made from flowers . . .
around your tender neck,

"And . . . with costly royal
myrrh . . .
you anointed . . .

"And on a soft bed
. . . tender . . .
you satisfied your desire . . .

"Nor was there any . . .
nor any holy . . .
from which we were away,

. . . nor grove . . ."

(Snyder 1989)

96

. . . [Sardis?]
Often turning her mind here . . .

[She honored you]
like an easily recognized goddess,
she rejoiced especially in your song.

But now she stands out among the Lydian women
as after sunset
the rosy-fingered moon

Surpasses all the stars; the light
spreads over the salty sea
equally as over the many-flowered fields.

And the dew grows beautifully liquid
and roses and tender chervil
flourish, and the flowery honey-lotus.

But she, roaming about far and wide,
remembers gentle Attis with desire;
her tender heart is surely heavy [because of your fate]
. . . to come . . .

(Snyder 1989)

Sappho's poems are marked by sympathetic dialogue and by mutuality of feeling between older and younger women. Comparable erotic poetry by contemporary or near-contemporary male poets seems to emphasize instead only the desire of the lover and his prowess in the sexual conquest of young men and women. (See Stigers 1981. For a parallel contrast, see the discussion of the elegaic poetry of Sulpicia in Chapter 11). Sappho develops the shared desire of lover and beloved and the beauty of their experience in an enchanted environment marked by the presence of flowers, fruits, and natural images like moons and stars. Aphrodite may be invoked to appear as a participant in this secure private world. The equally damaged papyrus fragments below stress the pleasures involved in attending festal occasions with other women, and the lovely dress and other adornments worn for the event.

2

Hither to me from Crete, to this holy
temple, where your lovely grove
of apple trees is, and the altars
smoke with frankincense.

Herein cold water rushes through
apple boughs, and the whole place is shaded
with roses, and sleep comes down
from rustling leaves.

Herein a meadow where horses graze
blooms with spring flowers, and the winds
blow gently . . .

Here, O Cyprian, taking [garlands],
in golden cups gently pour forth
nectar mingled together with our
festivities . . .

(Snyder 1989)

98a

. . . for my mother [said that]
in her youth it was indeed a great ornament if someone had tresses
wrapped in a purple [band].
But the girl who has hair
brighter than a fiery torch
should wear [?] wreaths
of blooming flowers.
Just now a many-colored
headband from Sardis . . .

(Snyder 1989)

Choruses of dancing maidens are a favorite subject of vase painters in many parts of the Greek world. As early as the time of Homer, Geometric vases show rows of women in dance formation, sometimes accompanied by a male aulos-player (an instrument similar to the modern oboe). In the Archaic period, one school of painters that especially favored this subject was at Clazomenai, on the Aeolian coast of Asia Minor, not far from Sappho's island of Lesbos (Fig. 1.1). The young women in their elegant, tight-fitting patterned chitons and delicate white flesh could be the kind of well-bred girls who constituted a social milieu like Sappho's. In Athens, choruses of dancing maidens are less common, but one krater of about 460 portrays a group that might well resemble the performers of Alcman's *Partheneia* (Fig. 1.2). Here the stiff poses of Archaic art have given way to a more relaxed classical style that better captures the rhythmic and graceful movements of such a chorus.

Figure 1.1. Archaic vase (ca. 550–540 B.C.E.) from Clazomenai showing young women dancing. The artist used white for their skin to distinguish them from men, whose red skin told of their outdoor lives; respectable women, the color suggests, stayed indoors and lived out of the public eye.

Figure 1.2. Red-figure Athenian vase (ca. 460 B.C.E.) with dancing women in the Classical style. This differs from the Archaic in its closer observation of human anatomy and the graceful fall of drapery.

Korai: Archaic Statues of Greek Maidens

Life-size standing marble statues of young women, often elaborately dressed in gaily painted garments, were made in many parts of the Greek world from the mid-seventh century to the early fifth. Today these figures are known as korai, although not all are korai in the literal sense of unmarried maidens, nor does any of them represent the goddess Kore/Persephone (on korai, see further Richter 1968 and Schneider 1975). Some were dedications in the sanctuary of a divinity, while others served as funerary markers.

The earliest extant kore is the dedication by Nicandre, a Naxian woman, to Artemis, in the goddess's sanctuary on Delos (cf. Fig. 1.10). She wears a tight-fitting belted peplos, giving her body a planklike effect. It has been suggested that the holes carved in each hand were for the attachment of metal attributes, a bow and arrow characterizing her as Artemis. But we cannot be certain if she represents the goddess or Nicandre herself. The dedicatory inscription carved on her garment (cf. Fig. 1.10C) describes the virgin goddess Artemis as a kore, but Nicandre was a married woman.

The largest series of surviving korai are those dedicated to Athena on the Acropolis of Athens from about 570 to 480 B.C.E. All stood in the open air and were damaged in the Persian sack of the Acropolis in 480 and subsequently buried on the slope of the hill, to be rediscovered in the excavations of the 1880s. The earliest korai wear the simpler Dorian peplos (a heavy woolen garment), sometimes in combination with other garments, such as a shawl, while from about 530 they regularly wear the thinner, more elaborate, and brightly painted Ionic chiton (usually linen) and himation. Very few of the Acropolis korai preserve an inscription recording the name of the dedicator or the sculptor. One that does is the largest of all that survive, standing over two meters with the plinth. Her inscription may be restored as follows:

> Nearchos the potter dedicated this
> Work as first-fruits to Athena.
> Antenor the son of Eumares made the statue.
> (Richter 1968: 69–70)

One of the latest in the series (Fig. 1.3), probably dedicated in the 480s, bears the simple inscription: "Euthydikos son of Thalarchos dedicated [me]." (Richter 1968: 99–100) When she was found, she was nicknamed "the pouting girl" *(la boudeuse)*, because the sculptor, in trying to suppress the "archaic smile" of earlier statues, turned down the corners of her mouth.

Of the funerary korai that have survived, one of the finest is Phrasicleia (Fig. 1.4), found in the Attic countryside in 1972. She must have stood in an Archaic cemetery at Merenda (modern Markopoulo), from which other finds (including a statue of a youth who could be Phrasi-

Figure 1.3. Kore from the Acropolis in Athens, dedicated in the 480s, and showing the growth of interest in naturalistic treatment of face and body in the fifth century. The "Archaic smile" of earlier korai (e.g., Fig. 1.4) is now gone.

Figure 1.4. Phrasicleia, the young woman who died before marrying (ca. 530 B.C.E.). The maiden's rich polos and jewelry signal the prosperity of her family as well as perhaps suggesting what she would have looked like if she had lived to be a bride.

cleia's brother) have come. Her epigram (which was known long before the discovery of the statue) reads:

> The tomb of Phrasicleia. I shall always be called kore,
> Having received this name as my lot from the gods,
> Instead of marriage.
> Aristion of Paros made [me].
>
> (Jeffery 1962: 138)

She wears an ornate costume, and the cylindrical polos (conical headdress—often an attribute of goddesses), decorated with buds, may be intended to portray her as a bride, the bride she never lived to be. A similar polos is worn by the famous Berlin kore (Richter 1968: 39–40 and figs. 139–146), who is also said to have been found in Attica and was probably also funerary. Yet another kore from an Attic cemetery is represented today only by the base and a finely carved pair of sandal-shod feet (Richter 1968: 58–59 and figs. 284–85). The dedication reads:

— set me up as a monument, beautiful to behold, to his daughter Phile. Phaidimos made me.

Another type of Archaic tomb monument, more common than a statue in the round, was the stele, a tall marble shaft carved in relief and often topped with a sphinx. One of the best known of these includes a fine representation of a young girl, alongside a youth who is probably her brother (Fig. 1.5). A fragmentary epigram may be restored to say that their parents set up the stele for the young siblings (Clairmont 1970: 13–15). In the Classical period, a new type of grave stele will become one of our principal sources for representations of Athenian women (cf. Fig. 3.2).

Relatively few korai have preserved an inscription telling us who put them up and why. But those that do have an inscription, along with the findspots of the others, indicate that these statues served two principal functions, both characteristic of Archaic Greek religion. Either they were dedications to a goddess in her sanctuary or they were grave markers placed on the tombs of wealthy women. In both instances, we may wonder how closely the statue approximates the actual dress and appearance of young women and what qualities it was meant to express.

A life-size marble statue was among the most expensive dedications made in Greek sanctuaries (typical dedications by poorer people were clay vases or plaques). Thus the korai themselves, in their dress, coiffure, and attributes, may be an accurate reflection of the appearance of young women of the aristocratic class whose families made such dedications. It has been suggested that the statues represent these young women in a specific situation known to us from Archaic literary sources, their appearance in religious sanctuaries on the occasion of public festivals (Schneider 1975). These were virtually the only times when a girl of marriageable age might appear in public, and the modest behavior expected of her is echoed in the demure downward gaze of many korai. Yet at the same time, paradoxically, she might call attention to herself with her elegant clothes, elaborately styled hair, expensive jewelry, makeup, and even a gesture of pulling her garment tight, emphasizing breasts, legs, and buttocks. Her beauty makes her an adornment to her family, to be appraised by prospective husbands; yet she should not call attention to herself, lest she invite unwanted admirers.

The Transition to Marriage

Both *Odyssey*, book 6, composed in the late eighth century B.C.E., and the Homeric *Hymn to Demeter*, probably composed at Eleusis in the later seventh or early sixth century B.C.E., address the complex transition from maidenhood to marriage. Yet whereas Homer's Nausicaa faces the prospect of marriage with a charming shy reserve mixed with eagerness, the Homeric *Hymn* dwells through its divine myth on the difficulties a young woman faced in leaving her natal home for a new, often distant environment and an unknown husband chosen for her by her father.

In the *Odyssey*, Homer's intelligent and lovely princess Nausicaa is shy about speaking of marriage to her parents, but they understand that her sudden desire to wash the family laundry in the company of her handmaidens and friends signals a readiness for a new life.

Figure 1.5. Funerary relief (540–530 B.C.E.) from Attica with a young man and a small girl in the Archaic style. He is nude, as is common for images of youthful gods, athletes, and heroes, and for young men of the Athenian ruling stratum; the girl is, predictably, fully draped, for female nudity was an exception reserved for prostitutes and dancing girls.

"Daddy dear, will you not have them harness me the wagon,
the high one with the good wheels, so that I can take the clothing
to the river and wash it? Now it is lying about, all dirty,
and you yourself, when you sit among the first men in council
and share their counsels, ought to have nice clean clothing about you;
and also, you have five dear sons who are grown in the palace,
two of them married, and the other three are sprightly bachelors,
and they are forever wanting fresh clean clothing, to wear it
when they go to dance, and it is my duty to think about all this."
So she spoke, but she was ashamed to speak of her joyful
marriage to her dear father, but he understood all and answered:
"I do not begrudge you the mules, child, nor anything
else. So go, and the serving men will harness the wagon,
the high one with the good wheels that has the carrying basket.
                    (*Odyssey* 6.57–70; Lattimore 1965)

Nausicaa looks for a husband who will be sympathetic to herself—
intelligent and socially graceful—and she mistakenly hopes for a brief
time that that husband might be the stranger Odysseus.

and he went a little aside and sat by himself on the seashore,
radiant in grace and good looks; and the girl admired him.
It was to her attendants with well-ordered hair that she now
spoke:
"Hear me, my white-armed serving women; let me say something.
It is not against the will of all the gods on Olympos
that this man is here to be made known to the godlike Phaiakians.
A while ago he seemed an unpromising man to me. Now he even
resembles one of the gods, who hold the high heaven,
If only the man to be called my husband could be like this one,
a man living here, if only this one were pleased to stay here."
                                                    (6.236–45)

The first scene between Odysseus and Nausicaa displays the princess's courage, beauty, and sensitivity, as well as her concern for how a
maiden's reputation can be maintained in the eyes of others. A young
woman's reputation can be harmed, she says, by encounters with men,
including her future husband, before marriage:

and it is their graceless speech I shrink from, the fear one may mock us
hereafter, since there are insolent men in our community,
and see how one of the worse sort might say when he met us,
"Who is this large and handsome stranger whom Nausicaa
has with her, and where did she find him? Surely he is
to be her husband, but is he a stray from some ship of alien men she
found for herself, since there are no such hereabouts?
Or did some god after much entreaty come down in answer
to her prayers, out of the sky, and all his days will have her?
Better so, if she goes out herself and finds her a husband
from elsewhere, since she pays no heed to her own Phaiakian
neighbors, although many of these and the best ones court her."

So they will speak, and that would be a scandal against me,
and I myself would disapprove of a girl who acted
so, that is, without the goodwill of her dear father
and mother making friends with a man, before being formally
married . . .

(6.273–89)

Nausicaa's fears for a maiden's reputation are not ill-founded. In Archaic Athens, the young sister of Harmodius was first invited and then declared to be unfit to carry a basket—a task for a virgin—in a festal procession. Her brother's enemy Hipparchus thus managed to cast a slur on her reputation for chastity (Thucydides 6.56.1, Pseudo-Aristotle *Athênaiôn Politeia, The Constitution of Athens* 18.2). The Archaic poet Archilochus wrote a series of poems defaming the reputation of his (very likely imaginary) fiancée, Neoboule. Her father Lycambes unjustly broke the engagement. Archilochus's poems were so brutal that Lycambes' daughters were said to have committed suicide out of humiliation. In the incomplete papyrus fragment below, Archilochus seduces an unprotected young woman, perhaps the sister of Neoboule; in the process he castigates and avenges himself on the less virtuous Neoboule. He apparently promises the unnamed girl that he will preserve her virtue by not going "all the way." (The narrator's reference to "the divine thing" is a euphemism for sexual intercourse, and the cornices, gates, and garden grass are also sexual metaphors.) Some have argued (the text of the final lines is uncertain) that he does not keep his promise.

> . . . .
> ". . . hold back completely;
> equally endure . . .
>
> but if you urge on and passion drives you,
> there's a woman in our house
> who now deeply desires . . .
>
> a lovely, delicate woman—I think her
> figure has no flaw—
> you may make her . . ."
>
> After she said that, I replied:
> "Daughter of Amphimedo,
> who was a noble and wise
>
> woman, now buried in the dank earth,
> there are many delights
> of the goddess for young men
>
> aside from the divine thing: one will do.
> But at our leisure
> when it grows dark . . .
>
> you and I will make our plans, god willing.
> I shall do as you say;
> much . . .

but beneath the cornice and gates . . .
Don't refuse me dear—
I'll hold to the garden grass,

you can count on it. Let another man
have Neoboule.
No, she is over-ripe . . .

her virgin bloom has flowed away
and her former charm.
She couldn't get her fill—

the mad woman showed her measure of . . .
To hell with her!
May this not . . .

that I, keeping such a woman,
will be the neighbor's joke.
I'd much rather have you

because you are not faithless or two-faced,
while she is much keener
and makes many men . . .

I fear that urging on in haste I may breed
blind and untimely things,
like the bitch's litter."

I said such things, and taking the girl
I laid her down, wrapped
in a soft cloak, in the blooming

flowers, my arms embracing her neck;
she was [still] with fear
like a fawn . . .

and I gently took her breasts in my hands,
. . . her fresh skin showed
the bloom of youth,

and caressing all her lovely body
I released my [white] force,
just touching her golden hair.
        (Cologne papyrus, Rayor 1991, modified)

The seventh-century Corinthian tyrant Periander, on the other hand, reportedly fell in love with Melissa when he saw her in a field wearing a simple garment and pouring wine for workmen; he later married her (Athenaeus, *Deipnosophistae* 13, 589F).

To turn back from Archilochus's literature of blame to that of praise, the encounter between Odysseus and Nausicaa discussed above also stresses that the ideal marriage should be marked by a likeness of mind between spouses and a set of shared social goals; above all, husband and wife should share in benefiting friends and harming enemies:

"and then may the gods give you everything your heart longs for;
may they grant you a husband and a house and sweet agreement
in all things, for nothing is better than this, more steadfast
than when two people, a man and his wife, keep a harmonious
household; a thing that brings much distress to the people who hate them
and pleasure to their well wishers, and for them the best reputation."

(6.180–85)

In the utopian island of Phaeacia where Nausicaa lives, men and women marry within their own society and marriage does not radically separate the bride from her family. Nausicaa's mother, the queen Arete, had married her own uncle, and if Nausicaa had married Odysseus, he would have lived with her, rather than taking his bride to his own residence, as happens in most Homeric marriages (Helen, the semi-divine daughter of Zeus, is another significant exception). The like-minded marriage that Odysseus idealizes is embodied not only in his own exceptionally harmonious marriage to Penelope but also in the union of Nausicaa's parents. Other marriages in the poem are less successful—both Helen and Clytemnestra are adulterous—and Odysseus seems to hold up this ideal to Nausicaa more as a hope than as a reflection of reality.

The *Hymn to Demeter*, on the other hand, highlights the pain that the transition to marriage can cause both mother and daughter (see further Richardson 1974, Arthur 1977, and Foley 1993). As seems often to have been the case in the human society of Archaic Greece, the divine father Zeus exercises his authority to promise his daughter Persephone (alternatively called Kore or "maiden") in marriage to his brother Hades without the permission (and here even the knowledge) of either mother or daughter. In this case, the separation between mother and daughter occasioned by marriage is heightened by the violence of Hades' abduction and the sequestering of Persephone in the impenetrable world of death.

Demeter I begin to sing, the fair-tressed awesome goddess,
herself and her slim-ankled daughter whom Aidoneus
seized. Zeus, heavy-thundering and mighty-voiced, gave her,
without the consent of Demeter of the bright fruit and golden sword,
as she played with the deep-breasted daughters of Ocean,   5
plucking flowers in the lush meadow—roses, crocus,
and lovely violets, irises and hyacinth—and the narcissus,
which Earth grew as a snare for the flower-faced maiden
in order to gratify by Zeus's design the Host-to-Many,
a flower wondrous and bright, awesome for all to see,   10
for the immortals above and for mortals below.
From its root a hundredfold bloom sprang up and smelled
so sweet that the whole vast heaven above
and the whole earth laughed, and the salty swell of the sea.
The girl marveled and stretched out both hands at once   15
to take the lovely toy. The earth with its wide ways yawned

over the Nysian plain; the lord Host-to-Many rose up on her
with his immortal horses, the celebrated son of Cronus;
he snatched the unwilling maid into his golden chariot
and led her off lamenting. She screamed with a shrill voice,   20
calling on her father, the son of Cronus highest and best.
Not one of the immortals or of humankind
heard her voice, nor the olives bright with fruit,
except the daughter of Persaius; tender of heart
she heard her from her cave, Hecate of the delicate veil   25
And lord Helios, brilliant son of Hyperion, heard
the maid calling her father the Son of Cronus. But he sat apart
from the gods, aloof in a temple ringing with prayers,
and received choice offerings from humankind.
Against her will Hades took her by the design of Zeus   30
with his immortal horses—her father's brother,
commander and host to many, the celebrated son of Cronus.

(trans. Helene P. Foley)

In this poem, the marriage of the daughter becomes temporarily a symbolic death, as marriage does in later Greek poetry as well, and Demeter laments over and responds to the event in precisely this fashion. After Hades' rape of her daughter Demeter disfigures her divine form by dressing as a mourning old woman; both mother and daughter refuse to eat for a long time.

So long as the goddess gazed on earth and starry heaven,
on the sea flowing strong and full of fish,
and on the beams of the sun, she still hoped   35
to see her dear mother and the race of immortal gods.
For so long hope charmed her strong mind despite her distress.
The mountain peaks and the depths of the sea echoed
in response to her divine voice, and her goddess mother heard.
Sharp grief seized her heart, and she tore the veil   40
on her ambrosial hair with her own hands.
She cast a dark cloak on her shoulders
and sped like a bird over dry land and sea,
searching. No one was willing to tell her the truth,
not one of the gods or mortals;   45
no bird of omen came to her as truthful messenger.
Then for nine days divine Deo roamed over the earth,
holding torches ablaze in her hands;
in her grief she did not once taste ambrosia
or nectar sweet-to-drink, nor bathed her skin.   50

The poem shows how Demeter and Persephone first resist and then finally accept the daughter's marriage. Unable to reach her daughter in the underworld, Demeter descends to earth in disguise as an old woman at Eleusis. Here Demeter observes the advantages that marriage can bestow on mortal women. The young daughters of Celeus, whom she first encounters at the Maiden Well in Eleusis, are represented with imagery that emphasizes their readiness for marriage and fertility. The daughters take pride in the way that wives preside over their households and make important decisions concerning the fate of their families. Even older women have an honored role as nurses of children or housekeepers, and they are cared for by their contemporaries.

> Withdrawing from the assembly of the gods and high Olympus
> she went among the cities and fertile fields of men,
> disguising her beauty for a long time. No one of men
> nor low-girt women recognized her when they looked,   95
> until she came to the house of skillful Celeus,
> the man then ruler of fragrant Eleusis.
> There she sat near the road, grief in her heart,
> where citizens drew water from the Maiden's Well
> in the shade—an olive bush had grown overhead—   100
> like a very old woman cut off from childbearing
> and the gifts of garland-loving Aphrodite.
> Such are the nurses to children of law-giving kings
> and the keepers of stores in their echoing halls.
> The daughters of Celeus, son of Eleusis, saw her   105
> as they came to fetch water easy-to-draw and bring it
> in bronze vessels to their dear father's halls.
> Like four goddesses they were in the flower of youth,
> Callidike, Cleisidike, fair Demo and Callithoe,
> who was the eldest of them all.   110
> They did not know her—gods are hard for mortals to see.
> Standing near her, they spoke winged words.
> "Who are you, old woman, of those born long ago?
> From where? Why have you left the city and do not
> draw near its homes? Women are there in the shadowy halls,   115
> of your age as well as others born younger,
> who would care for you both in word and in deed."
>
> . . . .
>
> "And all these have wives to manage their households.
> Of these not one at first sight would scorn
> your appearance and turn you away from their homes.
> They will receive you, for you are indeed godlike.
> But if you wish, wait here, until we come to the house   160
> of our father and tell Metaneira our deep-girt mother
> all these things straight through, in case she might bid
> you come to our house and not search after others'.
> For her only son is now nursed in our well-built hall,
> a late-born child, much prayed for and cherished.   165
> If you might raise him to the threshold of youth,
> any woman who saw you would feel envy at once,
> such rewards for his rearing our mother will give you."
> Thus they spoke and she nodded her head. The girls
> carried proudly bright jars filled with water and   170
> swiftly they reached the great house of their father.
> At once to their mother they told what they saw and heard.
> She bade them go quickly to offer a boundless wage.
> Just as hinds or heifers in the season of spring

bound through the meadow sated with fodder,   175
so they, lifting the folds of their shimmering robes,
darted down the hollow wagon-track, and their hair
danced on their shoulders like a crocus blossom.

In the palace at Eleusis, the maid Iambe cheers Demeter with jokes that almost certainly concern female fertility as well. (In other versions of the same myth, a woman named Baubo displays her genitals and pregnant belly to the goddess.) Demeter tries and fails to immortalize the human child Demophon, whom she has agreed to nurse. She then wins an ecstatic reunion with her daughter through withdrawing fertility from the earth. Zeus agrees that Persephone will spend two-thirds of the year with her mother and one-third with her husband in the world below. Persephone's suffering is mitigated by Hades' promise of new honors to herself in her role as queen of the underworld.

Mortals become beneficiaries of the divine experience of Demeter and Persephone. They are promised in perpetuity a stable agricultural cycle that parallels Persephone's annual separations from and returns to her mother and the world above. Through the Eleusinian Mysteries established by Demeter at the end of the poem, mortals of both sexes will be promised initiation into rites that will offer them a better lot after death through celebrating the story of the two goddesses.

At once she sent forth fruit from the fertile fields
and the whole wide earth burgeoned with leaves
and flowers. She went to the kings who administer law,
Triptolemus and Diocles, driver of horses, mighty
Eumolpus and Celeus, leader of the people, and revealed   475
the conduct of her rites and taught her mysteries to all of them,
holy rites that are not to be transgressed, nor pried into,
nor divulged. For a great awe of the gods stops the voice.
Blessed is the mortal on earth who has seen these rites,   480
but the uninitiate who has no share in them never
has the same lot once dead in the dreary darkness.
When the great goddess had founded all her rites,
the goddesses left for Olympus and the assembly of the other gods.
There they dwell by Zeus delighting-in-thunder, inspiring   485
awe and reverence. Highly blessed is the mortal
on earth whom they graciously favor with love.
For soon they will send to the hearth of his great house
Ploutus, the god giving abundance to mortals.

The site of Eleusis lies on the coast of Attica some 18 km northwest of Athens. Starting at the end of the last century, Greek archaeologists have uncovered virtually the entire sanctuary and distinguished building phases from the Bronze Age to the Roman period. The hypothetical locations of several places mentioned in the *Hymn to Demeter*, such as the Callichoron Spring (272), are indicated on the plan by George Mylonas

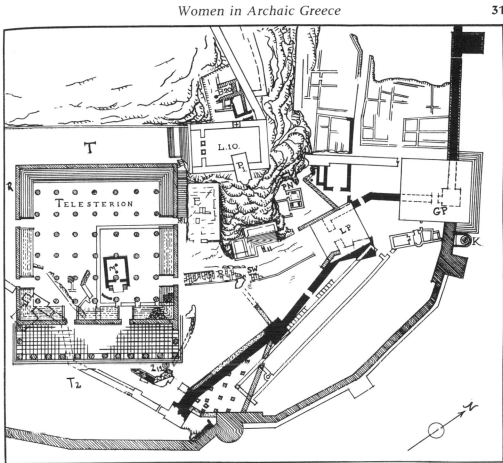

Figure 1.6. Plan of the sanctuary at Eleusis with the Telesterion or Hall of the Mysteries of Demeter, as well as the earlier and later buildings found on the site. K, the Callichoron; GP, the Greater Propylaea; LP, the Lesser Propylaea; PN, the Ploutonion; H11, rock-cut platform and the area of the "Mirthless Stone"; SW, the Sacred Way; F, the "Temple F"; P1, the Chapel of Panaghitsa; L10, Roman building on spur; B20, Prehistoric remains on the Akropolis; T, Terrace above the Telesterion; R1, Northern Stairway; R, Southern Stairway; M, the Megaron; T2, Terrace in front of main eastern façade of the Telesterion; Z12, the Callichoron of the Homeric hymn.

(Fig. 1.6). The Telesterion, first built in the sixth century and enlarged in the fifth, is the great hall where the Mysteries were performed.

We do not know exactly what went on in the Mysteries, since initiates were strictly forbidden to divulge anything about them; but the proceedings almost certainly included a reenactment of parts of the myth told above. Nevertheless, the *Hymn to Demeter* or the version it recounts was well known in Athens by the middle of the sixth century and inspired several vase paintings. A water jar (hydria) of about 520 B.C.E. (Fig. 1.7) shows Demeter (her name inscribed) in her chariot, after her reconciliation with the other Olympian gods, as she prepares to rejoin

Figure 1.7. Black-figure Attic vase (ca. 520 B.C.E.) showing the goddess Demeter in her chariot, her daughter Persephone returned to her from the underworld.

them (cf. *Hymn to Demeter* 470ff.). The way is led by Hermes, the messenger god, who conducts Persephone, freed from Hades (*Hymn to Demeter* 360ff.). Apollo, as a representative of the Olympian family, accompanies the festive procession on the kithara (a type of lyre); the goddess facing him may be his sister Artemis.

Cults of Demeter and of Persephone were particularly strong and widespread in the Greek colonies of South Italy and Sicily. Locri Epizephyrii was a Greek city in Southern Italy (near modern Reggio Calabria), founded in the early seventh century B.C.E. It had an important sanctuary of Persephone (Diodorus 27.4.3) that flourished especially in the sixth and fifth centuries. In the sanctuary were found hundreds of clay plaques dedicated to the goddess by women. Many of these show scenes relating to the wedding of the dedicator herself, such as the bride-to-be preparing her trousseau (cf. Chapter 7, and Fig. 7.10). But several other series of pinakes (plaques) depict the goddess Persephone, her mother Demeter, and occasionally other gods, such as Dionysus or Hermes, the messenger. One group (Fig. 1.8) shows the abduction of Persephone by Hades (*Hymn to Demeter* 15–20).

The story of Demeter and Persephone also served as the paradigm for many all-female fertility rituals throughout Greece, the most famous of which was called the Thesmophoria (see Chapter 3). Hence we can as-

Figure 1.8. Fragment of a fifth-century B.C.E. relief from the sanctuary of Persephone at Locri; its image of the abduction of Persephone by Hades stresses the frantic gestures of the maiden snatched away from her helpless friends.

sume that the goddesses' resistance to and final acceptance of marriage helped mortal women to define and accept their major social role, that of wife and mother who brought fertility to her society through her children and used her powers in rituals to ensure the success of the yearly crops.

Wives

The Archaic Ideal

As wife, the Homeric woman, at least as she appears in the *Iliad*'s Andromache or the *Odyssey*'s Penelope (see Chapter 2 for the different role of Spartan women), was meant not only to produce and raise heirs but also to preside over her household by weaving and watching over the domestic slaves and goods. This last role was particularly important, given the frequent absence of her husband on military or diplomatic missions. The *Odyssey* elaborates on the difficulties faced by Penelope during the extended absence of Odysseus, especially since his whereabouts are uncertain and he is presumed by many to be dead. Penelope wants to preserve marriage, household, and kingdom for Odysseus. Yet her son Telemachus is growing up and wants to come into his inheritance and control his household; suitors are pressing their courtship on Penelope, perhaps in part because the winner wants to use the marriage to secure the kingship of Ithaca; members of Odysseus's own household, including some of Penelope's handmaidens, are betraying their master and the suitors are consuming the wealth of the household; Odysseus's father is wasting away for lack of his son. It takes all the heroine's intelligence and strategy to forestall the suitors and preserve the integrity of her household (see further Foley 1978, Murnaghan 1987, and Katz 1991).

Of the domestic tasks assigned to the proper Homeric wife, the poems call attention to women's weaving. As the *Iliad*'s Hector says to his wife Andromache about the sexual division of labor between husband and wife, "But returning to the house, attend to your work, the loom and the distaff, and bid your handmaidens to do so also; but the men will have charge of the fighting, all of those from Ilium, but I more than others." (*Iliad* 6.490–93). Helen in *Iliad* 3 (125–28) weaves in her extraordinary web the battles fought at Troy over herself in the manner of a poet. Penelope's ruse with her weaving delays the threat of her marriage to the suitors for many years. In the period after the Trojan War in which the whereabouts of the wandering Odysseus are unknown, Penelope unravels each night the shroud for her father-in-law that she insists she must make before departure for marriage to one of the suitors.

The epic wife could influence in various ways the world outside her home. (The discussion of Classical Athens will emphasize the diminished role that the respectable wife had within her home, if not in the area of religion). When her husband was in residence, a wife could greet and converse with guests, tell stories, and even offer gifts of her own. In the *Odyssey*'s utopian Phaeacia, the wise Arete is said to determine the fate of suppliants to her hearth and even adjudicates quarrels among those she favors (7.73–74). Although she was meant to spend her time indoors, the Archaic wife could also serve her society by performing rites for the gods. Hector in the passage quoted above tells Andromache to return to her proper place within the house and leave war to the men (on this scene, see further Arthur 1981. A scene on Achilles' shield, however, depicts women and children defending their beseiged city from the ramparts [*Iliad* 18.514–15]; in another, wives watch a wedding from their doorways [*Iliad* 18.495–95].). Yet in *Iliad* 6, the women of Troy are assigned to leave their homes to propitiate the goddess Athena with gifts, and the Trojan women are often shown looking anxiously—or in the case of Helen, with magisterial interest—at the battles fought on the plains below the city wall.

The Trojan priestess who receives the women's gifts to Athena is named Theano. (For further discussion of Theano, as well as an illustration of an Archaic priestess of Athena in Athens, see Chapter 3.) Among the several figurines of priestesses from the archaic period, this ivory statuette (Fig. 1.9) from Ephesus holds a distaff to her breast in her left hand; a ball of wool is impaled on the rod, while a thread falls from the distaff through her left hand to a spindle dangling against her lower leg. Her high headdress, jewelry, decorated tunic, large eyes, and round face may be orientalizing features that characterize her as a priestess.

Religious Dedications by Aristocratic Women

The mission of Hecuba and her Trojan women to dedicate gifts to Athena was more than a fictional practice. Women are known to have made dedications to the gods and goddesses in sanctuaries throughout

Figure 1.9. A seventh-century B.C.E. ivory statuette of a priestess from Ephesus in Asia Minor; the combination of elaborate ornaments and the distaff and spindle of domestic work occur elsewhere for images of women and suggest that these are traditional attributes of women and femininity in the Greek world.

the Greek world during the Archaic period. Recent studies of dedicatory inscriptions of the eighth to fifth centuries B.C.E. showed that about eighty out of nearly one thousand were made by women. With few exceptions, women made dedications to female divinities, while men made dedications to both female and male divinities. The recipient of the largest number of dedications by women was Athena (especially on the

Acropolis of Athens); others were made to goddesses important in the female life cycle: Artemis, Hera, Aphrodite, Nemesis, the birth goddess Eileithyia, the Nymphs, Demeter, and Persephone.

The earliest and perhaps best-known dedication is a kore offered to Artemis on the island of Delos by a woman from neighboring Naxos named Nicandre (Fig. 1.10. See earlier under "Korai: Archaic Statues of Greek Maidens" for discussion of this statue). The dedicatory inscription, carved along one side of her dress, gives details of Nicandre's family, which must have been one of the wealthiest and most prominent on Naxos:

Nicandre dedicated me to the far-darter, the maiden who showers arrows, I, the daughter of Deinodicus of Naxos, distinguished among women, sister of Deinomenes and wife of Phraxos.

(Lazzarini 1976: no. 157; Richter 1968: 26)

The statue, put up in the middle of the seventh century B.C.E., is not only the earliest dedication by a Greek woman, but is the earliest example of Greek monumental stone sculpture.

From the evidence of Nicandre's dedication and one a century later on the island of Paros, it would seem that dedications by aristocratic women were more prevalent in the Cyclades than elsewhere in Greece. The later statue is lost, but the marble column that supported it bears this dedication:

Artemis, Telestodice dedicated this statue to you,
the mother of Asphalios and daughter of Thersiles.
I [the statue] boast I am the work of Critonides of Paros.

(Lazzarini 1976: no. 726)

Telestodice defines herself as daughter, wife, and mother of her male relatives. Since Artemis was born on Delos (with her brother Apollo), a main center of her worship was in the Cyclades, and dedications like Nicandre's suggest that she was the principal deity worshiped on Delos in the early Archaic period, before her brother took over.

Of smaller-scale objects dedicated by women, mirrors were considered specifically "female" because of their association with women's toilette and cosmetics. Seven bronze mirrors from all parts of the Greek world bear dedications by women to various goddesses and, in one instance, to Zeus. One mirror, dedicated by Hippylla, is from Brauron (Fig. 1.11), where we know from inscriptions that women dedicated articles of clothing to Artemis (probably in gratitude for a successful childbirth, an event over which the goddess presided), as well as to the heroine Iphigenia (Euripides, *Iphigenia among the Taurians* 1463–67; she received clothing from women who died in childbirth), though none survive (see the discussion of girls' rituals at Brauron in Chapter 3). In the sanctuary of Persephone at Locri in South Italy (cf. Fig. 1.8), Xenodoka dedicated a mirror to the goddess.

In the same sanctuary at Locri, a man and woman, Capron and Pro-

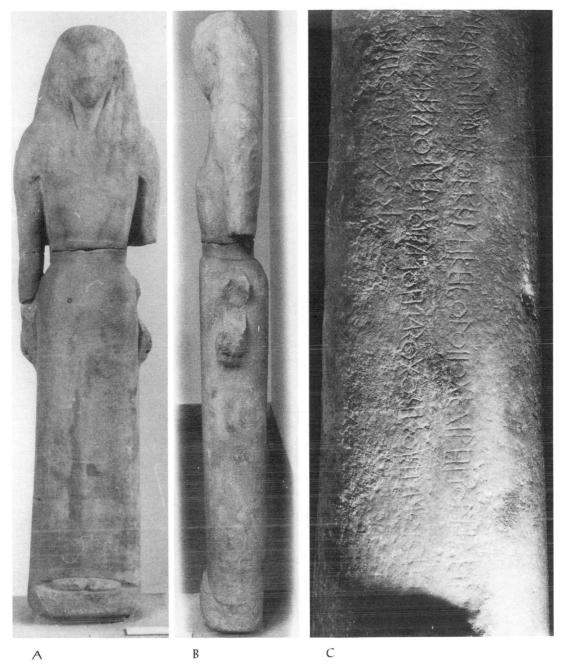

A   B   C

Figure 1.10. Nicandre offered this statue to the goddess Artemis, as she tells the viewer in an inscription on the side of her dress (**C**). This earliest remaining monumental Greek stone statue resembles Egyptian sculpture in its pose (**A**), and its flatness suggests its early date (**B**) (ca. 650 B.C.E.).

xena (presumably husband and wife) made a dedication to Persephone, and on Paros, the same Telestodice mentioned above dedicated a second statue together with her husband Democydes.

 The largest body of epigraphic evidence for such dedications comes

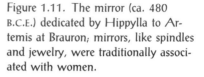

Figure 1.11. The mirror (ca. 480 B.C.E.) dedicated by Hippylla to Artemis at Brauron; mirrors, like spindles and jewelry, were traditionally associated with women.

from the Athenian Acropolis. There are fourteen certain dedications by women, and almost all belong to the late Archaic period, ca. 525–480 B.C.E. In most instances, the object dedicated is lost and we do not know what it was. In two cases the inscription is on a marble basin that is itself the dedication (perhaps used for holy water), and one inscription is on the pedestal that supported such a basin.

The relatively large number of dedications by Athenian women were probably inspired by the female divinity, Athena. The many korai set up on the Acropolis may have been dedications to Athena too (cf. Figs. 1.3 and 1.4), but we do not know how many of these, if any, were set up by women. Those few whose dedications are preserved were put up by men, who clearly controlled the financial resources to commission such expensive votives.

The latest of the Acropolis dedications by a woman was made ca. 470–450 B.C.E. Contemporaneous with this is an unusual inscription from the sanctuary of Demeter on the sloping hill between the Acropolis and the Agora. It records, in two elegiac couplets, a dedication to Demeter and Persephone by a priestess of the goddesses named Lysistrate (Pritchett 1940: 96–97):

> O Mistress Demeter, Lysistrate, the attendant of your secret rite,
> And of your daughter's, set up this offering of two wreaths
> As an ornament of the forecourt. She is not sparing of what she has,
> But is unstinting to the gods within her power.

Lysistrate had probably been awarded these two wreaths for her services as priestess of the cult of Demeter, which was a "branch" of the principal sanctuary in Eleusis (see Fig. 1.6).

Archaic Misogyny

The Homeric poems and early aristocratic lyric celebrate the importance of the woman's role as wife and mother, and praise her beauty, skill, and intelligence. Like men, these women are viewed as adult moral beings; their decisions may be subject to divine interference, but they are equally rational and can be praised for their moral integrity. In the *Odyssey* Penelope wins individual fame for her chastity, whereas the adultery of Clytemnestra, wife of Agamemnon and daughter of Tyndareus, casts a slur on womankind in general. Thus praise for the Homeric woman is individual, whereas blame is generalizable:

> The soul of Agamemnon, son of Atreus, answered him:
> "O fortunate son of Laertes, Odysseus of the many devices,
> surely you have won yourself a wife endowed with great virtue.
> How good was proved the heart that is in blameless Penelope,
> Ikarios' daughter, and how well she remembered Odysseus,
> her wedding husband. Thereby the fame of her virtue shall never
> die away, but the immortals will make for the people
> of earth a thing of grace in the song for prudent Penelope
> Not so did the daughter of Tyndareos fashion her evil
> deeds, when she killed her wedded lord, and a song of loathing
> will be hers among men, to make evil the reputation
> of womankind, even for those whose acts are virtuous."
> (*Odyssey* 24.191–202; Lattimore 1965)

One strand of the archaic tradition developed at length a considerably more ambivalent attitude to wives. These views are best represented in the story of the creation of the first woman in Hesiod's *Theogony* and *Works and Days* and Semonides' poem on the origin of the different tribes of womankind from different animals, earth, and sea.

Hesiod's two poems twice represent the creation of the first woman as a punishment to a group of mortal men (created in some versions by the god Prometheus). Woman's creation is part of man's fall from a Golden Age into a world marked by death, disease, labor, and the need to produce heirs from a creature whose seductive beauty conceals her unreliability, her greediness, and her uselessness. A wife can exhaust a man sexually and age him prematurely (*Works and Days*, 702–5); and, like a drone, she drains his hard-won accumulation of agricultural wealth. In contrast to other Archaic poetry, Hesiod mentions no contributions by wives to the economy of the household, not even cooking and weaving. Yet a wife is a necessary evil because without her a man cannot have a son to inherit his property. Suspicious of a wife's virtue and fidelity, Hesiod recommends a late marriage (thirty) to a young and virginal woman, preferably the daughter of a neighbor and therefore a known quantity (*Works and Days*, 699–701).

In Hesiod's creation myth the conflict between Zeus and the Titan god Prometheus or "Forethought" ultimately condemns mankind (as did Jehovah in Genesis) to three typically ambivalent gifts from the gods: agriculture, marriage and procreation, and sacrifice. Men appear to get the best parts of the sacrificial animal, but in fact they confirm their mortality with their portion, for the food they eat requires labor to produce; by contrast, the portions burned for the gods in sacrifice give them only the savor from the meat, while they continue to subsist on foods that ensure their immortality: nectar and ambrosia. Similarly, men retain fire; yet it is not the immortal fire of the gods, but a fire that man must labor to feed, just as he must also work to feed the useless and dronelike woman and produce children by her (see Vernant 1980b). In the following passage from the *Theogony*, a poem that is largely concerned with explaining the origins of the divine cosmos, the first woman resembles a bride. Although useless economically, a wife can, like other gifts of the gods to men, occasionally be good, even though a man's life continually alternates between good and bad. The *Works and Days* stresses the struggle of men living in an Iron Age to work and recover something of the lost Golden Age, a struggle to which women make no contribution beyond reproduction. In keeping with this theme, Pandora, the first woman, is a deceptive and hollow imitation of the goddesses she was made to resemble and the source of death and disease among humankind (See further Pucci 1977).

> Immediately he [Zeus] made in payment of fire an evil for men,
> for the famous Lame-Legged One fashioned of clay,
> as Zeus decreed, an image resembling a virgin demure.
> And the goddess gray-eyed Athena girdled and dressed her
> in a silver-white gown and over her head drew a veil,
> one that was woven with wonderful skill, a marvel to look at;
> and over this a garland of spring flowers, bright in their freshness,
> Pallas Athena set on her head a lovely adornment;
> and a gold crown, encircling the brow, she put in its place,
> which had been made by the famous Lame-Legged One himself,
> using the skill of his hands, gladly obliging Zeus Father.
> On it were made many intricate shapes, marvels to look at,
> resembling the terrible monsters spawned by earth and sea;
> many of these he put there all of them breathing with charm,
> marvelous beings which seemed to be living and able to roar.
> When he had finished this beauty, this evil to balance a good,
> Hephaistos brought her among the other gods and men,
> glorying in her adornment by the gray-eyed Daughter of Great Zeus.
> Then the gods and mortal men were struck with amazement
> when they beheld this sheer inescapable snare for men.
> From her descend the race of women, the feminine sex;
> from her come the baneful race and types of women.
> Women, a great plague, make their abodes with mortal men,

being ill-suited to Poverty's curse but suited to Plenty.
Compare how the honey bees in the protected cells of the hives
garner food for the drones, conspirers in evil works—
all day long they are active until the sun goes down
busily working and storing white honey during the daylight—
while the drones keep within the protected cells of the hives and
garner into their stomachs the food that others have worked for.
Even so Zeus the Thunderer on High created women
as an evil for men and conspirers in troublesome works.
And in exchange for a good he gave a balancing evil.
Whoever flees from marriage and women's mischievous works,
being unwilling to wed, comes to baneful old age with
no one to care for his needs, and though he has plenty to live on
while he is living, collateral heirs divide his possessions
when he is dead. As for the man who is fated to marry,
if he obtains a virtuous wife, one endowed with good sense,
throughout his life evil and good alternate endlessly.
But that man who obtains a wife who is thoroughly bad
lives having deep in his breast a pain which never subsides
fixed in his innermost heart, and this is an evil incurable.
Thus to deceive Zeus's mind is impossible or to get around it,
for not even the son of Iapetos, crafty Prometheus,
avoided his deep wrath, but in spite of his shrewdness
suffers under compulsion great inescapable bondage.

                      (*Theogony* 570–616; Frazer 1983)

Then, stirred to anger, Zeus of the Storm Cloud addressed him as follows:
"Son of Iapetos, you who surpass all others in planning,
you rejoice in your theft of my fire and in having deceived me,
being the cause of great pain to yourself and men in the future.
I shall give them in payment of fire an evil which all shall
take to their hearts with delight, an evil to love and embrace."
Thus the Father of Gods and Men addressed him, and laughed.
And he commanded far-famed Hephaistos immediately to make it
out of water and clay, and give it the voice of a human and
put in it strength and cause it to look like a goddess immortal,
having the lovely, desirable shape of a virgin. And then he
ordered Athena to teach her the skill of intricate weaving.
And Aphrodite the Golden he ordered to shed on her charm and
make her an object of painful love and exhausting desire.
And he ordered Hermes the Guide, the Slayer of Argos,
to put in her mind a dog's shamelessness and the deceit of a thief.
Thus spoke their king, Zeus, son of Kronos, and they obeyed him.
Immediately the famous Lame-Legged One moulded of clay
an image resembling a virgin demure, as Zeus had decreed.
And the goddess gray-eyed Athena girdled and dressed her:
the Graces divine along with our Lady Persuasion hung
golden necklaces on her, and the lovely Horai
crowned her head by setting upon it a garland of spring flowers,
all of which things Pallas Athena arranged in good order.
And the Guide, the Slayer of Argos, enclosed in her breast

lies and wheedling words and the treacherous ways of a thief,
following Zeus the Thunderer's decree; and he, heaven's herald,
gave her a speaking voice and announced that her name was Pandora,
"The Gift of All," because all the gods who dwell on Olympos
gave a gift to this plague for men who are eaters of bread.
But when he had completed this sheer inescapable snare,
Zeus Father had her led off as a gift to Epimetheus
by the famous Slayer of Argos, heaven's swift herald.
And Epimetheus took no heed of Prometheus' advice
not to receive any gift the Olympian Zeus might send him
but to reject it lest some evil shoould happen to mortals.
So he received it and learned by experience the evil he had.
For the tribes of men had previously lived on the earth
free and apart from evils, free from burdensome labor
and from painful diseases, the bringers of death to men.
In the power of these evils men rapidly pass into old age.
But then woman, raising the jar's great lid in her hands and
scattering its contents, devised anguishing miseries for men.
Only Hope was left within, securely imprisoned,
caught there under the lip of the jar, unable to fly
out and away, for before this could happen she let the lid drop,
as the Lord of the Aegis, Zeus of the Storm Cloud, decreed.
But as for those other, those numberless miseries, they wander among men,
for the earth is abounding in evils and so is the sea.
And diseases come upon men by day and by night,
everywhere moving at will, bringing evil to mortals
silently, for Zeus of the Counsels has deprived them of voices.
Thus in no way can anyone escape the purpose of Zeus.

                                    (*Works and Days*, 53–105; Frazer 1983)

Semonides' poem on women similarly stresses their tendencies to laziness, uncontrolled appetite, slovenliness, gossip, and adultery. Each tribe of women reflects the characteristics of its nonhuman origin (see further Loraux 1978). Mare women are aristocratic—a lovely and useless luxury; pig women reflect the slovenly environment in which they live; the donkey woman is reluctant to work but not to eat or engage in adultery; like Pandora, the vixen woman is unpredictably good or bad. Semonides hints in the final lines of the poem that his one virtuous woman, the industrious and sexless bee woman, may well be the product of imagination rather than reality (represented by the bad wives).

In the beginning God made various kinds of women
with various minds. He made one from the hairy sow,
that one whose house is smeared with mud, and all within
lies in dishevelment and rolls along the ground,
while the pig-woman in unlaundered clothing sits
unwashed herself among the dunghills and grows fat.

God made another woman from the mischievous
vixen, whose mind gets into everything. No act

of wickedness unknown to her; no act of good
either, because the things she says are often bad
but sometimes good. Her temper changes all the time.

. . . .

One was a donkey, dusty gray and obstinate.
It's hard to make her work. You have to curse and tug
to make her do it, but in the end she gets it done
quite well. Then she goes to her corner-crib and eats.
She eats all day, she eats all night, and by the fire
she eats. But when there's a chance to make love, she'll take
the first one of her husband's friends who comes along.

. . . .

One was begotten from the maned, fastidious mare.
She manages to avoid all housework and the chores
of slaves. She wouldn't touch the mill, or lift a sieve,
or sweep the dung from the house and throw it out of doors,
or kneel by the fire. Afraid the soot will make her dirty.
She makes her husband boon-companion to Hard Times.
She washes the dirt off her body every day
twice at least, three times somes days, and anoints herself
with perfume, and forever wears her long hair combed
and shadowed deep with flowers. A woman such as this
makes, to be sure, a lovely wife for someone else
to look at, but her husband finds her an expense
unless he is some baron or a sceptered king
who can indulge his taste for luxuries like her.

. . . .

One from a bee. The man is lucky who gets her.
She is the only one no blame can settle on.
A man's life grows and blossoms underneath her touch.
She loves her husband, he loves her, and they grow old
together, while their glorious children rise to fame.
Among the throngs of other women this one shines
as an example. Heavenly grace surrounds her. She
alone takes no delight in sitting with the rest
when the conversation's about sex. . . .

Even the wife who appears to be the best behaved
turns out to be the one who lets herself go wrong.
Her husband gawps and doesn't notice; neighbors do,
and smile to see how another man gets fooled.
Each man will pick faults in someone else's wife
and boasts of his own each time he speaks of her. And yet
the same thing happens to us all. But we don't see.
For women are the biggest single bad thing Zeus
has made for us; a ball and a chain; we can't get loose
since that time when the fight about a wife began
the great War, and they volunteered, and went to hell.
(Semonides 7.1–11, 43–49, 57–70, 83–91, 108–18; Lattimore
1960)

Scholars have speculated whether the different attitude that Hesiod (or Semonides) develops toward women is the product of his being less than an aristocrat, a farmer faced with difficult economic stresses posed by intensive agriculture on small holdings of land and a less than reliable social environment, in which kings were not above corruption and narrow self-interest; in which the interests of an individual household may be at odds with that of the society at large (Sussman 1978); in which the exogamous marriage and international diplomacy of epic are counterproductive or unimportant; and in which public and private worlds have apparently diverged far more radically than in the Homeric poems. They have questioned to what degree Hesiod's misogynistic perspective is the product of a poetic tradition that aims to persuade its hearers to be virtuous through negative as well as positive exempla. The nature of the audience may also affect the content of the poems: while the internal audiences of the Homeric poems explicitly include women, for example, Hesiod's works are addressed to kings and/or his brother. Finally, the larger themes that the poet is pursuing in the poem may shape his representation of women. Hesiod's first woman is a pawn in a larger game being played between gods and men. By contrast, Homer's portrait of Helen in the two great epics may be influenced by the need in the *Iliad* to avoid making the Trojan War appear fought for a worthless object, whereas the *Odyssey*'s more ambivalent portrait enhances its favoring of home, survival, and chaste wives relative to Iliadic military glory.

Mourners

Archaic art and literature also stress the important public role of women as mourners of the dead. Women not only laid out the bodies of the dead for burial, but played the major role in lamenting them. Women could be so effective at traditional mourning songs and gestures, such as tearing hair, cheeks, and clothing and beating the breast, that they were often hired to participate in the funeral lamentations and processions of important aristocrats and warriors. In the *Iliad*, Achilles' concubine Briseis plays an important role in mourning the hero Patroclus (19.282–303); in *Iliad* 24, the Trojan hero Hector's mother Hecuba, his wife Andromache, and his sister-in-law Helen praise the hero and lament his loss to family and city:

> By the gates they met Priam bringing the corpse of his son.
> Hector's dear wife and royal mother rushed up
> To the wheel-spinning wagon, and touching the head of the dead
> They wailed and tore at their hair, while the people crowded
> Around them and wept. And now all day long till sunset
> They would have stayed outside the gates, lamenting
> And weeping for Hector, had not the old King, still

In the chariot, spoken thus to his people:
    "Make way
For the mules to pass through. Later, when I've brought him home,
You may weep to your heart's content."
    He spoke, and the crowd
Opened up, making way for the wagon. Once at the palace
They laid Hector out on a corded bed and seated
Beside him singers to lead in the dirge, and they chanted
The funeral song with the women responding in chorus.
Then white-armed Andromache led their lament, holding
The head of man-killing Hector close in her arms,
And wailing:
    "My husband, early indeed you have left us,
Me a widow in your spacious halls, your son
Still a baby, the son we two so unluckily had,
Who now, I think will never live to be grown,
Since long before that this city shall topple in ruins.
For you, my husband, are dead, you that protected
The town and kept from harm its excellent wives
And little children. These, I fear, shall soon
Be riding the hollow ships, and I among them—
And you, my child, must go with me to where you shall toil
For some monstrous master, or have some Achaean seize
Your small arm and hurl you down from the wall to a miserable
Death, being bitter at Hector for killing his brother,
Perhaps, or his father, or else his son, since many,
Many Achaeans have bitten the dusty huge earth
At the hands of brave Hector, for your father was not at all gentle
In horrible war—so now the people are mourning
For you, Hector, throughout the city, and grief beyond words
You have brought on your parents, but I far more than all others
Have nothing left but miserable sorrow. For you
As you died neither stretched out your arms to me from the bed,
Nor did you say any word of sweet love that I
Might have kept in my heart through long days and nights of
      weeping."
    Thus she spoke in her wailing, and all of the women
Responded, moaning and weeping. Then Hecuba took up
The dirge and led the vehement keening, crying:
"Hector, the dearest by far to my heart of all
My children, you when alive were also dear
To the gods, and so they have cared for you now, though your fate
Was to die as you did. Whenever swift-footed Achilles
Took other children of mine, he sold them as slaves
Beyond the barren and unresting sea, into Samos,
Imbros, and Lemnos, lost in the haze. But when
With his tapering bronze he had taken your life, he dragged you
Daily about his comrade Patroclus's barrow—
Patroclus, whom you, my son, slew—though even this
Did not resurrect his friend. But now you lie
Fresh as the dew in our palace, like one merely sleeping,

Or one whom silver-bowed Phoebus Apollo has slain
With his gentle shafts."
    Even so she spoke in her wailing,
And roused the passionate keening. Then Helen was third
To lead the lament, crying: "O Hector, dearest
By far to my heart of all my husband's brothers,
My husband is Paris the godlike, who brought me to Troy—
Would I had died first! Now this is the twentieth year
Since I left my own country, but never once have I heard
From you an evil word or an ugly. In fact,
When the others reproached me here in the palace, some brother
Of yours, a sister, or a well-dressed sister-in-law,
Or even your mother—your father was kind to me always,
A father to me as well—at such times you
Would turn them away and restrain them with your gentle spirit
And courteous words. Hence now I weep for you
And my own luckless self, grieving at heart, for now
No longer is anyone left in wide Troy that is gentle
Or loving to me. All shudder whenever I pass."

(*Iliad* 24.719–776; Rees 1991)

Women Mourners in Archaic Funerary Iconography

The earliest figured scenes in Greek art, of the mid-eighth century B.C.E., show mourners at a funeral (Fig. 1.12), and in the centuries that follow, representations of death and its rituals occupy an important role in both painting and sculpture (see further Boardman 1955, Kurtz and Boardman 1971, Havelock 1981, Kurtz 1984, Mommsen 1984, Shapiro 1991). The Greek funeral is shown on painted clay vessels and other objects actually used in various aspects of funerary ritual, and these highlight the central role of women as mourners.

In the time of Homer, on large amphoras (Fig. 1.12) that marked the tomb of a wealthy Athenian, the deceased is shown lying in state upon his bier (on other vases the deceased is a woman). The mourners include both women and men, the women recognizable only by their long skirts and their position, kneeling beside the bier. Both men and women perform the ritual gesture of tearing their hair.

In the course of the seventh century, the role of mourner must have fallen increasingly to women, for at the beginning of the sixth century, Solon reportedly drafted laws regulating the conduct of female mourners at funerals (these laws are further discussed in Chapter 3. See Alexiou 1974 and Humphreys 1983). This legislation was aimed in part at curbing the ostentation of aristocratic funerals. One later source suggests that a major concern of the legislation was to regulate women's behavior in public:

He [Solon] also subjected the public appearances of women, their mourning, and their festivals, to a law which did away with disorder and license. When women went out, they were not to wear more than three garments, they were not to

Figure 1.12. Early Attic funerary vase (760 B.C.E.) showing mourners at a funeral; men and women tear their hair as a sign of inconsolable sorrow. The women kneel under the bier, their legs covered by long skirts.

carry more than an obol's worth of food and drink, nor a pannier more than a cubit high, and they were not to travel about by night unless they rode in a wagon with a lamp to light their way. Laceration of the flesh by mourners, the use of set lamentations, and the bewailing of anyone at the funeral ceremonies of another he forbade. The sacrifice of an ox at the grave was not permitted, nor the burial with the dead of more than three changes of raiment, nor the visiting of other tombs than those of their own family, except at the time of interment. Most of these practices are also forbidden by our [Attic] laws, but ours contain the additional proviso that such offenders shall be punished by the board of censors for women, because they indulge in unmanly and effeminate extravagances of sorrow when they mourn.

(Plutarch, *Solon* 21.4–5; Perrin 1982, modified)

Women were also forbidden to mourn for someone who was not a blood relative, a second cousin or closer, except for women over age 60 (Demosthenes *Against Macartatus*, 43.62.). This was evidently meant to curb the practice of hiring paid mourners. It is difficult to gauge from vase representations of funerals just how effective or strictly enforced these laws were. Women do regularly tear their hair and flesh, but this is always at the prothesis (wake), which took place in the home, not in public. There are too few depictions of the ekphora (funeral procession) to get a sense of the women's behavior. The limiting of the prothesis to family members does seem to have been adhered to: the number of

women surrounding the bier is relatively small on pinakes and loutrophoroi of the sixth century, and one plaque (Fig. 1.13) names all the
relations (mother, father, sister, aunts), as if to prove that all were
within the prescribed limits. The figures who come closest to the young
man laid out on his bier and actually touch him are all female (including a little girl), while the men and boys approach no closer than the
foot of the couch. Women were thought to be less threatened by the
ritual pollution (miasma) of contact with a corpse, especially women
who had given birth and had thus already incurred pollution.

In about 540 B.C.E., the black-figure vase painter Exekias was commissioned by a wealthy patron to execute a series of about fifteen terra-
cotta plaques to decorate a woman's tomb, forming a continuous frieze
around three sides of the structure. These plaques narrate the various
stages of the funeral, from the lying in state and preparation of the body
to the harnessing of the chariot to transport the body to the grave. Family members of both sexes mourn beside her bier, but the mourners accompanying the chariot are all women. One panel in the series is unique
in showing a vignette that is not strictly part of the funerary ritual (Fig.
1.14). Eight women have withdrawn into a room of the house to mourn
privately and to care for a small, now motherless child. In the foreground, two women sit quietly opposite each other, perhaps the mother
and a daughter or sister of the deceased. Unlike the ritualized gestures
of mourning prevalent in Archaic art, this intimate scene conveys the
grief of family and friends in a less formal fashion.

By the late sixth century, certain shapes of vases were clearly associ-

Figure 1.13. Funeral plaque (ca. 500 B.C.E.) with kin gathered at the wake of the deceased. Women
stand closer to the dead man than do the mourning men, whose arms are raised in a kind of farewell
salute.

Figure 1.14. Funeral plaque (ca. 540–530 B.C.E.) showing women mourning in private; the little boy held by the women at the upper right contributes to the sense of intimacy.

ated with funerary use and often decorated with appropriate scenes. One such shape is the phormiskos, a globular jug used to contain oil for anointing the corpse (Fig. 1.15). A dead woman named Myrrhine is surrounded by female mourners, one of them holding her child. Their streaming hair alludes to the standard gesture of mourning.

The favorite funerary shape in both black-figure and red is the lou trophoros, a tall, slender two-handled jug that held water to cleanse the corpse. One example shows two scenes from the funeral (Fig. 1.16). On the neck, a woman holds a loutrophoros while others around her mourn. Below, a youth lies on his bier, mourned by a group of women. Even when family members of both sexes mourn at the bier, it is always the women who stand nearest the deceased or touch his or her body. Woman's role in giving birth and caring for children seems to come full circle in her role of primary care for the dead. Both activities (at least after the Solonian legislation) generally took place within the home, the domain of women, while the primary activities of men, war and politics, took place outside the home.

Figure 1.15. On this unguent vase from the end of the sixth century B.C.E., the female mourners gather around the dead woman named Myrrhine. One of the mourners is a little girl, in the foreground.

Nonaristocratic Women

The Homeric poems stress the tragic effects war has on the lives of women and children, who will be forced to become slaves to the victors. When Achilles' concubine Briseis, a captive in war, laments the death of Patroclus, she recalls his promise to arrange her marriage to Achilles on their return to his homeland after the war (*Iliad* 19.282–300). Now neither Patroclus or Achilles will return home and fulfill her hopes. In *Iliad* 6, Hector imagines the piteous and humiliating lot Andromache will face as a slave (450–65). In the *Hymn to Demeter*, the disguised Demeter pretends that she has escaped from being captured by pirates who intend to sell her into slavery (122–34).

Yet epic poems claim that a slave's or concubine's lot could be mitigated by a beneficent master. In the aristocratic households of Homer, the children of concubines and slaves were often treated indistinguishably from noble children. In a lying Cretan tale, Odysseus tells the

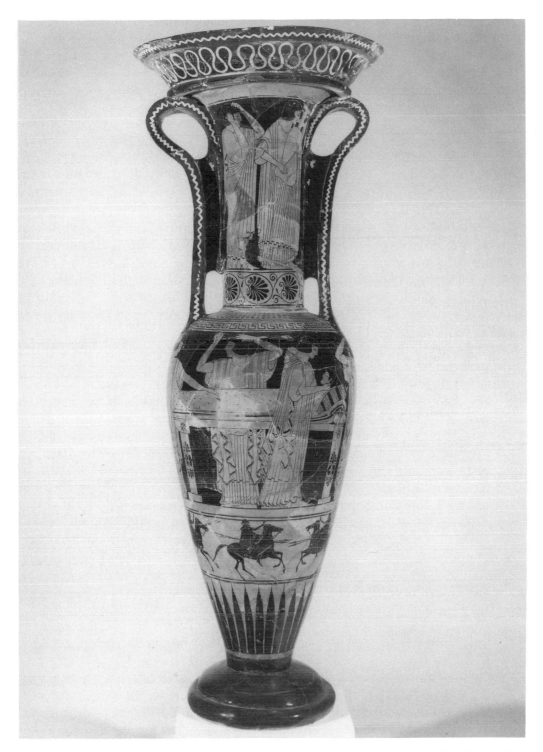

Figure 1.16. The loutrophoros (ca. 490–480 B.C.E.), holding water to wash the body of the deceased, appears on the neck of this loutrophoros, while on the body of the vessel the dead youth is shown with mourners.

swineherd Eumaeus that as the son of a concubine he was honored equally with the father's other sons, and eventually won a rich wife with his valor (*Odyssey* 14.199–213). Odysseus's mother cared for the once noble slave Eumaeus as one of her own children (*Odyssey* 15.365), just as Penelope once treated the now treacherous maidservant Melantho as her own child (*Odyssey* 18.321–25).

In the *Odyssey*, the disguised Odysseus tests the loyalty of his fifty female slaves, who assist Penelope in weaving, serving the suitors at table, and other household tasks. These female slaves are expected to conform to the standards of virtue required of free women, and those who slept with the suitors are brutally hanged by Odysseus. On the other hand, trusted servants can be treated with respect. We are told that Laertes, Odysseus's father, purchased the faithful slave Eurycleia for twenty oxen, honored her like a wife, yet did not sleep with her out of respect for his wife (*Odyssey* 1.430–33; see also *Iliad* 9.449–50, where Achilles' tutor Phoenix says that his father dishonored his mother by keeping a concubine). Menelaus only sired his bastard son Megapenthes from a slave woman after it was clear that Helen would bear no more children (*Odyssey* 4.11–14).

Literary sources give us little substantial evidence about the lives of free working women. In the *Hymn to Demeter*, to give an example of the kind of fragmentary evidence we have, Demeter, disguised as an old and homeless woman, suggests that she might become a nurse or housekeeper in Celeus's house (138–44). She is then offered a substantial wage to care for the only son of the household. Hesiod (*Works and Days* 602-03) recommends hiring a childless (nursing mothers cause trouble) female laborer for the summer. At *Iliad* 12.433-35 we hear of a virtuous widow weighing wool in scales in order to earn a meagre support for her children. Before the Solonian legislation, older women could earn wages as mourners. Two unusual inscriptions from the Athenian Acropolis give the women's occupations and show that in rare instances nonaristocratic women could also afford to make religious dedications:

Phrygia the baker dedicated me to Athena.

(Lazzarini 1976: no. 46)

Smycithe the washerwoman dedicated [me] as a tithe.
(Lazzarini 1976: no. 666; Raubitschek 1949: no. 380)

Phrygia's dedication is a small bronze shield decorated with a gorgoneion, not especially "female," but appropriate for the recipient. Smicythe dedicated a marble basin, appropriate to her own profession. Phrygia's name ("the Phrygian") suggests she was probably a foreigner living in Athens. The "tithe" in Smicythe's dedications is a substantial part of her earnings, and other dedications to Athena call themselves *aparchê* (first-fruits), implying that the dedication was something of value, the best the dedicator had to offer.

Thus even the slim evidence that we have for the lives of nonaristocratic women suggests that they imitated their richer sisters in dedications to the gods and were imagined in poetry as conforming to the same standards of praise and blame that regulated the behavior of free, legitimate wives.

NOTES

1. Griffiths 1972 argues that the poem is actually an epithalamium or marriage song for Agido on the morning after her wedding. See Page 1951 and Calame 1977 for further discussion.

2. For a citation of ancient sources on this insoluble question, see Campbell 1982.

TRANSLATIONS

Bing, Peter, and Rip Cohen. 1991. *Games of Venus*. New York.

Foley, Helene P. 1993. *The Homeric Hymn to Demeter*. Princeton, N.J.

Frazer, R. M. 1983. *The Poems of Hesiod*. Norman, Okla.

Lattimore, Richmond. 1960. *Greek Lyrics*. Chicago.

———. 1965. *The Odyssey of Homer*. New York.

Perrin, Bernadotte. 1982. *Plutarch's Lives*. Vol 1. Loeb Classical Library. Cambridge, Mass. (Originally published 1914)

Rayor, Diane. 1991. *Sappho's Lyre: Archaic Lyric and Women Poets of Ancient Greece*. Berkeley and Los Angeles.

Rees, Ennis. 1991. *The Iliad of Homer*. (First published 1963)

Segal, Charles. 1985. "Archaic Choral Lyric." In *The Cambridge History of Classical Literature*, 1: 165–85. Cambridge.

Snyder, Jane. 1989. *The Woman and the Lyre: Women Writers in Classical Greece and Rome*. Carbondale, Ill.

WORKS CONSULTED

Ahlberg, G. 1970. *Prothesis and Ekphora in Greek Geometric Art*. Göteberg.

Alexiou, Margaret. 1974. *The Ritual Lament in Greek Tradition*. Cambridge.

Arthur, Marylin B. 1973. "Early Greece: The Origins of the Western Attitude Towards Women." *Arethusa* 6: 7–58. [Also published in *Women in the Ancient World: The Arethusa Papers*, edited by John Peradotto and J. P. Sullivan, 7–58. Albany, N.Y., 1984.]

———. 1977. "Politics and Pomegranates. An Interpretation of the Homeric *Hymn to Demeter*." *Arethusa* 10: 7–48.

———. 1981. "The Divided World of *Iliad* VI." In *Reflections of Women in Antiquity*, edited by Helene P. Foley, 19–44. New York.

Boardman, John. 1955. "Painted Funerary Plaques and Some Remarks on Prothesis." *Annual of the British School of Archaeology at Athens* 50: 51–66.

Calame, Claude. 1977. *Les choeurs de jeunes filles en Grèce archaïque*. Vols. 1 and 2. Rome.

Campbell, D. A. 1982. *Greek Lyric*. Vol. 1. Loeb Classical Library. Cambridge, Mass.

Clairmont, C. W. 1970. *Gravestone and Epigram*. Mainz.

Donlan, Walter. 1981–82. "Reciprocities in Homer." *Classical World* 75: 137–75.

Foley, Helene P. 1978. "Reverse Similes and Sex Roles in the Odyssey." *Arethusa* 11:

7–26. [Also published in *Women in the Ancient World: The Arethusa Papers*, edited by John Peradotto and J. P. Sullivan, 59–78. Albany, N.Y., 1984.]

Griffiths, Alan. 1972. "Alcman's Partheneion: The Morning After the Night Before." *Quaderni Urbinati di Cultura Classica* 14: 7–30.

Havelock, Christine. 1981. "Mourners on Greek Vases: Remarks on the Social History of Women." In *The Greek Vase*, edited by S. L. Hyatt, 103–18. Latham, N.Y.

Jeffery, L. H. 1962. "The Inscribed Gravestones of Archaic Attica." *Annual of the British School of Archaeology at Athens* 57: 115–53.

Kurtz, D. C. 1984. "Vases for the Dead, an Attic Selection, 750–400 B.C." In *Ancient Greek and Related Pottery*, edited by H. A. G. Brijder, 314–28. Amsterdam.

———, and John Boardman. 1971. *Greek Burial Customs*. London.

Lacey, W. K. 1968. *The Family in Classical Greece*. Ithaca, N.Y.

Lazzarini, M. L. 1976. "Le formule delle dediche votive nella Grecia arcaica." *Memorie della R. Accademia dei Lincei*, ser. 8, 19: 47–354.

Leduc, Claudine. 1992. "Marriage in Ancient Greece." In *A History of Women in the West*, edited by P. Schmitt Pantel, 1: 233–94. Cambridge, Mass.

Loraux, Nicole. 1978. "Sur le race des femmes et quelques-unes de ses tribus." *Arethusa* 11: 43–88.

Mommsen, Heide. 1984. "Der Grabpinax des Exekias mit den trauernden Frauen." In *Ancient Greek and Related Pottery*, edited by H. A. G. Brijder, 329–33. Amsterdam.

Morris, Ian. 1986. "The Use and Abuse of Homer." *Classical Antiquity* 5, no 1: 81–138.

Page, D. L. 1951. *Alcman, the Partheneion*. Oxford.

Pritchett, W. Kendrick. 1940. "Greek Inscriptions." *Hesperia* 9: 97–133.

Prückner, H. 1968. *Die locrischen Tonreliefs*. Mainz.

Raubitschek, A. E. 1949. *Dedications on the Athenian Akropolis*. Cambridge.

Richardson, N. J. 1974. *The Homeric Hymn to Demeter*. Oxford.

Richter, G. M. A. 1968. *Korai*. London.

Ridgway, Brunilde S. 1987. "Ancient Greek Women and Art: The Material Evidence." *American Journal of Archaeology* 91: 399–409.

Schneider, Lambert A. 1975. *Zur sozialen Bedeutung der archaischen Korenstatuen. Hamburger Beiträge zur Archäologie*, suppl. 2. Hamburg.

Shapiro, H. A. 1991. "The Iconography of Mourning in Athenian Art." *American Journal of Archaeology* 95: 629–56.

Snodgrass, A. M. 1974. "An Historical Homeric Society?" *Journal of Hellenic Studies* 94: 114–25.

Sussman, Linda S. 1978. "Workers and Drones: Labor, Idleness and Gender Definition in Hesiod's Beehive." *Arethusa* 11: 27–42. [Also published in *Women in the Ancient World: The Arethusa Papers*, edited by John Peradotto and J. P. Sullivan, 79–94. Albany, N.Y., 1984.]

Vernant, Jean-Pierre. 1980a. "Marriage." In his *Myth and Society in Ancient Greece*, 45–70. Atlantic Highlands, N.J.

———. 1980b. "The Myth of Prometheus in Hesiod." In his *Myth and Society in Ancient Greece*, 161–85. Atlantic Highlands, N.J.

FURTHER READING

Bergren, Ann. 1983. "Language and the Female in Early Greek Thought." *Arethusa* 16: 69–95.

Burnett, Anne Pippin. 1983. *Three Archaic Poets*. Cambridge, Mass.

du Bois, Page. 1978. "Sappho and Helen." *Arethusa* 11: 89–100. [Also published in *Women in the Ancient World: The Arethusa Papers*, edited by John Peradotto and J. P. Sullivan, 95–106. Albany, N.Y., 1984.]

Humphreys, S. C. 1983. *The Family, Women and Death: Comparative Studies.* London.

Jenkyns, Richard. 1982. *Three Classical Poets.* Cambridge, Mass.

Katz, Marilyn A. 1991. *Penelope's Renown.* Princeton, N.J.

Kerényi, Karl. 1967. *Eleusis.* New York.

Lefkowitz, Mary. 1981. "Critical Stereotypes and the Poetry of Sappho." In her *Heroines and Hysterics*, 59–68. London.

Murnaghan, Sheila. 1987. *Disguise and Recognition in the Odyssey.* Princeton, N.J.

Pucci, Pietro. 1977. *Hesiod and the Language of Poetry.* Baltimore, Md. [chapter 4, "Pandora," 82–126]

Sourvinou-Inwood, Christiane. 1978. "Persephone and Aphrodite at Locri: A Model for Personality Definitions in Greek Religion." *Journal of Hellenic Studies* 98: 101–21.

Stigers, Eva. 1981. "Sappho's Private World." In *Reflections of Women in Antiquity*, edited by Helene P. Foley, 45–62. New York.

Vermeule, Emily. 1979. *Aspects of Death in Early Greek Art and Poetry.* Berkeley and Los Angeles.

Winkler, Jack. 1981. "Gardens of Nymphs: Public and Private in Sappho's Lyrics." In *Reflections of Women in Antiquity*, edited by Helene P. Foley, 63–90. New York.

2

EXCURSUS
SPARTAN WOMEN: WOMEN IN A WARRIOR SOCIETY

More than any other Greek women, Spartans have been the subject of praise or blame from antiquity to the present. This excursus begins with a note of praise from a twentieth-century feminist, but the last quotation is a strongly worded condemnation from a Greek philosopher.

Simone de Beauvoir (1952, p. 82) idealized Sparta:

Since the oppression of woman has its cause in the will to perpetuate the family and to keep the patrimony intact, woman escapes complete dependency to the degree in which she escapes from the family; if a society that forbids private property also rejects the family, the lot of women in it is found to be considerably ameliorated. In Sparta the communal regime was in force, and it was the only Greek city in which woman was treated almost on an equality with man. The girls were raised like the boys; the wife was not confined in her husband's domicile: indeed, he was allowed to visit her only furtively, by night; and his wife was so little his property that on eugenic grounds another man could demand union with her. The very idea of adultery disappeared when the patrimony disappeared; all children belonged in common to the city as a whole, and women were no longer jealously enslaved to one master; or, inversely, one may say that the citizen, possessing neither private wealth nor specific ancestry, was no longer in possession of woman. Women underwent the servitude of maternity as did men the servitude of war; but beyond the fulfilling of this civic duty, no restraint was put on their freedom.

Archaic to Hellenistic Sources

As we have seen in Chapter 1, fragments of early Archaic poetry are our first important sources for Spartan women; hence we have chosen to discuss them here. Later texts and brief reports about Spartan women are also extant, but archaeological and art historical sources are few. Of our sources only Alcman, who was probably born in Lydia but lived in Sparta at the end of the seventh century B.C.E., is a direct witness for women in the Archaic period. Xenophon lived in Sparta in the first quarter of the fourth century B.C.E. Other authors who comment on Sparta are late, but they often drew their information from earlier (though not necessarily trustworthy) sources. For example, Plutarch, who gives detailed information about women based on research in earlier literature, lived approximately one thousand years after the so-called constitution of the legendary Spartan lawgiver Lycurgus, which he describes. This excursus will survey what is reported about the history of Spartan women spanning approximately a 500-year period.

Our sources refer to Sparta of the Archaic, Classical, and Hellenistic periods, in several cases without raising the possibility that life in Sparta changed over time. This telescoping of history is one reason why the texts contain contradictions that are difficult to explain and reconcile on the nature of Spartan marriage, the choice of spouses, and women's relationship to real property. We have data about Spartan women who were upper class and royal, not about the women of the lower classes. (The population of Sparta was distributed into three groups: the Spartiates [or Spartans] were full citizens; the periokoi were free, non-citizens; and the helots were unfree workers.) Both poetic and prose texts give information on the life cycle from childhood through puberty, sexuality (including lesbianism), marriage, motherhood, and death.

The Education of Spartan Women

Alcman wrote choral lyrics that were performed by unmarried girls, and some fragments of these *Partheneia* still remain to offer glimpses of an all-female aristocratic world. (For longer excerpts of the poems from which the phrases below are quoted, see Chapter 1.) The beauty of Spartan women was legendary. Like the mythical Helen, the girls of *Partheneion* 1 are said to have had golden hair: "The tresses of my cousin Hagesichora blossom like pure gold. . . . She, with her gorgeous golden hair." Cosmetics were banished, and were, in any case, not needed, for exercising outdoors made women's complexions glow ("Her silvery face"). These handsome women, unsecluded, are named and their attractive features and accomplishments praised. The animal imagery used for them is complimentary: "Our glorious leader . . . who clearly stands out herself, as if you put among the herds a racehorse, sturdy, thundering, a champion. . . . The girl who's next to Agido in beauty shall race but as a Kolaxeian horse behind an Ibenian." Fine horses connote beauty and wealth, but, like the maidens who will be married, horses must be broken in or yoked.

The girls mentioned in *Partheneion* 1 seem to belong to at least two

different age groups (see Chapter 1). The oldest are Hagesichora and
Agido, who serve as models for the other girls, who are younger and who
vie for their leaders' attention. There is plenty of evidence for homoerotic friendships between men in many places and in all periods of
Greek history. Plutarch describes the relationship of younger with older
women in Sparta as sexual and educational and parallels it with the
better-known relationship of boys with men:

Whether a boy's standing was good or bad, his lover shared it. . . . Sexual relationships of this type were so highly valued that respectable women would in
fact have love affairs with unmarried girls. Yet there was no rivalry; instead, if
individual males found that their affections had the same object, they made
this the foundation for mutual friendship, and eagerly pursued joint efforts to
perfect their loved one's character.

> (Plutarch, *Life of Lycurgus*, 18; Talbert 1988: 30–31)

Some of Alcman's language is explicitly erotic. Competent transla-
tors convey these sentiments in various ways. The following selection
provides an example of one of the major problems confronting the reader
who must encounter the ancient evidence through the lens of translation. The first quotation from *Partheneion* 1 is from the translation by
Bing and Cohen (1991), which is quoted in full in Chapter 1:

> and no longer coming to Ainesimbrota's house will you say:
> "if only Astaphis were mine,
> if Philylla would look my way,
> or Demareta, or lovely Vianthemis—
> but Hagesichora wears me out with desire."

In Charles Segal's (1985: 174) version, the girls are more coy and
elusive:

Nor if you go to the house of Anesimbrota will you say, "May Astaphis be mine;
may Philylla cast her glances at me and Damareta and the lovely Vianthemis";
but rather you will say, "Hagesichora wears me down."

Richmond Lattimore's (1970) translations are usually close to the
Greek, but in this passage he adopts euphemisms:

> . . . nor go to Ainesimbrota's
> house and say:
> Let Astaphis be on my side;
> let Philylla look my way;
> give me Damareta, lovely Ianthemis.
> . . . Maidens, we have come to the peace desired,
> all through Hagesichora's grace.

The Greek text itself is difficult to establish. David Campbell prefers
an alternate version of the Greek (reading *terei* "guard" instead of *teirei*
"wears out").[1] The possibility that the text refers to an intimate relationship between Hagesichora and other women is mentioned only in
the commentary:

. . . nor will you go to Aenesimbrota's and say, "If only Astaphis were mine, if only Philylla were to look my way and Damareta and lovely Ianthemis"; no, Hagesichora guards me.

(Campbell 1988: 367)

However, the erotic allusion is probably correct, for such language is not confined to *Partheneion* 1, but appears in other *Partheneia:*

A girl declares her erotic feelings toward Astymeloisa who may be the leader of a chorus: . . . and with desire that looses the limbs, but she looks glances more melting than sleep and death. . . . If she should come near and take me by the soft hand, at once I would become her suppliant.

(*Partheneion* 2, frag. 3; Segal 1985: 178. See full quotation in Chapter 1)

Spartans were the only Greek girls for whom the state prescribed a public education. This education included a significant physical component. In *Partheneion* 1 girls are praised for swiftness in the comparisons with racehorses. Spartan women were the only Greek women we know of who stripped for athletics, as Greek men did, and engaged in athletics on a regular basis. Some sources report that total nudity, even in public in the presence of men, was not unthinkable for Spartans, as it was for other respectable Greek women. Thus in Plato's *Republic*, the proposal that women exercise in the nude is considered not only radical, but laughable. (See Chapter 3 "Ancient Critical Reactions to Women's Roles in Classical Athens".) When Spartan women participated in footraces at Olympia in honor of Hera, goddess of marriage, they wore a short chiton like those worn by the legendary Amazons (see Chapter 4):

Every fourth year the Sixteen Women weave a robe for Hera; and the same women also hold games called the Heraea. The games consist of a race between virgins. The virgins are not all of the same age; but the youngest run first, the next in age run next, and the eldest virgins run last of all. They run thus: their hair hangs down, they wear a shirt that reaches to a little above the knee, the right shoulder is bare to the breast. The course assigned to them for the contest is the Olympic stadium; but the course is shortened by about a sixth of the stadium. The winners receive crowns of olive and a share of the cow which is sacrificed to Hera; moreover they are allowed to dedicate statues of themselves with their names engraved on them. The attendants who help the Sixteen to run these games are women. As with the Olympic festival they trace back these girls' games to antiquity, declaring that Hippodameia in gratitude to Hera for her marriage to Pelops established the Committee of Sixteen and with their help inaugurated the Heraean festival.

(Pausanias 5.16.2; Frazer 1965: 1: 260)

The image of a young athletic woman shown in seminudity (Fig. 2.1) is extraordinary in the context of Archaic Greece. Compared with the heavily draped korai from other parts of the Greek world, the seminude woman in this statuette seems striking, but it was meant neither as "heroic," nor, as far as we can tell, erotic; rather it was a straightforword representation of the racing costume mentioned in the written texts. This statuette should be compared with the korai dis-

Figure 2.1. Statuette of a young female athlete shown in a short sleeveless dress, not unlike that of an Amazon. Such an image is unusual in the context of Archaic Greece, where female figures (other than prostitutes) are normally shown in layered garments that cover the whole body.

cussed in Chapter 1. (See further discussion of the female nude in Chapter 5.)

The naming of girls in the *Partheneia* and the fact that the names of victors in the footraces were inscribed on statues of themselves indicate that women were not excluded from the public sphere and suggest that some, at least, were literate. Women who participated in choirs that performed choral lyric certainly knew how to sing and dance and had memorized the myths and historical events narrated in the poems, for example those concerning the Pleiades mentioned in *Partheneion* 1. Unlike Athens, Sparta produced at least two female poets: their names are known, but their works are not extant. Athenaeus (13.600f.) refers to a poet named Megalostrata who was Alcman's contemporary, and Aristophanes (*Lysistrata* 1237) mentions a poet called Cleitagora. Iamblichus (*De Vita Pythagorica* 189–94, 267, 269) names several Spartan women who became Pythagoreans (Poralla, 1985: 72, 79, 118), while Plato (*Protagoras* 342D) remarked on the intellectual culture of Spartan women: "there are not only men but women also who pride themselves on their education; and you can tell that what I say is true and that the Spartans have the best education in philosophy." In view of the notorious lack of culture among Spartan men, it would appear that Spartan women were, in terms of their superior education, more like men in other Greek cities.

According to the reference to the "Sixteen Women" in the passage from Pausanias, quoted earlier, Spartans, like other Greek women, could weave. But Spartans were forbidden to engage in banausic, or money-making occupations: they gained their sustenance from the work of the lower classes on plots of land that were distributed to Spartans at birth, but which reverted to the community when they died. We do not know whether public land was allocated to female babies, or whether females were supported by the allocations made to men in their families. All male Spartans were educated to become warriors, and the women's principal task was to give birth to warriors. Xenophon draws attention to the eugenic goals of Spartan marriage and to elements in the education of Spartan women that were different from the experiences of Athenians:

For it was not by imitating other states, but by devising a system utterly different from that of most others, that he [Lycurgus] made his country preeminently prosperous.

First, to begin at the beginning, I will take the begetting of children. In other states the girls who are destined to become mothers and are brought up in the approved fashion, live on the very plainest fare, with a most meager allowance of delicacies. Wine is either withheld altogether, or, if allowed them, is diluted with water. The rest of the Greeks expect their girls to imitate the sedentary life that is typical of handicraftsmen—to keep quiet and do wool-work. How, then, is it to be expected that women so brought up will bear fine children?

But Lycurgus thought the labor of slave women sufficient to supply clothing. He believed motherhood to be the most important function of freeborn women. Therefore, in the first place, he insisted on physical training for the female no less than for the male sex: moreover, he instituted races and trials of strength for women competitors as for men, believing that if both parents are strong they produce more vigorous offspring.

He noticed, too, that, during the time immediately succeeding marriage, it was usual elsewhere for the husband to have unlimited intercourse with his wife. The rule that he adopted was the opposite of this: for he laid it down that the husband should be ashamed to be seen entering his wife's room or leaving it. With this restriction on intercourse the desire of the one for the other must necessarily be increased, and their offspring was bound to be more vigorous than if they were surfeited with one another. In addition to this, he withdrew from men the right to take a wife whenever they chose, and insisted on their marrying in the prime of their manhood, believing that this too promoted the production of fine children. It might happen, however, that an old man had a young wife; and he observed that old men keep a very jealous watch over their young wives. To meet these cases he instituted an entirely different system by requiring the elderly husband to introduce into his house some man whose physical and moral qualities he admired, in order to beget children. On the other hand, in case a man did not want to cohabit with his wife and nevertheless desired children of whom he could be proud, he made it lawful for him to choose a woman who was the mother of a fine family and of high birth, and if he obtained her husband's consent, to make her the mother of his children.

He gave his sanction to many similar arrangements. For the wives want to take charge of two households, and the husbands want to get brothers for their sons, brothers who are members of the family and share in its influence, but claim no part of the money.

Thus his regulations with regard to the begetting of children were in sharp contrast with those of other states.

(*Constitution of the Lacedaemonians* 1.2–10; Marchant 1984, 137–41)

Plutarch doubtless read Xenophon's description of Spartan society. His version agrees with Xenophon's: for example, both report with approval that girls were given a physical education and that newly married couples did not sleep together frequently. (For the education of girls at Athens, see Chapter 3, excerpt from Xenophon, *Oeconomicus*.) But Plutarch adds some curious antiquarian details about the transvestism of brides and a communal way of life for men that endured after marriage:

Aristotle claims wrongly that he (that is, Lycurgus) tried to discipline the women but gave up when he could not control the considerable degree of license and power attained by women because of their husbands' frequent campaigning. At these times the men were forced to leave them in full charge, and consequently they used to dance attendance on them to an improper extent and call them their Ladyships. Lycurgus, rather, showed all possible concern for them too. First he toughened the girls physically by making them run and wrestle and throw the discus and javelin. Thereby their children in embryo would make a strong start in strong bodies and would develop better, while the women themselves would also bear their pregnancies with vigor and would meet the challenge of childbirth in a successful, relaxed way. He did away with prudery, sheltered upbringing, and effeminacy of any kind. He made young girls no less than young men grow used to walking nude in processions, as well as to dancing and singing at certain festivals with the young men present and looking on. On some occasions the girls would make fun of each of the young men, helpfully criticizing their mistakes. On other occasions they would rehearse in song the praises which they had composed about those meriting them, so that they filled the youngsters with a great sense of ambition and rivalry. . . .

There was nothing disreputable about the girls' nudity. It was altogether modest, and there was no hint of immorality. Instead it encouraged simple habits and an enthusiasm for physical fitness, as well as giving the female sex a taste of masculine gallantry, since it too was granted equal participation in both excellence and ambition. As a result the women came to talk as well as to think in the way that Leonidas' wife Gorgo[2] is said to have done. For when some woman, evidently a foreigner, said to her: "You Laconian women are the only ones who can rule men," she replied: "That is because we are the only ones who give birth to men."

There were then also these inducements to marry. I mean the processions of girls, and the nudity, and the competitions which the young men watched, attracted by a compulsion not of an intellectual type, but (as Plato says) a sexual one. In addition Lycurgus placed a certain civil disability on those who did not marry, for they were excluded from the spectacle of the Gymnopaediae. . . .[3]

The custom was to capture women for marriage—not when they were slight or immature, but when they were in their prime and ripe for it. The so-called 'bridesmaid' took charge of the captured girl. She first shaved her hair to the scalp, then dressed her in a man's cloak and sandals, and laid her down alone on a mattress in the dark. The bridegroom—who was not drunk and thus not impotent, but was sober as always—first had dinner in the messes, then would slip in, undo her belt, lift her and carry her to the bed. After spending only a short time with her, he would depart discreetly so as to sleep wherever he usually did along with the other young men. And this continued to be his practice thereafter: while spending the days with his contemporaries, and going to sleep with them, he would warily visit his bride in secret, ashamed and apprehensive in case someone in the house might notice him. His bride at the same time devised schemes and helped to plan how they might meet each other unobserved at suitable moments. It was not just for a short period that young men would do this, but for long enough that some might even have children before they saw their own wives in daylight. Such intercourse was not only an exercise in self-control and moderation, but also meant that partners were fertile physically, always fresh for love, and ready for intercourse rather than being sated and pale from unrestricted sexual activity. Moreover some lingering glow of desire and affection was always left in both. . . .

What was thus practiced in the interests of breeding and of the state was at that time so far removed from the laxity for which the women later became notorious, that there was absolutely no notion of adultery among them.

(Plutarch, *Life of Lycurgus*, 14–15; Talbert 1988: 24–26)

It is important to read such descriptions in the light of the authors' desire to contrast Sparta with their own societies. In Athenian thought, Spartan women served as the "Other" vis-à-vis Athenian women. For example, Spartan women spent their time out-of-doors and spoke freely to men; Athenians ideally stayed indoors and scarcely spoke to their husband. (See further, Chapter 3.) Therefore, writers exaggerated the differences between them. Like Amazons (see Chapter 4), Spartans were also exploited as a means of praising or blaming the women in an author's own state or women in general. Some ancient commentators considered that Sparta, when ordered by the Lycurgan constitution, had been a utopia. Thus some of the provisions in Plato's ideal *Republic* resemble those ascribed to the archaic constitution of Lycurgus. (See Chapter 3, "Ancient Critical Reactions to Women's Role in Classical Athens.") Xenophon and Plutarch praised and criticized the treatment of women and women's influence in Spartan society.

Included in the works of Plutarch are a collection of quotations purported to be the words of Spartan women, most of whom are undatable. They are consistent with the report in the *Life of Lycurgus* and other sources quoted earlier in showing that wit (not silence) was attributed to women; they were not "laconic." The quotations also indicate that some women, at least, subscribed to the Spartan ideal that encouraged men to be brave in war. Cowardice, for example abandoning one's shield and running from the battle, was not tolerated. Unlike most other Greek women, Spartans refused to lament over men who died in war (cf. Chapters 1 and 3). Rather, they took pride in the bravery of their sons:

After hearing that her son was a coward and unworthy of her, Damatria killed him when he made his appearance. This is the epigram about her:
Damatrius who broke the laws was killed by his mother,
She a Spartan lady, he a Spartan youth.

Another [Spartan] woman, when her sons fled from a battle and reached her, said, "In making your escape, vile slaves, where is it you've come to? Or do you plan to creep back in here where you emerged from?" At this she pulled up her clothes and exposed her belly to them.

A woman, when she saw her son approaching, asked how their country was doing. When he said: "All the men are dead," she picked up a tile, threw it at him and killed him, saying: "Then did they send you to bring us the bad news?"

As a woman was burying her son, a worthless old crone came up to her and said, "You poor woman, what a misfortune!" "No, by the two gods, a piece of good fortune," she replied, "because I bore him so that he might die for Sparta, and that is what has happened, as I wished."

When an Ionian woman was priding herself on one of the tapestries she had made (which was indeed of great value), a Spartan woman showed off her four most dutiful sons and said they were the kind of thing a noble and good woman ought to produce and should boast of them and take pride in them.

Another woman, as she was handing her son his shield and giving him some encouragement, said, "Son, either with this or on this."

(Plutarch, *Sayings of Spartan Women* 240–41; Talbert 1988: 159–61)

The Fourth Century and the Hellenistic Period

"Spartan" in English connotes asceticism and self-denial. According to Plutarch, under the Lycurgan constitution, this definition applied to the women as well as the men. But in the fourth century B.C. and the Hellenistic period some Spartan women were extremely wealthy and were conspicuous consumers. For example, Spartan women were the first women to own racehorses that were victorious at Panhellenic festivals. Like wealthy male owners, they did not themselves participate in the race, but employed charioteers (for other women who owned racehorses see Chapter 5).

Inscription recording one of the Olympic victories (in 396 and 392 B.C.E) of the horses of Cynisca:

> My father and brothers were kings of Sparta.
> I, Cynisca, victorious with my chariot of fleet horses,
> erected this statue. I declare that I am the only woman
> in all of Greece, who has won this crown.
>
> (*Inscriptiones Graecae* 5.1.1564a;
> Moretti 1953: p. 40, no. 17)

Sparta's power declined in the fourth century, and Aristotle and other commentators felt that the distribution of wealth among women was at least partly responsible. As we have seen, Plutarch quotes Aristotle and agrees with him in pointing out that a man's continual absence in military service, eating and sleeping in the barracks with his fellow soldiers, and going away for lengthy campaigns, affected family relationships and women's status. He asserts that the men of Sparta obeyed their wives and allowed them to intervene in public affairs more than they intervened in private ones (*Agis* 7.3) But Plutarch, who was a Neoplatonist and who was optimistic about women's moral and intellectual potential, rejected Aristotle's conclusion that women were responsible in large part for the decline of Sparta. Aristotle viewed Sparta as a gynaikokratia (that is, a state ruled by women), and as such, contrary to the natural hierarchy in which men were to rule women. (See excerpts from Aristotle in Chapter 3, "Ancient Critical Reactions to Women's Roles in Classical Athens.") In Athens and some other Greek states women were not permitted to own land or to manage substantial amounts of wealth. Aristotle also criticized the Spartan system of land-tenure, which permitted women to own land and to manage their own property:

Again, the license of the Spartan women hinders the attainment of the aims of the constitution and the realization of the good of the people. For just as a husband and a wife are each a part of every family, so may the city be regarded as about equally divided between men and women; consequently in all cities where the condition of women is bad, one half of the city must be regarded as not having proper legislation. And this is exactly what happened in Sparta. There, the lawgiver who had intended to make the entire population strong in character has accomplished his aims with regard to the men, but has neglected the women, who indulge in every kind of luxury and intemperance. A natural consequence of this lifestyle is that wealth is highly valued, particularly in societies where men come to be dominated by their wives, as is the case with many military and warlike peoples, if we except the Celts and a few other races who openly approve of male lovers. In fact, there seems to be some rational justification for the myth of the union of Ares with Aphrodite, since all military peoples are prone to sexual activities with either men or women. This was evident among the Spartans in the days of their supremacy, when much was managed by women. But what is the difference between women ruling, or rulers being ruled by women? The result is the same. Courage is a quality of little use in daily life, but necessary in war, and yet even here the influence of the Spartan women has been negative. This was revealed during the Theban invasion of Laconia[4] when the women of Sparta, instead of being of some use like women in other cities, caused more confusion than the enemy. It is not surprising, however, that the license of the women was characteristic of Spartan society from the earliest times, for the men of Sparta were away from home for long periods of time as they fought first against the Argives and then against the Arcadians and Messenians. When they returned to a peaceful life, having grown accustomed to obedience by military discipline, which has its virtue, they were prepared to submit themselves to the legislation of Lycurgus. But when Lycurgus attempted to subject women to his laws they resisted and he gave up, as tradition says. These, then, are the causes of what happened and thus it is clear that the constitutional shortcoming under discussion must be assigned to them. Our task, however, is not to praise or blame, but to discover what is right or wrong, and the position of women in Sparta, as we have already noted, not only contravenes the spirit of the constitution but contributes greatly to the existing avarice. This problem of greed naturally invites an attack on the lack of equality among the Spartans with regard to the ownership of property, for we see that some of them have very small properties while others have very large ones, and that as a result a few people possess most of the land. Here again is another shortcoming in their constitution; for although the lawgiver rightly disapproved of the selling and buying of estates, he permitted anyone who so desired to transfer land through gifts or bequests, with the same result. And nearly two-fifths of all the land is in the possession of women, due to the fact that heiresses are numerous the customary dowries are large. The regulation of dowries by the state would have been a better measure, abolishing them entirely or making them, at any rate, small or moderate.

(Aristotle, *Politics* 2.6.5–11 [1269b–1270a];
Spyridakis and Nystrom 1988: 183–84)

The Problem of Spartan Women

The difficulties we face in evaluating the status of women in antiquity are nowhere more compelling than in the case of Sparta. Objectivity has eluded both ancient and modern commentators who have picked through the conflicting fragments of ancient evidence to select "facts" that corroborate their views. Their opinions vary according to their conceptions about "the good life" within "the properly governed state." According to legends associated with the Lycurgan constitution, Sparta, like Plato's *Republic*, was a totalitarian state, where the totality of life was subject to regulation and supervision: neither protection of private property nor freedom of the individual were matters for concern. But, as we have seen, Aristotle, with the advantage of hindsight, criticized Sparta's failure to curtail women's freedom and to regulate women's ownership of private property. In contrast, a feminist like Simone de Beauvoir, focusing on traditions about communal property and the amelioration of women's lot, might prefer it to Classical Athens.

NOTES

1. Malcolm Davies (p. 26, line 77) reads *teirei*.
2. Born in 506 B.C.E.
3. The festival of the naked boys, or boys without armor.
4. Under Epaminondas in 369 B.C.E.

TRANSLATIONS

Bing, Peter, and Rip Cohen. 1991. *Games of Venus*. New York.
Campbell, David A. 1988. *Greek Lyric*. Vol. 2. Loeb Classical Library. Cambridge, Mass.
Davies, M. 1991. *Poetarum Melicorum Graecorum Fragmenta*. Vol. 1 Oxford.
Frazer, J. G. 1965. *Pausanias's Description of Greece*, New York (originally published 1898).
Lattimore, Richmond. 1970. *Greek Lyrics*. Chicago and London (originally published 1955).
Marchant, E. C. and G. W. Bowersock, 1968. *Xenophon VII. Scripta Minora*. Loeb Classical Library. Cambridge, Mass. (originally published in 1925 without supplement).
Moretti, L. 1953. *Iscrizioni Agonistische Greche*. Rome.

Segal, Charles. 1985. "Archaic Choral Lyric: Alcman." In *The Cambridge History of Classical Literature*, vol. 1, *Greek Literature*, edited by P. E. Easterling and B. M. W. Knox, Cambridge, 168–85.

Spyridakis, Stylianos V., and Bradley P. Nystrom. 1988. *Ancient Greece: Documentary Perspectives*. Dubuque, Ind.

Talbert, Richard. 1988. *Plutarch on Sparta*. London.

WORKS CONSULTED

Beauvoir, Simone de. 1952. *The Second Sex*. New York. (Originally published as *Le Deuxième Sexe*, Paris, 1949)

Poralla, Paul. 1985. *A Prosopography of Lacedaemonians*. 2d edition by Alfred S. Bradford. Chicago.

FURTHER READING

Calame, Claude. 1977. *Les choeurs de jeunes filles en Grèce archaïque*. Vols. I and II. Rome.

Kunstler, Barton Lee. 1987. "Family Dynamics and Female Power in Ancient Sparta." In *Rescuing Creusa*, edited by Marilyn B. Skinner, 31–48 [Also published in *Helios*, n.s. 13, no. 2: 31–48.]

Mossé, Claude. 1991. "Women in the Spartan Revolutions of the Third Century B.C." In *Women's History and Ancient History*, edited by Sarah B. Pomeroy, 138–53. Chapel Hill, N.C.

Page, Denys L. 1951. *Alcman. The Partheneion*. Oxford.

Scanlon, Thomas F. 1988. "Virgineum Gymnasium. Spartan Females and Early Greek Athletics." In *The Archaeology of the Olympics*, edited by W. Raschke, 185–216. Madison, Wis.

3

WOMEN IN CLASSICAL ATHENS: HEROINES AND HOUSEWIVES

The Tragic Wife: The Nature and Limitation of the Sources

Corinthian women, I have come out of the house
lest you criticize me for anything. For many people
I know have become proud, some out of the public eye,
others openly. Private people, however,
get a bad reputation for inactivity.
For there is no justice in mortal eyes
when someone suffering no wrong hates a person
at first sight before he has understood his temperament.
A foreigner above all must adapt to the city, but
I would not even approve a person who offends
his fellow citizens out of pride and insensitivity.
Yet on me this disaster has fallen unexpectedly
and broken my heart. I am done for, my friends,
and giving up all joy in life, I wish to die.
My whole life was bound up in him, as he well knows;
yet my husband has proved to be the worst of men.
Of all beings who breathe and have intelligence,
we women are the most miserable creatures.
First we have to buy a husband at a steep price,
then take a master for our bodies.
This second evil is worse than the first, but
the greatest struggle turns on whether we get a bad
husband or a good one. Divorce is not respectable
for a woman and she cannot deny her husband.
Confronting new customs and rules,
she needs to be a prophet, unless she has learned
at home how best to manage her bedmate.
If we work things out well and the husband
lives with us without resisting his yoke,
life is enviable. Otherwise it is better to die.
A man, when he is tired of being with those inside
goes out and relieves his heart of boredom,

or turns to some friend or contemporary.
But we have to look to one person only.
They say we have a life secure from danger
living at home, while they wield their spears in battle.
They are mistaken! I would rather stand three
times beside a shield than give birth once.
(Euripides, *Medea* 214–51. [431 B.C.E.];
trans. Helene P. Foley)

Every respectable woman in classical Athens (ca. 480–323 B.C.E.) became a wife if she could; not to marry, as Medea argues, provided no real alternative. In this passage, Euripides' Medea has come out from seclusion in her house to express to the women of Corinth her pain over her husband Jason's betrayal. Medea has maintained the modesty and retirement appropriate to the life of a proper Athenian wife, who should, at least ideally, have spent most of her time indoors unless she were participating in religious events. She also does not want other women to think her proud, when they come to offer their sympathy. For, as the tragic heroine Iphigeneia says in another play by Euripides, voicing a view about female solidarity standard in drama (Euripides, *Iphigeneia Among the Taurians*, 1061–62, ca. 414–410 B.C.E.):

We are women, a tribe sympathetic to each other
and most reliable in preserving our common interests.

Medea is a foreigner in Corinth. She helped Jason win the Golden Fleece after she fell in love with him in her native Colchis and fled with him to Greece. Now he is leaving her to marry the only child of the King of Corinth. Yet her complaints about marriage are not alien to the Greek chorus. A woman, Medea complains, must buy an unknown husband with a dowry; every bride lives the life of a foreigner in her new home; husbands can escape from the house if the marriage goes badly, but wives cannot. They are dependent on one person, for whose sake they must undertake the pains and risks of childbirth.

This passage raises central questions about the lives of women in Classical Athens. How secluded was the proper wife's existence? How much was she able to escape the confines of her house for the supportive companionship of other women? To what degree could she expect help and legal protection from her society when mistreated? Did Athenian wives fear or resent being married off young (early teens) to a considerably older husband (late twenties or above) whom they (in contrast to Medea) did not choose or know before the wedding?

Drama is a problematic source for the lives of both women and men in Classical Athens (see further Foley 1981, Zeitlin 1985, Just 1989, Des Bouvrie 1990). Classical tragedies and comedies generally are based on myths from the remote past or (in the case of comedy) fantastic invented scenarios. The plays may simply represent what male poets (and, on stage, male actors) imagined about women, or used them to imagine. Some have argued, for example, that Medea's speech is Euripides' clever reply to the objections contemporary Sophists made to marriage as an institution that curtailed male freedom, not a serious response to women's plight. We are not even certain that women were present at the theater festivals in honor of the god Dionysus to see these plays (although there is evidence on both sides, it seems more likely that some women did do so); and no female voice has survived to give us a hint of a woman's perspective in her own words. At the same time, the vivid portraits of women in drama—often more assertive, articulate, or rebellious than those we have from sources that claim to represent historical reality more directly—may have reflected real social and historical issues and tensions, even if in a somewhat indirect fashion.

We know, for example, that Medea exaggerates somewhat in this speech. Although divorce was easy to obtain, Athenian women at least (if not the foreigner Medea), were legally and financially protected in such cases. Their dowry had to be returned with them and court cases repeatedly cite male responsibility for the welfare of female relatives (see Demosthenes [Dem.] 30.21; the eponymous archon oversaw the welfare of orphans, widows, and pregnant widows), even if we know that some guardians failed to carry out that responsibility (for example, the abuse of Demosthenes' mother by her guardian [Dem. 27 and 28]. See also Isaeus 8.36, Aeschines 1.95–99, Andocides 1.124–27, and Dem. 48.54–55). Among the upper classes at least, marriage patterns in Athens became increasingly endogamous, and husbands may not always have been complete strangers to their wives, or the move to a new household such a radical transition. Citizen wives visited with neighbors and participated frequently in religious events, sometimes in the company of other women, and sometimes at large civic festivals; thus, a wife's existence may not have been so restricted as Medea suggests. Nevertheless, Medea is not the only tragic wife to criticize her lot, and passages in other plays emphasize in different ways the difficulties that both the transition to marriage and a wife's subsequent isolation presented for her.

Procne in Sophocles' *Tereus* asserts that the transition to marriage was a shock after the girl's carefree childhood:

> Now outside [my father's house] I am nothing. Yet I have often
> observed woman's nature in this regard,
> how we are nothing. When we are young in our father's house,
> I think we live the sweetest life of all humankind;
> for ignorance always brings children up delightfully.
> But when we have reached maturity and can understand,
> we are thrust out and sold
> away from the gods of our fathers and our parents,
> some to foreigners, some to barbarians,
> some to joyless houses, some full of reproach.
> And finally, once a single night has united us,
> we have to praise our lot and pretend that all is well.
>   (Frag. 524N [583R]. [early 420s B.C.E.?]; trans. Helene P. Foley)

Clytemnestra (at Aeschylus' *Agamemnon* 855ff.) gives a lengthy speech about the tortures women experience when their husbands are at war, and in Sophocles' *Women of Trachis* the heroine Dejaneira expresses anxiety over the frequent absences of her husband:

> Chosen partner for the bed of Heracles,
> I nurse fear after fear, always worrying
> over him. I have a constant relay of troubles;
> some each night dispells—each night brings others on.
> We have had children now, whom he sees at times,
> like a farmer working an outlying field,
> who sees it only when he sows and when he reaps.
> This has been his life, that only brings him home
> to send him out again, to serve some man or other.
> (*Women of Trachis*, 27–35 [ca. 420s B.C.E.];
>
> Jameson 1959)

Such passages probably do not simply represent poetic fantasies. Women did react to the absence and death of their men at war; a woman's husband was often absent. The historian Herodotus reports that once, after a disastrous Athenian raid on Aegina, the new widows took out their brooches and stabbed to death the one male survivor. Each woman asked as she stabbed where her own husband was. The Athenians then changed the style of women's dress so that in the future they would not need brooches (5.87). Furthermore, agricultural work and civic and military duties took husbands out of the house for extended periods. Popular culture in Athens emphasized the desirability of a man's dedication to the interests of the city-state and to work outside the house. Xenophon, in the *Oeconomicus*, a treatise on household management, for example, argues for a strict division of labor by sex: the husband's role is to take care of what is outside the house and the wife's to care for what is inside; once he has trained his wife to perform her job properly, he can leave her in charge of her own sphere (7.17ff.; see further under "Domestic Activities" in this chapter).

Euripides' Phaedra, who has had the misfortune to fall in love with her stepson, Hippolytus, and is struggling to resist her passion, also shows how difficult a wife's life might be. Surrounded by suspicion (see also Euripides, *Ion* 398–400), with too little opportunity for achievement and too much time to brood and fantasize, the wife may find it difficult to adhere to the moral principles that she had been raised to accept. Phaedra wishes to preserve the reputation of herself (and, she later adds, her children), but she finds it impossible to distract herself from her sufferings. Even the company of other women only makes virtue more difficult to attain (see also Euripides, *Andromache* 943–53).

> Many a time in night's long empty spaces
> I have pondered on the causes of a life's shipwreck.
> I think that our lives are worse than the mind's quality
> would warrant. There are many who know virtue.

We know the good, we apprehend it clearly.
But we can't bring it to achievement. Some
are betrayed by their own laziness, and others
value some other pleasure above virtue.
There are many pleasures in a woman's life—
long gossiping talks and leisure, that sweet curse.
. . . .
It would always be my choice
to have my virtues known and honored. So
when I do wrong I could not endure to see
a circle of condemning witnesses.
I know what I have done: I know the scandal:
and all too well I know that I am a woman,
object of hate to all.

(Euripides, *Hippolytus*, 375–84, 403–7 [428 B.C.E.];
Grene 1959)

And indeed, she seems to be partially correct in her fears, for when Hippolytus hears (against her will) of Phaedra's passion he pours out a tirade against women: he wishes that children could be acquired in other ways, since women are an economic drain, dangerous when clever, and prone to adultery (616ff.). This speech provokes Phaedra to take action, for she is afraid that Hippolytus will inform her husband Theseus. She commits suicide, leaving behind a tablet that claims that Hippolytus tried to rape her. It is hard to tell whether such plays confirm the popular fears about women and the need to supervise their behavior closely, or whether they attack the cultural confinement of women as dangerous in itself, or both.

Although drama generally represented potential problems and crises in life, it could also reflect or even exaggerate popular ideology about the normal role of women. Legally, wives in Athens were not permitted to make important social and financial decisions without the supervision of a guardian, and Aristotle argues in his *Politics* that the virtue of a wife consists in her obeying her morally superior husband (see especially, 1252a–b, 1254b). Some wives on the Greek stage, unlike Medea, actually revel in subordinating themselves to their husband's needs and wishes, as popular culture thought that they should. Alcestis, who agreed to die in her husband's stead, was a mythical ideal. (For the embarrassing consequences this sacrifice could have for her husband Admetus, see Euripides' *Alcestis*. For representations of Alcestis as a marital ideal in art, see Fig. 3.15 and Chapter 13). In the passage below, Euripides' Andromache, former wife of the dead Trojan hero Hector and now concubine to Achilles' son Neoptolemus, tries to persuade his wife Hermione to defer consistently to her husband. The rich young Spartan Hermione, the spoiled darling of her parents Menelaus and Helen, has been trying to manipulate her husband and to get rid of his concubine and her child, since she is childless; she turns to her father whenever she is in trouble.

Your husband does not despise you on account of my drugs,
but because you are not fit to live with.
That's my magic charm. It is not beauty, my good woman,
but virtues that keep our husbands happy.
When you get annoyed at something, Sparta's the big deal
in your mind and Skyros counts for nothing.
You are a have among have nots. For you Menelaos
is greater than Achilles! This is why your husband hates you.
A woman must be content, even when married off
to a poor husband, and not fight over family resources with him.
If you had a husband who ruled in snowbound Thrace,
where one man shares his bed with many women
in rotation, would you kill them all? You'd be caught
tainting all women with your own incontinence.
How shameful! Though admittedly we've got a worse
case of this disease than men, even if we conceal it well.
Dearest Hector, for your sake I assisted in your love affairs
when Aphrodite tripped you up and many times
I nursed your bastards at my breast,
rather than betray some bitterness toward you.
With such virtuous conduct I won my husband's
approval. But you, you're even afraid to let
a drop of rain fall on your husband.

(Euripides, *Andromache* 205–28 [ca. 419 B.C.E.];

trans. Helene P. Foley)

The passage suggests that a wealthy wife might use her family position and her dowry as leverage against her husband. When Xenophon in the *Oeconomicus* proposes that a couple would do best to treat the wife's dowry as joint property (7.13), he also seems to hint that it could, in less ideal circumstances, become a bone of contention. Furthermore, since a Greek wife was only "lent" in marriage to her husband's family for the purpose of producing legitimate heirs, that family continued to have some stake in her future and could potentially reappropriate her to serve their own needs (see later under "Silenced Women" in this chapter).

It should be noted in considering Andromache's advice that men could and did have concubines in Athens. If the women were not Athenians, their children were not Athenian citizens after Pericles' citizenship law of 451–450 B.C.E. which defined as legitimate the children of two Athenian citizens. The foreign Medea in the passage quoted at the beginning of this chapter has been rejected in favor of a Corinthian wife, who could give Jason a socially advantageous marriage and children. The famous statesman Pericles, however, divorced his wife and took up with the foreign hetaira, Aspasia; in defiance of his own law, he eventually had his child by her declared legitimate after the death of his children by his first wife. Isaeus 6 demonstrates the problems that could arise when a husband allegedly adopted the children of his mistress, whom he preferred to his wife, and tried to make them his legitimate heirs.

Although, as was said above, there are many cases where male poets invented fantastic female characters to argue out difficult social conflicts and create women who act in ways not permitted to them in life, these striking pictures of the complex problems of a wife's existence seem to express genuine contradictions in her role, if only in the male imagination. As we shall see, Classical Athenian sources consistently give us conflicting views on women (for a general discussion of interpretive issues, see Pomeroy 1975, Gould 1980, Blok 1987, and Just 1989). And virtually all of those sources, with the exclusion of archaeology, are tendentious. Historians' views are constrained by their conception of what events are worthy to be recorded. Thucydides rarely mentions women in his history of the Peloponnesian Wars, for he writes about political and military events from which women were largely excluded. The anthropologically oriented Herodotus, on the other hand, considers both family and public life worthy of his investigations. The second-century c.e. historian Plutarch (whose sources are often early) was particularly interested in the status of women in the various societies that he discusses. Rhetoricians and orators—we rely on the law court speeches of Lysias, Demosthenes, Isaeus, and others here—shape their testimony to convince an audience of their cause, and philosophers such as Plato, Aristotle, and Xenophon generally argue for and refine social ideals, rather than attempt to reflect the status quo. The fine arts may idealize, fantasize, or romanticize, and it is often hard to draw the line between depictions of life and representations of myth or even between wives, slaves, and prostitutes in Attic vase paintings (Williams 1983). Yet if we take all of these sources together, Classical Athens seems to have attempted, far more strictly than in Archaic Greece, to define both legally and informally the relation of the family and the individual to the state and of private life to public life. These changes affected the relations between men and women and may well have created the kinds of tensions that we have seen in the dramatic representations of distressed wives quoted earlier.

Women in Relation to the Polis

The Athenian democracy was a "men's club" whose active members were restricted to men descended from parents who were both Athenian citizens. After Pericles' citizenship law of 451–450 B.C.E., citizen women were carefully distinguished from those who were not, such as slaves, and residents of foreign descent, for the purpose of determining the citizenship of their children; but female citizens did not participate in governing the democracy. Indeed, before the Hellenistic period women were excluded from government and the military throughout Greece. Yet, unlike the laws attributed to Lycurgus at Sparta, which prescribed a public system of education for women, the laws attributed to Solon in sixth-century Athens were largely restrictive and may have aimed to reduce outward manifestations of inequality among men, as well as to strengthen the individual oikos (family, household, or estate) and to control family life. Under oligarchic, aristocratic, or monarchic governments, some women belonged to the ruling elite and wielded informal power such as we saw in the Homeric poems of the Archaic age. Since most of the population had no political rights, the possession of such rights did not pointedly distinguish men from women. The attempt by democratic Athens to buttress the equality of all its male citizens and to give them substantial responsibilities in the public sphere apparently, except in the case of religion, increasingly relegated to the private sphere all other free Athenians, whether women or resident aliens (free men or women protected by Athenian law but not entitled to the privileges of male citizens). (See further Just 1989: 22–23.) Solon's laws affecting women seem to have been designed for a number of purposes. One important function was to ensure the preservation of individual households and provide them with legitimate heirs.

That law, too, seems absurd and ridiculous, which permits an heiress, in case the man under whose power and authority she is placed by law is himself unable to consort with her, to be married by one of his next of kin. Some, however, say that this was a wise provision against those who are unable to perform the duties of a husband, and yet, for the sake of their property marry heiresses, and so under cover of law, do violence to nature. For when they see that the heiress can consort with whomever she pleases, they will either desist from such a marriage, or make it to their shame, and be punished for their avarice and insolence. It is a wise provision, too, that an heiress may not choose her consort at large, but from the kinsmen of her husband, that her offspring may be of his family and lineage.

(Solon 20.2)

Still further, no man is allowed to sell a daughter or a sister, unless he finds that she is no longer a virgin.

(Solon 23.2; Perrin 1982)

Law-court cases from the fourth century B.C.E. in Athens still reflect tensions over which relatives should be permitted to marry an heiress (epikleros; see further under "Silenced Women" in this chapter).

Another purpose of Solon's legislation was to curb women's informal influence on their husbands.

On the other hand, he did not permit all manner of gifts without restriction or restraint, but only those which were not made under the influence of sickness, or drugs, or imprisonment, or when a man was the victim of compulsion or yielded to the persuasion of his wife. He thought, very rightly and properly, that being persuaded into wrong was no better than being forced into it, and he placed deceit and compulsion, gratification and affliction, in one and the same category, believing that both were alike able to pervert a man's reason.

(Solon 21.3; Perrin 1982)

Isaeus 6 is one of a number of court cases presenting the idea that the whole political system is threatened if an individual man's reason is undermined by a woman's influence: "the woman who destroyed Euc-

-eason and laid hold of so much property is so insolent, that . . .
; her contempt not only for the members of Euctemon's family,
'or the whole city" (6.48; see also Demosthenes 46.14, Isaeus

Solon's laws were also intended to control public appearances of
women, including their expression of private emotion in public (for Solon's laws curbing such behavior, especially in the context of funerals,
see Chapter 1).

Mourning

In some cases, it seems certain that Solon's laws prevented women from
acting as they had earlier. As has already been shown in Chapter 1, Solon's legislation on funerals prescribed that only close kin could mourn
for the dead, thus prohibiting the ostentatious practice among the aristocracy of hiring women mourners and denying older women a source of
income. Nevertheless, sources indicate that funerary legislation continued to be passed at Athens in the three centuries after Solon, and there
is both archaeological (the shifting degree of ostentation in funerary
monuments, discussed further below) and literary evidence that the regulation of women's role in lamenting the dead and of funerary practices
in general continued to be a disputed issue (see further, Humphreys 1983,
Loraux 1986, and Foley 1993). Drama, for example, continued to represent women who resist the limited role permitted to them and/or persist
heroically in carrying out the special responsibilities to dead kin that
their culture assigned to them. The most famous case is Sophocles' Antigone. After the battle at Thebes for succession between her brothers
Eteocles and Polyneices, her uncle Creon pronounces an edict that bans
burial for the traitor Polyneices, who attacked his own city. Antigone
defies the edict and publicly embarrasses her uncle. Particularly cha-
grined to be challenged by a woman, Creon moves quickly to silence the
voice of his niece. In the end, Antigone's championing of the rights of
the dead receives divine support. The prophet Tiresias tells Creon that
the gods are offended by the pollution from the corpse. Creon must bury
Polyneices and rescue Antigone from the cave in which he has imprisoned her to die. Too late, Creon finds Antigone dead and his son Hai-
mon, Antigone's fiancé, kills himself over her body. In her first confron-
tation with Creon, Antigone offers the following defense of her
disobedience to the edict:

> For me it was not Zeus who made this proclamation.
> Nor did Justice dwelling with the gods below
> define such laws for humankind.
> I did not think your orders had such power
> that you, a mortal, could outrun
> the gods' unwritten and unfailing rules.
> Not merely of today or yesterday, they live
> forever, and no one knows from where they came.

For their sake I was not about to pay a penalty
to the gods, fearing the will of any man.
I knew that I would die; how could I fail to know,
even if you had not decreed it? If I die
before my time, I call this death a gain.
When someone lives with many sorrows
as I do, how could dying be unprofitable?
For me to meet this fate is thus a trivial grief.
But if I had permitted my mother's dead son
to remain an unburied corpse, I would
have grieved at that; at this I do not grieve.
Now if I seem to have played the fool,
perhaps it is a fool who charges me with folly.
          (Sophocles, *Antigone* 450–70 [ca. 442–41 B.C.E.];
                              trans. Helene P. Foley)

Similarly, in Euripides' *Suppliants*, the mothers of the seven champions who attacked Thebes come to Athens for help. Thebes has refused to allow their sons to be buried. The mothers expect to acquire the right to mourn their sons extravagantly in public. Instead, Theseus appropriates the bodies of the slain from them. He has Adrastus, the surviving leader of the champions, pronounce a public funeral oration, and then takes the bodies away for cremation. The mothers remain to the end of the play eager to embrace the remains of their sons; but they are not even permitted to hold the urns containing their ashes. Theseus excuses his actions in a fashion that serves to justify Athens' own contemporary restriction of women's public lamentation of the dead:

ADRASTUS: Sorrowful mothers! Draw near your children!
  THESEUS: Adrastus! That was not well said.
ADRASTUS: Why? Must parents not touch their children?
  THESEUS: To see their state would be mortal pain.
ADRASTUS: Yes, corpse wounds and blood are a bitter sight.
  THESEUS: Then why would you increase the women's woe?
ADRASTUS: I yield.

                    (lines 941–47 [420s B.C.E.]; Jones 1959)

Such passages raise interesting questions. Funeral orations and funerary legislation recommended or required curtailment of public grief. Tragedy and other sources represent contradictory views on women's public expression of emotion. In Aeschylus's *Seven Against Thebes*, for example, the hero Eteocles first encounters the chorus of young women praying excitedly to statues of the gods and bringing them offerings in the hope of acquiring their protection from the enemy encamped outside Thebes' walls. Eteocles views their activities as disastrous to the effort of the Theban warriors to defend their city. Plutarch even argues that women's mourning for the god Adonis, a religious rite discussed later in this chapter, threatened the war effort during the Peloponnesian Wars: "the women were celebrating . . . the festival of Adonis, and in many places throughout the city little images of the god were laid out for burial, and funeral rites were held about them, with wailing cries of women, so that those who cared anything for such matters were distressed, and feared lest all that powerful armament, with all the splendor and vigour that were so manifest in it, should speedily wither away and come to naught" (Nicias 13, Perrin 1982).

Similarly, Athenian democracy celebrated its war dead and did not wish grief to undermine its heroizing of the dead and the dedication of its soldiers to the interests of the state. Plutarch also tells us that when Pericles returned to Athens after subduing Samos and delivered a funeral oration in 440 B.C.E., many of the women crowned him with garlands. But Elpinice, the sister of Cimon, one of the few women of Athens to have a (dubious) reputation of her own (see Plutarch, Cimon 4.5–7), reportedly came up to him and said,

"This was a noble action, Pericles, and you deserve all these garlands for it. You have thrown away the lives of these brave citizens of ours, not in a war against the Persians or the Phoenicians, such has my brother Cimon fought, but in destroying a Greek city which is one of our allies." Pericles listened to her words unmoved, so it is said, and only smiled and quoted to her Archilochus's verse, "Why lavish perfumes on a head that's grey?"

(Plutarch, Pericles 28. Scott-Kilvert 1960)

In a fashion traditional to Athens's archaic past, the aristocratic Elpinice wielded political influence for and through her brother Cimon (even long after his death, as here), for whom she twice interceded with Pericles; her advanced age may also explain the liberties she feels free to take here. Pericles, as a representative of the new ideology of Athens, dismisses her speech and her claims to authority.

Like the words of the elderly Elpinice, women's lamentations also potentially challenged the war effort, because they stressed the consequences of death for the survivors. Yet when male characters in tragedy imagine their own deaths, they hope for burial, care after death, and lamentations from the women of their family (for example, Orestes in Euripides' *Iphigeneia Among the Taurians*, 700–705). And what if a man died in a private context or a whole country became exhausted by war and its rhetoric, as may have happened during the long (431–404 B.C.E.) Peloponnesian Wars between Sparta and Athens? The families of such men may have resented the absence of a public opportunity to display grief over private deaths (the reemergence of ostentation in private grave monuments during the last quarter of the fifth century may also indicate resistance to funerary legislation curtailing such display). The overall dramatic contexts in which the actions of Antigone or Theseus occur suggest (although this case cannot be made here) that poets may be expressing ambivalence about the state control of burial practice and the suppression of women's lamenting voices in the public arena of Athens. We know that women continued to have an important informal influence on private funerals, for the speaker of Isaeus 8.21–22 claims that, although he had been planning to conduct his grandfather's funeral from his own house, he acceded to the wishes of his grandmother, who wished to lay out and deck the corpse, to conduct it from the house of the deceased.

Silenced Women

Advice to the parents of the dead was a traditional feature of public funeral orations, and Pericles urged those couples who were physically capable to produce more children. Exploiting the traditional view that young women who lacked male supervision and a male relative to conduct transactions that required meeting men were in danger of losing their respectability, Pericles offers to war widows a warning unique in extant funeral orations:

> If I also must say something about a wife's virtue to those of you who will now be widows, I will state it in a brief exhortation. Your reputation is glorious if you do not prove inferior to your own nature and if there is the least possible talk about you among men, whether in praise or blame.
>
> (Thucydides 2.45.2, 431 B.C.E.)

In contrast to the public praise and blame of women in the Archaic period, poets, law-court speeches, and philosophers all express the view that respectable women (wives, mothers, daughters, sisters, and other close female relatives of the speakers) should remain silent or subdued in public and avoid being discussed by men. Orators avoid naming living respectable women unless they wish to cast a slur on their names (Schaps 1977). Not only women's names, but women themselves were supposed to keep out of public view, with the important exception of their appearances at funerals and festivals as various cults and rituals required. "A woman who travels outside the house must be of such an age, that onlookers might ask, not whose wife she is, but whose mother." (Hyperides, frag. 205 Jensen; Golden 1990: 122). Thus in vase painting, respectable women are rarely portrayed out-of-doors, except at festivals or in cemeteries and wedding processions.[1] At Lysias 3.6, the speaker claims that his sister and nieces had lived in the women's quarters with so much concern for their modesty that they were embarrassed even to be seen by their male relatives (see also Demosthenes 47, Isaeus 3.13–14, Lysias 1.22–23):

> Hearing that the boy was at my house, he came there at night in a drunken state, broke down the doors, and entered the women's rooms: within were my sister and my nieces, whose lives have been so well-ordered that they are ashamed even to be seen by their kinsmen. This man, then, carried insolence to such a pitch that he refused to go away until the people who appeared on the spot, and those who accompanied him, feeling it a monstrous thing that he should intrude on young girls and orphans, drove him out by force.
>
> (first quarter of the fourth century B.C.E.; Lamb 1960)

Lycurgus (*Against Leocrates* 40) tells us that after the battle of Chaeronea in 338 B.C.E. free women stood in their doorways to ask from passersby news of their relatives, thus behaving in a fashion "unworthy of themselves and of the city." Only courtesans went to parties with men, opened the front door themselves, or spoke to passersby in the street (see Isaeus 3.13–14 and Theophrastus, *Characters* 28.) This anonymity protected women from contact with men who were not family members, but it also makes it extremely difficult to study the history of Athenian women. In court cases, for example, speakers often found it hard to document the lives of respectable women. Laws governing the inheritance of property were not strictly agnatic (exclusive to the male line), but males preceded females in the right to inherit and relationships traced through males took precedence over those through females. Women were sufficiently obscure that it was possible to contest a rival's claim to an inheritance by arguing that his mother had not been a legitimate child of her father or that his mother had not been a lawful wife of his father but had been a hetaira or concubine. In the following speech of 375 B.C.E. a grandson claims a large inheritance from his mother's father, who was named Ciron. Endogamous marriage was common among the upper class. Ciron's first wife was his cousin; she gave birth to one daughter who became the speaker's mother. The speaker bases his claim on the presumption that if his mother had lived she would have been an epiklêros (heiress or, literally, "attached to the estate" of her father) when Ciron died, since there was no son to inherit the estate. In families where the surviving children were female, the estate of the father passed through such daughters to their sons. (See the laws of Solon quoted earlier in this chapter.) Wealthy heiresses were likely to be claimed in marriage by their next of kin (who would have inherited the property if the heiresses were not alive), even if they were already married. (See Isaeus 3.64–67.) Although according to law, children were members of their father's family and remained with them after the death of their father just as they would have stayed with their father in case of divorce, the speaker argues that his mother and her offspring retained ties to Ciron:

As was natural, seeing that we were the sons of his own daughter, he [that is, Ciron] never performed a sacrifice without us, but whether the occasion was trivial or important, we were always at his side, taking part with him in the ceremony. . . . The conduct of our father and the knowledge that the married women of the district had of our mother shows that she was Ciron's legitimate daughter. When he married her, our father celebrated a marriage feast with his relatives and three friends and presented the marriage sacrifice to the members of his tribe in accordance with their laws. Later, his wife was selected, along with the wife of Diocles of Pitthos, by the women of the district to preside at the Thesmophoria and to carry out the customary rites with her colleagues. When we were born he introduced us to his tribe with the usual oath that we were born of an Athenian woman legally betrothed.

(Isaeus 8.15–19 [383–363 B.C.E.]; trans. Sarah B. Pomeroy)

Here the speakers find it necessary to prove that their mother was Ciron's legitimate daughter, and they make their case not only by citing Ciron's actions, but by referring to the activities of the women of the district.

Named Women

Inscriptional evidence is exceptional in naming and even celebrating individual citizen women. An inscription on a black-figure vase of the fifth
century B.C.E. celebrates the victory of a girl named Melosa in a girl's
carding (wool-working) contest (Attic, fifth-century B.C.E. Friedländer /
Hofleit 1948: p. 165 177m). Priestesses (unlike other respectable women)
are named in a number of religious contexts (see below), and after she
died, a woman's name might be inscribed on her tombstone along with
the names of her closest male relatives (see Mnesarete's stele in the Introduction to Part I). The genealogy of some women can be established
in this way. For example, her mother and father set up the tombstone of
a little girl named Aristylla (Fig. 3.1), who died about 430–425 B.C.E.,
perhaps in the plague that ravaged Athens in the early years of the Peloponnesian War. A brief epigram gives the names of her parents, Ariston
and Rhodilla. Aristylla stands before her mother, their hands clasped.
The handshake is a common motif on Athenian gravestones, symbolizing
both the leave-taking of the dead who must journey to the Underworld

Figure 3.1. Tombstone of Aristylla (ca.
430–425 B.C.E.) shows the dead girl
taking the hand of her mother. The
meditative character of the image is typical of funerary imagery of the period;
the wakes with mourners tearing their
hair have largely disappeared from the
art of the fifth century.

and the union of family members that continues even in death. Arystilla's tender age is indicated by her close-cropped hair and the small bird she holds in her left hand, a favorite plaything of young girls. Her mother Rhodilla is characterized as a proper Athenian matron by her backed chair with footstool, the mantle draped over her legs, and the veil pulled up over her head.

The woman commemorated by another gravestone was named Pausimache (Fig. 3.2). The epigram carved just above her head reads:

Figure 3.2. Tombstone of Pausimache (ca. 390–380 B.C.E.), who holds a mirror and whose inscription speaks of her goodness and good sense.

It is fated that all who live must die; and you, Pausimache, left behind pitiful grief as a possession for your ancestors, your mother Phainippe and your father Pausanias. Here stands a memorial of your goodness and good sense for passers-by to see.

(Clairmont 1970: No. 13, p. 77)

Pausimache probably died unmarried, since no husband or children are mentioned. She is shown gazing into a mirror, not a symbol of vanity as in Renaissance art, but of the beauty and grace admired in Greek women. The mirror may also have a more specific reference, to the wedding of which Pausimache has been deprived by her early death, for brides are often shown holding a mirror as they prepare for the ceremony.

Often, when the inscription on the tombstone is metrical the woman alone is named, but without the addition of the names of male relatives she could not be identified, either by strangers who were her contemporaries or by later historians. An epigram on a relief from the Athenian port of Piraeus from the beginning of the fourth century B.C.E. is typical in emphasizing the dead woman's decorum and productivity:

> The memory of your virtue, Theophile, will never die
> Self-controlled, good, and industrious, possessing every virtue.
> (Peek 1955: 1490)

Civic Religion

Despite the attempt to regulate women's public activity and reputation, women in classical Athens legitimately appeared in public contexts when they engaged in ritual activities. Women's participation in civic cults and their role as religious officials often represented a significant opportunity to contribute, at least symbolically, to the welfare of the city-state as a whole. The Athenian state religion, with its many cults, festivals, and rituals, was an integral part of everyday life, and women participated as much as men. Women of all social positions, both native Athenians and foreigners, worshiped together, though some cults and rituals were restricted to a more limited group, such as married women (possibly including concubines) at the Thesmophoria. These rituals apparently helped to mark and facilitate a girl's transition to marriage and motherhood, to celebrate her role as weaver, and to harness women's reproductive powers to promote the fertility of the entire society.

From early childhood, girls took part in religious rituals. Aristophanes mentions three activities in which groups of girls of the same age participated.[2] Some of these activities were probably similar to those of Spartan girls. (See Chapter 2 discussion of Alcman, *Partheneia*.) Girls wove, ground grain, carried burdens, and danced in ritual contexts (choruses of girls danced at the Greater Panathenaia and perhaps at other festivals). In this passage the girl is probably meant to be understood as grinding grain and carrying figs (a symbol of fertility) for Athena:

> Once I was seven I became an arrêphoros.
> Then at ten I became a grain grinder for the goddess (lit. the
>   Archegetis or "first leader").
> After that, wearing a saffron robe, I was a bear at Brauron.
> And as a lovely young girl I once served as a basket bearer, wearing
>   a string of figs.
> (Aristophanes, *Lysistrata* 641–47 [412 B.C.E.]; trans. Helene P. Foley)

Several monuments and artifacts give additional evidence for these activities. A section of the Parthenon frieze (ca. 440–432 B.C.E., Fig. 3.3) represents the culmination of the Panathenaic procession in honor of Athena. At the right, the Archon Basileus, the chief magistrate of the Athenian state religion, assisted by a small child, folds the new peplos, a robe woven especially for the goddess. Behind the Archon, the priestess of Athena Polias receives two girls who bring stools on their heads. The girls are probably the Arrephoroi, who had helped in the weaving of the peplos, along with their other duties in the cult of Athena. Each year two (or four) girls between seven and about ten were chosen as Arrephoroi in the cult of Athena Polias on the Acropolis. They lived for a time near the Erechtheum, no doubt under the supervision of the priestess of Athena, and were present when the weaving of the peplos began. The culmination of their service was a secret ritual described by Pausanias (1.27.3): they carried something given them by the priestess down an underground passage on the slope of the Acropolis, deposited it at a special place, and brought something else back up. Two Loutrides or Plyn-

Figure 3.3. A detail of the east frieze of the Parthenon (ca. 440–432 B.C.E.) in Athens shows part of the Panathenaic procession for Athena; the frieze wrapped around the outside of the cella (the inner chamber housing the statue of the goddess) and presented the idealized citizenry of the city as handsome young men with their horses, beautiful young women with baskets and other gifts for Athena, and the mature men who governed the city.

trides also removed garments from the statue of Athena on the Acropolis
and washed them.

Since there were only two (or four) Arrephoroi per year, it was a
great honor reserved for girls of noble families. Any girl, by contrast,
could take part in the rites of Artemis at Brauron, although sources differ
on what proportion of eligible girls may have participated.[3] Because the
sanctuary was on the east coast of Attica, far from Athens, the girls
stayed at least overnight, in a stoa built for this purpose. Girls of different ages, but still before puberty, participated in races in honor of Artemis at her sanctuary at Brauron (Fig. 3.4). The ritual was known as
the Arkteia (playing the she-bear), and the girls were dubbed "bears"
after the animal that was associated with the huntress Artemis. Sometimes the girls ran nude, as here, at other times in a short garment, the
chitoniskos (the nudity may indicate the girl's wild, premarital state).
These girls hold crowns of leaves and probably ran around an altar that
is not preserved. The palm tree at right stands for Delos, the sacred island where Artemis and her brother Apollo were born (on the Arkteia,
see further Kahil 1977 and Sourvinou-Inwood 1988b). Choruses of young

Figure 3.4. Vase fragment (ca. 430 B.C.E.) with racing girls, probably at the sanctuary of Artemis at
Brauron. This is one of the rare cases of female nudity in an image unconnected with prostitution; its
outdoor setting is marked by a tree.

girls participated in an all-night vigil on the Acropolis during the Great Panathenaia (Euripides, *Heracleidae* 777–83), and in spring maidens carried branches of sacred olive wrapped in wool in the procession to the temple in the Delphinium, where they supplicated Apollo and Artemis (Plutarch, *Theseus* 18.2).

As an adult, a woman had the opportunity to participate in many cults, some alongside men and others limited to women. In the Panathenaic procession in honor of Athena, while men rode horseback and led the sacrificial oxen, women carried various objects for use in the sacrifice, including offering trays (cf. Fig. 3.5) and incense-burners. Women are most numerous on the east frieze of the Parthenon, which represents the head of the Panathenaic procession and the final preparations for sacrifice. The two young women shown at left in Figure 3.5 are the kanêphoroi, named for the offering trays (kanoun) they carry. These marriageable young women were given the exceptional honor of a share in the Panathenaic sacrifice. Each pair of women is met by one of the marshals who organize the procession and keep it moving according to plan. The marshal at the left holds a kanoun that he has taken from one of the women. Metic girls (resident aliens) carried water-jars and stools and parasols for aristocratic girls in the procession.

Perhaps the most famous festival restricted to women was the Thes-

Figure 3.5. East frieze of the Parthenon (ca. 440–432 B.C.E.), with the maidens who carried trays as part of the procession in honor of Athena. The woman at the head of this group (left) has handed the tray to the marshal facing her.

mophoria, a fertility rite for Demeter, travestied by Aristophanes in his *Women at the Thesmophoria*. Women, almost exclusively married citizens (concubines may have been included), organized their own festival, and spent three days living in Demeter's hilltop sanctuary near the Pnyx. All public business in the Agora was suspended for the rite. We know very little of the well-kept secrets of this festival. A late source (scholion to Lucian, Rabe 275–76; Winkler 1990) tells us:

The Thesmophoria are a Greek festival containing mysteries. . . . They are celebrated, according to the more mythical account, because when Kore [the goddess Persephone] was seized by Plouto [god of Hades, the Greek underworld] while picking flowers, there was a swineherd named Eubouleus tending his pigs in that place and they were all swallowed up in the chasm along with Kore. Women known as Bailers, who have stayed pure for three days, bring up the rotten remains of objects that had been thrown down into the pits. Descending into the secret chambers, they bring the material back and place it on the altars. They believe that whoever takes some of it and scatters it along with his seed will have a good crop. They also say there are serpents down in the chasms, who eat most of what is thrown in: therefore the celebrants clap and shout when the women are bailing and when they replace those figures—to make the serpents go away, whom they consider to be the guardians of the secret chambers.

The passage goes on to say that the unspeakable objects thrown into the pits with the pigs are replicas of snakes and male genitals made from dough; all these, including the pigs, which are associated with female genitalia, help to promote fertility. Elsewhere we learn that during the Thesmophoria the women camped out on the hillside, imitating the life of humankind before agriculture, fasted and mimicked the mourning of Demeter for her lost daughter, and finally celebrated a feast in honor of birth (kalligeneia). (See further Brumfield 1981: 70–103)

Dionysus was another important deity in the lives of women in classical Athens. Women may have attended the theatrical festivals in his honor (see earlier), and if so, they could have acquired considerable knowledge of contemporary literature. Although the evidence for historical maenadism (maenadic rituals performed by actual women and recorded in inscriptions, rather than represented in art and literature) does not begin before the fourth century B.C.E., women played important roles in cults such as the Lenaia and the Anthesteria. The Lenaia was a festival of Dionysus in which women were especially prominent; the name derived from *lenai*, a synonym for maenad, the god's female devotee. In Fig. 3.6A the focus of the ritual is a mask of Dionysus affixed to a column and decorated with leaves and branches. The woman at the left ladles wine from a stamnos (the same type of vessel as this one), perhaps into the kantharos carried by the middle women on the reverse of the vase. This is the ritual shape of wine cup associated with the god Dionysus (cf. Fig. 3.6B). Other offerings are the meat and breads heaped on the table in front of him. The seated woman playing the flutes is crowned with the god's sacred ivy. On the ground in the center is a long

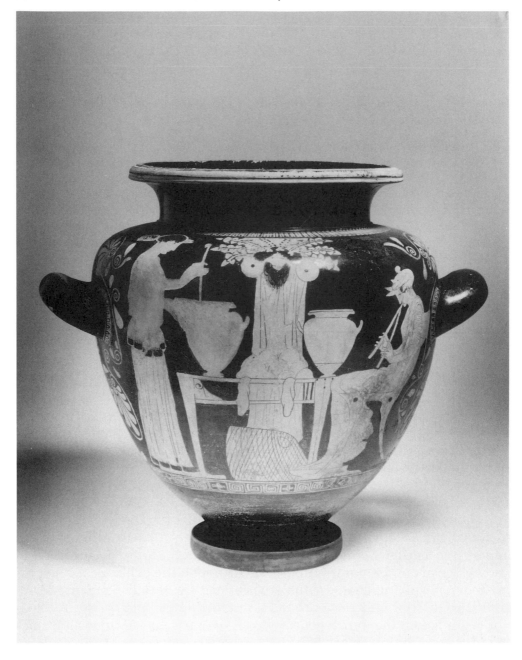

Figure 3.6. **A:** Vase (ca. 450 B.C.E.): Cult rituals in honor of the god Dionysus, a favorite of women in both Greek and Roman culture.

object like a flat basket, which was used to carry the mask of Dionysus to the sanctuary where it would be set up for worship.

The Basilinna, the wife of the Archon Basileus, played a key role in the celebration of the Anthesteria, a three-day festival of Dionysus in late winter. She made secret offerings on behalf of the city at Dionysus's

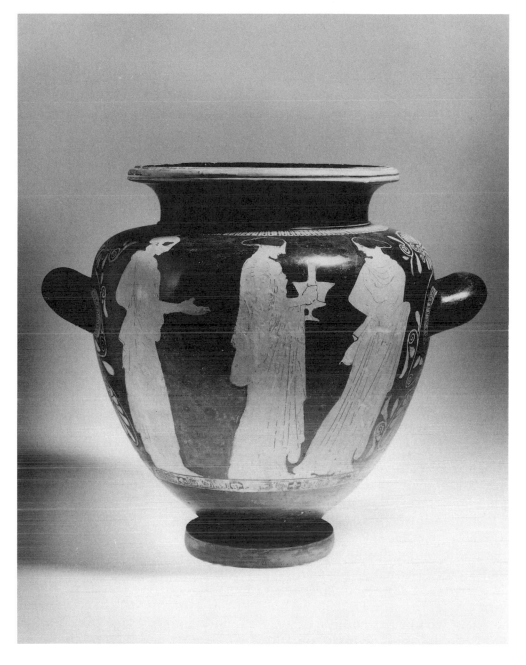

Figure 3.6 **B**: Vase (ca. 450 B.C.E.) as in **A**. Woman with a ritual wine cup, or kantharos.

sanctuary, administered a sacred oath to fourteen women (the Gerarai) who performed rituals under her direction, and became for one night the symbolic wife of the god. The wedding of Dionysus and the Basilinna took place at the Boukoleion, a building that otherwise served as the headquarters of the King Archon (Basileus). In a red-figure vase of c. 440,

Figure 3.7. Vase (ca. 440 B.C.E.) showing the drunken Dionysus coming to
visit his bride, the Basilinna, who
waits within the doorway of the
house.

the Basilinna sits on the bridal bed that we glimpse through open doors,
awaiting the god. He approaches unsteadily, after a generous sample of
the new wine that was celebrated in this festival (Fig. 3.7). Dionysus is
preceded by a young satyr holding a wine pitcher called a *chous* (this
second day of the festival was called *Choes*, after the shape), and an old
satyr casually guards the door to the chamber (see further Simon 1963
and 1983).

Both vase paintings and literary passages generally suggest that Dionysiac rites involved release from ordinary life and its cares. Dionysus
was the god of wine, and his worship could include departure from
household tasks, dancing to the excited rhythms of the aulos (often
translated "flute," but actually closer to the modern oboe) and drums.
For these reasons, we can understand some of its special appeal to the
relatively confined and secluded women of Athens (Kraemer 1979). In
poetry and vases female worshipers of Dionysus wear fawnskins, wreathe
their hair with ivy and snakes, and carry a thyrsus, a branch topped
with ivy leaves (see Fig. 3.8). Although the actual worship of Dionysus
by Attic women was more subdued, the following passage from Euripides' *Bacchae*, in which the chorus of women try to convert Thebes to
Dionysus, may convey something of the spirit of Dionysiac worship:

> O Thebes, nurse of Semele,
> wreathe yourselves with ivy!
> Abound in bryony, green
> and brilliant with berries!
> Make yourself a bacchant with branches
> of oak and pine and
> fringe your dappled fawn skins
> with tufts of white wool!
> Treat your violent wands

Figure 3.8. Interior of an Attic white-ground cup by the Brygos Painter, ca. 480 B.C.E., A maenad, a female follower of the wine god Dionysus, appears wearing an animal-skin cape, a snake in her hair, and carrying a thyrsus and panther in her hands; all these testify to the maenad's wildness.

> with reverence. The whole earth will dance at once!
> Bromius is he who leads his bands
> to the mountain, to the mountain where
> the crowd of women waits
> driven from their looms and shuttles
> by Dionysus!
>
> Euripides, *Bacchae* 105–19 [ca. 406 B.C.E.];
> trans. Helene P. Foley)

In the late fifth century, when Athens had a large foreign population, many cults from abroad were introduced, such as that of the Asiatic vegetation god Adonis (see the passage from Plutarch quoted earlier, and the discussion of Theocritus 15 in Chapter 5), whom the goddess Aphrodite loved and lost. His worship seems to have been especially popular with nonaristocratic women and hetairai. The rites for Adonis were held at night during the hot season of late July. Groups of women celebrated on the rooftops, lamenting for the beautiful young dead god Adonis. Special miniature "gardens for Adonis," broken terra-cotta pots with seeds, were made to sprout quickly and then set out to wither in the sun on the roofs of houses. On a red-figure lekythos (Fig. 3.9),

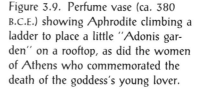

Figure 3.9. Perfume vase (ca. 380 B.C.E.) showing Aphrodite climbing a ladder to place a little "Adonis garden" on a rooftop, as did the women of Athens who commemorated the death of the goddess's young lover.

Aphrodite herself, assisted by Eros, carries the little gardens up a ladder as mortal attendants, devotées of the divine couple, look on (see further Weill 1966).

The Haloa, a festival named for the threshing floor on which it took place, was celebrated for Demeter and Dionysus at Eleusis. Again, we only have a glimpse of women's roles in this ritual from a late ancient source, which expresses embarrassment at important fertility rites that would have made far more sense to those who performed them:

On this day there is also a women's ceremony conducted at Eleusis, at which much joking and scoffing takes place. Women process there alone and are at liberty to say whatever they want to: and in fact, they say the most shameful things to each other. The priestesses covertly sidle up to the women and whisper into their ear—as if it were a secret—recommendations for adultery. All the women utter shameful and irreverent things to each other. They carry indecent images of male and female genitals. Wine is provided in abundance and the tables are loaded with all the foods of the earth and sea except those that are forbidden in the mystical account, that is, pomegranate, apple, domestic birds, eggs, and of sea creatures red mullet, eruthinos [a hermaphrodite fish], blacktail, crayfish, and dogfish. The archons set up the tables and leave them inside for the women while they themselves depart and wait outside, showing to all inhabitants that the types of domestic nourishment were discovered by them [the Eleusinians] and were shared by them with all humanity. On the tables there are also genitals of both sexes made of dough.

(Rabe 279–81; Winkler 1990)

Priestesses

Cults of female divinities regularly had priestesses as their chief personnel, but, like their male counterparts, these women were not chosen for extraordinary piety or after special religious training. Generally the priesthood was either hereditary within a family or was "bought" by a wealthy family for one of its members, for a limited term in office (see further, Turner 1984). Although they were subject to state audits (Aeschines 3.18), there is little evidence that the priestesses profited from their office in any way, although the decree for the building of the Temple of Athena Nike on the Acropolis specifies that the priestess shall receive the skins of sacrificial animals (*Inscriptiones Graecae* I³ 35; Meiggs and Lewis 1969, no. 44) and the Priestess of Demeter at Eleusis apparently received fees from initiates (see the Chapter 13).

Before the fifth century, references to priestesses in Athens are few and vague, e.g., Herodotus's mention that when the Spartan king Cleomenes tried to enter the Acropolis in 508, the priestess of Athena told him it was unlawful for a Spartan (5.72). Yet by the middle of the sixth century, in the wake of the reorganization of the Panathenaic festival in 566, we find numerous depictions in vase painting of the cult of Athena, including a woman who may be identified as her priestess on the Acropolis (Fig. 3.10). Here a sacrificial procession led by the priestess approaches a statue of the goddess on the Acropolis. Two men lead an ox that will be sacrificed at the altar that stands between priestess and statue. The priestess does not wear any sacerdotal clothing, but is marked by her proximity to altar and statue and by her gesture of holding out purificatory branches toward the goddess she serves. The subject is essentially the same as that depicted much more grandly on the Parthenon frieze a century later (cf. Figs. 3.3 and 3.5).

In the fifth century and later, many priestesses are known by name from inscriptions. By far the most famous, and the subject of much scholarly controversy, is Lysimache, who was priestess of Athena for sixty-four years in the later fifth and early fourth centuries (Pliny, *Natural History* 34.76). She appears in an inscription on a statue base; the statue, now lost, may well have depicted Lysimache as priestess of Athena. She has been identified as the model for Lysistrata, in Aristophanes' play, and both names, Lysimache and Lysistrata, meaning "disbander of armies," occur in later generations of the Eteoboutad family that held the hereditary priesthood of Athena Polias (see Lewis 1955).

Figure 3.10. Black-figure vase (ca. 550–540 B.C.E.) with the cult statue of Athena on the Acropolis; a priestess and two men with an ox approach the altar before the statue. The most sacred statue of Athena was a small and crude wooden one. This image may reflect another statue of Athena that stood in a second temple on the Acropolis or in the open.

One other priestess of the fifth century whom we know by name was Theano. When Alcibiades was condemned in absentia in 415 for parodying the mysteries of Demeter, Theano refused to curse him publicly, as had been required of all priests and priestesses (Plutarch, *Alcibiades* 22.1).[4] The name Theano can hardly be accidental, since in Homer this is the name of the priestess of Athena at Troy (*Iliad* 6.297–300). This suggests that some priestesses may have taken on "professional" names during their term in office.[5]

We should not underestimate the importance of women's religious role in Athens. (See the section on religious dedications by women in Chapter 1 for an example of a religious dedication made by a Classical woman.) Plutarch tells us that during a struggle between the followers of Megacles and Cylon in the seventh century, those followers of Cylon who took refuge at altars were slaughtered; but those who supplicated the wives of the archons were spared. (Solon 12.1) In passages cited earlier, women's role as lamenters of the dead was viewed by moralizing writers as potentially disruptive; other writers suggest that religion could lead women into adultery. In Lysias 1 (see later under "Adultery") the defendant's wife was first seen by her future lover at her mother-in-law's funeral. Plutarch dismisses allegations that the architect Pheidias arranged assignations for Pericles with freeborn Athenian women who came to the Acropolis on the pretext of looking at works of art (Pericles 13.15). Yet it is less the unreliable allegation than the reported pretext for the women's presence that is of interest here (see also the interest of the chorus of women at Euripides' *Ion* 184ff. in observing the religious monuments at Delphi).

In drama women often cite their important role in religion when they protest against their literary reputation for adultery, drinking, or irresponsibility. Sometimes they recall the city's interest in their religious upbringing (Aristophanes, *Lysistrata* 641–47, quoted earlier). In the passage below, Euripides' Melanippe offers the most powerful defense of her sex for its role in religion (women did not serve as prophets in Athens, but they did at the other places in Greece mentioned here):

> Men's blame and abuse of women is vain—
> the twanging of an empty bowstring.
> Women are better than men and I will prove it.
> . . . .
> They manage the house and guard
> within the home goods from the sea.
> No house is clean and prosperous without a wife.
> And in divine affairs—I think this of the first importance—
> we have the greatest part. For at the oracles of Phoebus
> women expound Apollo's will. At the holy seat of Dodona
> by the sacred oak the female race conveys
> the thoughts of Zeus to all Greeks who desire it.
> As for the holy rituals performed for the Fates
> and the nameless goddesses, these are not holy

in men's hands; but among women they flourish,
every one of them. Thus in holy service woman
plays the righteous role. How then is it fair for
the race of women to be abused? Will not
the empty censure of men cease; and those who think
all women should be blamed alike if one is found
erring? Let me make further distinctions.
There is nothing worse than a bad woman,
and nothing better than a good one.
Only their natures differ . . .

> (*The Captive Melanippe*, frag. 13,
> Page *Greek Literary Papyri* [420s B.C.E.?];
> trans. Helene P. Foley)

As additional defenses against their reputation, women cite the contributions they make to the city in the form of sons (Aristophanes, *Women at the Thesmophoria*), or their thrifty management of the household, which is far less corrupt and more generous than the actions of men in the assembly *(Women at the Assembly)*. Sometimes they announce that if they had been allowed a public voice in poetry, they would have sung an answer to the other sex, who are just as guilty of adultery and betrayal as women (*Medea* 410–30).

Domestic Activities

Women also participated in religious rituals more closely associated with their roles in the family. Domestic cults required daily tending. Marriages, funerals, and the care of the dead at family tombs may have been less ostentatious and less assertively public than in the Archaic period, but they still offered occasions to mark women's contribution to the continuity of individual oikoi, a continuity Athenian law and custom made a point of protecting.

Care of the Dead

We have already discussed women's more subdued role as lamenters of the dead. Yet the care of the dead did not end with the funeral and burial. The grave had to be continually visited and provided with offerings, and this responsibility fell primarily to Athenian women. On a typical funerary vase (Fig. 3.11), the visitor arrives with a large basket of offerings at a particularly elaborate tomb, a tall stele standing atop a stepped platform and crowned by a floral acroterion. The offerings that fill the steps are of two types, wreaths and small jugs of perfumed oil, the same shape as the vase on which this scene is painted. Another lekythos of this type floats in the background. This shape, especially when covered with a white slip, as here, was made exclusively for funerary use. The visitor is dressed only in the sleeveless fine linen chiton that

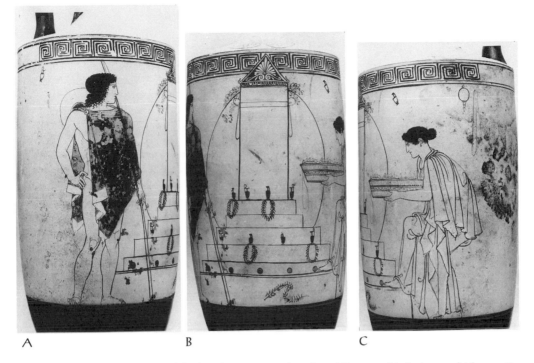

A   B   C

Figure 3.11. Funerary vase, or lekythos (ca. 440 B.C.E.) in the white-ground technique, which permitted delicate use of outline for depictions of scenes of mourners. The youth at left, nearly nude and carrying a spear (A), is perhaps an apparition of the deceased, a male relative of the woman who visits his tomb (B and C).

became fashionable in Athens during the fifth century. From the middle of the century, in both sculpture (cf. Fig. 3.5) and vase-painting, the sheer garment clings to the body, revealing the forms underneath. But this should be taken more as a reflection of artistic taste than as a deliberate attempt to eroticize women's bodies, especially on a solemn occasion like this. We should not assume that women actually went out in public dressed in transparent clothing, any more than the nude male warriors in Greek art reflect actual battle practice.

On another vase of similar type (Fig. 3.12), a young woman, coming to lay an offering at the tomb of a dead relative (her mother?) is confronted by an apparition of the deceased. The offering is a kind of sash that will be tied around the stele, which already has two such ornaments. Such epiphanies of the deceased at their tombs are not uncommon on white lekythoi of the late fifth century. They are not to be taken literally, but simply offer the viewer a "portrait" of the deceased that often corresponds to the types found on contemporary marble gravestones (cf. Fig. 3.1 and Mnesarete in the Introduction to Part I). Here the woman rests her chin on her fist in a dejected pose, as if brooding over her own death.

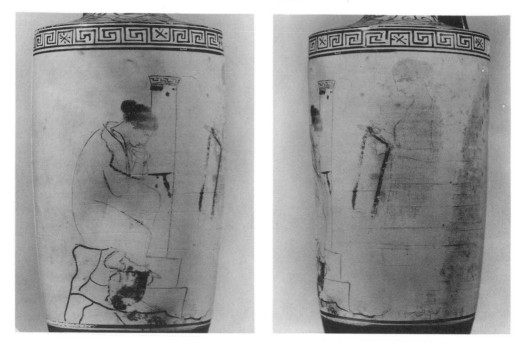

Figure 3.12. White-ground lekythos (ca. 430 B.C.E.) with a scene of a beribboned stele to which a woman comes bearing another sash. At left is a seated woman, perhaps the deceased.

Weddings

The central event of an Athenian wedding was the procession in a simple chariot from the home of the bride to that of the groom (Figs. 3.13 and 3.14), and court cases often cite this moment as proof of a wife's legitimacy. The procession traditionally took place at night; hence the presence of figures carrying torches to light the way. The bride, still veiled, stands in the car as her husband mounts it in preparation for the journey. Other relatives follow the chariot on foot, bringing gifts for the couple. This small cylindrical vase with lid is a pyxis, a box for women's toiletries. Such an object would have been a typical gift for the bride. On the day after her wedding, an Athenian woman was visited by her female friends and relatives. In Figure 3.15 the bride stands at the right, in front of the doors to her bedroom, receiving her guests. The gifts include nuptial vases filled with greenery, and one woman plays with a pet bird. On the wall behind are hung a mirror, attribute of the bride (cf. Fig. 3.2) and a wreath. All the women have been given mythological names; the bride is Alcestis, prototype of the virtuous wife because of her loyalty to her husband and willingness to die in his place. This un-

$\longrightarrow$

Figure 3.13. Pyxis (ca. 440–430 B.C.E.) for cosmetics, ornamented with a bridal scene. The attendant family and friends bear gifts including a large jar and a box, perhaps containing jewelry, household goods, or the bride's trousseau. The door to the left is a sign for the house.

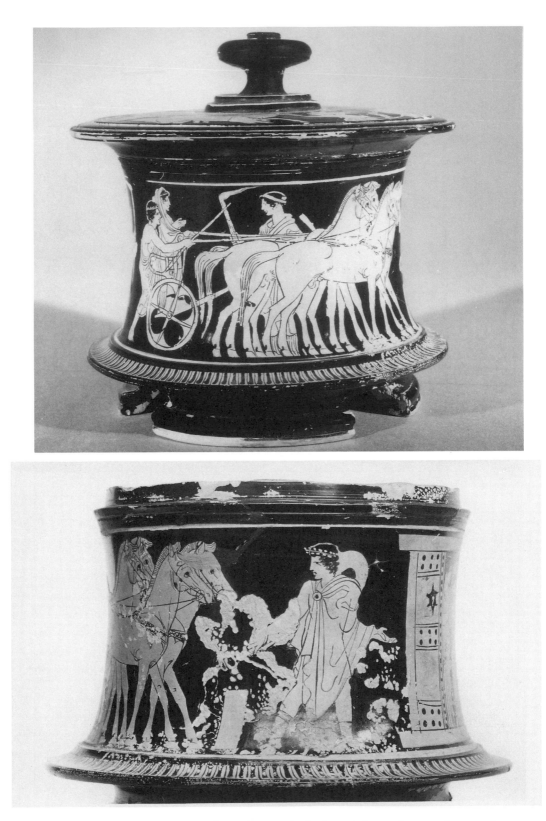

Figure 3.14. Pyxis as in Figure 3.13, here showing the bride carried in a chariot to her new home. The composition of bride and charioteer is reminiscent not only of other wedding scenes but also of the abduction of Persephone by Hades as it appears in Greek art (cf. Fig. 1.8). The god Hermes leads the couple to their new home.

Figure 3.15. Epinetron (ca. 420 B.C.E.) with scenes of a bride and her guests and gifts. The epinetron is a curved piece of ceramicware placed over the leg of a woman who then cards the raw wool on it.

usual object is known as an *epinetron* because it was meant to be placed over a woman's knee, the roughened upper surface used for carding wool.

In the last third of the fifth century, young brides and grooms are shown together in moments of quiet intimacy that convey a new, more romantic and idealized notion of heterosexual love (see Sutton 1981). In creating the imagery of the ideal couple, artists take liberties with some of the realities of life. The groom, for example, is regularly shown as a beardless ephebe, a young man of approximately seventeen to nineteen years of age, although we know that most Athenian men did not marry before their mid- to late twenties, when they certainly had a full beard. The bride, on the other hand, may well seem more mature than the fourteen- or fifteen-year-old girl she often was. On a loutrophoros, the vessel used to hold water for the bridal bath (Fig. 3.16), the groom typically leads his new bride gently by the hand toward the marriage chamber. The little Erotes (Cupids) that flutter about the bride add a touch of romantic fantasy. Such scenes, decorating gifts for the new bride, were no doubt meant to calm her fears of the unknown by painting a rosy picture of her wedding day and of the handsome stranger she had yet to meet.

Women in the Household

The life of respectable women (the wives and female relatives of citizens, and very probably of resident aliens as well) within the household was secluded, primarily in order to protect their role as producers of le-

A   B

Figure 3.16. Vase for water for a bride's bath (loutrophoros), probably a wedding gift; **A.** The groom leads the bride toward the bedroom, **B.** indicated by the doorway (ca. 430 B.C.E.).

gitimate heirs; it was less secluded, however, than popular ideals might have allowed. Furthermore, as might be expected, women had informal opportunities to influence the men in their families and sometimes violated the laws attempting to regulate their reproductive powers.

After marriage, a young woman assumed responsibility for the prosperity of her husband's household and for the well-being of its members. The *Oeconomicus* of Xenophon, a Socratic dialogue written in the second quarter of the fourth century B.C.E., describes the management of the oikoi of the wealthiest Athenians. Young wives, apparently with little training for the job, sometimes managed large households. Xenophon and his interlocutor Socrates are critical of the girl's lack of domestic education:

Socrates said, "As for a wife—if she manages badly although she was taught what is right by her husband, perhaps it would be proper to blame her. But if he doesn't teach her what is right and good and then discovers that she is ignorant of these qualities, wouldn't it be proper to blame the husband? Anyhow,

Critobulus, you must tell us the truth, for we are all friends here. Is there any-one to whom you entrust a greater number of serious matters than to your wife?

Critobulus replied, "No one."

"Is there anyone with whom you have fewer conversations than with your wife?"

Critobulus answered, "No one, or at least not very many."

"And you married her when she was a very young child who had seen and heard virtually nothing of the world?"

"Yes."

(3.11–13; trans. Sarah B. Pomeroy)

Socrates tells Critobulus of the conversation Ischomachus had once had with his wife when they were newly married and he was describing her function in his household:

" 'Certainly, you will have to stay indoors and send forth the group of slaves whose work is outdoors, and personally supervise those whose work is indoors. Moreover, you must receive what is brought inside and dispense as much as should be spent. And you must plan ahead and guard whatever must remain in reserve, so that the provisions stored up for a year are not spent in a month. And when wool is brought in to you, you must see that clothes are produced for those who need them. And you must also be concerned that the dry grain is in a good condition for eating. However, one of your proper concerns, perhaps, may seem to you rather thankless: you will certainly have to be concerned about nursing any of the slaves who becomes ill.' "

(*Oeconomicus* 7.35–37. On nursing the sick, see also [Dem] 59.56)

Women are repeatedly said to inhabit "women's quarters" in the most remote and protected part of the house. The wife, other freewomen in the household, and female slaves normally lived and worked in these women's quarters. Plato (*Laws* 781c) captures the nature of these con-fined spaces when he describes women as a race "accustomed to a sub-merged and shadowy existence." Although these quarters are not always easy to locate in the archaeological remains, some traces can be seen in the plan of a house excavated on the north slope of the Areopagus in Athens (see Fig. 3.17). The men's quarters on the north side of the house and the women's quarters on the south side each have their own en-trance. There is no access to the Andron (men's quarters) from the women's quarters.[6] Even a household of modest means usually included a female slave so that the wife was not obliged to perform chores out-of-doors where she might encounter men who were not close kin and who therefore posed potential threats to her chastity and the legitimacy of the family's heirs.

As might be expected, scenes depicting husband and wife together after the wedding are rare, but portrayals of women together in the women's quarters without any men present are common. The principal activity portrayed on vase paintings as characteristic of respectable Athenian women who stayed at home was weaving and the making of clothing for the family. This was a woman's most important contribu-tion to the economy of the household and, from the time of Homer's

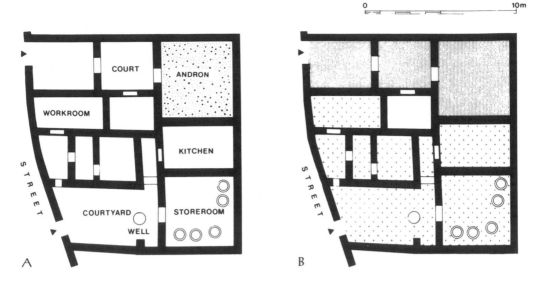

Figure 3.17. **A.** Plan of a house (fifth century, B.C.E.) on the north slope of the Areopagus in Athens, with indications of the separation of men's and women's quarters and the placement of the latter in an area with no direct connection to the andron, the room for men's gatherings. **B.** Women's quarters are marked by + and men's are shaded.

Penelope, the symbol of the virtuous and industrious wife. Socrates advises a man who is having trouble supporting a large group of female relatives to put them to work making wool; they will contribute to the household and be happy to be occupied (Xenophon, *Memorabilia* 2.7.2–14.) On a red-figure cup (Fig. 3.18), a seated woman draws strands of wool from a basket *(kalathos)* and smoothes them over her leg, as a friend watches.

Child care was of course a main preoccupation of the women's quarter of an Athenian house, though the subject is not commonly shown in vase painting. In one unusual example (Fig. 3.19), the mother is handed her child by a slave girl. The kalathos in the middle is not in use, but is simply a token of the respectable housewife. The babies depicted on Athenian vases are inevitably male, perhaps reflecting the concern of all Athenians to produce a male heir.

Playing with dolls and nurturing pet animals prepared a girl for marriage and motherhood. Dolls were dressed as girls of marriageable age. Little girls are often distinguishable from grown women in Greek art only by their small stature. Their chignons and long dresses are those of mature women, and Greek artists of the classical period still had difficulty in rendering convincingly a child's face. A girl on a gravestone, in one example (Fig. 3.20), wears a fine linen chiton, girded high above the waist, as was fashionable in this period, and a fillet in her wavy hair. But the girl is probably meant to be only five or six. Her name is Plangon (Doll), and the doll that she so prominently displays may be a play on the name. Beside the toy, she is shown with her favorite pet, a goose.

Figure 3.18. Interior of a cup (ca. 470 B.C.E.), with a woman watching as another works wool from a wool-basket. The furniture, a klismos chair with its saber curved legs and a padded stool, indicates in abbreviated form the decoration of the house.

Figure 3.19. Vase (ca. 450 B.C.E.), with a baby brought to his seated mother. The swirling skirt of the hurrying attendant and the outstretched arms of mother and infant give the scene a sense of emotional immediacy as attractive as the composition, in which the chair curve and the flip of the servant's hem follow the curves of the vase.

Figure 3.20. Grave stele of Plangon, a young girl with a doll and a pet goose (325–320 B.C.E.).

Hanging in the background are textiles that may include the sakkos, worn loosely over the hair. Unlike boys of the same age, girls were rarely portrayed nude (the vases found at Brauron discussed above are an exception, see Fig. 3.4).

The evidence of vase painting also suggests, however, that women at home engaged in more intellectual activities than we would suspect from written sources, especially reading and playing music. For example, in Figure 3.21, the seated woman hunches over an opened bookroll. She is no doubt reading aloud to the three women who accompany her, one of them holding a chest that could contain jewelry or other valuables. Scenes in the women's quarters seldom include any men, but they do show that it was common for small groups of women to gather, whether for work (weaving) or for relaxation.

Women's Work Outside the Home

The complete seclusion of women was only possible in households of some means, and both vase paintings and literary texts suggest a variety of exceptions. A large group of black-figure vases shows women fetching water at a public fountain house (Fig. 3.22). In most instances the vase itself is a hydria, the three-handled pitcher with broad belly and narrow

Figure 3.21. Vase (ca. 450 B.C.E.), with a woman seated on a klismos and reading from a scroll amid other women; the group suggests the women's quarters and the social environment of respectable married women for whom exposure to men not directly related to them seems to have been rare.

neck used for transporting water. Here several women are ready to leave, balancing the full hydria on their heads. Two others are waiting their turn, the empty vessels sitting sideways on their heads, as yet another fills her hydria. It is evident that this is also a social occasion, the

Figure 3.22. Water-jar (ca. 520 B.C.E.) from Athens, depicting women at a fountain house.

women chatting animatedly with one another. The sudden appearance of these scenes in the years 520–500 may commemorate the building of a beautiful fountain house in the Agora by the tyrant Hippias about 520. The scene loses popularity in the fifth century. The fountain house was known as a dangerous place, where men might lurk. These women, though attractively dressed, could be either slaves or free women too poor to afford a slave (Hannestad 1984). Nevertheless, some respectable women apparently did brave the difficulties of fetching water at wells or streams. In Aristophanes' *Lysistrata* (327ff.), the chorus of older wives complain of the crowds of slaves and rogues that they encounter fetching water at a spring on the side of a hill; Euripides' Electra, lamenting her domestic duties as wife of a peasant farmer, goes to get water at a stream (*Electra* 140ff.)

In the more rural parts of Attika, women must have also participated in agricultural work on the family property. On one vase (Fig. 3.23), a group of women is shown picking fruit in an orchard. The work does not look very strenuous, but in other such scenes the women are shown actually climbing the trees. One woman, dressed in black, carries away a full basket, straining under the weight (see Fracchia 1972).

Women from poor families sometimes had to work outside the home. (Aristotle remarks at *Politics* 1300a that in democracies it is impossible to keep poor women from going out when they wish to.) Demosthenes 57.45 refers to a period when citizen women were forced to become wet nurses, wool-workers, or grape-pickers "owing to the misfortunes of the city in those days." In the same speech, the mother of Euxitheus is said to have served as a nurse and sold ribbons due to her poverty (57.31–34). A woman selling bread in Aristophanes' *Wasps* (1396–98) is clearly of citizen status; in Aristophanes' *Women at the Thesmophoria*, a garland-seller complains that the poet Euripides' attacks on traditional religion are ruining her business (443–58); in his *Lysistrata* the heroine's older married allies are designated at one point as vendors (447–48). On one side of a red-figure vase (Fig. 3.24A), the seated woman is the proprietor of a shop selling perfumed oil. Her customer, a young woman, has brought a small cylindrical container, called an *alabastron*, which has been filled by the seller from a large pelike (the same shape as this vase) on the ground. The seller's humble status is suggested by her short, cap-like hair. On the reverse (Fig. 3.24B), the customer has returned home and presents the alabastron to her mistress, who has sent her on this errand. The domestic setting is indicated by the mirror hanging on the wall and the kalathos, or wool-basket, at the right.

Women, Law, and Politics

Women from different households seem to have had far more contact with one another than Pericles' funeral oration and other sources might lead us to suspect. Aristophanes' plays assume that women mix with each other not only at festivals, but to borrow and exchange household goods, or to serve as midwives for each other (for example, Aristophanes *Women at the Assembly*, esp. 446–48, 460, 528 and Theophrastus, *Characters* 10). And as we see in a speech of the orator Demosthenes, rural women who were neighbors knew a good deal about each others' lives: "Before they undertook this malicious action against me, my mother and

Figure 3.23. Vase showing women picking fruit (ca. 460 B.C.E.). The light-colored clothing and erect poses of the pickers seem meant to differentiate them from the woman carrying the fruit, but whether the dark-clad one is a slave and the others are not is unclear.

theirs were intimate friends and used to visit one another, as was natural, since they both lived in the country and were neighbors, and since, furthermore, their husbands had been friends while they lived. Well, my mother went to see theirs, and the latter told her with weeping what had happened, and showed her the effects'' (Demosthenes 55.23–4; Mur-

A   B

Figure 3.24. **A.** Vase (ca. 460 B.C.E.) with a woman selling perfumes and unguents in a shop. Such commercial scenes are rare in Greek vase painting, as are references to the work women did outside the home. **B.** Reverse of the vase in Figure 3.24.A. The domestic environment, indicated by mirror and wool-basket, differs from the shop, where the jar hanging on the wall and the large jar on the floor use a typically abbreviated visual language to depict a commercial environment.

ray 1988). In Aristophanes' *Lysistrata* (700–02), a mother speaks of inviting her daughter's friend, a neighbor, to share in a celebration of Hecate. Aristotle complains that in radical democracies women dominate the house and spread gossip about their men (*Politics* 1313b). (See also Demosthenes 53.4 and 58.40, Theophrastus 10.13, Lysias 32.10, Plato *Theatetus* 149, Euripides, *Electra* 1130.) On rare occasions, groups of women may even have spontaneously taken action. Herodotus tells us that during the Persian Wars, after the Athenian men stoned a councillor to death for advocating submission to Persia, the Athenian women ran to his house in order to stone his wife and children (*Histories* 9.5).

Although not legally competent to transact serious business, citizen women also participated in and were knowledgeable about economic exchanges among relatives and about matters of inheritance; they were also brought into court to elicit sympathy for defendants. One of the orations of Demosthenes (41) makes clear that both a mother and two daughters were familiar with family wills; the mother lent money and jewelry to her son-in-law and kept accounts of these loans. Aeschines (1.170) refers to wealthy young men whose fathers were dead and whose mothers were administering their property. In Lysias 32, the children of a widow had been defrauded of their inheritance by their guardian, Diogeiton, her deceased husband's brother and her own father (she had married her paternal uncle.) At a family council she criticized Diogeiton over the treatment of her two sons: "And when we assembled she asked him what sort of man he was to think it right to act in the way he had acted towards the boys. . . . If you have no feeling of embarrassment towards any man, you ought to have feared the gods; you received, when your brother set sail, five talents from him on deposit. And in support of this I am willing to put forward my children . . . and swear on oath upon their heads anywhere you care to name." After proving her point with records from an account book, she says: "And then you had the audacity to claim, though you have all this money, that their father left two thousand drachmae and thirty staters, the sum which was bequeathed to me, and I handed over to you when he was dead." The speaker then adds that "all of those present were so affected by what this man had done and by the things which she said to him, when we saw the boys and the injuries inflicted on them, and remembered the deceased and how unworthy a trustee he had left for his possessions, and when we reflected on how difficult a thing it is to find a man who could be trusted with what he ought to be trusted, none of us who were there could utter a word, gentlemen of the jury, we could only weep as sadly as the victims and depart in silence." (Lysias 32.12ff. [ca. 400 B.C.E.]; Lacey 1968: 160–61. See Demosthenes 40.10, Isaeus 12.5, Lysias 13.39–42, and Demosthenes 36.14 for other examples of women's participation in issues relating to inheritance.)

Women and their priorities also had informal influence on their menfolk in other contexts as well. Demosthenes 59.110 suggests that the jurymen will have to justify their decision on the infamous Neaera (see below) to their wife, daughter, or mother (see also Lycurgus, *Against Leocrates* 141). Isaeus 12.5 insists that women would not allow their husbands to give false evidence about family matters. Isaeus 7.14–15 (see also Demosthenes 40.10 and 50) shows that men consulted respected women in a range of family matters: "so he came to my mother, his own sister, for whom he had a greater regard than for anyone else, and expressed a wish to adopt me, and asked her permission, which was granted" (Murray 1988). In Isaeus 2 a man named Menecles reportedly gave his wife back to her family for remarriage because he could not give her children: "Menecles, with many expressions of praise for our sister, approached us and said that he viewed with apprehension his increasing age and childlessness: she ought not, he said, to be rewarded for her virtues by having to grow old with him without bearing children; it was enough that he himself was unfortunate. He, therefore, begged us to do him the favor of marrying her to someone else with his consent." (2.7–8; Forster 1983) Indeed, as Andromache puts the whole issue of wifely influence in Euripides' *Trojan Women*:

> I gave
> my lord's presence the tribute of hushed lips, and eyes

quietly downcast. I knew when my will must have its way
over his, knew also how to give way to him in turn.
(lines 653–56 [415 B.C.E.]; Lattimore 1959)

Adultery

Law-court cases on the subject of adultery or concerning the violation of
marriage laws give us a good idea of the male concerns over honor and
the legitimacy of their children that led to women's confinement in the
oikos and of the complex relations that could develop between women
of different social status in the household. In the story told in the following law-court speech written by the orator Lysias in the first quarter of
the fourth century, a young wife was seduced only after the seducer had
caught sight of her at her mother-in-law's funeral. (An older widow who
had a son could continue to live in the same house with him, even after
he married.) The husband, Euphiletus, murdered his wife's seducer, a
man named Eratosthenes. Although orations written for law courts are
usually tendentious, Euphiletus expects that his household and activities
will appear normal to the members of the jury who are, like himself,
Athenian men of moderate means. He describes his house as follows: "I
have a little two-story house, both storys are the same size, the women's
quarters are on the upper story and the men's on the ground floor" (Lysias 1.9; trans. Sarah B. Pomeroy). The husband was free to enter the
women's quarters and to have sexual relations with his wife and slaves
(see further, the house-plan, Fig. 3.17). Euphiletus describes how he had
gradually come to learn about his wife's affair. He emphasizes that the
adultery began after the birth of his baby and he never gives his wife's
name:

> When I, Athenians, decided to marry and brought a wife into my house, for
> some time I was disposed neither to vex her nor to leave her too free to do just
> as she pleased. I kept a watch on her as far as possible, with such observation
> of her as was reasonable. But when a child was born to me, thenceforth I began
> to trust her and placed all my affairs in her hands, presuming we were now in
> perfect intimacy. (Lysias 1.6; Lamb 1960)

. . . .

> One day, when I had come home unexpectedly from the country, after din-
> ner, the baby was crying and colicky. Actually the slave girl was bothering him
> on purpose to make him behave so, because—as I found out later—this man was
> in the house. Well, I told my wife to go and nurse the baby, to stop his crying.
> But at first she refused, pretending that she was so glad to see me back after my
> absence. At last I began to get annoyed, and I insisted on her going.
> "So that you may assault the little slave girl," she exclaimed. "When you
> were drunk, in the past, you grabbed her."
> (Lysias 1.11–12; trans. Sarah B. Pomeroy)

Doubtless because she spent so much time with her mistress and because
her master was so violent, the slave girl attempted to conceal the affair,
even though her master threatened her with the usual punishments "to

be whipped, to be thrown into a mill [that is, to work as a beast of burden, turning the millstone], and to be constantly subjected to such punishments" (Lysias 1.18). But when the slave realized that Euphiletus knew the details of the affair, for he had been told by "an old hag who had been sent by a woman—Eratosthenes' previous mistress" (Lysias 1.15), she told all and helped him catch the seducer naked in bed with his wife. The murdered man's relatives prosecuted Euphiletus for homicide, but he argued before the court that the law not only justified, but required him to murder his wife's seducer and that seduction is a more heinous crime than rape:

"If anyone shames by force a free adult or child, he is liable to a double penalty [that is, double the damages owed for inflicting similar violence on a slave]. If he shames by force a woman in one of the cases where it is permitted to kill him, he shall be liable to the same penalty. . . . The lawgiver [Athenian laws on homocide were attributed to Draco, who had been appointed to write the first law code in 621 B.C.E.] thought that those who use violence deserve a smaller penalty than those who use persuasion . . . , thinking that those who make their conquest by violence are hated by the persons who are violated; but those who use persuasion corrupt the souls of their victims, making other men's wives more closely attached to themselves than to their own husbands, and get control of the house, and make it dubious who the fathers of the children really are, the husbands or the adulterers."

(Lysias 1.32–33; trans. Sarah B. Pomeroy)

The law required the husband to divorce an adulterous wife and the adulteress was forbidden to wear jewelry and to participate in public religious activities. (Dem. 59.86–87. See Cole 1984 and Harris 1990) But despite the law, it was difficult to force a husband to testify in court that his wife had had extramarital sexual relations (Aeschines 1.107), for such relations made the parentage and citizenship of children dubious and diminished the honor of the cuckolded husband. Similarly, we do not hear of daughters who were sold into slavery in accordance with the provisions of Solon's law, quoted above.

Like Lysias 1, other speeches emphasize the special roles of the wife as producer of legitimate children and guardian of the household property, and the dangers that ensue if these roles are violated. In this speech written around 340 B.C. and included among the speeches of Demosthenes, the prosecution alleges that Neaera had been raised as a prostitute in Corinth. Hence neither she nor her children were Athenian citizens, although Stephanus had given Neaera's daughter in marriage to an Athenian cult official under the pretext that she was his legitimate daughter and an Athenian citizen. If the prosecution proved their case, Neaera would be sold into slavery, her children would lose their citizenship, and Stephanus would be deprived of his political rights. The defendant is Neaera, but through attacking her, the prosecutors Apollodorus and Theomnestus intend to inflict dishonor and loss of civic rights on their political enemy, Neaera's husband Stephanus. The prosecutors stress the importance of maintaining the distinction between women of different social status in Athens, a distinction that Neaera has violated:

For this is what living with a woman in marriage is: for a man to beget children by her and to present his sons to his fellow clansmen and members of his district and to give daughters as his own in marriage to their husbands. Mistresses we have for pleasure, concubines for daily service to our bodies, but wives for the procreation of legitimate children and to be faithful guardians of the household.

(Dem. 59; trans. Sarah B. Pomeroy)

The prosecution casts doubt on Neara's respectability by naming her repeatedly in the speech:

Nicarete, who was the freedwoman of Charisius of Elis and the wife of his cook Hippias, bought seven girls when they were small children. She was an astute judge of natural beauty in little girls and furthermore she understood how to bring them up and train them skillfully, for she made this her profession and got her livelihood from the girls. She used to address them as daughters, implying that they were free women, so that she might extract the largest fees from those who wished to get close to them. When she had reaped the profit of the youthful prime of everyone of them, she sold all seven of them: Anteia, Stratola, Aristocleia, Metaneira, Phila, Isthmias, and this Neaera here.

In the course of my speech I will tell you who bought each of them and how they were set free by those who purchased them from Nicarete. . . . At the moment I wish to return to the defendant Neaera here and prove that she belonged to Nicarete, and that she worked by letting out her body for hire to those who wished to get close to her.

The rhetorician Lysias was the lover of Metaneira. In addition to all the other expenses he had incurred for her, he wished to have her initiated in the Mysteries, for he thought that everything else he had spent on her was taken by the woman who owned her, but that for whatever he spent on her for the festival and the Mysteries the woman herself would be grateful. So he asked Nicarete to come to the Mysteries bringing Metaneira with her so that she might be initiated, and he promised that he himself would initiate her. When they arrived, Lysias did not bring them to his own house, out of respect for his wife, the daughter of Brachyllus who was his own niece, and for his mother who was elderly and lived in the same house. Instead he housed the two, Metaneira and Nicarete, with Philostratus of Colonus, who was his friend and still a bachelor. The defendant Neaera here accompanied them, for she was already working with her body, although she was still very young, for she had not yet reached puberty.

(Dem. 59.18–22;)

Hetairai

Apparently relying on the anonymity of respectable wives, the former prostitute Neaera temporarily succeeded in passing her daughter off as an Athenian wife. Yet most prostitutes could only imitate respectability by engaging in respectable domestic practices like weaving and spinning, as we see them doing in many vase paintings. There were many types of prostitutes in Athens. Hetairai, or "female companions," at the top of the social scale of these professional sexual entertainers, were well trained and possessed artistic talents; pornai were at the bottom. Some were free foreign women or resident aliens or metics, and others were slaves. They could entertain men at symposia or drinking parties in the men's quarters of a respectable house, in houses rented for them by patrons, or at their own establishments. Of these women, only one played a significant role in Athenian history: the famous hetaira and later madam, Aspasia. Here is how Plutarch described her liaison with Pericles:

> Sources claim that Aspasia was highly valued by Pericles because she was clever and politically astute. After all, Socrates sometimes visited her, bringing along his pupils, and his close friends took their wives to listen to her—although she ran an establishment that was neither orderly nor respectable, seeing that she educated a group of young female companions to become courtesans. Aeschines says that Lysicles the sheep dealer, a man lowly born and humble of nature, became the most important man of Athens by living with Aspasia after the death of Pericles. Consequently there is a good deal of truth contained in the *Menexenus* of Plato (even if the first part is written tongue in cheek) when it states that she had the reputation of associating with many Athenians as a teacher of rhetoric. Nevertheless, it appears as if Pericles' affection toward Aspasia was chiefly erotic in nature. . . . The story goes that he would kiss her warmly both when he left for the marketplace and when he returned home each day.
>
> (*Pericles* 34.3–6; trans. Hallett in Sarah B. Pomeroy,
> *Goddesses, Wives, Whores and Slaves*, p. 89)

The lives of Athenian prostitutes, both at work in the company of male clients and at home among themselves, are best documented by hundreds of red-figure vase paintings from the late sixth century to the late fifth. These make it clear that most hetairai were hired for entertainment, companionship, and sex at (or after) a symposium, or men's drinking party. In one typical scene (Fig. 3.25), three couples are shown. One hetaira has just undressed and is about to join her partner on his couch, while the two other couples are already reclining together. The affectionate gestures of the couple in the middle are somewhat unusual and may present a romanticized view of a relationship that is portrayed with brutal realism on many other vases (cf. Fig. 3.27). The hetaira at the right is playing kottabos, a favorite Athenian party game, flicking the dregs of the wine at a target. The wreathed wine-bowl (krater) under one handle and the slave boy who serves the wine, under the other, are standard attributes of the symposium setting. On these occasions, drinkers used cups like this one, and the scenes decorating the exterior would have provided visual entertainment and perhaps helpful hints to one's partner.

Drinking cups also offer many images of naked hetairai by themselves, which must have functioned like pinups for male consumers. One

Figure 3.25. Symposium vase (490–480 B.C.E.), with men and their hired female companions. The popularity of these vases testifies to the common practice among citizen men of entertaining themselves under circumstances utterly separated from the household and family.

pair faces each other, relaxed on pillows, as if having their own private, all-girl symposium (Fig. 3.26), probably a male fantasy. Hetairai are also pictured in all the same domestic contexts in which respectable (that is, citizen) women are seen, though sometimes their nudity makes clear their status. The distinction between hetairai and matrons is far from obvious in many scenes that show women performing domestic chores like spinning and weaving (cf. Fig. 3.18). Since hetairai like Neaera tried to pass themselves off as Athenian citizens, they would have affected the same manners and styles as their reputable counterparts. An unusual epitaph of the late fifth century, apparently recording the devotion of an hetaira to her dead friend, further testifies to the desire of hetairai to emulate customs relating to respectable women.[7]

Because of your true and sweet friendship, your companion (hetaira) Euthylla placed this tablet on your grave, Biote, for she keeps your memory with tears, and weeps for your lost youth.

(Peek 1415/IG II² 10954; trans. M. R. Lefkowitz,
in Lefkowitz and Fant, 1982, no. 25, pp. 11–12)

The hetairai in Figure 3.26 display the ideal of youthful female beauty that dominates fifth-century Greek art: slim and graceful, with small and firm breasts. Often the proportions are curiously masculine, as

Figure 3.26. Drinking cup (520–510 B.C.E.), with a pair of hetairai amusing themselves as if at a symposium; their nudity and poses, as well as the drinking vessels they hold, make it clear that these are not what the Athenians would consider respectable women.

if the artist had used an ephebe's body as his model and simply added, not always convincingly, the breasts.

But young slender hetairai did not stay that way forever, and vase-painters seem to enjoy the ruthless caricature of the fat, aging, and toothless prostitute forced to make up for her lost beauty with other skills (Fig. 3.27). Here and in other, more brutal scenes, we witness the degradation to which prostitutes could be subjected once the niceties of the symposium were over (see Keuls 1983b and 1985, Peschl 1987).

Ancient Critical Reactions to Women's Roles in Classical Athens

Classical Athens was a place of great intellectual ferment. Both drama and philosophy undertook to question women's roles and the relation of private to public life that shaped the relations between the sexes and organized their activities. For example, in Plato's *Republic*, a Socratic dialogue written in the same period as Xenophon's *Oeconomicus*, Socrates imagines the institutions of the "Just Society," in which each person fulfills a function appropriate to his or her aptitude. The inhabitants of the Republic are distributed into three classes. Among the highest class,

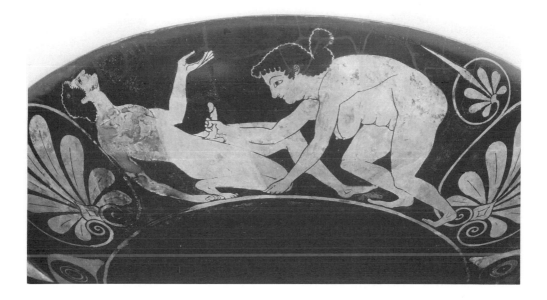

Figure 3.27. Detail of a symposium vase (ca. 500 B.C.E.), with an older hetaira whose body and double chin place her far from the idealized young women of Fig. 3.26. Unlike them, older prostitutes appear on other symposium vases as the objects of sexual penetration by two or more men at once.

or Guardians, the nuclear family and private property are eliminated. Thus interfamilial squabbles over legitimacy, inheritance, and the chastity of women such as those described in speeches from the law courts quoted earlier, would not exist. Instead, men and women of procreative age have intercourse at intervals regulated by the state; children are raised in common in state-run nurseries. Plato, like Xenophon and other followers of Socrates, argued that the soul has no gender. The minds of men and women have the same moral and intellectual potential. Therefore, in the Republic, men and women of the Guardian class are given the same education. Some of the provisions governing women and the family are similar to those thought to have existed in the ideal Spartan society (see Chapter 2). Thus, in the Republic women are even given the athletic training that conventional Athenian thought deemed appropriate only for males. Because there is no private sphere, women perform jobs in the public sphere, serving in the military and the government (see further Okin 1979). The government is totalitarian, authoritarian, and hierarchical; the highest official in the Republic is a philosopher-king, or, conceivably, a philosopher-queen. Although Plato was not a feminist in the contemporary sense of the word, some of the assumptions about androgyny and the provisions in the Republic resemble those in twentieth-century utopian feminist thought:

So if we are going to use men and women for the same purposes, we must teach them the same things.

Yes.

We educated the men both physically and mentally.

Yes.

We shall have to train the women also, then, in both kinds of skill, and train them for war as well, and treat them in the same way as the men.

It seems to follow from what you said, he agreed.

I dare say, I rejoined, that their novelty would make many of our proposals seem ridiculous if they were put into practice

There's no doubt about that, he said.

And won't the most ridiculous thing of all be to see the women taking exercise naked with the men in the gymnasium? It won't only be the young women; there will be elderly women too, just as there are old men who go on with their exercises when they are wrinkled and ugly to look at.

Lord! he said, that's going to be a funny sight by present standards.

Still, I said, now we've launched out on the subject we must not be afraid of the clever jokes that are bound to be made about all the changes that follow in the physical training and education of women, and above all about them being trained to carry arms and ride.

. . . .

Well, let's see if we can find a way out. We admit that different natures ought to have different kinds of occupation, and that men and women have different natures; and yet we go on to maintain that these admittedly different natures ought to follow the same occupations. That is the charge we have to meet, isn't it?

That is it.

. . . .

We are sticking obstinately to the verbal debating point that different natures should not be given the same occupations; but we haven't considered what kind of sameness or difference of nature we mean, and what our intention was when we laid down the principle that different natures should have different jobs, similar natures similar jobs.

No, we've not taken that into consideration.

Yet we might just as well, on this principle, ask ourselves whether bald men and long-haired men are of the same or opposite natures and, having agreed that they are opposite allow bald men to be cobblers and forbid long-haired men to be, or vice versa.

That would be absurd.

But the reason why it is absurd, I pointed out, is simply that we never meant that natures are the same or different in an unqualified sense, but only with reference to the kind of sameness or difference which is relevant to various employments. For instance, we should regard a man and a woman with medical ability as having the same nature. Do you agree?

Yes. But a doctor and a carpenter we should reckon as having different natures.

Yes, entirely.

Then if men or women as a sex appear to be qualified for different skills or occupations, I said, we shall assign these to each accordingly; but if the only difference apparent between them is that the female bears and the male begets, we shall not admit that this is a difference relevant for our purpose, but shall

still maintain that our male and female Guardians ought to follow the same occupations.

And rightly so, he agreed.

. . . .

There is no administrative occupation which is peculiar to woman as woman
or man as man; natural capacities are similarly distributed in each sex, and it
is natural for women to take part in all occupations as well as men, though in
all women will be the weaker partners.

Agreed.

Are we therefore to confine all occupations to men only?

How can we?

Obviously we can't; for we are agreed, I think, that one woman may have
a natural ability for medicine or music, another not.

Yes.

And one may be good at athletics, another have no taste for them; one be
good at soldiering, another not.

I think so.

Then may a woman not be philosophic or unphilosophic, high-spirited or
spiritless?

She may.

Then there will also be some women fitted to be Guardians: for these natural qualities, you will remember, were those for which we picked our men
Guardians.

Yes, they were.

. . . .

As law-giver, you have already picked your men Guardians. You must now pick
women of as nearly similar natural capacities as possible to go with them. They
will live and feed together, and have no private home or property. They will
mix freely in their physical exercises and the rest of their training, and their
natural instincts will necessarily lead them to have sexual intercourse.

. . . .

We must, if we are to be consistent, and if we're to have a real pedigree herd,
mate the best of our men with the best of our women as often as possible, and
the inferior men with the inferior women as seldom as possible, and bring up
only the offspring of the best. And no one but the Rulers must know what is
happening, if we are to avoid dissension in our Guardian herd.

That is very true.

(extracts from Plato, *Republic* 452, 453e–456a, 458c–d, 459e; Lee 1987)

Poets as well as philosophers imagined women performing roles that
were not permitted to them in contemporary society. The comic poet
Aristophanes imagines women staging a sex strike for peace *(Lysistrata)*,
convicting the poet Euripides of misogyny during the Thesmophoria
(Women at the Thesmophoria), or taking over the government and creating a communist utopia when they have become disgusted with men's
abuse of state interests *(Women at the Assembly)*. Tragedy imagines
women who take revenge on their enemies *(Medea, Hecuba)*, kill their
husbands for sacrificing a child (Clytemnestra), resist marriage (Aeschylus, *Suppliants)*, argue against the views offered by men *(Antigone,
Phoenician Women)*, and save members of their family *(Iphigenia*

Among the Taurians, Helen). One of the most poignant figures in tragedy is the maiden who voluntarily sacrifices herself for family, city, or nation. In the following passage, Iphigenia agrees to sacrifice herself to the goddess Artemis so that the Greek army can go to Troy. She imagines that she will win the fame for heroism denied to women in the real life of classical Athens:

> I have decided to die. But I want to die
> gloriously, putting aside what is ignoble.
> Look here, mother, and consider with me if I calculate well.
> All Greece turns to me now in her greatness;
> on me depends the departure of the fleet and the defeat of Troy.
> Because of me barbarians will no longer have the license
> to abduct women from the blessed land of Greece;
> they will expiate the loss of Helen, whom Paris stole.
> By my death I will achieve all these things;
> as liberator of Greece I shall win a glorious name.
> Surely I should not love life too much.
> You bore me for all the Greeks, not for yourself only.
> Innumerable soldiers armed with shields
> and plying oars dare to challenge the enemy
> and die for their country when it has been wronged.
> Shall my life, my single life, hold all this back?
> (Euripides, *Iphigeneia in Aulis* 1376–90; trans. Helene P. Foley)

Despite such radical challenges to tradition, Plato's student Aristotle could be said to have the last word on these issues, for his more traditional views on women's roles retained greater influence—in theory if not necessarily in reality—in the coming eras. Aristotle's ideas about women and gender were consistent: they appear in his writing on politics, biology, and theory of tragedy (see Chapters 2 and 6). In his *Politics*, Aristotle criticized Socrates' ideas on gender. In his view, Plato's utopian Republic is unworkable; patriarchy is natural and in the best interests of all who inhabited a Greek city-state. Women are suited by nature for their private role in the household and because they are naturally inferior to men, they should be trained to moral obedience to their husbands and fathers:

We shall, I think, in this as in other subjects, get the best view of the matter if we look at the natural growth of things from the beginning. The first point is that those which are incapable of existing without each other must be united as a pair. For example, (a) the union of male and female is essential for reproduction and this is not a matter of *choice*, but is due to the *natural* urge, which exists in the other animals too and in plants, to propagate one's kind. Equally essential is (b) the combination of the natural ruler and ruled, for the purpose of preservation. For the element that can use its intelligence to look ahead is by nature ruler and by nature master, while that which has the bodily strength to do the actual work is by nature a slave, one of those who are ruled. Thus there is a common interest uniting master and slave.

Nature, then, has distinguished between female and slave: she recognizes different functions and lavishly provides different tools, not an all-purpose tool like the Delphic knife; for every instrument will be made best if it serves not many purposes but one. But non-Greeks assign to female and slave exactly the same status. This is because they have nothing which is by nature fitted to rule; their association consists of a male slave and a female slave. So, as the poets say, "It is proper that Greeks should rule non-Greeks," the implication being that non-Greek and slave are by nature identical.

Thus it was out of the association formed by men with these two, women and slaves, that a household was first formed; and the poet Hesiod was right when he wrote, "Get first a house and a wife and an ox to draw the plough," (The ox is the poor man's slave) This association of persons, established according to nature for the satisfaction of daily needs is the household, the members of which Charondas called "bread-fellows" and Epimenides the Cretan "stable-companions."

. . . .

There are, as we saw, three parts of household-management, one being the rule of a master, which has already been dealt with, next the rule of a father, and a third which arises out of the marriage relationship. This is included because rule is exercised over wife and children—over both of them as free persons, but in other respects differently: over a wife, rule is as by a statesman; over children, as by a king. For the male is more fitted to rule than the female, unless conditions are quite contrary to nature; and the elder and fully grown is more fitted than the younger and undeveloped. It is true that in most cases of rule by statesmen there is an interchange of the role of ruler and ruled, which aims to preserve natural equality and non-differentation; nevertheless, so long as one is ruling and the other is being ruled, the ruler seeks to mark distinctions in outward dignity, in style of address, and in honours paid. . . . As between male and female this kind of relationship is permanent.

. . . .

Thus it becomes clear that both ruler and ruled must have a share in virtue, but that there are differences in virtue in each case, as there are also among those who by nature rule. An immediate indication of this is afforded by the soul, where we find natural ruler and natural subject, whose virtues we regard as different—one being that of the rational element, the other of the non-rational. It is therefore clear that the same feature will be found in the other cases too, so that most instances of ruling and being ruled are natural. For rule of free over slave, male over female, man over boy, are all different, because, while parts of the soul are present in each case, the distribution is different. Thus the deliberative faculty in the soul is not present at all in a slave; in a female it is present but ineffective, in a child present but undeveloped.

We should therefore take it that the same conditions inevitably prevail in regard to the moral virtues also, namely that all must participate in them but not all in the same way, but as may be required by each for his proper function. The ruler then must have moral virtue in its entirety; for his function is in its fullest sense that of a master-craftsman, and reason is a master-craftsman. And the other members must have such amount as is appropriate to each. So it is evident that each of the classes spoken of must have moral virtue, and that restraint is not the same in a man as in a woman, nor justice or courage either, as Socrates thought; the one is the courage of a ruler, the other the courage of a servant, and likewise with the other virtues.

. . . .

For these relationships are part of the household, and every household is part of a state; and the virtue of the part ought to be examined in relation to the virtue of the whole. This means that both children and women must be educated with an eye to the constitution—at least if it is true that it makes a difference to the soundness of a state that its children should be sound, and its women too. And it must make a difference; for women make up half the adult free population, and from children come those who will participate in the constitution.

(Aristotle, *Politics* 1252a24–b14, 1259a37–1259b10, 1260a3–24, 1260b12–25; Sinclair, rev. Saunders 1981)

NOTES

1. For occasional outdoor scenes depicting fetching water, fruit picking, market selling, or swimming (not shown), see further under "Women's Work Outside the Home."
2. Golden 1990: 47 suggests that this passage is partially ironic, because the chorus of women claim the benefits of participating in more rituals than one child could participate in.
3. In general, it appears that whereas all citizen-boys participated in civic rituals, only a select number of girls did so. A scholiast to Aristophanes tells us that selected maidens went to Brauron, but later sources say that all girls participated (considerations of space make this less likely). In a procession every four years to Brauron, all those who had served the goddess in the intervening time marched.
4. See Sourvinou-Inwood 1988a for the view that the whole episode is a fiction.
5. See Nagy 1979 for the alternative view that parents named their daughters Theano in hope that they would become priestesses.
6. See Walker 1983. For another perspective on domestic space in the Greek house, see Jameson 1990a and b.
7. The word *hetaira* here could simply mean female companion or friend in a more neutral sense.

TRANSLATIONS

Forster, E. S. 1983. *Isaeus*. Loeb Classical Library. Cambridge, Mass. (Originally published 1927)

Grene, David. 1959. *Hippolytus*. In *The Complete Greek Tragedies: Euripides I*, edited by David Grene and Richmond Lattimore, 157–221 Chicago.

Jameson, Michael. 1959. *The Women of Trachis*. In *The Complete Greek Tragedies: Sophocles II*, edited by David Grene and Richmond Lattimore, 71–119. Chicago.

Jones, F. W. 1959. *The Suppliant Women*. In *The Complete Greek Tragedies: Euripides IV*, edited by David Grene and Richmond Lattimore, 51–104 Chicago.

Lamb, W. R. M. 1960. *Lysias*. Loeb Classical Library. Cambridge, Mass. (Originally published 1930)

Lattimore, Richmond. 1959. *The Trojan Women*. In *The Complete Greek Tragedies: Euripides III*, edited by David Grene and Richmond Lattimore, 121–175 Chicago.

Lee, Desmond. 1987. *Plato: The Republic*. New York.

Murray, A. T. 1988. *Demosthenes*. Vol. 6. Loeb Classical Library. Cambridge, Mass. (Originally published 1935)

Perrin, Bernadotte. 1982. *Plutarch's Lives*. Vols. 1 and 2. Loeb Classical Library. Cambridge, Mass. (Originally published 1914)

Scott-Kilvert, I. 1960. *Pericles*. In his *Plutarch, Rise and Fall of Athens*, 165–206 Harmondsworth, Middlesex.

Sinclair, T. J. 1981. *Aristotle: The Poetics*. Revised by T. J. Saunders. London.
Winkler, John J. 1990. *The Constraints of Desire*. New York.

WORKS CONSULTED

Blok, Josine. 1987. "Sexual Asymmetry: A Historiographical Essay." In *Sexual Asymmetry: Studies in Ancient Society*, edited by Josine Blok and Peter Mason, 1–57, Amsterdam.

Boardman, John. 1974. *Athenian Black-figure Vases*. London.

———. 1975. *Athenian Red-figure Vases: The Archaic Period*. London.

———. 1989. *Athenian Red-figure Vases: The Classical Period*. London.

Brommer, Frank. 1977. *Der Parthenon Fries*. Mainz.

Brumfield, Allaire Chandor. 1981. *The Attic Festivals of Demeter and Their Relation to the Agricultural Year*. Salem, N.H.

Clairmont, Christoph. 1970. *Gravestone and Epigram*. Mainz.

Cole, Susan G. 1984. "Greek Sanctions against Sexual Assault." *Classical Philology* 79: 97–113.

Foley, Helene P. 1981. "The Conception of Women in Athenian Drama." In *Reflections of Women in Antiquity*, edited by Helene P. Foley, 127–68. New York.

———. 1993. "The Politics of Tragic Lamentation." In *Tragedy, Comedy and the Polis*, edited by A. Sommerstein, J. Henderson, and B. Zimmermann, 101–44. Bari.

Fracchia, Helena. 1972. "The San Simeon Fruit Pickers." *California Studies in Classical Antiquity* 5: 103–11.

Friedländer, P., with H. B. Hofleit. 1948. *Epigrammata: Greek Inscriptions in Verse*. Berkeley and Los Angeles.

Golden, Mark. 1990. *Children and Childhood in Classical Athens*. Baltimore, Md.

Gould, John. 1980. "Law, Custom and Myth: Aspects of the Social Position of Women in Classical Athens." *Journal of Hellenic Studies* 100: 38–59.

Hague, Rebecca. 1988. "Marriage Athenian Style." *Archaeology* 41: 32–36.

Hannestad, Lise. 1984. "Slaves and the Fountain House Theme." In *Ancient Greek and Related Pottery*, edited by H. A. G. Brijder, 252–55. Amsterdam.

Harris, E. M. 1990. "Did the Athenians Regard Seduction as a Worse Crime than Rape?" *Classical Quarterly*, n.s. 40: 370–77.

Harrison, A. R. W. 1968. *The Law of Athens*. Vol 1, *The Family and Property*. Oxford.

Humphreys, S. C. 1983. *Women, the Family and Death*. London.

Jameson, Michael. 1990a. "Domestic Space in the Greek City-state." In *Domestic Architecture and the Use of Space*, edited by S. Kent, 92–113. Cambridge.

———. 1990b. "Private Space and the Greek City." In *The Greek City*, edited by Oswyn Murray and Simon Price, 171–95. Oxford.

Just, Roger. 1989. *Women in Athenian Law and Life*. London.

Kahil, Lilly. 1977. "L'Artemis de Brauron: rites et mystère." *Antike Kunst* 20: 86–98.

Keuls, Eva. 1985. *The Reign of the Phallus*. New York.

Kraemer, Ross. 1979. "Ecstasy and Possession: The Attraction of Women to the Cult of Dionysus." *Harvard Theological Review* 72: 55–80.

Kurtz, Donna. 1975. *Athenian White Lekythoi*. Oxford.

Lacey, W. K. 1968. *The Family in Classical Greece*. New York.

Lazzarini, M. L. 1976. *Le Formule delle dediche votive nella Grecia arcaica. Atti della Accademia Nazionale Dei Lincei*, ser. 8, vol. 10.

Lefkowitz, M. R., and M. B. Fant. 1982. *Women's Life in Greece and Rome: A Source Book in Translation*. Baltimore.

Lewis, D. M. 1955. "Notes on Attic Inscriptions (II)." *Annual of the British School of Athens* 50: 1–7.

Lezzi-Hafter, Adrienne. 1988. *Der Eretria Maler*. Mainz.

Loraux, Nicole. 1986. *The Invention of Athens*. trans. Alan Sheridan, Cambridge, Mass.

Maas, P. 1946. "Stephano, title of a priestess." *Hesperia* 15: 72.

Meiggs, Russell, and D. M. Lewis. 1969. *A Selection of Greek Historical Inscriptions.* Oxford.

Nagy, Blaise. 1979. "The Naming of Athenian Girls: A Case in Point." *Classical Journal* 74: 360–64.

North, Helen. 1966. *Sophrosyne.* Ithaca, N.Y.

Page, D. L. 1970. *Select Papyri III. Literary Papyri.* Loeb Classical Library. Cambridge, Mass.

Parker, Robert. 1983. *Miasma: Pollution and Purification in Early Greek Religion.* Oxford.

Peek, W. 1955. *Griechische Vers-Inschriften.* Vol. 1, *Grab-epigramme.* Berlin.

Peschl, Ingeborg. 1987. *Die Hetäre bei Symposion und Komos in der attisch-rotfigurigen Vasenmalerei.* Frankfurt.

Pomeroy, Sarah P. 1975. *Goddesses, Wives, Whores and Slaves.* New York.

———. Forthcoming. 1994. *Xenophon, Oeconomicus: A Social and Historical Commentary.* Oxford.

Reinsberg, Carola. 1989. *Ehe, Hetärentum und Knabenliebe im antiken Griechenland.* Munich.

Schaps, D. M. 1977. "The Woman Least Mentioned: Etiquette and Women's Names." *Classical Quarterly* 27: 323–31.

———. 1979. *Economic Rights of Women in Ancient Greece.* Edinburgh.

Shapiro, H. A. 1991. "The Iconography of Mourning in Athenian Art." *American Journal of Archaeology* 95: 629–56.

Simon, Erika. 1963. "Eine Anthesterien-Skyphos des Polygnotos." *Antike Kunst* 6: 6–22.

———. 1966. "Neue Deutung zweier eleusinischer Denkmäler des 4. Jahrhunderts v. Chr." *Antike Kunst* 9: 72–92.

———. 1983. *Festivals of Attica.* Madison, Wis.

Sourvinou-Inwood, Christiane. 1988a. "Priestess in the Text: *Theano Menonos Agrylethen.*" *Greece and Rome* 35: 28–39.

———. 1988b. *Studies in Girl's Transitions. Aspects of the Arkteia and Age Representations in Attic Iconography.* Athens.

Sutton, Robert F. 1981. "The Interaction between Men and Women Portrayed on Attic Red-figure Pottery." Ph.D. Dissertation, University of North Carolina.

———. 1989. "On the Classical Athenian Wedding: Two Red-figure Loutrophoroi in Boston." In *Daidalikon: Studies in Memory of Raymond V. Schoder, S. J.*, edited by R. F. Sutton, 333–59. Wauconda, Ill.

Turner, Judy Ann. 1984. "Hiereai: The Acquisition of Feminine Priesthoods in Ancient Greece." Ph.D. dissertation, University of California, Santa Barbara.

van Straten, F. T. 1981. "Gifts for the Gods." In *Faith, Hope, and Worship: Aspects of Religious Mentality in the Ancient World*, edited by H. S. Versnel, 65–151. Leiden.

Walker, Susan. 1983. "Women and Housing in Classical Greece: the Archaeological Evidence." In *Images of Women in Antiquity*, edited by A. Cameron and A. Kuhrt, 81–91. London.

Weill, Nicole. 1966. "Adonaziasouzai." *Bulletin de Correspondance Hellénique* 90: 664–74.

Williams, Dyfri. 1983. "Women on Athenian Vases: Problems of Interpretation." In *Images of Women in Antiquity*, edited by A. Cameron and A. Kuhrt, 92–106. London.

FURTHER READING

Blok, Josine, and Peter Mason, eds. 1987. *Sexual Asymmetry: Studies in Ancient Society.* Amsterdam.

Clark, Gillian. 1989. "Women in the Ancient World." *Greece and Rome. New Surveys in the Classics*, No. 21. Oxford.

Cole, Susan G. 1981. "Could Greek Women Read and Write?" In *Reflections of Women in Antiquity*, edited by Helene P. Foley, 219–45. New York.

Des Bouvrie, Synnøve. 1990. *Women in Greek Tragedy*. Symbolae Osloenses Fasc. Suppl. XXVI. Oslo.

Cohen, David. 1991. *Law, Sexuality, and Society: The Enforcement of Morals in Classical Athens*. Cambridge.

Goldhill, Simon. 1986. In his *Reading Greek Tragedy*, "Sexuality and Difference," 107–37. Cambridge.

Harvey, David. 1988. "Painted Ladies, Fact, Fiction and Fantasy." In *Ancient Greek and Related Pottery*, edited by J. Christiansen and T. Melander, 242–57. Copenhagen.

Keuls, Eva. 1983a. "Attic Vase-Painting and the Home Textile Industry." In *Ancient Greek Art and Iconography*, edited by W. G. Moon, 209–23. Madison, Wis.

———. 1983b. " 'The Hetaera and the Housewife': The Splitting of the Female Psyche in Greek Art." *Mededelingen van het Nederlands Instituut te Rome* 9–10: 23–40.

Lefkowitz, M. L. 1981. *Heroines and Hysterics*. London.

Okin, Susan. 1979. *Women in Western Political Thought*. Princeton, N.J.

Patterson, Cynthia B. 1991. "Marriage in Athenian Law." In *Women's History and Ancient History*, edited by Sarah B. Pomeroy, 20–47. Chapel Hill, N.C.

Schaps, D. M. 1982. "The Women of Greece in Wartime." *Classical Philology* 77: 193–213.

Schmitt-Pantel, Pauline, ed. 1992. *A History of Women: From Ancient Goddesses to Christian Saints*. Cambridge, Mass.

Sutton, Robert. 1992. "Pornography and Persuasion in Attic Pottery." In *Pornography and Representation in Greece and Rome*, edited by A. Richlin, 3–35. Oxford.

Zeitlin, Froma. 1985. "Playing the Other: Theater, Theatricality, and the Feminine in Greek Drama." *Representations* 11: 63–94.

4

EXCURSUS
AMAZONS:
WOMEN IN CONTROL

In ancient times there were Amazons, daughters of Ares, dwelling beside the river Thermodon; they alone of the people around them were armed with iron and they were the first of all to mount horses, with which, due to the inexperience of their foes, they surprised them and either caught those who fled or outstripped those who pursued. They were considered men for their high courage, rather than women for their sex; for they seemed to outdo men in their spirit more than to be at a disadvantage in their form. Ruling over many nations, they enslaved those around them; yet hearing by report of the great renown of our country, they mustered the most warlike of the nations and marched them against this city for the sake of great glory and through high ambition. But having met with valiant men they came to possess spirits suitable to their own nature; the reputation they won was the reverse of their previous one, and by their disasters rather than by their bodies they were deemed to be women. They alone failed to learn from their mistakes, and thus to be better advised in their future actions. They did not return home and report their own misfortune and our ancestors' courage; for they died on the spot and were punished for their folly, thus making our city's memory imperishable for its valor, while due to their disaster in this region they made their own country nameless. And so those women, by their unjust greed for others' land, justly lost their own.

(Lysias 2.4–6, *Funeral Oration* [early fourth century B.C.E.];
Lamb 1960 modified)

The mythical defeat of the Amazons became in the rhetoric of Classical Athenian funeral orations one of the great achievements of the Attic past, which symbolized the rescue of the Greeks from slavery at the hands of foreign conquerors. In these funeral speeches Amazons were imagined, through their greed for fame and empire, to have fallen: the very kind of enterprise in which Athens itself engaged in the second half of the fifth century. Amazons played a central role in the art and ideology of Archaic and Classical Athens, but they were continually reimagined to serve a changing culture and politics. Amazon myths of a society ruled by women are a case study in understanding ways in which gender was used to conceptualize central cultural issues and problems in the Classical period (for further discussion and interpretation, see Boardman 1982, du Bois 1982, von Bothmer 1957, Carlier-Detienne 1980–81, Hardwick 1990, Just 1989, Lefkowitz 1986, Merck 1978, Shapiro 1983, and Tyrrell 1984).

Our earliest representations of Amazons appear in Archaic epic and Attic vase paintings of the sixth century B.C. Epic views Amazons as a band of great female warriors. The tomb of the Amazon queen Myrrhina is a landmark (like the tombs of other heroes who died young and glorious) at Troy (*Iliad* 2.814). At *Iliad* 3.184–89ff. King Priam describes how he battled Amazons in his youth. Some of those Amazons came to fight on the Trojan side in the war at Troy, and their queen, Penthesilea, met her death at the hands of the great Greek warrior Achilles, who fell in love with his victim as he killed her. Battles against the Amazons were an important labor for the heroes Bellerophon and Heracles. In his ninth labor, Heracles captured the girdle of the Amazon queen and brought it back to Greece for the daughter of Eurystheus. Beginning at about 575 B.C.E. Heracles' battles with the Amazons, sometimes in single combat, became a popular subject in Attic black-figure vase painting. An Attic black-figure hydria, for example, shows Heracles and Telamon fighting Amazons dressed as hoplites (Fig. 4.1), warriors in heavy armor, and differentiated by their white flesh. Visually these Amazons do not differ from Greek heroes; they wear Greek armor, carry Greek weapons, and engage in pursuits typical of male warriors. Although their femininity is not stressed, the artist may dwell on the moment of defeat, as the Amazons fall to the ground in submission, their heads bent back.

Yet Amazons were soon to lose their status as great, if somewhat exotic, warriors, a match for all but the greatest of Greek heroes. Athens repeatedly used Amazons to serve its own ideology. First the Attic hero Theseus appropriated some of the deeds of Heracles. At about 490 B.C.E. on the metopes of the Athenian treasury at Delphi, both Theseus and Heracles are shown involved in an expedition to Amazon country. In later Attic versions of the story Theseus, his friend Pirithous, and his charioteer Phorbas abduct an Amazon by trickery (Fig. 4.2, Theseus and the Amazon Antiope). The Amazons retaliate by invading Attica. Tamed by her love for Theseus, the Amazon intercedes in the battle and arranges a treaty (Plutarch, *Theseus* 26–28). Later the Amazon, abandoned by Theseus, was said to have interrupted his marriage with the Cretan Phaedra and to have been killed by Heracles, who was one of the guests. Yet the story of Theseus's engagement with the Amazons, which seems to have been promoted by the Pisistratid tyrants who ruled Athens for much of the sixth century, put the hero awkwardly at fault as the abductor of an innocent Amazon. As we saw in Lysias's oration at the beginning of this excursus, however, the ambitious Amazons soon became responsible for their own fall.

Shortly after the two Persians wars between the Greeks and the Per-

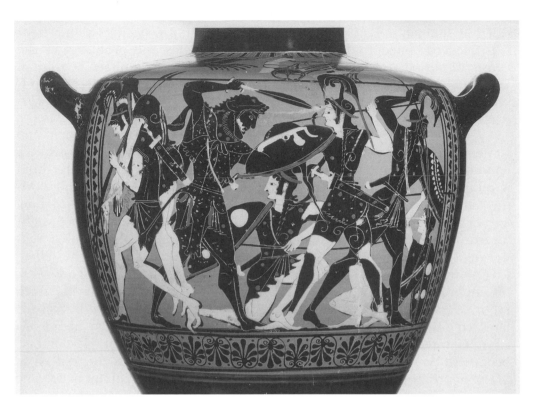

Figure 4.1. Vase (ca. 520–500 B.C.E.) in the black-figure technique with the heroes Heracles and Telamon fighting Amazons.

Figure 4.2. Outside of a cup (ca. 510 B.C.E.), on which Theseus abducts the Amazon Antiope; she wears the exotic garments of an eastern warrior to mark her difference from Greek women.

sians from 490 to 480 B.C.E., Athenian art made a point of suggesting analogies between the eastern Amazons and the defeated Persians.[1] Amazons, dressed in Eastern garb and carrying bows and arrows, by their defeat hinted at the feminized nature and the incapacity for self-control of the Greeks' barbarian opponents. A red-figure amphora, for example, shows a Greek warrior between two Amazons dressed in Persian style (Fig. 4.3). Paintings made in the 460s B.C.E. in the Stoa Poikile at Athens showed Amazons before the Acropolis, the Greeks and Persians at Marathon, the Greek capture of Troy, and Athens fighting the Spartans at Oinoe. Later artistic programs such as the metopes of the Parthenon linked the battle against the Amazons with battles between Greeks and centaurs, Greeks and Trojans (now viewed as eastern and barbarian), or Gods and Giants. Centaurs were mythical horsemen. Unable to control the violence and sexuality inherent in their half-bestial nature, they invaded the wedding of the Lapiths and were prevented from raping the Lapith women by the intervention of Heracles. Just as centaurs embodied masculinity out of control, in these artistic programs the violent, promiscuous, and war-loving Amazons became an analogous female challenge to the order of civilization. The centrality of the defeat of the Amazons in Athenian propaganda is confirmed by the fact that the battle against the Amazons appeared on the outside of the shield held by the statue of the city's divine protectress, Athena Parthenos, in her temple on the Acropolis (Fig. 4.4 shows a reconstruction of the shield by E. B. Harrison).

In particular, Amazons were viewed as hostile to men and marriage. The fifth-century historian Hellanicus, in a description that typified the views of his contemporaries, called the Amazons "a golden-shielded, silver-axed, male-infant-killing host." The unfeminine Amazons were said to cauterize their right breasts (the word *a-mazon* means "without breast") in order to remove any impediment to effective fighting (Frags. 16, 17; F. Jacoby *Die Fragmente der griechischen Historiker* 3B 45–46); or they allegedly fed their female infants on horse's milk to prevent the enlargement of their breasts (Philostratus, *Heroikos* 330). Hence they denied the social function of Attic women as nurturers of their children. The tragic poet Aeschylus imagined the Amazons' defeat to have occurred at the Areopagus, the site of the first trial by jury for murder in Athens. In his play the *Eumenides*, the hero Orestes is exonerated from killing his mother Clytemnestra (a rebel against marriage who killed her husband Agamemnon and turned against her own son), and her female advocates, the Furies or Erinyes, divine spirits of familial vengeance, meet their defeat. Orestes' victory is linked with the earlier Greek victory over the Amazons. The god Apollo argues in Orestes' defense that Clytemnestra's crime against marriage is more serious than Orestes' killing of a woman who is not a true relative, since women simply serve to nurture the seed of their men. In Attic art and literature the taming of the Amazons by war or love, which returned these women to their "natural" state (see Lysias above), came to represent a renewal of the proper

Figure 4.3. Attic vase (ca. 440–430 B.C.E.), with a Greek warrior between two Amazons; their Persian garments provided the Greek viewer during and after the Persian Wars with an image of the non-Greek that conflated foreignness, femininity, and moral laxity with defeat.

order of patriarchal civilization, in which women were subordinated to marriage to produce offspring who were certainly legitimate. In this respect the story of the Amazons' fall and ultimate extermination through their own errors was a "myth of matriarchy" that served to explain, by

Figure 4.4. The shield of Athena Parthenos from the gold and ivory statue (mid-fifth century B.C.E.) in the Parthenon in Athens; in this reconstruction drawing, the inevitable defeat of the Amazons is made clear by their falling and dead figures.

positing an earlier era in which women could dominate or exclude men, the inevitability and desirability of the civilized status quo.

Fifth-century and later Greek writers developed an entire ethnography for Amazons. These ethnographies sometimes represented Amazon "culture" as systematically inverting that of the Greeks, sometimes as a complex alternative to it. In the fifth-century historian Herodotus's account of an encounter between Scythians and Amazons, the Scythian young men become enamored of the beautiful warriors with whom they engage in battle. When they wish to marry their sexual partners, with whom they have (typically of Amazons) mated at random outdoors, the Amazons refuse to become conventional wives: "We could not live with your women—our customs are quite different from theirs. To draw the bow, to hurl the javelin, to ride a horse, these are our arts. Of women's work we know nothing. Your women, on the contrary, do none of these things, but stay at home in their wagons, and never go out to hunt, or to do anything. We should never get along together. But if you truly wish to have us as your wives and will conduct yourselves with strict justice towards us, go home to your parents, ask them to give you your inheritance, and then come back to us, and let us live together by ourselves." (*Histories* 4.114, Rawlinson 1942, modified) Inverting the usual practice of Greek marriage, the Scythian husbands bring their goods with them (the equivalent of a woman's dowry) and move to a place where the Amazons can continue to exercise their military ways. The Amazons are the dominant partners in these marriages, although they lose their language because they are quicker to learn their partners' tongue than the reverse. In some versions of Amazon ethnography, Amazons live without men, except for periodic promiscuous forays to become pregnant. They keep their girl children, and kill, emasculate, or send away for adoption their male children. In Diodorus's first-century B.C.E. account, on the other hand, Amazon men in Libya live the lives of Greek women—they stay at home, weave, and tend the children, deprived of the right to govern—while the women fight and demonstrate a remarkable capacity for just and orderly rule.

Amazons are often envisioned as less civilized than the Greeks. They practice an orgiastic religion, worshiping Ares, the Phrygian Magna Mater, Cybele, and the virginity-loving Artemis in a fashion that recalls the dangerous attraction of Greek women to the worship of Dionysus. Although Strabo (*Geography* 11.5.1) has Amazons engage in agriculture, Diodorus makes them less civilized eaters of meat alone, and Herodotus's Amazons have not yet learned how to navigate ships. Amazons' weapons, the bow, the ax, and sometimes the javelin and the spear, tend to associate them with light-armed soldiers or with those, like bowmen, who had less military prestige than the heavy-armored hoplite. Amazon communities are typically located at the borders of the known world— for example, in the North East on the southern shore of the Black Sea on the Thermodon River or in the South West in Libya. Geographers and medical writers tried to explain the Amazon phenomenon by the inferior climate from which they come: for example, saying that the colder climates of the North West produced more virile women.

Insofar as Amazons are untamed, virginal, and aggressive, they could serve to represent a phase of life for both young men and women: the androgynous state of life between childhood and adulthood. Yet Amazons serve as important paradigms precisely because they generally fail to make the transition to "maturity." Both erotic and virginal, heroic on the Greek model and yet less civilized than their opponents, Amazons were a parodoxical mixture of youthful attractiveness and a danger that must be surpressed.

Although many later Greek writers scoffed at the unlikelihood of Amazon myths (for example, Strabo, 11.5.3), the stories of Amazons were remarkably persistent. Alexander the Great was said to have been chosen as a mate by the Amazon Queen Thalestris, who approached his camp with the hope of conceiving an heroic child. Amazon myths, while largely imaginary, may have originated in Greek encounters with the nomadic Scythians in the area north of the Black Sea. Archaeological remains confirm that some Scythian aristocratic women, who were buried with horse trappings and weapons, rode horses and fought in war. Indeed, Plato uses the example of these Scythian women in the *Laws* (805A and 806B), when he wants to give proof that women are capable of fighting for their country.

NOTES

1. Amazons had also been depicted in eastern dress on black-figure vases (see Shapiro 1983). Boardman 1982 suggests that the equation between Persians and Amazons began after the Ionian revolt in the early fifth century B.C.E.

TRANSLATIONS

Lamb, W. R. M. 1960. *Lysias*. Loeb Classical Library. Cambridge, Mass. (Originally published 1930)

Rawlinson, George. 1942. *Herodotus: The Persian Wars*. New York.

WORKS CONSULTED

Bamberger, Joan. 1974. "The Myth of Matriarchy: Why Men Rule in Primitive Society." In *Women, Culture and Society*, edited by M. Rosaldo and L. Lamphere, 263–80. Stanford.

Boardman, John. 1982. "Herakles, Theseus and Amazons." In *The Eye of Greece*, edited by D. Kurtz and B. Sparkes, 1–28, Cambridge.

Bothmer, Dietrich von. 1957. *Amazons in Greek Art*. Oxford.

Carlier-Detienne, Jeanne. 1980–81. "Les Amazons font la guerre et l'amour." *L'Ethnographie* 76: 11–33.

du Bois, Page. 1982. *Centaurs and Amazons: Women and the Pre-History of the Great Chain of Being*. Ann Arbor, Mich.

Hardwick, Lorna. 1990. "Ancient Amazons—Heroes, Outsiders or Women?" *Greece and Rome* 37: 14–36.

Just, Roger. 1989. *Women in Athenian Law and Life*. London.

Lefkowitz, Mary. 1986. *Women in Greek Myth*. London.

Merck, Mandy. 1978. "The City's Achievements: The Patriotic Amazonomachy and Ancient Athens." In *Tearing the Veil*, edited by Susan Lipshitz, 95–115. London.

Shapiro, H. A. 1983. "Amazons, Thracians and Scythians," *Greek, Roman, and Byzantine Studies*: 105–14.

Tyrell, W. Blake. 1984. *Amazons: A Study in Athenian Myth-Making*. Baltimore, Md.

5

THE HELLENISTIC PERIOD:
WOMEN IN A COSMOPOLITAN WORLD

The Hellenistic is the only period in Greek and Roman history defined by the reign of a woman. It begins with the death of Alexander the Great on June 10, 323 B.C.E. and ends after the Roman conquest of Egypt, with the suicide of Cleopatra VII on August 12, 30 B.C.E. and the subsequent eighteen-day reign of her children. The late Sir Moses Finley opened his essay "The Silent Women of Rome" with the observation that Cleopatra was the most famous woman in Roman history (Finley 1968: 129). Because of her fame (and infamy) she will be discussed again in Part II of this book (see Chapter 10). Plutarch's description of Cleopatra suggests that her powerful attraction for great men like Julius Caesar and Mark Antony came not so much from conventional physical beauty as from her charm and intelligence. Living in Alexandria and traveling widely in the Mediterranean, she was at home in several languages and diverse cultures:

For her beauty, as we are told, was in itself not altogether incomparable, nor such as to strike those who saw her. There was a sweetness also in the tones of her voice; and her tongue, like an instrument of many strings, she could readily turn to whatever language she pleased, so that in her interviews with barbarians she very seldom had need of an interpreter, but made her replies to most of them herself and unassisted, whether they were Ethiopians, Troglodytes, Hebrews, Arabians, Syrians, Medes or Parthians. It is said that she knew the speech of many other peoples also, although the kings of Egypt before her had not even made an effort to learn the native language, and some actually gave up their Macedonian dialect.

(Plutarch, *Antony* 27.2; Perrin 1968 modified)

Images of Cleopatra survive in large numbers and in various media, from marble busts (Fig. 5.1) to bronze coins (Fig. 5.2). The well-preserved head in Berlin (Fig. 5.1) was probably made in Alexandria itself and is a good example of the soft, gentle quality that was the hallmark of the Alexandrian style in sculpture. Cleopatra shares the so-

A   B

Figure 5.1. Marble bust of Cleopatra, perhaps from Alexandria **A.** front view and **B.** profile. The oval face, with its prominent nose and short chin, are repeated on several images of the queen to convey a distinctly recognizable portrait type beneath the overlay of youthful idealization.

Figure 5.2. Silver tetradrachm of Cleopatra, minted at Askelon (39–37 B.C.E.), which shares the same portrait type as the bust shown in Figure 5.1.

called melon coiffure, with a bun at the back, with many of her Ptolemaic ancestors two centuries earlier, as well as Roman women, and her face conforms to the Alexandrian ideal of the youthful queen. Yet there is also a strong individuality that makes her unmistakable. This is evident in a comparison with a coin she probably had minted in 39 or 38 B.C.E. that shows all the same features (Fig. 5.2). By contrast, a slightly later coin, from the time of her involvement with Mark Antony (Fig. 5.3), has both "Romanized" Cleopatra and "Orientalized" her, especially in the exaggeratedly large, hooked nose, in order to portray her as a "client" (subject ally) of the Romans (Smith 1988: 133–34). Through her involvement with Julius Caesar and Mark Antony, and her rivalry with Octavian (the future emperor Augustus), she was indeed as important in shaping the course of Roman history as that of her native Egypt. Like other Ptolemaic queens, Cleopatra was also portrayed in purely Egyptian style (cf. the portrait of Arsinoë II, Fig. 5.10), in sculptures made for the native Egyptians (cf. Bieber 1961, fig. 371). She could even be shown as the Egyptian (male) Pharaoh, with bare chest and short kilt, taking up a tradition that went back to the New Kingdom Queen Hatshepshut, ca. 1500 B.C.E. (cf. *Cleopatra's Egypt*, cat. no. 78).

Although Cleopatra was heir to some ancient Egyptian traditions (Fig. 5.4), she was not an anomaly in a long line of Greek queens (Pomeroy 1984: 3–40). Thus, it is not a distortion of history—even history defined in the traditional sense as political change—to put women like Cleopatra at the center of the inquiry, then to look at other elite women for whom such queens served as models, and finally to discuss how the lives of lower-class and anonymous women differed from those of their counterparts in preceding periods of Greek history.

Figure 5.3. Silver tetradrachm of Cleopatra minted at Antioch (37 B.C.E.) with the very large nose and enlarged jaw that was preferred by moneyers in the period when the queen was involved with Mark Antony.

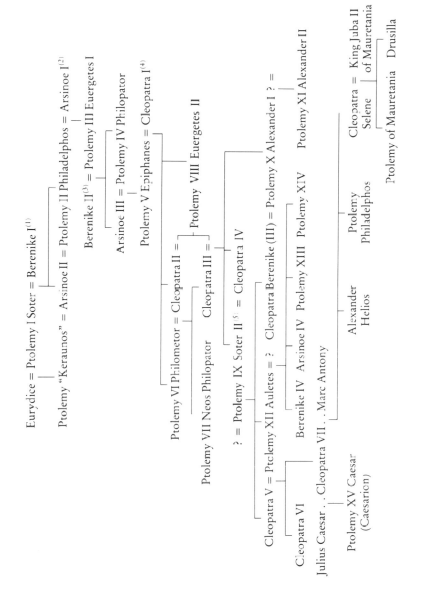

Eurydice = Ptolemy I Soter = Berenike I[1]

Ptolemy "Keraunos" = Arsinoe II = Ptolemy II Philadelphos = Arsinoe I[2]

Berenike II[3] = Ptolemy III Euergetes I

Arsinoe III = Ptolemy IV Philopator

Ptolemy V Epiphanes = Cleopatra I[4]

Ptolemy VI Philometor = Cleopatra II =

Ptolemy VIII Euergetes II

Cleopatra III =

Ptolemy VII Neos Philopator

? = Ptolemy IX Soter II[5] = Cleopatra IV

Cleopatra Berenike (III) = Ptolemy X Alexander I ? =

Ptolemy XI Alexander II

Cleopatra V = Ptolemy XII Auletes = ?

Berenike IV Arsinoe IV Ptolemy XIII Ptolemy XIV

Cleopatra VI

Julius Caesar . . Cleopatra VII . . Marc Antony

Alexander Helios

Ptolemy Philadelphos

Cleopatra = King Juba II Selene | of Mauretania

Ptolemy XV Caesar (Caesarion)

Ptolemy of Mauretania   Drusilla

(1) A Macedonian Greek noblewoman
(2) Daughter of King Lysimachos of Thrace (Greece)
(3) Daughter of the Greek King Magas I of Cyrene, the son of Berenike I
(4) Daughter of the Greek King Antiochus III of Syria
(5) It is possible that Ptolemy IX is actually the son of Ptolemy VIII and Cleopatra II

Figure 5.4. The Ptolemies: an abbreviated genealogy.

139

The Cosmopolis: The Range of the Sources

Cleopatra VII is paradigmatic of her time. Information about her is found in a wide variety of sources, visual and textual, and in languages of the western, eastern, and southern Mediterranean world. Thus it is clear that the extant sources for the history of Hellenistic women are much more diverse than those for Greek women in earlier historical periods. Our evidence for the Classical period was mainly for Athenians and Spartans. In the wake of Alexander's defeat of Persia, Greeks began to settle in areas such as Egypt that had formerly belonged to the Persian Empire, and to found new cities like Alexandria.

The Hellenistic was a period of migration for Greek women as well as for men. In the Classical period, respectable women—at least those of Athens—had been able to look forward to only two journeys: the first from their father's house to their husband's, the next from their husband's house to the grave. But in the Hellenistic period both women and men migrated to the newly conquered territories and forged new lives for themselves in the frontier outposts of Hellenism. In the new cosmopolitan cities, some restrictive conventions of the old city-states were retained, but others were altered or discarded in response to changing societal and individual needs. For example, in Alexandria nonroyal Greek women still needed to conduct their legal and economic transactions through the intermediary of a male guardian, but royal women and women who used the Egyptian or Jewish legal systems did not do so. Among the Greeks, a dowry was still a prerequisite for marriage, but respectable unmarried women who chose to work in the liberal arts and professions are noted with admiration in the historical sources. Poetic sources, however, including Theocritus and the poets of the *Greek Anthology* (Paton 1968), portray the vicissitudes of women living independently and outside the strictures and protection of the Classical oikos. These women are the predecessors of the "New Women" of the late Roman Republic (see Chapter 10). Our evidence for women's history at this period is also ethnically diverse: thus it is possible to compare the legal status of Greek women living in Egypt with the status of Egyptian, Jewish, and Roman women who were their contemporaries. It is not, however, always possible to determine the ethnicity of individual women, unless they are Greeks at the top of the ruling class. Furthermore, the documentary material from non-Greek sources that could provide information about lower-class and native women has not yet been fully exploited by historians, because very few can read the demotic script in which the Egyptian language was written in this period.

New types of primary historical sources appear in abundance. The climate of the Egyptian countryside was conducive to the preservation of papyri. Documents written on papyrus including those recording marriage contracts, divorces, wet-nursing contracts, and private letters are a rich source for women's history (Pomeroy 1984). A major problem in dealing with these texts is that most often a woman is known from only one document. Thus it is not clear whether the source describes a common phenomenon or an idiosyncratic situation. Papyri also often provide the only texts of literary works such as Callimachus's "Victory of Berenice" and "Lock of Berenice." Though some scholars will inevitably ask whether evidence from Greco-Roman Egypt is typical of that which might have been found in the rest of the ancient world if the climate had been favorable to the preservation of papyri, with the exception of the Canopus decree and the depictions of Blacks in the cult of Isis (which will be discussed later in this chapter), the documents cited in the present chapter do not seem exotic and probably had their analogues in the rest of the Hellenistic world.

In the wake of Alexander the Great, workshops of Greek artists throughout the Mediterranean recorded the rhythms of urban life with a new sophistication and realism. Terra-cotta figurines from all corners of the Greek world give insights into women's daily lives and testify, for example, to women's literacy (Fig. 5.5: a girl holding a book roll; see below, "Education and Professions"). They often show ethereally pretty young women engaged in carefree activities like dancing, playing games (Fig. 5.6),[1] or talking with one another. The same spirit of intimacy between women is depicted by Hellenistic poets, such as Herodas, who, writing for a largely male audience, imagines two women having a frank discussion about sex:

METRO: Please tell me the truth, dear Koritto, who stitched you the scarlet baubon?[2]
KORITTO: Where have *you* seen it, Metro?
METRO: Oh, it was Nossis, Erinna's daughter, who had it given me a couple of days ago—la! a pretty present![3]
KORITTO: Nossis! From whom did she get it?
METRO: Will you betray me if I tell you?
KORITTO: By these sweet eyes, Metro dear, not a soul shall hear from Koritto's mouth anything you say.
METRO: It was Eubule, wife of Bitsas, who gave it to her, and told her that no one was to know about it.
KORITTO: Women, women, this woman will be the death of me one day. I had pity on her entreaties and gave it to her, Metro, before I used it myself, and she snatches it like some treasure-trove and makes a present of it to improper people; I bid goodbye, dear, for ever to such a woman as this; let her choose some other friend instead of me henceforward. I shan't lend anything to Nossis, daughter of Medokes—if I speak more strongly than a woman should, may Nemesis forgive me—not even a rotten baubon, if I had nine hundred and ninety-nine besides.
(Herodas 6.12–36; Headlam and Knox, 1922, modified)

A scene in one of Theocritus's *Odes* illustrates how women were free to move about and to address male strangers in public in a large cosmopolitan city like Alexandria. (Contrast, in Chapter 3, the situation of respectable women whose names could not even be mentioned outside

Figure 5.5. Terra-cotta figurine from Benghazi (330–300 B.C.E.) of a woman with a writing tablet.

the family circle.) In this passage, two friends accompanied by their slave women are on their way to the palace, to attend a festival of Adonis sponsored by Queen Arsinoë II (on the patronage of Arsinoë II, see Pomeroy 1984: 17–20):

PRAXINOA: Heavens, what a crowd! How and when are we to get through this plague? They're like ants—there's no numbering or counting them.

Figure 5.6. Terra-cotta figurine from Tanagra (ca. first half of third century B.C.E.) of young women playing a game resembling piggyback (ephedrismos). The long and elegant figures, clearly beyond early childhood, mix innocent conduct with a touch of sensuality.

You've done us many a good turn, Ptolemy, since your father was in heaven. Nowadays no ruffian slips up to you in the street Egyptian-fashion and does you a mischief—the tricks those packets of rascality used to play, one as bad as another with their nasty tricks, a cursed lot.

Dear Gorgo! what will become of us? The king's chargers! My dear sir, don't tread on me. The chestnut's reared; see how wild he is. Keep clear, Eunoa, you reckless girl. He'll go for the man that's leading him. It's lucky I left the baby at home.

GORGO: It's all right, Praxinoa; we've got behind them now, and they've gone to their place.

PRAXINOA: And now I'm collecting myself again too. A horse and the cold snake I've been afraid of more than anything else ever since I was a child. Let's hurry; we're being swamped in this mob.

GORGO: Are you from the palace, mother?

AN OLD WOMAN: I am, my children.

GORGO: Is it easy to get in?

OLD WOMAN: The Greeks got into Troy by trying, my pretties; everything's done by trying.

GORGO: The old lady has pronounced her oracles and gone off.

PRAXINOA: Women know everything—even how Zeus married Hera.

GORGO: Look, Praxinoa, what a crowd there is round the doors.

PRAXINOA: Terrific. Give me your hand, Gorgo, and Eunoa take Eutychis's, and mind you don't get separated from her. We must all go in together. Eunoa, stick close to us. Oh dear, oh dear, my shawl is torn in two already, Gorgo. For heaven's sake, sir, mind my wrap as you hope for happiness.

(Theocritus 15.44–71; Gow 1952)

Literary sources for this period, however, are relatively meager and fragmentary. We do not have the dramas or orations that we know reflected the views of a large part of the population of a city like Classical Athens. Nor do we have a historian who commands the respect due a Thucydides and gives a consistent interpretation of events. Instead, we quote, for example, from the epitome that Justin (third century, C.E.) made of Pompeius Trogus's moralizing narrative. Although Plutarch wrote biographies of great men rather than history, and lived in a later period, his work continues to provide crucial evidence for the history of women of this period, as it did for those of preceding generations. Thus the history of women, like the following account, must be pieced together from diverse sources, Greek and Latin, of uneven worth.

Berenice II

Berenice II (ca. 273–221 B.C.E.) of Egypt is a good example of a Hellenistic queen who exercised real political power and who left her mark on poetry and religion. She had access to a large fortune, which she spent as she chose on perfume made of roses and on racehorses that competed in Panhellenic games on the Greek mainland.[4] (Owning racehorses was a traditional form of conspicuous consumption among men; cf. Chapter 1, Semonides on the mare-woman.) Berenice was sole heir to the city of Cyrene and also derived some of her income from shipping. Like some other elite and royal women, Berenice owned ships that transported grain on the Nile (*P. Rylands* 4.576; see Hauben 1979). Her life, like that of her famous descendant Cleopatra VII, included intrigue, incestuous adultery, with mother and daughter vying for the same man, and intra-familial homicide: themes formerly found in myth and tragedy became historical reality in the days of the Ptolemies.

Berenice was the daughter of Magas of Cyrene, and Apame. The political fate of Cyrene was linked to Berenice's marriage and decided by a struggle between Berenice and Apame. Berenice's father had betrothed her to her cousin Ptolemy III—a marriage that would reunite Cyrene with Egypt.

After the death of Magas, his widow Apame invited the Macedonian Demetrius the Fair to Cyrene to marry her daughter in order to thwart the plan to reunify the two kingdoms. The mother competed with her daughter for the same man.

Magas, king of Cyrene, died. Before his illness he had betrothed Berenice, his only daughter, to the son of Ptolemy II after ending a dispute with him. But after the death of the king, Arsinoë [that is, Apame] the mother of the unmarried girl, because she was opposed to the betrothal, had it annulled and sent envoys to fetch Demetrius (who was the brother of King Antigonus and himself descended from a daughter of Ptolemy I), so that he could marry the girl and become king of Cyrene. Demetrius did not delay. With the help of the winds, he came at once to Cyrene, and relying on his good looks he began to ingratiate himself with his mother-in-law. From the very start he was proud of his royal descent, had no power with the army, and shifted his desire to please from the girl to her mother. When the liaison was discovered, first by the girl, then by the populace and the army, it caused disgust. Accordingly, when everyone favored the son of Ptolemy, a plot was prepared against Demetrius. When he had retired in his mother-in-law's bed, assassins were sent in. But when Arsinoë heard the voice of her daughter standing at the door and warning the assassins to spare her mother, she shielded the adulterer a little while with her own body. When he was killed and Berenice had piously avenged the adultery of her mother, in her subsequent marriage she carried out her father's plan.

(Justin [Pompeius Trogus] 26.3.2–8; trans. Sarah B. Pomeroy)

There are portraits of Berenice II on coins (Fig. 5.7), in stone (Fig. 5.8), and on some of the best preserved faience oinochoai, small blue jugs used in the ruler cult at Alexandria (Fig. 5.9). All these portraits share certain characteristics: the full, fleshy face; large, dreamy eyes, and a simple coiffure enhanced by a metal diadem (missing from the marble bust, Fig. 5.8). They are not so idealized, however, as to conceal signs of middle age, like the sagging flesh under the chin, to indicate that her influence and power continued to increase with age. Her own ample proportions echo the material prosperity of Egypt that is intimately linked with her, in the cornucopia that she carries on the oinochoe (Fig. 5.9) and that also appears on the reverse of her coins (Fig. 5.7B). The cornucopia alludes to the queen's role as preserver of fertility and incarnation of the goddess of good fortune, Tyche. The two caps

A   B

Figure 5.7. **A.** Silver tetradrachm minted at Alexandria (246–221 B.C.E.) of Queen Berenice II. Signs of maturity help to convey the queen's power. **B.** Reverse of the same coin. The cornucopia, which also appears on the vase in Figure 5.9, connects the queen with the goddess of good fortune, Tyche, and with fertility.

beneath it on the coin may refer to Castor and Polydeuces, sons of Zeus and protectors of seafaring (hence to Berenice's own descent from Zeus and her association with Aphrodite and the sea). On the oinochoe, an inscription identifies Berenice as queen and invokes good fortune, while another associates her with the "Benevolent Gods." She stands near an altar and pours a libation from a *phiale*. Such vessels, perhaps containing wine, would have been offered by worshipers for the well-being of the royal house (Thompson 1975: 118).[5] The Egyptian technique of blue faience is combined with a purely Hellenizing style that likens the queen to maternal goddesses of fertility such as Demeter (cf. "Canopus Decree" [quoted later this chapter] and Pollitt 1986: 273).

For her courageous deeds Greek and Roman authors awarded Berenice the most extravagant praise any Greek woman ever enjoyed (see, for example, Callimachus, "The Lock of Berenice," below, lines 25–28). She was herself an accomplished equestrian and rode horses on the battlefield.[6] She also owned racehorses that competed in the Nemean and Olympian games. Callimachus of Cyrene celebrated the victory of her quadriga at Nemea. The "Victory of Berenice" was, apparently, the first epinician (victory ode) written in honor of a woman owner (for the fragments and bibliography see Lloyd-Jones and Parsons 1983, nos. 254–269). The reconstruction of the fragments of this poem indicates that it was a traditional epinician similar to those celebrating men. Callimachus related the story of Hercules who slew the Nemean lion and of the foundation of the Nemean Games. The poem is now fragmentary; it probably began and ended with references to Berenice's victory at Nemea.

Figure 5.8. Portrait bust (provenance unknown) (second half of the third century B.C.E.) of Queen Berenice II showing the typical full face with large eyes and simple hairstyle; the diadem is missing here but is present on the coin portrait in Figure 5.7.

Figure 5.9. Faience jug from Alexandria, found at Xanthos (ca. 240 B.C.E.), with an image of Berenice II making an offering at an altar. The cornucopia indicates the prosperity of Egypt under the queen's beneficent rule, as do the inscriptions that connect Berenice II with the "Benevolent Gods."

Berenice governed Egypt when her husband went off to campaign in the Third Syrian War (246–241 B.C.E.). She vowed to dedicate a lock of her hair to Arsinoë II–Aphrodite at Zephyrium upon his safe return. (Dedications of hair were normal offerings to Greek divinities, and Arsinoë had by this time been deified and assimilated to Aphrodite; see later under "Religion: Imperial Cult and the Goddess Isis"). Berenice made the dedication, but the hair disappeared. The winged horse of Arsinoë II–Aphrodite had carried it off. Conon the astronomer, grateful for imperial patronage, flattered the queen by identifying her lock of hair among the constellations and Callimachus narrates the vicissitudes of the lock in "The Lock of Berenice." The poet expects Berenice to understand the erudite allusions to astronomical, mythical, and historical matters in the elegy, and to have so cultivated a taste for poetry that she can appreciate his work.

Callimachus's "Lock of Berenice" is too fragmentary to be reproduced in its entirety here (Fragment 110, Pfeiffer). Instead, we print a
translation of excerpts from the Latin version by Catullus, who knew
personally Roman women who (like Berenice) exercised economic
power, were involved in politics, and could appreciate erudite poetry
(see Chapter 10). The poem is not only arcane but amusing, as the lock
of hair comments on personal and historical events. (Aphrodite is referred to as Venus in Catullus's Latin version):

> Conon the astronomer, who has observed every star
>   in the sky, determined their risings and settings,
> is the expert on solar eclipses, the corona's splendor,
>   the slow precession of the constellations,
> and into what cave on Latmos the Moon-Goddess descends
>   when love's vibrations disturb her orbit—
> this Conon has also observed in the velvet night sky
>   yours truly, a lock of hair from Berenice's head,
> glowing serenely, which she dedicated to All Goddesses,
>   stretching out her slender arms in supplication,
> what time the king, her newlywed husband, sated and proud,
>   sallied forth to annex Syria to his realm,
> displaying, I might add, on his royal person the marks
>   of the previous night's struggle for virgin spoils.
> Query: is Aphrodite really distasteful to brides? Are those
>   crocodile tears they shed at the bridal chamber's threshold,
> blubbering away while their parents are weeping for joy?
>   Dissimulated groans, so help me gods,
> as I deduced from my mistress's pitiful lamentations
>   the day her new husband went off to war.
> Oh, but you say you weren't mourning your desolate bed
>   but the poignant departure of a cherished brother?
> And yet the sorrow consumed you down to the marrow,
>   your bosom heaved with exquisite anxiety,
> you were senseless with grief! And this from a woman
>   I've known as courageous from girlhood on.
> Or have you forgotten the noble crime by which you secured
>   your royal marriage? Who else would have dared it?
> What a fit of *tristesse*, what a maudlin send-off you gave him!
>   Zeus! How many times did your hanky dab your eyes?
> A character change wrought by some god? Or do lovers
>   simply resent the absence of the body loved?
> Anyway, you dedicated me to All Goddesses (with a good deal
>   of bull's blood) toward your husband's return,
> and return he did, in fairly short order, having annexed
>   half of Asia to his eastern frontier.
> For which exploits and in expiation of which vow
>   I have been enrolled as a member of this celestial club.
> . . . .
> My sister strands, just recently parted, were bewailing my fate,
>   When Memnon's brother, Arsinoë's dainty mount, pumping

dappled wings, whisked me away through the ethereal dark
　　and deposited me in Aphrodite's chaste lap.
Zephyritis herself had comissioned this flight,
　　the Hellenic lady who haunts Egypt's shores.
And Aphrodite, lest the crown from Ariadne's temples
　　be the only such fixture to light the night sky,
arranged that I too, blonde consecrated spoils dripping
　　with tears, should illumine the precincts divine,
installing me as a new constellation 'midst the old.

. . . .

　　And now, Virgin Nemesis, forgive me
for the outspoken candor of what I feel I must say,
　　And may the stars spare me their scalding gossip:
I am not so happy with this state of affairs that I don't
　　suffer terribly at the permanent separation
from my mistress's head, together with whom I have imbibed
　　perfumes galore (though we abstained when she was a virgin).
So this is my plea: You virgins blessed by the bridal torch,
　　before offering your bodies to your ardent husbands,
before you even pull off your dress to bare your nipples,
　　offer me some ointment from your onyx jar—
but only if you're devoted to what a chaste bed allows.
　　If any adulteress should pour a libation,
may dry dust soak it up and render it void. I want
　　no propitiation from disreputable women.
My wish is rather that conjugal harmony inhabit
　　the homes of all brides, and constant devotion.
And you, my queen, when on your way with festal lamps
　　to appease Aphrodite you look up at the stars,
do not allow me, once yours, to remain unperfumed,
　　but propitiate me from your royal largesse!
　　　　　A prisoner of the stars!
If only I could be on a queen's head again, Orion
　　could shine up to Aquarius for all that I care.
　　　(Catullus 66.1–39; 51–61; 79–93; Lombardo and Rayor 1988)

Berenice II and Ptolemy III had four children: Ptolemy IV, Arsinoë III, Magas, and Berenice. The younger Berenice predeceased her parents and was deified (see the "Canopus Decree" below). Arsinoë III eventually married her brother Ptolemy IV (on brother-sister marriage, see the next section). After the death of Ptolemy III in 222 B.C.E. Berenice attempted to gain the support of the army for her favorite Magas (Plutarch, *Cleomenes* 33; Polybius 15.25). But his brother ordered him to be scalded to death. The subsequent murder of Berenice by her son's command is indicative of the political power she continued to wield:

At the time when they [Ptolemy IV and his advisers] were plotting the murder of Magas [Berenice's younger son] and Berenice, being in great fear of their project failing chiefly owing to the courage of Berenice, they were compelled to conciliate the whole court.

　　　　　　　　　　　　　　　　　(Polybius 5.36; Paton 1967: 89)

Although Ptolemy IV was responsible for his mother's murder, he created a priestesshood in her honor. The athlophoros (prize-bearer) of Berenice the Benefactor was awarded precedence over priestesses of all other queens. The title of the priestess, athlophoros, may refer to the victories of Berenice's horses at Nemea and Olympia. Ptolemy IV also built a temple for Berenice with the epithet "Savior" on the shore at Alexandria (Fraser 1972: 1: 238–39). Thus, following the model of male heroes in Greek tradition who underwent multiple trials and survived thanks to their courage and cunning, Berenice truly earned her apotheosis.

Religion: Imperial Cult and the Goddess Isis

"The Lock of Berenice" (lines 56–58) alludes to the deification of Arsinoë II as Aphrodite-Zephyritis, and the Canopus Decree refers to the deification of Berenice, daughter of Ptolemy III and Berenice II, and of Berenice's daughter and namesake. Portraits of the queens often indicate their divinity through their clothing and the attributes they hold (cf. Fig. 5.10).

The cults of the queens as divine required the appointment of priestesses. The priestesses were usually young daughters of the Alexandrian aristocracy. Their principal function, from which their titles derived, was carrying items such as baskets in processions. Thus their religious activities were similar to those of the girls on the Parthenon frieze, and probably were created in conscious imitation of their Classical predecessors (cf. Figs. 3.3 and 3.5).

Unlike the Athenians, however, the names of the Alexandrian girls were widely known, for they appear frequently in the dating formulas of inscriptions and documents written on papyrus. For an example, we turn now to the Canopus Decree, which indicates that the Egyptians accepted the Ptolemies' claim to divinity as descendants of the Pharaohs and as incarnations of both Greek and native Egyptian gods. Berenice herself is linked to Demeter through the imagery of ears of grain. Note the many echoes of earlier rituals, such as the singing of hymns by choruses, fertility offerings to the goddess, and the reference to the kanephoros of Arsinoë (cf. the kanephoroi on the Parthenon Frieze—fig. 3.5), as well as new Egyptian elements in the cult.

Decree of Egyptian Priests in honor of
Ptolemy III and Berenice II, Canopus, March 4, 238 B.C.E.

In the ninth year of the reign of Ptolemy, son of Ptolemy and Arsinoë the Brother-and-Sister Gods, the priest of Alexander and the Brother-and-Sister Gods and the Benefactor Gods being Apollonidas son of Moschion and the kanephoros of Arsinoë Philadelphos being Menecrateia daughter of Philammon, on the seventh of the month Apellaios, the seventeenth of the Egyptians' (month) Tybi: decree: the chief-priests and the prophets[7] and those who enter the shrine for

Figure 5.10. Portrait (provenance unknown) (ca. 270–246 B.C.E.) of Ptolemaic queen Arsinoë II in a traditionally Egyptian (Pharaonic) style.

the adoring of the gods and the feather-bearers and the sacred scribes and the
other priests who come together from the temples in the country for the fifth of
(the month) Dios, on which day is celebrated the birthday of the king, and for
the 25th of the same month, on which day he received the kingdom from his
father, (all these) having assembled together on this day in the temple of the
benefactor Gods in Canopus spoke: Whereas King Ptolemy, son of Ptolemy and
Arsinoë the brother-and-Sister Gods, and Queen Berenice, his sister and wife,
the Benefactor Gods, continually bestow many and great benefactions on the
temples in the country and increase ever more the honors of the gods, and in all
respects they exercise concern, with great expense and abundance, for Apis and
for Mnevis[8] and for the other renowned sacred beasts of the country; and the
king marched out and brought back safe to Egypt the sacred images, which had

been carried out from the country by the Persians; and returned them to the temples whence each had originally been taken away; and he has maintained the country in a state of peace, fighting wars on its behalf against many peoples and those who rule among them; and they provided law and order for all those in the country and for the others who are ranged under their rule; and when the river once overflowed its banks insufficiently and all those in the country were terrified at this happening and were thinking upon the destruction that had taken place under some of the former kings, in whose reign those dwelling in the country met with droughts, exercising provident care over those in the temples and the others inhabiting the country, by exercising much forethought and forgoing not a little of their revenues for the sake of the safety of the people, and by sending for grain for the country from Syria and Phoenicia and Cyprus and many other places at rather high prices they saved the inhabitants of Egypt, leaving behind an immortal benefaction and the greatest record of their virtue both for contemporaries and for future generations; in return for which the gods have granted them their kingdom peacefully established and will give them all the other good things for all time; with good fortune, be it resolved by the priests of the country:

To increase the already existing honors (paid) in the temples to King Ptolemy and Queen Berenice, the Benefactor Gods, and to their parents the Brother-and-Sister Gods, and to their grandparents the Savior Gods; . . . be it resolved: To perform everlasting honors to Berenice, the princess born of the Benefactor Gods, in all the temples in the country, and, since she went to the gods in the month of Tybi, the very month in which also the daughter of Helios, whom her father lovingly called sometimes his crown and sometimes his sight, in the beginning departed from life, and (since) they hold in her honor a feast and a boat-procession in the month of Tybi in all the temples in the country for four days from the seventeenth, on which day the boat-procession and the conclusion of the mourning for her originally took place; and to fashion a sacred image of her, of gold and precious stones, in each of the first- and second-rank temples and to set it up in the holy place; the prophet or (one) of those who [enter the shrine] for the adorning of the gods shall carry it in his arms, whenever there are processions or festivals of the other gods, in order that, being seen by all it may be honored and obeisance may to done to it, being called (the image) of Berenice Mistress of Maidens; and for the royal crown set upon her image, as distinct from the one set upon the images of her mother Queen Berenice, to consist of two ears of grain, in the middle of which shall be the asp-shaped insignia and behind which a commensurate papyrus-shaped scepter, such as the goddesses are wont to hold in their hands, about which the tail of the (asp-shaped) insignia shall be wound, so that the name of Berenice, in accordance with the symbol of the sacred script, will be signified by the arrangement of her royal crown; and, when the Kikellia are celebrated in the month of Choiach before the boat-procession of Osiris, for the maiden daughter of the priests to fashion another image of Berenice, Mistress of Maidens, to which they shall likewise perform a sacrifice and the other rites performed at this feast; and for it to be permitted in the same way to the other maidens, who so wish, to perform the rites to the goddess; and for her to be hymned by the chosen sacred maidens who are in the service of the gods, when they have put on the individual royal crowns of the goddesses whose priestesses they are accounted as being; and, when the early sowing is at hand, for the sacred maidens to carry up ears of grain to be laid before the image of the goddess; and for the men and women singers to sing to her each day, during the feasts and festivals of the other gods, whatever hymns the sacred scribes write and give to the teacher of songs, of which also copies shall be entered in the sacred books.

And whereas provisions are given to the priests from the sacred (revenues) whenever they are brought to the group (of priests of each temple) (be it resolved) for there to be given to the daughters of the priests from the day of their birth food from the sacred revenues, such as shall be determined by the councillor priests in each temple in proportion to the sacred revenues; and for the bread given to the wives of the priests to have its own particular shape and to be called the bread of Berenice. And let the appointed supervisor and chief priest in each temple and the scribes of the temple inscribe this decree on a stone or bronze stele, in sacred characters[9] and in Egyptian (characters),[10] and in Greek (characters), and let them set it up in the most conspicuous place in the first- and second- and third-rate temples, in order that the priests in the country may be seen to honor the Benefactor Gods and their children, as is just.

(*Orientis Graeci Inscriptiones Selectae 56.*
Bagnall and Derow 1981: 222–26, no. 136)

This syncretism of Greek and Egyptian elements is also evident in royal iconography. A Ptolemaic queen deified after her death, such as Berenice II or Arsinoë II, could be depicted in purely Egyptian style. In the portrait of Arsinoë (fig. 5.10), the corkscrew locks of hair were painted black, and the face would originally have been gilded. The facial features—large, wide-open eyes, arched brows, and full, curved lips—all conform to Egyptian, rather than Greek conventions. A hieroglyphic inscription on the back pillar indicates that the figure was dedicated after the death and deification of Arsinoë in 270, but during the lifetime of her husband/brother Ptolemy II (d. 246). From the beginning of the Ptolemaic dynasty, the old Egyptian gods and goddesses were enthusiastically honored by the Macedonian rulers. According to the most complete account of Alexander's campaigns, that of Arrian, writing in the second century C.E., Alexander himself laid out the plan of Alexandria in Egypt in 330 B.C.E., designating temples for the Greek gods and for "Isis of Egypt" (3.1.5). Under Ptolemy I and II, the museum (an association dedicated to the Muses, i.e., to intellectual and artistic pursuits) sponsored scientific research under the patronage of Isis. At least by the time of Ptolemy III, Isis was established in the role of divine protectress of the king, as she had been for the pharaohs (Solmsen 1979: 21–25).

In this period of syncretism and cosmopolitanism, the Greeks identified Aphrodite with the Egyptian goddess Isis. However, as the following inscription demonstrates, in Egyptian and Hellenistic thought the single goddess Isis embodied forces and exercised powers that the Greeks had distributed among many divinities, both male and female:

Demetrius, the son of Artemidorus, who is also (called) Thraseas, a Magnesian from (Magnesia on the) Maeander, an offering in fulfillment of a vow to Isis. He transcribed the following from the stele in Memphis which stands by the temple of Hephaestus:

I am Isis, the tyrant of every land; and I was educated by Hermes and together with Hermes I invented letters, both the hieroglyphic and the demotic, in order that the same script should not be used to write everything. I imposed laws on men, and the laws which I laid down no one may change. I am the eldest daughter of Cronus. I am the wife and sister of King Osiris.[11] I am she who discovered (the cultivation of) grain for men. I am the mother of King Horos. I am she who rises in the Dog Star.[12] I am she who is called goddess by women. By me the city of Bubastis was built. I separated earth from sky. I designated the paths of the stars. The sun's and the moon's course I laid out. I invented navigation. I caused the just to be strong. Woman and man I brought together. For woman I determined that in the tenth month she shall deliver a baby into the light. I ordained that parents be cherished by their children. For parents who are cruelly treated I imposed retribution. Together with (my) brother Osiris I stopped cannibalism. I revealed initiations to men. I taught (men) to honor the images of the gods. I established precincts for the gods. The governments of tyrants I suppressed. I stopped murders. I compelled women to be loved by men. I caused the just to be stronger than gold and silver. I ordained that the true be considered beautiful. I invented marriage contracts. Languages I assigned to Greeks and Barbarians. I caused the honorable and the shameful to be disguised by Nature. I caused nothing to be more fearful than an oath. He who unjustly plotted against others I gave into the hands of his victim. On those who commit unjust acts I imposed retribution. I ordained that suppliants be pitied. I honor those who justly defend themselves. With me the just prevails. Of rivers and winds and the sea I am mistress. No one becomes famous without my knowledge. I am the mistress of war. Of the thunderbolt I am mistress. I calm and stir up the sea. I am in the rays of the sun. I sit beside the course of the sun. Whatever I decide, this also is accomplished. For me everything is right. I free those who are in bonds. I am the mistress of sailing. The navigable I make unnavigable whenever I choose. I established the boundaries of cities. I am she who is called Thesmophoros. The island from the depths I brought up into the light. I conquer Fate. Fate heeds me. Hail Egypt who reared me.

(*Die Inschriften von Kyme* 41. White marble stele from the temple of Isis, late first century B.C.E. or first century C.E.; Burstein 1985: 146–48, no. 112)

Images of Isis in Hellenistic art show her both in Hellenizing style and with Egyptian features (Figs. 5.11 and 5.12). On a carved marble votive relief (Fig. 5.11), a goddess in purely Greek style, usually identified as Isis, leans on a pillar beside an august seated god, an amalgam of Zeus and Osiris (Havelock 1970: no. 168). The mortal worshipers, on a much smaller scale, include a family with two children, as well as more women and children observing. The relief was probably made in Athens and shows the spread of the more popular Egyptian divinities, especially Isis, north from Egypt. A figure that may show a Ptolemaic princess wears an outfit characteristic of Isis in Egyptian art, a sheer, tight-fitting dress with a knot between the breasts (Fig. 5.12; see Bieber 1961: 97). The syncretism of Isis with Aphrodite is also manifested in the minor arts (cf. Fig. 5.18).

Women in Public

Like the Hellenistic queens and priestesses other wealthy, elite, women were awarded public honors, including magistracies. Some of these hon-

Figure 5.11. Marble votive relief (late second century, B.C.E.) from Athens, showing Isis and an enthroned god worshiped by a family with women and children.

ors were the result of their kinship with men who enjoyed similar honors; some were probably granted as a result of the women's generosity. For example, Phile was the first woman to be selected as the stephanephoros, the eponymous magistrate[13] at Priene.

Decree of Priene in honor of Phile, first century B.C.E.

Phile daughter of Apollonius and wife of Thessalus, the son of Polydectes, having held the office of stephanephoros, the *first* woman (to do so), constructed at her own expense the reservoir for water and the city aqueduct.

(*Die Inschriften von Priene* 208; Burstein 1985: 59, no. 45)

Gravestones attest to a new level of prosperity for nonroyal women in the Hellenistic period. Large numbers of gravestones from all over the Greek world give a sense of the norms and values expected of women, especially in the urban, middle-class society typical of most Hellenistic centers. One such center was Smyrna (modern Izmir) in Asia Minor (Fig. 5.13; on these monuments, see Pfuhl and Möbius 1977). The deceased, seated on a large chair with footstool, demonstrates her modesty by wrapping both arms in her voluminous garments. Not one but two small slave girls attend her, one displaying the spindle that alludes to

Figure 5.12. Statue in black granite
(Ptolemaic period) of a woman in the
costume of Isis, the dress with the so-
called Isis-knot between the breasts.
She may represent a woman of the
Ptolemaic court.

the age-old convention of the noble wife as spinner and weaver. The
other displays a large chest with its lid open, as if inviting a glance at
the mistress's jewels. Her name and her father's name—Phile, daughter
of Apollas—are inscribed above, along with another inscription, "the
people," suggesting that she or her family held a prominent position in
the city.

   Independence of action in public is envisioned for the married

Figure 5.13. Tombstone (second century B.C.E.) from Izmir (ancient Smyrna) showing a seated woman with two slaves, one holding a spindle to remind the viewer of the virtuous domestic life of the deceased who, like all other good wives, spun and wove the cloth for her family.

woman. The earliest extant Greek marriage contract gives detailed provisions for self-help. The aggrieved wife will be obliged to have dealings with men who are not her close kin when she seeks retribution from her husband:

In the seventh year of the reign of Alexander, son of Alexander, the fourteenth year of Ptolemy's administration as satrap, in the month of Dius.

Contract of marriage of Heraclides of Temnos and Demetria. Heraclides takes as his lawful wife Demetria of Cos from her father Leptines of Cos and her mother Philotis. He is free; she is free. She brings with her to the marriage clothing and ornaments valued at 1,000 drachmas. Heraclides shall supply to Demetria all that is suitable for a freeborn wife. We shall live together in whatever place seems best to Leptines and Heraclides, deciding together.

If Demetria is caught in fraudulent machinations to the dishonor of her husband Heraclides, she shall forfeit all that she has brought with her. But Heraclides shall prove whatever he charges against Demetria before three men whom they both approve. It shall not be lawful for Heraclides to bring home another woman for himself in such a way as to inflict contumely on Demetria, nor to beget children by another woman, nor to indulge in fraudulent machinations against Demetria on any pretext. If Heraclides is caught doing any of these things, and Demetria proves it before three men whom they both approve, let Heraclides return to Demetria the dowry of 1,000 drachmas which she brought, and forfeit 1,000 drachmas of the silver coinage of [Ptolemy bearing a portrait head of] Alexander. Demetria, and those representing Demetria, shall have the right to exact payment from Heraclides and from his property on both land and sea, as if after a legal action.

This contract shall be decisive in every respect, wherever Heraclides may produce it against Demetria, or Demetria and those helping Demetria to exact payment may produce it against Heraclides, as though the agreement had been made in that place.

Heraclides and Demetria shall each have the right to keep a copy of the contract in their own custody, and to produce it against one another.
Witnesses:
Cleon of Gela, Anticrates of Temnos, Lysis of Temnos.
Dionysius of Temnos, Aristomachus of Cyrene, Aristodicus of Cos.

        (*P. Elephantine* 1 [311–310 B.C.E.]; Pomeroy 1984: 86–87)

A new current of autonomy and assertiveness can be detected even in the letters and petitions of ordinary women who are widowed or who seem to live in households without men. A request from a widow for the appointment of a male guardian which Greek law required:

To King Ptolemy greetings from Nicaea daughter of Nicias, Persian. My husband Pausanias died in the 23rd year, leaving a will of the same year, of the month of Panemos [in which] he designated . . . Naius his son as my guardian. It has now happened that he has died in the 4th year, in the month of Daisios which is Hathyr of the Egyptians, and I have no relative who can be registered as my [guardian. Therefore, so that] the legacy to me from my husband may not be dissipated for that reason, [since I have] no guardian with whom I can make arrangements about these things, I ask you, O king, to order Diophanes the *strategus*[14] to give me as guardian Demetrius the Thracian, a 60-aroura holder of the troop of Ptolemaeus son of Eteoneus of the . . . th hipparchy, to whom Pausanias married his sister, and for the *strategos* to make written records about these things, so that this may be in the official register; and since, being old and getting infirm, I am not able to make the trip to Crocodilopolis, I have sent the aforesaid Demetrius to deliver the petition, for Diophanes to write to Dioscurides the *epistates*, to make a description of me and of the guardian whom I am requesting, and to send them to Diophanes. If this is done, I shall have benefited, O king, from your kindness. Farewell. (Response) To Dioscurides. Taking some of the elders of the village go to Nicaea and if ——, their descriptions, and send me a report. Year 4, Daisios 27, Hathyr 29. (Docket) Year 4, Daisios 27, Hathyr 29. Nicaea, daughter of Nicias, Persian, about a request.

        (*P. Enteuxis* 22 [218 B.C.E.]; Bagnall and Derow 1981: 200, no. 123)

A woman who works with her hands lodges a complaint against a male bath attendant concerning bodily injury:

To King Ptolemy greeting from Philista daughter of Lysias resident in Tricomia. I am wronged by Petechon. For as I was bathing in the baths of the aforesaid village on Tubi 7 of year 1, and stepped out to soap myself, he being bathman in the women's rotunda and having brought in the jugs of hot water emptied one (?) over me and scalded my belly and my left thigh down to the knee, so that my life was in danger. On finding him I gave him into the custody of Nechthosiris the chief policeman of the village in the presence of Simon the epistates.[15] I beg you therefore, O king, if it please you, as a suppliant who has sought your protection, not to suffer me, who am a working woman, to be thus lawlessly treated, but to order Diophanes the strategus to write to Simon the epistates and Nechthosiris the policeman that they are to bring Petechon before him in order that Diophanes may inquire into the case, hoping that having sought the protection of you, O king, the common benefactor of all, I may obtain justice. Farewell. (Docketed) To Simon. Send the accused. Year 1, Gorpiaeus 28 Tubi 12. Philista against Petechon, bathman, about having been scalded.
                    (*P. Enteuxis* 82 [220 B.C.E.]; Hunt and Edgar 1968: 235–37, no. 269)

An abandoned wife scolds her husband for using religion as a pretext to avoid coming home:

Isias to her brother Hephaistion [greeting]. If you are well and other things are going right, it would accord with the prayer which I make continually to the gods. I myself and the child and the household are in good health and think of you always. When I received your letter from Horos, in which you announce that you are in *katoche*[16] in the Serapaeum at Memphis, for the news that you are well I straightway thanked the gods, but about your not coming home, when all the others who had been secluded there have come, I am ill-pleased, because after having piloted myself and your child through such bad times and been driven to every extremity owing to the price of wheat, I thought that now at least, with you at home, I should enjoy some respite, whereas you have not even thought of coming home nor given any regard to our circumstances, remembering how I was in want of everything while you were still here, not to mention this long lapse of time and these critical days, during which you have sent us nothing. As, moreover, Horos who delivered the letter has brought news of your having been released from detention, I am thoroughly ill-pleased. Notwithstanding, as your mother also is annoyed, for her sake as well as for mine please return to the city, if nothing more pressing holds you back. You will do me a favor by taking care of your bodily health. Farewell. Year 2, Epeiph 30. (Address) To Hephaistion.
                    (*UPZ* 1.59 [168 B.C.E.] = *Select Papyri* 97; Bagnall and
                    Derow 1981: 235, no. 144)

In 220 B.C.E. a father complained that he was abandoned by his daughter:

To King Ptolemy greeting from Ctesicles. I am being wronged by Dionysius and my daughter Nice. For though I had nurtured her, being my own daughter, and educated her and brought her up to womanhood, when I was stricken with bodily infirmity and my eyesight enfeebled she would not furnish me with any of the necessities of life. And when I wished to obtain justice from her in Alexandria, she begged my pardon and in year 18 she gave me in the temple of Arsinoë Actia a written oath by the king that she would pay me twenty drachmae every month by means of her own bodily labor; if she failed to do so or transgressed any of the terms of her bond, she was to forfeit to me 500 drachmae on pain of incurring the consequences of the oath. Now, however, corrupted by Dionysius, who is a comic actor, she is not keeping any of her engagements to me, in contempt of my old age and my present infirmity. I beg you therefore, O king, not to suffer me to be wronged by my daughter and Dionysius the comedian who has corrupted her, but to order Diophanes the strategus to summon them and hear our case; and if my words are true, let Diophanes deal with her corrupter as seems good to him and compel my daughter Nice to yield me my rights . . . For by this means I shall no longer be wronged, but having sought your protection, O king, I shall obtain justice. (Docketed) We have delegated . . . (Endorsed) Year 1, Gorpiaeus 30 Tubi 13. Ctesicles against Dionysius and Nice his daughter concerning a written oath.

(*P. Enteuxis* 26; Hunt and Edgar 1968: 2:233, no. 268, modified)

Despite such indications of female autonomy in the public sphere, society was still strongly patriarchal, and female infants, in particular, continued to be devalued. The Greeks, in Egypt and elsewhere, practiced infanticide, especially in order to reduce the number of females. In contrast to the Greeks, the Egyptians reared all their children. Diodorus Siculus draws attention to this peculiar practice and attributes the lack of infanticide to the fertility of the soil and the ease of rearing children in Egypt:

The Egyptians are required to raise all their children in order to increase the population, on the ground that large numbers are the greatest factor in increasing the prosperity of both country and cities. Nor do they hold any child a bastard, even though he was born of a slave mother; for they have taken the general position that the father is the sole author of procreation and that the mother only supplies the fetus with nourishment and a place to live, and they call the trees which bear fruit "male" and those which do not "female," exactly the opposite to the Greek usage. They feed their children in a sort of happy-go-lucky fashion that in its inexpensiveness quite surpasses belief; for they serve them with stews made of any stuff that is ready to hand and cheap, and give them such stalks as the *byblos* plant as can be roasted in the coals, and the roots and the stems of marsh plants, either raw or boiled or baked. And since most of the children are reared without shoes or clothing because of the mildness of the climate of the country, the entire expense incurred by the parents of a child until it comes to maturity is not more than twenty drachmas. These are the leading reasons why Egypt has such an extraordinarily large population.

(Diodorus Siculus 1.80.3–6; Oldfather 1968 1:275–77)

Evidence for infanticide in Egypt appears just after the Roman conquest. In the following letter a husband instructs his wife to expose a baby if it is female. The husband addresses his wife as "sister." This term may merely indicate closeness and affection, or it may be a reflection of reality; brother-sister marriage occurred among both Greeks and Egyptians. (See Fig. 5.4; the Canopus decree, above, for references to Arsinoë

II and her brother and husband Ptolemy II as "Divine Siblings"; and the "Praises of Isis" [this chapter] for the marriage of Isis to her brother Osiris; and see further, Carney 1987).

Letter of Hilarion to Alis:

Hilarion to his sister Alis very many greetings, likewise to my lady Berous and Apollonarion. Know that we are still in Alexandria. Do not be anxious; if they[17] really go home, I will remain in Alexandria. I beg and entreat you, take care of the little one, and as soon as we receive our pay I will send it up to you. If by chance you bear a child, if it is a boy, let it be, if it is a girl, cast it out.

(*P. Oxyrhynchus* 4.744.1–10 (1 B.C.E.); Hunt and Edgar 1968: 1:no. 105)

Like papyri, New Comedy, which began in Athens in the late fourth century, shows that older traditions about women were preserved while new ones were introduced. In the third century B.C.E. a poet of New Comedy wrote: "Everyone, even a poor man, raises a son, everyone, even a wealthy man, exposes a daughter" (Poseidippus, *Hermaphroditus*, frag. 12 Kassel-Austin).

But New Comedy also includes female characters who try to act for themselves and manipulate their world. This new genre, which originated in Athens, was characterized by typical plots and typical bourgeois or lowlife characters. In a standard plot, a young man falls in love with a woman who is unsuitable for him to marry until it is discovered that she is actually of high birth. Or a young man rapes a young woman at a festival. After the birth of the child, other characters—typically slaves or a courtesan with a heart of gold—contrive to bring the couple together in a satisfactory marriage. The fragmentary remains of plays in the second group, such as Menander's *Samia* or *Epitrepontes*, are notable for the alliances built between respectable wives, young women, and courtesans. In other plays, henpecked husbands complain about the tyranny or treachery of their wives with all the vigor of Euripides' misogynistic Hippolytus (for example, Alexis, frag. 146 Kock; Menander, frag. 333 Körte). In New Comedy the young hero and heroine are often displayed as passive victims of circumstances; but occasionally even a young woman could stand up for herself.

The following papyrus fragment of the second century B.C.E. has sometimes been attributed to a tragic imitator of Euripides and sometimes to a New Comedy, but all agree that the scenario is predictably New Comic. The heroine tries to persuade her father not to marry her off to a man richer than her present husband:

The words I speak, father, you should be speaking: it is fitting that you should be wiser than I, and speak what the time demands. Now, in your default, it remains for me, I think, perforce to plead myself the cause of justice. If my husband has done me a great injury, is it not for me to exact a penalty therefor? And if he has wronged me, must I not perceive it? Perhaps I am a fool and know it not. I will not answer no: and yet a woman, father, though a fool in judgment of all else, may perhaps have good sense about her own affairs. But be it as you will. Only tell me this, wherein he wrongs me? For wife and husband there is a law laid down: for him, to love his woman for ever till the end; for her, to do whatever gives her husband pleasure. All I demanded, my husband has been to me; and all that pleases him, father, pleases me. You say he is good to me but he is poor! So now (you tell me) you give me in marriage to a man of wealth, that I may not live all my life in distress. Where in the world is all that money, father, which—if I have it—will cheer me more than the man I love? How is it just or honorable, that I should take my share of the good things he had, but in his poverty take no share at all? Say, if the man who is now about to take me (which dear God forbid, nor shall it ever be!—at least not of my will, nor while I can prevent it)—if he should lose his substance hereafter, will you give me to another man? And then to another, if he too loses all? How long will you use my life, father, for your experiments with fortune? When I was a child, that was the time for you to find a husband to give me to, for then the choice was yours. But when you had once given me, father, at once it was for me to look to my own fate. And justly so, for if I judge not well, it is my own life that I shall injure. There is the truth. So by the goddess of our home, do not rob me of the man to whom you wedded me. This favor I ask of you—a just one, father, and full of loving kindness. If you refuse, you shall do your pleasure by force: and I shall try to endure my fortune as I ought, without disgrace.

> (Menander; Sandbach 1972: 328; Page 1970: 185–87)

Education and Professions

Increased opportunities for education as well as the focus on the individual contributed to the emergence of women poets in several parts of the Greek world (Pomeroy 1977). Some of the women traveled to festivals and recited their poetry. For celebrating the city in her poetry, Aristodama was awarded public honors usually reserved for men by Lamia.[18]

Decree in honor of Aristodama of Smyrna, 218–217 B.C.E.

Of the Aitolians the strategus is Hagetas, a citizen of Kallion. With good fortune. Resolved [by the city] of the Lamians. Since Aristodama, daughter of Amyntas, a citizen of Smyrna in Io[nia], epic poet, while she was in our city, gave several [public recitations] of her poems in which the nation of the Aitolians [and] the People's ancestors were worthily commemorated and since the performance was done with great enthusiasm, she shall be a proxenos[19] of the city and benefactor, and she shall be given citizenship and the right to purchase land and [a house] and the right of pasture and inviolability and security on land and sea in war and peace for herself and her descendants and their property for all time together with all other privileges that are given to other proxenoi and benefactors and Diony[sios], her brother, and his descendants shall have the rights of a proxenos, citizenship, inviolability.

> (*Sylloge Inscriptionum Graecarum* 3 532.
> Trans. adapted from Burstein 1985: 86–87, no. 64)

At the end of the first century B.C.E. Antipater of Thessalonica described the canon of women poets:

These are the divine-voiced women that Helicon fed with song, Helicon and Macedonian Pieria's rock: Praxilla; Moero; Anyte, the female Homer; Sappho, glory of the Lesbian women with lovely tresses; Erinna; renowned Telesilla; and you Corinna, who sang the martial shield of Athena; Nossis, the tender-voiced, and dulcet-toned Myrtis—all craftwomen of eternal pages. Great Heaven gave birth to nine Muses and Earth to these nine, the deathless delight of mortals.

(Adapted from Paton 1968: 3:17, Book 9:epigram 26)

Erinna of Teos, or Telos, who probably lived at the end of the fourth century B.C.E., was highly praised by Ancient critics. Her poetry contains echos of Sappho. In the "Distaff," she takes the traditional female theme of spinning and turns it into a piercing, never-ending lament for her friend Baucis who had died soon after her marriage. Erinna recalls their childhood together when they played the tortoise game and played with dolls, and describes Baucis's abrupt transition from girl to wife. The "Distaff" once consisted of 300 hexameters, but is now fragmentary.

of a girl . . . maidens [or dolls?] . . . tortoise . . .
tortoise . . . wave
from white horses
I shouted loudly . . . tortoise . . .
the yard of the great court . . .
wretched Baucis, I cry out this lament . . .
these games lie in my heart
still warm. But [those are] already ashes.
of dolls . . . in the bed-chambers . . .
maidens [or dolls] . . . once at dawn
Mother . . . to the wool-workers
. . . sprinkled with salt
little . . . Mormo brought fear.[20]
. . . she roamed on her four feet
and changed her visage from [one thing to another].
But when into the bed . . . , you forgot everything which still
in your innocence . . . having heard your mother,
dear Baucis. Forgetfulness . . . Aphrodite.
Therefore you, weeping . . . but other things I leave;
for my feet [are] not permitted . . . for the house,
nor [am I able] to look upon a corpse, nor to lament
with uncovered hair . . . shame
tears me around my cheeks . . .
nineteen . . . Erinna . . . distaff . . . shame . . .
maiden-songs . . . looking . . . hair . . . dear Baucis . . .
flame . . . Hymenaios . . . Hymenaios . . . alas,
wretched Baucis . . .

(Erinna, "Distaff"; Snyder 1989: 93)

Erinna, like most of the other poets of the period, also wrote epigrams (short poems on a variety of themes). Erinna wrote two sepulchral epigrams for Baucis:

O stele and Sirens and mournful urn of mine,
    you who hold this small heap of ashes that belong to Hades,
Give greetings to those who pass by this my grave,
    whether they are citizens or visitors from other towns.

Say that this tomb holds me, who was a bride; say also this,
　　that my father called me Baucis, and that my family
　　Was of Tenos, so that they may know, and that my companion
　　Erinna inscribed these words upon my tomb.
　　　　　　　　　(*Palatine Anthology* 7.710; Snyder 1989: 91)

I am the tomb of the bride Baucis; passing by
　　this much lamented stele, say this to Hades beneath the earth:
"Hades, you are envious." But to you who see them,
　　these beautiful monuments will announce the cruel fate of
Baucis:
How with the pine-torches with which Hymenaios was hymned
　　her father-in-law set the girl ablaze upon this pyre,
And you yourself, Hymenaios, changed the tuneful song of marriage
　　into the mournful sound of lamentation.
　　　　　　　　　(*Palatine Anthology* 7.712; Snyder 1989: 90)

Other women poets also give intimate glimpses of women's worlds.
Not much seems to have changed since the Classical period in the daily
lives of women. What is new, however, is the existence of women poets
who wrote for and about women. Nossis of Locri in Italy (ca. first half
of third century B.C.E.) wrote lyrics and epigrams. Only the latter are
extant. She defines herself as a poet in relation to Sappho. The form
of the poem is that of a funerary epigram, similar to those by Erinna
quoted above:

　　Stranger, if you sail to Mytilene of the lovely dances
　　　to be inspired with the flower of Sappho's graces,
　　say that the Locrian land bore me, one dear to the Muses
　　　and to her. Having learned that my name is Nossis, go.
　　　　　　　(Epigram 11 [Gow and Page]; Skinner 1991: 34)

As the quotation from Herodas (see earlier) suggests, Nossis gained
a reputation as a poet of love, perhaps of lesbian relationships. Epigram
1 is frankly erotic: the poet rejects honey, because she finds Eros is
sweeter. The allusions to Aphrodite, flowers, and roses evoke echoes of
Sappho:

　　Nothing is sweeter than desire. All other delights are second.
　　　From my mouth I spit even honey.
　　Nossis says this, whom Aphrodite does not love,
　　　knows not her flowers, what roses they are.
　　　　　　　(Epigram 1 [Gow and Page]; Skinner 1991: 33)

In Epigram 3 Nossis dedicates a valuable garment that she and her
mother had woven as a gift to the goddess Hera at Lacinia in southern
Italy. "Noble" indicates that, like most other women who had time to
devote to poetry, Nossis was upper-class. She proudly refers to herself,
and to her mother, in turn, by matronymics (Skinner 1987; Skinner 1991:
20–47). Matrilineal naming was the local custom at Locri though patri-
lineal naming was the usual practice in the rest of Greece (see Chapter
3):

> Most reverend Hera, you who often descending from Heaven
> behold your Lacinian shrine fragrant with incense,
> receive the linen wrap that with her noble child Nossis
> Theophilis daughter of Cleocha wove for you.
> (Epigram 3 [Gow and Page]; Skinner 1991: 22)

Anyte of Tegea in Arcadia was probably a contemporary of Nossis. Like male poets, she celebrated war and was one of the first Hellenistic poets to write bucolic poetry. She also wrote epigrams, among them several for girls who died before marriage. These poems were probably genuine grave inscriptions. Because marriage was the most important event in a woman's life, dying unwed occasioned great lamentation over an unfulfilled life (cf. Chapter 1 on Phrasicleia and Chapter 3 on loutrophoroi as funeral vases for the unmarried). In the following poems the pathos is increased because the daughter predeceased her parents. Although the scenario is the same, the epigrams are not repetitive. Note in particular the attention paid to Antibia's intelligence, a quality prized in the Hellenistic period among families where daughters were educated.

> Throwing her arms around her dear father,
> Erato, melting away in moist tears, spoke these last words.
> "Father, I am no more; dark black Death
> covers my eyes as already I perish."
> (*Palatine Anthology* 7.486)

> Often in lamentation upon this girl's tomb her mother Cleina
> bewails her beloved child who dies before her time.
> She calls forth the soul of Philanis, who—before her marriage—
> crossed the pale stream of the River Acheron.
> (*Palatine Anthology* 7.649)

> No bed-chamber and sacred rites of marriage for you.
> Instead, your mother put upon this marble tomb
> A likeness which has your girlish shape and beauty,
> Thersis; you can be addressed even though you are dead.
> (*Palatine Anthology* 7.490)

> I mourn for the maiden Antibia, to whose
> father's house many suitors came, drawn by
> Report of her beauty and wisdom. But deadly Fate
> whirled away the hopes of all of them.
> (*Palatine Anthology*, epigrams 1–4 [Gow and Page];
> Snyder 1989: 68)

Corinna of Tanagra was probably Anyte's contemporary (West 1990). She wrote narrative lyrics replete with Boeotian myth. In a brief fragment she proclaims:

> But I myself [sing] the excellent deeds
> of male and female heroes.
> (Frag. 664b *Poetae Melici Graeci*;
> Snyder 1989: 44)

Much of Corinna's poetry, like Anyte's, was probably directed to audiences of men and women. Perhaps this is one of the reasons that her work, like that of other women poets, survived, became famous, and was incorporated into the cultural mainstream. For Roman poets of the Augustan age, her name was synomymous with talent and erudition. Ovid calls his mistress "Corinna," and Propertius 2.3.22 claims that his mistress wrote verses that were as good as Corinna's. Fragment 2 was addressed to a group of girls who are probably members of a chorus who will learn to perform Corinna's songs (for similar *partheneia*, see Chapters 1 and 2):

> Terpsichore [summoned me] to sing
> beautiful tales of old
> to the Tanagraean girls in their white robes.
> And the city rejoiced greatly
> in my clear, plaintive voice.
> For great things . . .
>
> . . . the broad-plained earth . . .
> I, having done honor to the oracles
> in the time of our fathers . . .
> . . . to the maidens . . .
> I myself often honored with words
> the leader Cephissus [the river god]
> but also often great Orion
> and the fifty mighty youths
> whom   [he   begat]   by   mating   with
> nymphs . . .
>
> (Frag. 664b *Poetae Melici Graeci*;
> Snyder 1989: 50)

Women poets probably read the works of other writers and wrote their own poetry in the privacy of their homes. But some respectable, educated women pursued professions that required them to work in the public sphere and to have dealings with men who were not kinsmen. In Classical Athens, a few women had studied at Plato's Academy: "Among his disciples were . . . two women Lasthenia of Mantineia and Axiothea of Phlius who dressed like a man" (Diogenes Laertius 3.46, similarly, 4.2).

A third female student is mentioned in *Papyrus Oxyrhynchus* 52.3656. Starting in the later fourth century B.C.E. even more women became philosophers. Hipparchia (ca. 300 B.C.E.) learned about Cynic philosophy and was attracted to Crates through her brother, but her decision involved rebelling against her parents and convention. She shaped her own life and created her own identity:

Hipparchia too, sister of Metrocles, was captured by their doctrines. Both of them were born at Maroneia. She fell in love with the discourses and the life of Crates, and would not pay attention to any of her suitors, their wealth, their high birth or their beauty. But to her Crates was everything. She used even to threaten her parents she would make away with herself, unless she were given in marriage to him. Crates therefore was implored by her parents to persuade the girl, and did all he could, and at last, failing to persuade her, he got up, took off his clothes before her face and said. "This is the bridegroom, these are his possessions; make your choice accordingly; for you will be no helpmeet of mine, unless you share my pursuits."

(Diogenes Laertius 6.96–98; Hicks 1922)

Some Hellenistic women also became artists. Most of the women painters we know of were the daughters of male artists and seem to have worked on the same sorts of subjects as their male contemporaries. However, the most famous woman artist of all, Laia, or Lala, of Cyzicus, is not known by a patronymic; nor did she marry. Her subjects were predominantly female:

There were also women painters: Timarete the daughter of Micon, who painted the very ancient picture of Artemis at Ephesus; Irene, daughter and pupil of the painter Cratinus, who did the girl at Eleusis, a Calypso, an old woman, and Theodore the juggler and Alcisthenes the dancer; and Aristarete, daughter and pupil of Nearchus, who painted an Asclepius. When Marcus Varro was a young man [mid-first century B.C.E.], Iaia [Laia or Lala] of Cyzicus, who never married, painted pictures with the brush in Rome, chiefly portraits of women, as well as a large picture on wood of an old woman, at Naples, and a self-portrait done in a looking glass. No one else had a quicker hand in painting, while her artistic skill was such that the prices she obtained far outstripped the most celebrated portraitists of the day.

(Pliny, *Natural History* 35.147–48; Rackham 1968)

The painters grouped together here range in date from the fifth century to the first B.C.E., and most are otherwise unattested. It is striking, however, that, as in the Renaissance and Baroque, most women artists are daughters of male artists who taught them their art.

In the Hellenistic period women also began the formal study of medicine. Hagnodice, the first female obstetrician in Athens, studied with Herophilus, probably in the last quarter of the fourth century B.C.E. (see Chapter 6). Some details about women being excluded by law (rather than by custom as was probably the case) from practicing medicine in Athens are likely to be fabrications. Nevertheless, Athenian women did begin to practice obstetrics in the fourth century B.C.E.:

The ancients had no midwives, and therefore women died [in childbirth], led on by their sense of shame. For the Athenians had taken heed that no slave or woman should learn the science of medicine. A certain girl, Hagnodice, as a young woman desired to learn the science of medicine. Because of this desire, she cut her hair, put on male clothing, and entrusted herself to a certain Herophilus for her training. After learning this science, when she heard that a woman was having labor-pains, she used to go to her. And when the woman refused to entrust herself [to Hagnodice], thinking that she was a man, Hagnodice lifted her undergarment and revealed that she was a woman. In this way she used to cure women.

(Hyginus, *Fabula* 274.10–11; p. 167 Rose; von Staden 1989: 53)

The Female Body

A new interest in the female body and the problems of reproduction is suggested by a group of grave stelai and other funerary monuments from the mid-fourth through the third centuries that show a woman in labor (Fig. 5.14). The funerary context implies that she has died in childbirth. These are almost unique among Greek grave monuments in alluding so directly to the manner and moment of death. The transparent garment focuses our attention on the belly, even if it is not shown as realistically pregnant. The awkward pose and dishevelment of hair and clothing are quite different from the quiet, composed grief of Classical gravestones (cf. Introduction, Fig. 1; Chapter 3, Figs. 3.1 and 3.2). The dying woman is surrounded by members of her family, who sometimes grieve openly. It has been suggested that these scenes heroize the dead woman, in a manner analogous to the heroization of men who have died in battle (Vedder 1988). For most women, the noblest service to the community continued to be the production of male offspring.

From the fifth century on, Hippocratic and later doctors used the female reproductive system (see Chapter 6) to explain women's apparently erratic behavior, propensity for Dionysiac ecstasy, and susceptibility to romantic love. Stimulated by these interests, as well as by the fascination with the symptoms of erotic passion in the Archaic lyric poets (especially Sappho), Hellenistic writers repeatedly elaborated upon the literary portrait of the female victim of Aphrodite, who is generally pitifully abandoned after her clandestine seduction or her bold leap into love regardless of family, friends, and social mores. The fascination with female eroticism, seduction, and desertion is perhaps understandably characteristic of a period of shifting and sometimes unsettled social lives in the Greek community, and other poetic genres generally do not offer the comic and bourgeois solution to the abandoned or raped female found in New Comedy. Apollonius of Rhodes's *Medea* (to be abandoned at Corinth by Jason) is not the angry and articulate wife of Euripides' play, but a young girl overwhelmed by her first experience of passion:

And fast did her heart throb within her breast, as a sunbeam quivers upon the walls of a house when flung up from the water, which is just poured forth in a cauldron or a pail maybe; and hither and thither on the swift eddy does it dart and dance along; even so the maiden's heart quivered in her breast. And the tear of pity flowed from her eyes, and ever within anguish tortured her, a smouldering fire through her frame, and about her fine nerves and deep down beneath the nape of her neck where the pain enters keenest, whenever the unwearied Loves direct against the heart their shafts of agony.

(*Argonautica* 3.755–65; Seaton 1980)

Similarly, in Theocritus 2, Simaetha, a poor but respectable virgin who lives alone with a maid, falls in love with and solicits a young athlete named Delphis. Here she narrates her own first reaction to her soon-to-be faithless lover:

Figure 5.14. Tombstone from late fourth or third century, B.C.E. Attica showing a woman who may have died in childbirth.

Hardly halfway along the road—about at Lycon's—
I saw Delphis: he was walking with Eudamippus.
Their beards were more golden than curling honey-suckle,
and their chests had such a sheen—brighter than you, Moon,
for they were fresh returned from the genteel toil of the gym.

Tell, how Eros fell on me, Lady Moon!
The moment my eyes lit on them, madness lit on me,
and fire was laid to my heart, poor wretch that I am!
My looks were a faded flower; I took no more note of my possessions,
and I know not how I got home; a burning fever was shaking me,
and I lay in my bed for all of ten days and nights.

· ·
. . . And I, as soon as I was aware,
by the light foot fall, it was he crossing the threshold.

· ·
I froze, through and through to the bone, colder than snow,
and the sweat ran from my forehead, more like a heavy dew.
I couldn't utter a word, not so much as a broken word
children whimper in sleep to their mother. My once fresh
complexion became like a wax doll, exactly.

(Theocritus 2.76–86, 103–110; Rist 1978)

Simaetha is only one of the young women in Hellenistic poetry who apparently live without male supervision and engage in love affairs with men without being courtesans or prostitutes.

The following fragmentary pastoral poem entitled the "Oaristus" or "Whispered Erotic Dialogue" was attributed to Theocritus, but in fact was composed by an imitator of a later but uncertain date. Here a cowherd gradually seduces a young girl who is pasturing goats. The youth wears down the maiden's reluctance with themes that also appear in marriage songs (epithalamia)—the woman's fear of losing her virginity and of childbirth is countered with reminders of the short bloom of youth and the rewards of children. This poem leaves the result of the seduction unclear. Daphnis mimics in a pastoral mode all the protestations of a responsible suitor, but both the girl's aged father and the cowherd's homestead are quickly ignored in favor of the physical consummation that the "little satyr" has been aiming at from the start. By contrast, in Longus's later Greek novel *Daphnis and Chloë*, the poet makes a point of delaying the consummation of the pastoral couple's desire until after marriage.

MAIDEN: Paris, another cowherd, abducted chaste Helen.
DAPHNIS: No, Helen of her own free will captured the cowherd with a kiss.
MAIDEN: Don't be so sure, you little satyr. They say a kiss is a trivial thing.
DAPHNIS: Yet there is sweet pleasure even in trivial kisses.
MAIDEN: I wipe off my mouth and spit out your kiss.
DAPHNIS: You're wiping your mouth? Give it back to me to kiss.
MAIDEN: A kiss is a good thing for your calves, not for an unwed girl.
DAPHNIS: Don't be so sure. Soon life will pass you by like a dream.
MAIDEN: Supposing I am growing a bit older, I drink milk and honey now.
DAPHNIS: A half-ripe grape will be a raisin. What is now a rose will dry up and fade.
MAIDEN: Don't put a hand on me. Still on me? I'll tear your lip.
DAPHNIS: Come here under the wild olives so I can tell you a story.
MAIDEN: I don't want to. You tricked me with a lovely story once before.
DAPHNIS: Come here under the elms so you can hear my pipe.

MAIDEN: Please yourself. A woeful song does not please me.

DAPHNIS: Unfortunately even you must respect the Paphian's [Aphrodite's] anger, maiden.

MAIDEN: Never mind the Paphian, as long as Artemis protects me.

DAPHNIS: Don't say that, lest she strike you and put you in a net from which you cannot escape.

MAIDEN: Let her strike as she wished. Artemis will protect me.

DAPHNIS: Your won't escape love. No virgin ever has.

MAIDEN: By Pan, I will escape. But may you bear his yoke.

DAPHNIS: I am afraid he will give you to a lesser man.

MAIDEN: Many have courted me, but not one was pleasing to my mind.

DAPHNIS: And I too, one of many, have come as your suitor.

MAIDEN: What am I to do, my friend? Marriages are full of pain.

DAPHNIS: Not pain. Marriage does not bring grief but dancing.

MAIDEN: Yes, they say wives fear their bedfellows.

DAPHNIS: No, they always control them. What do wives fear?

MAIDEN: I am afraid to give birth. The bolt of Eileithyia [the goddess of childbirth] is harsh.

DAPHNIS: But Artemis, your queen, lightens the pains of childbirth.

MAIDEN: But I fear to give birth lest I destroy my lovely flesh.

DAPHNIS: Yet if you bear children, you will see a new dawn of youth.

MAIDEN: And what bridal gift do you bring me, worth marriage, if I do say yes.

DAPHNIS: You will have my whole herd, and all my groves and pasture land.

MAIDEN: Swear that after marriage you won't leave me against my will.

DAPHNIS: No, by Pan himself, even if you want to get rid of me.

MAIDEN: And will you build me a bridal chamber? Will you build me a house and farm?

DAPHNIS: I will build you a bridal chamber. And I shall tend your beautiful flocks.

MAIDEN: And my old father, what, oh what story shall we tell him?

DAPHNIS: He will praise your marriage when he hears my name.

MAIDEN: Say your name. Even a name is often pleasing.

DAPHNIS: I am Daphnis. My father is Lycidas, my mother Nomaea.

MAIDEN: You are from a good family. Mine's no worse than yours.

DAPHNIS: I know. You are Acrotime and your father is Menalcas.

MAIDEN: Show me your grove, where your cowherd's hut stands.

DAPHNIS: Come and see how my slender cypresses bloom.

MAIDEN: Keep feeding, my goats. I am going to look over the cowherd's farm.

DAPHNIS: Feel well, bulls, so I can show my groves to the maiden.

MAIDEN: What are you doing, you little satyr? Why are you touching my breasts inside my clothes?

DAPHNIS: First of all, I will give those velvety apples a lesson.

MAIDEN: I feel faint, by Pan. Take your hand out.

DAPHNIS: Take courage, dear girl. Why are you afraid of me? How very fearful you are.

MAIDEN: You are throwing me into a ditch and dirtying my lovely clothes.

DAPHNIS: But don't you see that I am putting a soft fleece under your clothes?

MAIDEN: Oh dear, you have taken off my girdle. Why have you loosed it?

DAPHNIS: I am making this my very first offering to the Paphian.

MAIDEN: Wait, you fool. Maybe someone is coming. I hear a sound.

DAPHNIS: The cypresses are prattling about your marriage to each other.

MAIDEN: You have made a rag of my clothes. And I am naked.

DAPHNIS: I'll get you another robe larger than your own.

MAIDEN: You say you'll give me everything. But perhaps later on you won't give me salt.

DAPHNIS: If only I could add my very life to the gifts.

MAIDEN: Artemis, do not be angry that I no longer rely on your precepts.

DAPHNIS: I will give a heifer to Love and a cow to Aphrodite herself.

MAIDEN: I came here a virgin, and I go home a wife [or woman].

DAPHNIS: Wife, mother and nurse of children. A girl no more.

And so delighting in their fresh young bodies they whispered to each other. Their furtive mating was accomplished. She got up and went back to pasture her flocks with downcast eyes, but the heart within was glad. And he, delighted with his marriage bed, went to his herds of bulls.

([Theocritus] 27; trans. Helene P. Foley)

In an epigram, Asclepiades, a contemporary of Nossis and Anyte, also played with the theme of virginity and seduction:

> Pretty maiden, what's the good
> of hoarding up your maidenhood?
> Once in Acheron we must,
> maiden, come to bones and dust.
> (Epigram 2; trans. J. S. Philli-
> more, in Wallace and Wallace
> 1941: 9)

The portrayal of the female body in Greek art underwent radical changes starting about the middle of the fourth century (Bonfante 1989). In the art of the Ancient Near East, nudity for goddesses was not taboo or unusual, so that occasionally, under Eastern influence, there are examples in early Greek art of the eighth and seventh centuries. But in Archaic and Classical Greek art, there are only a few specific contexts in which female nudity may occur: hetairai and other prostitutes on Attic pottery made for men's use at symposia (cf. Chapter 3, Figs. 3.25–3.27); and narrative contexts that require nudity, such as the Rape of Cassandra at Troy (Fig. 5.15). Here, on a vase of about 500 B.C.E., the frontal nudity of the Trojan princess about to be violated during the sack of Troy is intended to be shocking rather than erotic. The beauty of the female body was not explored for its own sake, and only the youthful, athletic male body was considered an object of admiration in publicly displayed monuments. Statues of women that were set up in public, such as the korai on the Athenian Acropolis, are always modestly dressed, and the drapery itself becomes the principal vehicle for conveying female grace and beauty (cf. Chapter 1).

The first experiments with the nude female in monumental art are to be found in statues of Aphrodite by the sculptor Praxiteles in the mid-fourth century, such as the famous Cnidia (Fig. 5.16). The proportions of the body are still closer to the athleticism of male statuary than the soft features of the face, for which Praxiteles was renowned. As the first

Figure 5.15. Athenian vase (ca. 500 B.C.E.) showing the sack of Troy; the nude figure of Cassandra, the doom-predicting priestess whose punishment for her transgression was that no one would believe her, clings, at the lower left of the figure, to the city's cult statue of Athena, but it cannot save her from her Greek attacker, the Lesser Ajax. Her nudity stands as the sign of her imminent rape.

entirely nude female in Classical sculpture, the Cnidia gave rise in antiquity to many romantic anecdotes: Praxiteles' mistress, Phryne, was said to be the statue's model; a man supposedly became enamored of the statue, Pygmalion-like, and made love to it; and the goddess Aphrodite herself, on seeing the statue, allegedly asked indignantly, "Where did Praxiteles see me naked?" (Paton 1968: Book 16.160).

Praxiteles did not continue to work into the Hellenistic period, but through the influence of his son, also a sculptor, and his workshop, the type of the nude Aphrodite became one of the central images of Hellenistic and Roman art. The choice of Aphrodite, goddess of love and sexual desire, is of course not accidental, and no other female divinities were shown nude. Even Aphrodite's nudity is always motivated by a narrative element (for example, she was born from the sea and is portrayed bathing or preparing to bathe), to mitigate the exhibitionistic quality and overt eroticism of what must at first have seemed a shocking exposure.

The body type that evolved for the nude Aphrodite by the third cen-

Figure 5.16. Statue of Aphrodite from Cnidos (Asia Minor) by Praxiteles (ca. 350 B.C.E.). The type of nude Aphrodite spawned a series of similar statues in the Hellenistic period and of copies made in the Roman period.

tury is assumed to express contemporary standards of female beauty, which look very different from the standards for Classical women who, when nude, are usually lean and athletic, the physique differing little from that of young men. The High Hellenistic Aphrodite (late third to second century B.C.E.) is fleshy and emphasizes certain feminine features such as wide hips, large buttocks, and, in the crouching pose, creases in the Rubensesque torso (Fig. 5.17). It is not certain whether this awkward pose was intended to be erotic or unflattering, or simply to explore the reaction of the body to certain movements that had been neglected in Classical sculpture. The invention of the crouching Aphrodite was traditionally ascribed to the sculptor Doidalsas of Bithynia and dated to the mid-third century, but it may be no earlier than the beginning of the second (Ridgway 1990: 230–32). In Hellenistic Egypt where, as we have seen, Aphrodite became merged with Isis, the result may hark back to the earliest Near Eastern nude female figures, with unabashed emphasis on fertility (Fig. 5.18).

Along with the preoccupation with ideals of youthful feminine beauty in Hellenistic art came a fascination with its opposite: the grotesque caricature (Fig. 5.19). This is part of a broader interest in all physical types that deviate from the norm (handicapped people, emaciated beggars, etc.), as if in deliberate reaction to the two centuries of

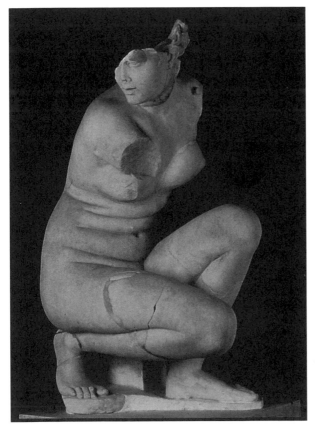

Figure 5.17. Statue of the crouching Aphrodite, said to be bathing. Found in Vienne in Gaul, the statue may testify to the circulation of Hellenistic originals and Roman copies to provincial areas.

Figure 5.18. Terra-cotta statuette from Naucratis (first century B.C.E. to first century C.E.) of Aphrodite-Isis. The broad hips and heavy breasts assert the connection of this composite goddess with fertility.

Classical idealism that had gone before. Particularly noticeable is the exploration of old age and the toll it takes on the body, whether male or female. The well-known figure of a drunken old woman convincingly renders such traits as the bony chest and sagging breasts, ravaged face and toothless mouth (Fig. 5.20). At the same time, we are not meant to

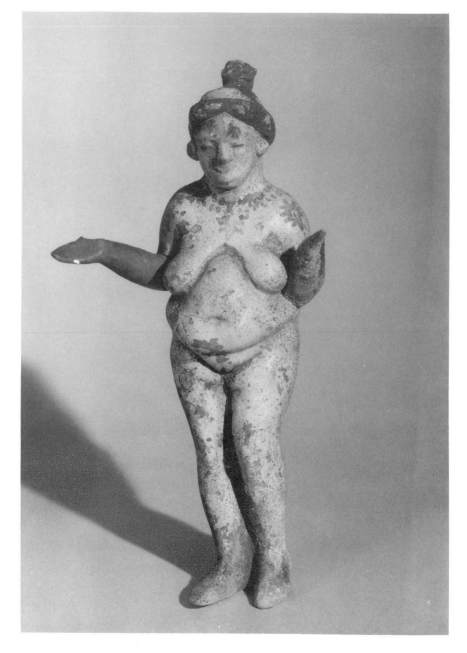

Figure 5.19. Hellenistic terra-cotta statuette from Tanagra (ca. 350–325 B.C.E.) of a woman with a heavy and aging body. The contrast with the idealized attenuation of the figurines of young women (see Figures 5.5 and 5.6) is striking, and, along with other images of older women (see Figure 5.20), it seems reminiscent of the ridicule implicit in the images of aging prostitutes in earlier Greek vase painting (Fig. 3.27).

Figure 5.20. Statue (third century B.C.E.) of a drunken old peasant woman, probably made for the decoration of a villa or for a private art collection of the sort known from the Roman empire.

pity her, for the splendid wine vessel she caresses suggests that her inebriation is the gift of the god Dionysus, a happy consolation for the infirmity of age (Zanker 1989). Appreciation of old women and of a life well spent appeared as well in poetry:

Stranger, know that I who rest here
Was once a priestess of Demeter,
And Priestess too of the Cabiri
And later also of Cybele;

That this old woman, now dust in earth,
helped many through the pains of birth
And bore two sons, in whose arms I
Closed my eyes. Farewell. Pass by.
                    (*Palatine Anthology* 7.728; Lombardo and
                                                    Rayor 1988)

Miccos kept his Phrygian nurse Aischra
Well cared for all her life, and when she died
Set up her statue in perpetual gratitude
For the old woman and her nursing breasts.
                    (*Palatine Anthology* 7.458; Lombardo and
                                                    Rayor 1988)

NOTES

1. The game, known as *ephedrismos*, was a kind of piggyback ride and was played by both little girls and young women, but less often by boys or men.

2. A baubon is a leather dildo.

3. Erinna and Nossis were poets (see "Education and Professions"), but not related. The use of their names here may be facetious.

4. Athenaeus 15.689a. Arsinoë II, Berenice's predecessor as the queen of Egypt, had also been fond of horses and of perfume made of roses. For the horses, see Hesychius, s.v. *hippia* and Callimachus, "The Lock of Berenice," line 54. See the excursus on Sparta for Spartan queens who owned horses that were victorious at Panhellenic games and, for recent epigraphic evidence, Tracey and Habicht (1991).

5. For the role of the empress in the Roman imperial cult see Chapter 13.

6. Hyginus, *Astronomy* 2.24. Although Hyginus is not a trustworthy source, similar stories about Macedonian and Ptolemaic queens riding in combat help to confirm Hyginus's report about Berenice II. See further, Pomeroy 1984: chap. 1.

7. Interpreters of writings concerning gods.

8. Apis and Mnevis were sacred bulls.

9. Hieroglyphics.

10. Demotic Egyptian script.

11. Osiris was King of the Dead.

12. Sirius, which rose on July 19 and signaled the beginning of the new year.

13. The calendar year was identified by her name. See, for example, the dating formula at the beginning of *P. Elephantine* 1, quoted on pp. 158–159.

14. Local governor.

15. Local magistrate.

16. Perhaps "in confinement" or "in detention" by the god's order.

17. Probably his companions.

18. Chalaion also honored Aristodama: *Supplementum Epigraphicum Graecarum* 2 (1925) 263 (Delphi, third century B.C.E.).

19. "Friend of the state," an honor awarded to foreigners as acknowledgment of their benefactions or importance.

20. Mormo was a female bogey traditionally used to frighten children into obedience.

TRANSLATIONS

Hicks, R. D. 1922. *Diogenes Laertius: Lives of Eminent Philosophers.* Loeb Classical Library. Cambridge, Mass.

Hunt, A. S., and C. C. Edgar. 1968. *Select Papyri.* Loeb Classical Library. Cambridge, Mass.

Lombardo, Stanley, and Diane Rayor. 1988. *Callimachus: Hymns, Epigrams, Select Fragments.* Baltimore, Md.

Oldfather, C. H. 1968. *Diodorus Siculus, Biblioteca historica.* Loeb Classical Library. Cambridge, Mass.

Paton, W. R. 1967. *Polybius: The Histories.* Loeb Classical Library, Vol. 5. Cambridge, Mass.

————. 1968. *The Greek Anthology.* 5 vols. Loeb Classical Library. Cambridge, Mass.

Perrin, Bernadotte. 1968. *Plutarch's Lives.* Loeb Classical Library. Cambridge, Mass.

Rackham, H. 1968. *Pliny: Natural History.* Loeb Classical Library. Cambridge, Mass.

Rist, Anna. 1978. *The Poems of Theocritus.* Chapel Hill, N.C.

Rose, H. J. 1934. *Hyginus Fabulae.* Lugduni Batavorum.

Seaton, R. C. 1980. *The Argonautica.* Loeb Classical Library. Cambridge, Mass. (Originally published 1912.)

Staden, Heinrich von. 1989. *Herophilus: The Art of Medicine in Early Alexandria.* Cambridge.

WORKS CONSULTED

Bagnall, Roger S., and Peter Derow. 1981. *Greek Historical Documents: The Hellenistic Period.* Chico, Calif.

Bieber, Margarete. 1961. *The Sculpture of the Hellenistic Age.* 2d ed. New York.

Bonfante, Larissa. 1989. "Nudity as a Costume in Classical Art." *American Journal of Archaeology* 93: 543–70.

Burstein, Stanley. 1985. *The Hellenistic Age from the Battle of Ipsos to the Death of Kleopatra VII.* New York.

Cameron, Alan. 1981. "Asclepiades' Girl Friends." In *Reflections of Women in Antiquity,* edited by Helene P. Foley, 275–302. New York.

Carney, Elizabeth D. 1987. "The Reappearance of Royal Sibling Marriage in Ptolemaic Egypt." *Parola del Passato* 42: 420–39.

Cleopatra's Egypt. 1988. Exhibition catalogue. Brooklyn Museum.

Dittenberger, W. 1903–05. *Orientis Graeci Inscriptiones Selectae.* Leipzig.

Dittenberger, W., ed. 1915. *Sylloge Inscriptionum Graecarum³.* Leipzig. Rep. 1982 Olms, Hildesheim.

Finley, M. I. 1968. *Aspects of Antiquity.* London.

Fraser, P. M. 1972. *Ptolemaic Alexandria.* 3 vols. Oxford.

Gow, A. S. F., ed. 1952. *Theocritus.* 2 vols. Cambridge.

Gow, A. S. F., and D. L. Page. 1968. *Greek Anthology, Hellenistic Epigrams.* 2 vols. Cambridge.

Hauben, H. 1979. "Le transport fluvial en Egypt ptolémaïque: les bateaux du roi et de la reine." In *Actes du XV e Congrès internationale de papyrologie.* (*Papyri Bruxellenses Graecae* 19), 68–77. Brussels.

Havelock, Christine M. 1970. *Hellenistic Art.* Greenwich, Conn.

Headlam, Walter, and A. D. Knox. 1922. *Herodas: Mimes and Fragments.* Cambridge.

Hondius, J. J. E. et al, eds. 1923– *Supplementum Epigraphicum Graecum.* Leiden.

Kassel, R., and C. Austin. 1989. *Poetae Comici Graeci.* Berlin.

Kock, T. 1884. *Comicorum Atticorum Fragmenta,* vol. 2. Leipzig.

Körte, A. 1957. *Menandri reliquiae.* Leipzig. Teubneri.

Lloyd-Jones, Hugh, and Peter Parsons. 1983. *Supplementum Hellenisticum.* Oxford.

Page, D. L. 1970. *Greek Literary Papyri*. Loeb Classical Library. Cambridge, Mass. (Originally published 1941)

Page, D. L. 1962 (rep. 1975). *Poetae Melici Graeci*. Oxford.

Pfeiffer, R. 1949–58. *Callimachus*, 2 vols. Oxford.

Pfuhl, Ernst, and Hans Möbius. 1977. *Die ostgriechischen Grabreliefs*. Vol. 1. Mainz.

Pollitt, J. J. 1986. *Art in the Hellenistic Age*. Cambridge.

———. 1990. *The Art of Greece: Sources and Documents*. Cambridge.

Pomeroy, Sarah B. 1977. "Technikai kai Mousikai: The Education of Women in the Fourth Century and in the Hellenistic Period." *American Journal of Ancient History* 2: 51–68.

———. 1984. *Women in Hellenistic Europe from Alexander to Cleopatra*. New York. (paperback ed., Detroit, 1989)

Ridgway, Brunilde S. 1990. *Hellenistic Sculpture*. Vol. 1. Madison, Wis.

Rist, Anna. 1978. *The Poems of Theocritus*. Chapel Hill, N.C.

Rose, H. G. *Hyginus Fabulae*.

Sandbach, F. H. 1972. *Menandri reliquiae selectae*. Oxford.

Skinner, Marilyn B. 1987. "Greek Women and the Matronymic." *Ancient History Bulletin* 1: 39–42.

———. 1991. "Nossis Thelyglossos." In *Women's History and Ancient History*, edited by Sarah B. Pomeroy, 20–47. Chapel Hill, N.C.

Smith, R. R. R. 1988. *Hellenistic Royal Portraits*. Oxford.

Snyder, Jane McIntosh. 1989. *The Woman and the Lyre: Women Writers in Classical Greece and Rome*. Carbondale, Ill.

Solmsen, Friedrich. 1979. *Isis among the Greeks and Romans*. Cambridge, Mass.

Thompson, Dorothy B. 1975. *Ptolemaic Oinochoai and Portraits in Faience*. Oxford.

Tracey, Stephen V., and Christian Habicht. 1991. "New and Old Panathenaic Victor Lists." *Hesperia* 60: 187–236.

Vedder, Ursula. 1988. "Frauentod—Kriegertod im Spiegel der attischen Grabkunst des 4. Jhs. V. Chr.," *Mitteilungen des Deutschen Archäologischen Instituts (Athens. Abt.)* Grabkunst 103: 161–91.

Wallace, W., and M. Wallace. 1941. *Asklepiades of Samos*. Oxford.

West, M. L. 1990. "Dating Corinna." *Classical Quarterly*, n.s. 40: 553–57.

Zanker, Paul. 1989. *Die trunkene Alte*. Munich.

FURTHER READING

Fantham, Elaine. 1975. "Sex, Status and Survival in Hellenistic Athens: A Study of Women in New Comedy." *Phoenix* 29: 44–74.

Fowler, Barbara Hughes. 1989. *The Hellenistic Aesthetic*. Madison, Wis.

Griffiths, Frederick T. 1981. "Home before Lunch: The Emancipated Woman in Theocritus." In *Reflections of Women in Antiquity*, edited by Helene P. Foley, 247–73. New York.

Onians, John. 1979. *Art and Thought in the Hellenistic Age*. London.

Thompson, Dorothy J. 1988. *Memphis under the Ptolemies*. Princeton, N.J.

6

EXCURSUS
MEDICINE:
THE "PROOF" OF ANATOMY

LESLEY DEAN-JONES

The medical texts of Greece and Rome span the period from the mid-fifth century B.C.E. to the last years of late antiquity, though some periods are better represented than others. Like the rest of Greco-Roman literature, these writings were overwhelmingly male-authored.[1] Unlike the majority of ancient literature, however, the gynecological material within the medical corpora would be derived from and aimed at a female audience. Of course, women's experience would be refracted through authors and practitioners who were male, but if the latter were to maintain a clientele of any size, they would have to work with images with which women themselves concurred. Thus, if only to a limited extent, the gynecological treatises of antiquity give us some access to women's perception of themselves.

Moreover, where individual women are mentioned in the medical texts, we catch a glimpse of events and circumstances of the daily life of women from all classes of society. In the Classical period a doctor was called in to attend the niece of a certain Temenes:

The niece of Temenes was asthmatic. The hypochondria seemed strained tight after a time. And if she had an infant, I do not know.
(*Epidemics* IV. 26; trans. Lesley Dean-Jones, from Littré 1962: 5:170)

Note that even when the patient died (as in this case) the physician avoided using her name and referred to her by her relationship to a man (see also Chapter 3, "Silenced Women"). This comment is interesting in that while the author thought it possible that the woman (probably a young unmarried girl as she is not referred to as somebody's wife) could have given birth, he forbore to ask, though this information would surely have been relevant to his treatment of the case. He apparently believed that a family might want to conceal the fact that a woman had borne a child, rather than selling her into slavery (see Chapter 3) and tried to work within a delicate situation.

Another incidental remark made by an author challenges the notion that, except for a few clearly defined occasions (see Chapters 1 and 3) unmarried girls were kept secluded until marriage at a young age.

The beautiful maiden daughter of Nerios, twenty years of age, was struck on the front of the head with the flat of the hand by a young female friend while they were playing.[2] Upon this she became blind and breathless, and when she got home she immediately developed a fever, her head ached and she was red around the face.

(*Epidemics* V 50; trans. Lesley Dean-Jones, from Littré 1962: 5:236)

Ancient medical texts, therefore, can be a rich source for women's social history. The gynecological texts cover pathology, therapy, embryology, and obstetrics. For the purposes of this excursus, however, I will focus on the development of anatomical and physiological theory, suggesting how, in different periods, the dominant medical image of women reflected contemporary conceptions of female nature and women's role in society. This will bind the excursus together as a coherent unity since most of Herophilus's extant fragments concerning women are anatomical in nature, and he forms an essential bridge between the medical writings of the Greek and the Roman periods.

The Hippocratics

The Hippocratic Corpus is the name given to a collection of sixty to seventy medical treatises (many more would have been available in antiquity) written by several anonymous doctors from different parts of the Greek world in the fifth and fourth centuries B.C.E. Because of this diversity of authorship, the corpus does not display any unanimity of doctrine, but in theories concerning women a dominant model can be identified. Eleven of the treatises are specifically gynecological, but women are also mentioned in the general works of the corpus, and in the seven books of the *Epidemics* (a collection of case histories) one-third of the patients discussed are female.

During the Classical period the artistically ideal proportions for the female body were markedly masculine (see Chapter 2; cf. Fig. 3.26). The medical opinion of the time, however, suggests that it was just as difficult for ordinary women of the period to meet these ideal proportions as it is for average women today to mimic the supposed ideal of feminine beauty. One ancient doctor describes the difference between male and female flesh thus:

I say that a woman's flesh is more porous and softer than a man's: since this is so, the woman's body draws moisture both with more speed and in greater quantity from the belly than does the body of a man. For if anyone should set clean wool and a piece of cloth which is clean, thickly-woven, and equal in weight to the wool, over water or on top of a damp place for two days and nights, when he takes them off and weighs them, he will discover that the wool is much heavier than the cloth. The reason this happens is that water in a wide-mouthed jar always escapes in an upward direction. Now the wool, on the one hand, because it is both porous and soft, receives more of the escaping water, while the cloth, because it is solid and thickly-woven, will be filled up, although it does not take on much of the escaping water. It is in this way, then, that a woman, because she is more porous, draws more moisture and draws it with greater speed from her belly to her body than does a man.

(*Hippocrates: Diseases of Women* I.1; Hanson 1975 572)

Another Hippocratic author describes a type of flesh similar to that of a woman's body in the glands of a man:

The nature of glands is spongy, and they are porous and fat, and there is no flesh like it in the rest of the body, nor anything else similar in the body, but they are of loose texture and have numerous veins. If you were to cut through one, it would bleed profusely. In appearance they are white and like phlegm, to the touch they are like wool. And if you knead a gland with your fingers and apply considerable force, it gives out an oily liquid and breaks into many pieces and is completely destroyed.

(*Glands* 1; trans. Lesley Dean-Jones, from Joly 1978: 13:114)

Whereas a man has flesh of this weak nature only in a few appropriate parts of his body, where it serves the specific function of absorbing excess moisture, a woman's whole physical being is constituted from such flesh. Those surface body parts thought to exhibit this glandular nature in men (that is, the breasts), are further pronounced in women:

The glands on the chest are called breasts and they fill out in those who produce milk, but not in those who do not produce milk. Women do produce milk and men do not. In women the nature of these glands is extremely porous, just like the rest of the body, and the nourishment which they draw to themselves they convert to milk . . . In men the denseness and compactness of the body contribute greatly to these glands not becoming large. For the male is firm and like close-woven cloth both to the sight and to the touch. But the female is porous and loose and like wool to the sight and touch, with the result that as a porous and soft thing she does not give up moisture, while the male does not absorb any, being compact and hard; moreover, labor strengthens his body so that he does not have anything from which he might take any excess fluid. This account demonstrates that of necessity both the chest and the breasts and the rest of a woman's body are loose and soft both on account of her inactivity and on account of what has been said. With men the opposite is the case.

(*Glands* 16; trans. Lesley Dean-Jones, from Joly 1978: 13:121–22)

The author did not believe the excessive porosity of a woman's body was due to nature alone (although, since it was a part of nature, it could never be completely eradicated), but also to the supposedly inactive lifestyle pursued by women. This point of view is shared by another Hippocratic author:

The males of all species are warmer and drier, and the females moister and colder, for the following reasons: originally each sex was born in such things and grows thereby, while after birth males use a more rigorous regimen, so that they are well warmed and dried, but females use a regimen that is moister and less strenuous, besides purging the heat out of their bodies every month.

(*Regimen* I.34; Jones 1979–84: 4:281)

Generally, then, contrary to the pictorial representations of women in the Classical period, the medical texts of the period describe a female body that is rounder, plumper, and softer than a male's. An exceptionally active woman (and many women would have had a more active life-style than that assumed by the medical texts; see Chapter 2, "The Education of Spartan Women;" Chapter 3, "Women's Work Outside the Home" and Figure 3.23) might minimize the amount of moisture her body soaked up, but it would still soak up some because of the nature of her flesh. The moisture that resulted from nourishment and that was used to build and maintain the body was blood. Consequently, women were thought to be constantly absorbing blood into their flesh. The blood was stored in the numerous passages of a woman's flesh until it was evacuated once a month as menstrual fluid. If a women conceived, the menstrual fluid was not evacuated but was drawn on steadily for nourishment by the developing fetus. The fetus itself was constituted when male and female seed intermingled in the woman's womb. A woman was thought to ejaculate semen directly into her womb when she reached orgasm during sexual intercourse, but despite the numerous therapies in the Hippocratic gynecology for causing women to conceive, there is no indication of how to bring about female orgasm other than the simple act of intercourse. One author advised:

The best time [for conception] is when the menstrual flow has stopped. It is especially during these days that one should see if [a woman] is able to conceive, for they are most successful [for fertility]. If she does not conceive straight away, and everything else is well with her, nothing stops her from going to her husband on other days, for the habit will excite her desire and cause her passages to open. If the ejaculate from the man runs together directly with that from the woman, she will conceive.

(*On Diseases of Women* I.17; trans. Lesley Dean-Jones from Littré 1962: 8:56)

Thus, even in a context that demanded female seed, the Hippocratics realized that the time of the month was more significant for conception. As the month progressed, the woman's passages would become congested with menstrual blood, making it difficult for the seed to be drawn together and ejaculated into the womb.

Greek men generally considered themselves more rational than women and this theory supplied them with anatomical "proof" that by their nature women were predisposed to irrationality. Within the body the passages to the breasts were particularly important in explanations of madness.

There is a thick vein in each breast. These contain the greatest portion of intelligence. . . . In one who is about to go mad the following is a warning indication: blood collects in the breasts.

> (*Epidemics* II. vi. 19 and 32; trans. Lesley Dean-Jones, Littré 1962: 5:136 and 138)

Since women would always be susceptible to an accumulation of blood in their breasts, this could be taken to account for the supposedly erratic behavior of women, much as culturally stereotyped female behavior today is attributed by some to female hormones.

In a healthy woman, the blood was evacuated from the body once a month through the womb, which actively drew the blood to itself through the passages that led to it and discharged it through the vagina. This process caused most women considerable discomfort, if not actual pain, especially if the passages of the body were still narrow due to the fact that they had not been broken down by the copious lochial flow that takes place after giving birth. However, it was even worse for a woman if menstruation did not take place, for then the menses could flow out of her womb back through her body via the passages and accumulate in various sites, causing a variety of illnesses. Often the accumulation of menstrual blood manifested itself not in a physical illness but in aberrant behavior. Virgins whose cervix had not yet been opened by the warmth, friction, and moisture of sexual intercourse were apt to try to hang themselves and jump down wells because of the blood that accumulated around their hearts. This reflects the cultural association of female puberty with both marriage and death. Further evidence of the power of menstrual blood to affect the mind is shown in the case histories of two women suffering similar symptoms. Both suffered some mental derangement, as evidenced by rambling and the uttering of obscenities—a feature of some female rituals (see Chapter 3, "Civic Religion"). One woman is cured when menstruation takes place; the other never menstruates and dies.

In Thasos a woman of gloomy temperament, after a grief with reason for it, without taking to bed, lost sleep and appetite and suffered thirst and nausea. She lived near the place of Pylades on the plain.

First day. As night began there were fears, much rambling, depression and slight feverishness. Early in the morning frequent convulsions; whenever these frequent convulsions intermitted, she wandered and uttered obscenities; many pains, severe and continuous.

Second day. Same symptoms; no sleep; fever more acute.

Third day. The convulsions ceased, but were succeeded by coma and oppression, followed in turn by wakefulness. She would jump up; could not restrain herself; wandered a great deal; fever acute; on this night a copious, hot sweating all over; no fever; slept, was perfectly rational, and had a crisis.[3] About the third day urine black and thin, with particles mostly round floating in it, which did not settle. Near the crisis copious menstruation.

In Thasos the wife of Delearces, who lay sick on the plain, was seized after a grief with an acute fever with shivering. From the beginning she would wrap herself up, and throughout, without speaking a word, she would fumble, pluck, scratch, pick hairs, weep and then laugh, but she did not sleep; though stimulated the bowels passed nothing. She drank a little when the attendants suggested it. Urine thin and scanty; fever slight to the touch; coldness of the extremities.

Ninth day. Much wandering followed by return to reason; silent.

Fourteenth day. Respiration rare and large with long intervals, becoming afterwards short.

Seventeenth day. Bowels under a stimulus passed disordered matters, then her very drink passed unchanged; nothing coagulated. The patient noticed nothing; the skin tense and dry.

Twentieth day. Much rambling followed by recovery of reason; speechless; respiration short.

Twenty-first day. Death.

The respiration of this patient throughout was rare and large; took no notice of anything; she constantly wrapped herself up; either much rambling or silence throughout.

(*Epidemics* III.17, cases 11 and 15; Jones 1979–84: 1:277, 283–85)

In Hippocratic theory the physical differences between men and women accounted for women's physical and mental inferiority to men. However, that women menstruated meant that they had a self-regulating purging mechanism which prevented them falling as seriously ill or being afflicted with life-threatening diseases as readily as men. To this extent the Hippocratics viewed menstruation as a good thing for all women, and in fact may have tried to emulate it by venesection and other forms of purging in men.

Though many women fell ill, they were fewer than the men and less frequently died. But the great majority had difficult childbirth and after giving birth they would fall ill and these especially died, as did the daughter of Telebulus on the sixth day after delivery. Now menstruation appeared during the fevers in most cases, and with many maidens it occurred then for the first time. Some bled from the nose.[4] Sometimes both epistaxis and menstruation appeared together; for example, the maiden daughter of Daitharses had her first menstruation during fever and also a violent discharge from the nose. I know of no woman who died if any of these symptoms showed themselves properly, but all to my knowledge had abortions if they chanced to fall ill when with child.

(*Epidemics* I.16; Jones 1979–84: 1:171)

Another aspect of female anatomy that was seen as a threat to female health and a cause of erratic behavior was her womb. The Hippocratics believed that if a woman's womb became too dry and light because she was not having enough intercourse, the womb could be attracted to the moister organs of her body—her liver, heart, brain, diaphragm, or bladder. If it settled on any of the first four of these a woman could become voiceless, lose consciousness, or exhibit any of those symptoms we designate by the word "hysteria."[5]

If suffocation occurs suddenly, it will happen especially to women who do not have intercourse and to older women rather than to young ones, for their wombs are lighter. It usually occurs because of the following: when a woman is empty and works harder than in her previous experience, her womb, becoming heated from the hard work, turns because it is empty and light. There is, in fact, empty space for it to turn in because the belly is empty. Now when the womb turns, it hits the liver and they go together and strike against the abdomen—for the womb rushes and goes upward towards the moisture, because it has been dried out by hard work, and the liver is, after all, moist. When the womb hits the liver, it produces sudden suffocation as it occupies the breathing passages around the belly.

Sometimes, at the same time the womb begins to go toward the liver, phlegm flows down from the head to the abdomen (that is, when the woman is experiencing the suffocation) and sometimes, simultaneously with the flow of phlegm, the womb goes away from the liver to its normal place and the suffocation ceases. The womb goes back, then, when it has taken on moisture and has become heavy. . . . Sometimes, if a woman is empty and she overworks, her womb turns and falls toward the neck of her bladder and produces strangury—but no other malady seizes her. When such a woman is treated she speedily becomes healthy; sometimes recovery is even spontaneous.

In some women the womb falls towards the lower back or towards the hips because of hard work or lack of food, and produces pain.

(Hippocrates: Diseases of Women I.7; Hanson 1975: 576)

If the womb did not return to its proper place spontaneously there were various measures a doctor could follow to draw it back. One of the most common was to use sweet and foul-smelling substances at either end of a woman—sweet to entice the womb in the direction it should go, foul to drive it from the place where it had lodged.

Whenever the womb falls against the hypochondria, it causes suffocation. When in this case the crisis of the disease occurs, hot and bitter vomiting seizes the patient, and though she gets better for a short time, then piercing pain seizes her head and throat. Apply fomentations, if the suffocation is in the upper part of the body. Under the nose burn foul-smelling substances gradually, for if they are burned en masse the womb is displaced to the lower parts of the body and trouble follows. Burn sweet-smelling substances below the woman. And give her castor and fleabane to drink. When the womb is drawn down the body, fumigate the woman from beneath with putrid substances and burn sweet-smelling substances under her nose.

(On Diseases of Women II.125; trans. Lesley Dean-Jones
from Littré 1962: 8:268)

There were other more mechanical means of treating a womb that had become displaced (such as bandaging a woman tightly beneath her breasts and applying pressure to the offending organ if it moved up the body, or hanging a woman upside-down on a ladder if it prolapsed) but the apparent favor in which odor-therapies were held suggests that the womb itself was thought to be endowed with some sense of smell. Accordingly, the Hippocratics conceived of the female reproductive organ as an entity within a woman that had a consciousness of its own beyond her control.

Aristotle

The philosopher Aristotle (384–322 B.C.E.) was a contemporary of some of the later Hippocratics and disputed their understanding of the female body. He was not a doctor, but took a particular interest in natural history. As a result, he was less concerned with pathology than were the Hippocratics and used his researches (including dissections) on other animals for comparative purposes and to supplement his knowledge of the human body. His theories and observations pertaining to the female body are recorded primarily in his major biological treatises.

Aristotle differed from the Hippocratics in seeing a closer resemblance between the bodies of men and women. He believed the difference between the two sexes lay simply in the amount of heat in their bodies. The hotter a body was the more it could "concoct" the food it ate into blood, and the easier it could convert this blood into flesh, hair, nails, etc., and perfect its form. Aristotle believed that the male was demonstrably more perfect than the female in almost all species.

As a general rule, in red-blooded animals furnished with feet and not oviparous, the male is larger and longer-lived than the female. . . . Furthermore, in all animals the upper and front parts are better, stronger and more thoroughly equipped in the male than in the female, whereas in the female those parts are the better that may be termed hinder-parts or underparts. And this statement is applicable to man and to all vivipara that have feet. Again, the female is less muscular and less compactly jointed, and more thin and delicate in the hair—that is, where hair is found; and where there is no hair, less strongly furnished in some analogous substance. And the female is more moist of flesh, and more knock-kneed, and the shin-bones are thinner; and the feet are more arched and hollow in such animals as are furnished with feet. And with regard to voice, the female in all animals that are vocal has a thinner and sharper voice than the male; except, by the way, with kine, for the lowing and bellowing of the cow has a deeper note than that of the bull. With regard to organs of defence and offence, such as teeth, tusks, horns, spurs, and the like, these in some species the male possesses and the female does not; as, for instance, the hind has no horns and where the cock-bird has a spur the hen is entirely destitute of the organ; and in like manner the sow is devoid of tusks. In other species such organs are found in both sexes, but are more perfectly developed in the male; as, for instance, the horn of the bull is more powerful than the horn of the cow.
     (*History of Animals* 538a22–24 and 538b1–25; Thompson 1984: 1:851)

Aristotle believed male upper-body strength is relevant because it mirrors the disposition of the natural order of the universe in which more honorable objects are placed above and before those things less worthy of honor. Of the two sexes, then, the male was the more perfect representative of any species and as such was also the hotter.

As a more perfect animal would use up most of its nourishment in building a bigger, stronger, better equipped body, it would have less left over to be further concocted into seminal residue. Its greater amount of heat working on this smaller amount of material could produce a very potent hot fluid, so hot that it was capable of passing on the form of the animal into a new individual. This ability to pass on its form to another is what made an animal "complete." In humans a man was complete when he could concoct white hot semen. A woman's cooler body could only concoct blood into menstrual fluid, which remained bloody in appearance, though it was capable of carrying more of the human soul than ordinary blood.[6] Because of her incapacity to fully concoct blood to the point it could carry the soul of a new individual, Aristotle termed woman a "deformed man."

> Just as it sometimes happens that deformed offspring are produced by deformed parents, and sometimes not, so the offspring produced by a female are sometimes female, sometimes not, but male. The reason is that the female is as it were a deformed male.
>
> (*Generation of Animals* 737a25–28; Peck 1979: 175)

Aristotle did not mean that women were deformed because of their physical appearance. The aspect in which they were "deformed" (vital heat) had far-reaching effects because it was the very principle of generation. It was because of this "deformity" that women were weaker; their weakness was not, in itself, their deformity.

The most important physical result of a woman's lesser heat and her inability to concoct her seminal residue was the menstrual flow. Unlike the Hippocratics, Aristotle did not think menstruation was beneficial for all women. For some women it could seriously weaken the body.

> After puberty some lads who were thin before grow stout and healthy, and the converse also happens; and the same is equally true of girls. For when in boy or girl the body is loaded with superfluous matter, then, when such superfluities are got rid of in the spermatic or menstrual discharge, their bodies improve in health and condition owing to the removal of what had acted as an impediment to health and proper nutrition; but in such as are of opposite habit their bodies become emaciated and out of health, for then the spermatic discharge in the one case and the menstrual flow in the other take place at the cost of natural healthy conditions.
>
> (*History of Animals* 581b26–582a5; Thompson 1984: 911)

In fact, Aristotle viewed menstruation as a distressing time for all women.

> With those in whom the ailment [that is, menstruation] lasts but a little while, two days or three, recovery is easy; but where the duration is longer, the ailment is more troublesome. For women are ailing during these days; and sometimes the discharge is sudden and sometimes gradual, but in all cases alike there is bodily distress until the attack be over.
>
> (*History of Animals* 582b5–9; Thompson 1984: 912)

Moreover, Aristotle thought that the human female was smaller and weaker than the human male to a degree not observable in other animals because in women a comparatively larger amount of their nourishment was directed to their seminal residue than to building their own bodies. Here Aristotle is confusing menstruation and the estrus discharge of other mammals, which is much smaller in volume.

The discharge is wont to be more abundant in women than in the females of any other animals . . . in such animals the females are sometimes larger than the males.

(*History of Animals* 582b29–33; Thompson 1984: 913)

The lack of vital heat meant that a woman could not exhibit the perfect human form in the intellectual arena either. She could not perfect the supremely human faculty of deliberation, and so she remained naturally subject to men as ruled to ruler (see Chapter 3, "Ancient Critical Reactions to Women's Roles in Classical Athens"). Elsewhere Aristotle lists traits that are typical of male and female.

In all cases, excepting those of the bear and leopard, the female is less spirited than the male; in regard to the two exceptional cases, the superiority in courage rests with the female. With all other animals the female is softer in disposition, is more mischievous, less simple, more impulsive, and more attentive to the nurture of the young; the male, on the other hand, is more spirited, more savage, more simple and less cunning. The traces of these characters are more or less visible everywhere, but they are especially visible where character is more developed, and most of all in man.

The fact is, the nature of man is the most rounded off and complete and consequently in man the qualities above referred to are found most clearly. Hence woman is more compassionate than man, more easily moved to tears, at the same time is more jealous, more querulous, more apt to scold and to strike. She is, furthermore, more prone to despondency and less hopeful than the man, more void of shame, more false of speech, more deceptive, and of more retentive memory. She is also more wakeful, more shrinking, more difficult to rouse to action and requires a smaller quantity of nutriment.

As was previously stated, the male is more courageous than the female, and more sympathetic in the way of standing by to help. Even in the case of cephalopods, when the cuttlefish is struck with the trident the male stands by to help the female; but when the male is struck the female runs away.

(*History of Animals* 608a32–b19; Thompson 1984: 773–75)

Thus, not only did the lack of heat cause women to be weaker and less intelligent than men, but it also resulted in those negative personality traits associated with women since the Archaic period.

A body that was going to be able to concoct semen developed testicles, spermatic passages, and a penis. A body that would only be able to concoct blood into menstrual fluid developed a womb and a vagina.

Now male and female differ in respect of their *logos*, in that the power or faculty possessed by the one differs from that possessed by the other; but they differ also to bodily sense, in respect of certain physical parts. They differ in their *logos,* because the male is that which has the power to generate in another (as was stated above), while the female is that which can generate in itself, i.e., it is that out of which the generated offspring, which is present in the generator, comes into being. Very well, then: they are distinguished in respect of their faculty, and this entails a certain function. Now for the exercise of every function instruments are needed, and the instruments for physical faculties are the parts of the body. Hence it is necessary that, for the purpose of copulation and procreation, certain parts should exist, parts that are different from each other, in respect of which the male will differ from the female; for although male and female are indeed used as epithets of the whole animal, it is not male or female in respect of the whole of itself, but only in respect of a particular faculty and a particular part—just as it is "seeing" and "walking" in respect of certain parts—and this part is one which is evident to the senses. Now in the female this special part is what is called the uterus, and in the male the regions about the testes and the penis.

(*Generation of Animals* 716a18–34; Peck 1979: 11–13)

Although uterus and penis were different organs fulfilling different functions, the complementary nature of their roles led to a certain similarity of formation.

The uterus is always double without exception, just as in males there are always two testes without exception. . . . Now in males the seminal passages must have a fixed position and not stray about, and the same is true of the uterus in females.

(*Generation of Animals* 716b32–33 and 720a12–14; Peck 1979: 17 and 41)

Obviously, here Aristotle is challenging the Hippocratic conception of a mobile womb. The belief that the womb was "double" (that is, contained two compartments) was generally accepted throughout antiquity and was often cited to explain the occurrence of twins. This image may have developed from some rudimentary knowledge of the Fallopian tubes (particularly as the compartments are often referred to as "horns"), but neither Aristotle nor any author before Herophilus describes the Fallopian tubes per se. It is possible, however, that Aristotle observed ovaries in pigs.

The ovaries of sows are excised with the view of quenching in them sexual appetites and of stimulating fatness. The sow has first to be kept two days without food, and, after being hung up by the hind legs, it is operated on; they cut the lower belly, about the place where the boars have their testicles, for it is there that the ovary grows, adhering to the two divisions of the womb; they cut off a little piece and stitch up the incision. Female camels are mutilated when they are wanted for war purposes, and are mutilated to prevent their being got with young.

(*History of Animals* 632a21–28; Thompson 1984: 982)

The result of removing the ovaries might lead one to expect that Aristotle would develop a theory of some parallelism between the function of these female organs and the male testicles, but in Aristotle's philosophy this was impossible. The testicles were involved in the production of semen, which by definition women were incapable of producing. The fact that the Greek word translated as "ovaries" is a singular term (ka-pria) indicates that, if it indeed designates the ovaries, their duality was not considered significant; that is, they were not generally looked upon as analogous to testicles, which were often designated by the term "twins" *(didymi)*.

So, while Aristotle acknowledged that female bodies were much more similar to men's than the Hippocratics had allowed, the point at which male and female diverged—vital heat—had far-reaching conse-quences in the female that justified women's physical and intellectual subordination to men.

Herophilus

Herophilus lived and worked at Alexandria at the end of the fourth and the beginning of the third century B.C.E. Unlike any of his predecessors, or successors until the late thirteenth century C.E., Herophilus was able to dissect the human body. We know from various testimony that he was particularly interested in gynecological matters, but we do not have the same extensive works for him as we do for the Hippocratics and Aris-totle. What has survived is chiefly fragmented quotations on specific contentious issues in antiquity, and most of those dealing with women are anatomical in nature.

Although, as a physician, he considered himself to be following in the tradition of Hippocrates, where the difference between male and fe-male was concerned he accepted Aristotle's theory that the significant fact was that males possessed greater heat. Even the womb, the defini-tively female organ, was formed from the same materials as the rest of the human body and was subject to the same principles of health and disease.

And in his *Midwifery* Herophilus says that the uterus is woven from the same thing as the other parts, is regulated by the same faculties, has the same mate-rial substances at hand, and is caused to be diseased by the same things, such as excessive quantity, thickness, and disharmony in similars. Accordingly, says Herophilus, there is no affection peculiar to women, except conceiving, nourish-ing what has been conceived, giving birth, "ripening" the milk, and the oppo-sites of these.

(Soranus, *Gynecology* III.3; von Staden 1989: 365)

Moreover, like Aristotle, he observed a certain parallelism between the male and female reproductive tract. The parallelism he noted, however, far exceeds anything described by Aristotle.

In females the two "testicles" [that is, ovaries] are attached to each of the two shoulders of the uterus, one on the right, the other on the left, not both in a single scrotum but each of the two separate, enclosed in a thin membranous skin. They are small and rather flat, like glands, sinewy at their surrounding covering, but easily damageable in their flesh, just like the testicles of males. In mares they are also quite sizeable. And they are attached to the uterus with no small number of membranes and with a vein and an artery implanted from the uterus into these "testicles." You see, the attachment is from the vein and the artery that go to each of the two "testicles," a vein from the vein and an artery from the artery.

The spermatic duct [that is, Fallopian tube] from each "testicle" is not very apparent, but it is attached to the uterus from the outside, one duct from the right, the other from the left. Like the seminal duct of the male, its anterior part is also convoluted, and almost all the rest up to its end looks varicose. And the spermatic duct from each "testicle" grows into the fleshy part of the neck of the bladder, just like the male duct, being thin and winding in its anterior part where it touches the hipbones. Here [at the neck of the bladder] it also terminates, like the pudendum penetrating to the interior from either side.

(Galen, *On the Seed* II.1; von Staden 1989: 185–86)

Herophilus thus recognized organs in the female analogous to testicles in the male, and that there were ducts leading from these organs. But although he describes the ducts as being attached to the uterus, they empty out (as do the male ducts, which discharge their seed into the penis for ejaculation) into the neck of the bladder, whence the female seed will be voided from the body. Following a theory articulated by Apollo in Aeschylus' *Eumenides* (see Chapter 4) and established as the medical norm by Aristotle, Herophilus believed that a woman's only contribution to reproduction was the menstrual fluid, so female seed was unnecessary for conception; it therefore had to be diverted past the uterus. Unfortunately, we do not know what function, if any, Herophilus believed female seed fulfilled.

Herophilus's view on menstruation was also much closer to Aristotle's than to the Hippocratics'. In fact, whereas the Hippocratics believed the onset of menstruation was invariably a cure for any disease a woman was suffering, Herophilus believed it could make a woman susceptible to falling ill.

Herophilus, however, says that at certain times and for certain women, menstruation is harmful. Some women, he says, are actually in a state of unimpeded health when they are not menstruating, whereas the opposite often happens while they are menstruating: they become paler and thinner and contract the beginnings of diseases. At other times, however, and in certain cases, menstruation is beneficial, so that women who previously were wan and emaciated, later, after menstruation, have good colour and are well nourished.

(Soranus, *Gynecology* I.29; von Staden 1989: 374)

By the Hellenistic period, then, the bodies of women were considered far more analogous to the bodies of men than they had been in the Classical period, which may have bolstered the increased autonomy many women enjoyed in affairs that had traditionally been reserved for men (see Chapter 5, "Women in Public"). But this assimilation of the interior space of the two sexes contrasts sharply with the development in the artistic representation of the female, which in the Hellenistic period began to diverge from the masculinized proportions of the Classical era (see Chapter 5, Figs. 5.16 and 5.17).

Soranus

Herophilus was extremely influential on succeeding generations of physicians, particularly in descriptions and understandings of the female reproductive system. He had written a practical manual for midwives (incidentally indicating that he expected at least some of them to be able to read and that he viewed them as colleagues rather than as rivals[7]) and in this he was followed by the Greek doctor Soranus, who lived at Rome at the beginning of the second century c.e. The confidence Soranus placed in midwives is shown in his discussion of what makes the best midwives.

It is necessary to tell what makes the best midwives, so that on the one hand the best may recognize themselves, and on the other hand beginners may look upon them as models, and the public in time of need may know whom to summon. Now generally speaking we call a midwife faultless if she merely carries out her medical task; whereas we call her the best midwife if she goes further and in addition to her management of cases is well versed in theory. And more particularly, we call a person the best midwife if she is trained in all branches of therapy (for some cases must be treated by diet, others by surgery, while still others must be cured by drugs); if she is moreover able to prescribe hygienic regulations for her patients, to observe the general and the individual features of the case, and from this to find out what is expedient, not from the causes or from the repeated observations of what usually occurs or something of the kind. . . . And it is not absolutely essential for her to have borne children, as some people contend, in order that she may sympathize with the mother because of her experience of pain; for ⟨to have sympathy⟩ is ⟨not⟩ more characteristic of a person who has given birth to a child.

(*Gynecology* I.4; Temkin 1956: 6)

Soranus, therefore, seems to imagine midwives performing much the same service as a doctor would, with some education in theory and with the same capacity for intelligent observation and decision making.

Soranus himself had never dissected a human body (and is, indeed, rather dismissive of the benefits to be gained from it), but he follows Herophilus's description of the disposition of the ovaries, uterus and "spermatic ducts." However, he goes a little further in likening the cervix and vagina to the penis and the prepuce, again, basing his description on analogy with the male.

Furthermore, the "testicles" are attached to the outside of the uterus, near its isthmus, one on each side. They are of loose texture, and like glands are covered by a particular membrane. Their shape is not longish as in the males; rather they are slightly flattened, rounded and a little broadened at the base. The spermatic duct runs from the uterus through each "testicle" and extending along the sides of the uterus as far as the bladder, is implanted in its neck.

Therefore, the female seed seems not to be drawn upon in generation since it is excreted externally. . . . [The vagina] is a sinewy membrane, almost as round as the intestine, comparatively wide inside, comparatively narrow at the external end; and it is in the vagina that intercourse takes place. The inner part of the vagina grows around the neck of the uterus like the prepuce in males around the glans.

(*Gynecology* I.12 and 16; Temkin 1956: 11–12, 14)

Although, like Herophilus, Soranus does not believe the female semen ever enters the womb and contributes to conception, he does give us an explanation of the significance of women becoming excited during intercourse and releasing their fluid.

Just as without appetite it is impossible for the seed to be discharged by the male, in the same manner, without appetite it cannot be conceived by the female. And as food swallowed without appetite and some aversion is not well received and fails in its subsequent digestion, neither can the seed be taken up or, if grasped, be carried through pregnancy, unless urge and appetite for intercourse have been present. For even if some women who were forced to have intercourse have conceived, one may say with reference to them that in any event the emotion of sexual appetite existed in them too, but was obscured by mental resolve. . . .

As movement of the whole body is wont to provoke sweating, whereas lack of motion holds it back and prevents it, and as the performance of the vocal function stimulates to an increased excretion the saliva which by nature accompanies the passage of the breath—in the same way, during intercourse the associated movement around the female genitals relaxes the whole body. And for this reason it also relaxes the uterus.

(*Gynecology* I.37 and 31; Temkin 1956: 36, 28)

As far as a material contribution to conception was concerned, however, Soranus concurred in the theory of Aristotle and Herophilus that the only thing a woman contributed was her menstrual fluid. Indeed, he advises prospective bridegrooms to inquire into a woman's menstrual flow, among other things, before marrying her.

Since women usually are married for the sake of children and succession, and not for mere enjoyment, and since it is utterly absurd to make inquiries about the excellence of their lineage and the abundance of their means but to leave unexamined whether they can conceive or not, and whether they are fit for childbearing or not, it is only right for us to give an account of the matter in question. One must judge the majority from the ages of 15 to 40 to be fit for conception, if they are not mannish, compact and oversturdy, or too flabby and very moist. . . . Furthermore they seem fit if their uteri are neither very moist or dry, not too lax or constricted, and if they have their catharsis regularly, not through some moisture or ichors of various kinds, but through blood and of this neither too much, nor, on the other hand, extremely little. Also those in whom the orifice of the uterus is comparatively far forward and lies in a straight line.

(*Gynecology* I.34; Temkin 1956: 32)

It is difficult to imagine many bridegrooms seeking such information from the family of a young girl. Presumably, in cases where he did, an independent expert, probably a midwife, would have to be engaged to examine the woman.

Soranus did not believe menstruation served any useful purpose beyond procreation. In this he went beyond Herophilus who had thought it beneficial for some women.

In regard to health menstruation is harmful to all, although it affects delicate persons more, whereas its harmfulness is entirely hidden in those who possess a resistant body. Now, we observe that the majority of those not menstruating are rather robust, like mannish and sterile women. And the fact that they do not menstruate any more does not affect the health of women past their prime, nay on the contrary, the drawing off of blood makes the majority more delicate. Besides, virgins not yet menstruating would necessarily be less healthy; if, on the other hand, they enjoy perfect health, menstruation, consequently, does not contribute to their health, but is useful for childbearing only; for conception does not take place without menstruation.

(*Gynecology* I.29; Temkin 1956: 26–27)

It is interesting to note that in some sense Soranus considers sterile women to be healthier than those who can bear children. He admits that if menses are impeded they cause disease, but he claims it is the impediment that has to be treated. Simply bringing on the menses will not cure a woman, nor keep her healthy. He does not, however, go so far as some other "persons of distinction" who contended that menstruation is purely pathological, resulting from an ulcerated uterus.

Menstruation does not occur because the uterus is ulcerated, rather it occurs through diapedesis and profuse perspiration, in the same manner in which the gums too, when rubbed, emit blood without ulceration and as in fractures without wounds we find the bandages bathed in blood when the dressing is changed.

(*Gynecology* I.28; Temkin 1956: 25)

The lessening of the importance of menstruation in defining what it was to be a woman, to the point where some thought it was the pathological product of an ulcerated womb, may go some way to explaining the increased awe and disgust in which menstruation seems to be held in the Roman period. A person could now be a healthy woman without menstruating (though she might be sterile). In some ways this could make the regular monthly appearance of blood seem inexplicable and frightening. Pliny, a nonmedical encyclopedist of the first century C.E., says there is nothing more remarkable than the periodic bleeding of women, and he lists among its attributes the capability of withering plants, stopping hail, killing caterpillars, removing bitumen, dimming mirrors, blunting knives, souring wine, drying up seeds, and driving dogs mad. His description of the effects of menstrual blood was used by the Inquisition during the Renaissance to identify witches.

Like Herophilus, Soranus does not indicate that he believed woman shared any particular behavioral characteristics because they shared anatomy, and although he believes they share "conditions" that can be termed gynecological, these are restricted to their reproductive tract. In other aspects their bodies are just like men's.

Now we say that there exist natural conditions in women peculiarly their own (as conception, parturition, and lactation if one wishes to call these functions conditions), whereas conditions contrary to nature are not generically different but only in a specific and particular way. For in regard to generic differences, the female has her illness in common with the male, she suffers from constriction or from flux, either acutely or chronically, and she is subject to the same seasonal differences, to gradations of disease, to lack of strength, and to the different foreign bodies, sores, and injuries. Only as far as particulars and specific variations are concerned does the female show conditions peculiarly her own, i.e. a different character of symptoms. Therefore she is subject to treatment generically the same.

(*Gynecology* III.5; Temkin 1956: 132)

Soranus believed all the illnesses in the body resulted from some part of the body being in either a constricted or a lax state. In therapy what was constricted had to be relaxed, what was lax had to be tightened. Relocation of the womb was not a possible source of disease. However, Soranus did believe that the womb was particularly susceptible to constriction, and he recognized the female disease "hysterical suffocation," connecting it with what were perceived as abnormalities in a woman's life.

Hysterical suffocation has been named after both the affected organ and one symptom, viz. suffocation. But its connotation is: obstructed respiration together with aphonia and a seizure of the senses caused by some condition of the uterus. In most cases the disease is preceded by recurrent miscarriages, premature birth, long widowhood, retention of menses and the end of ordinary childbearing or inflation of the uterus. . . . The hysterical disease, on account of the aphonia and seizure of the senses, is related to epilepsy, apoplexy, catalepsy, lethargy and the aphonia caused by worms. . . . The majority of the ancients and almost all followers of other sects have made use of ill-smelling odors (such as burnt hair, extinguished lamp wicks, charred deer's horn, burnt wool, burnt flock, skins and rags, castoreum with which they anoint the nose and ears, pitch, cedar resin, bitumen, squashed bed bugs, and all substances which are supposed to have an oppressive smell) in the opinion that the uterus flees from evil smells. Wherefore they have also fumigated with fragrant substances from below, and have approved of suppositories of spikenard (and) storax, so that the uterus fleeing the first mentioned odors, but pursuing the last-mentioned might move from the upper to the lower parts. . . . We, however, censure all these men who start by hurting the inflamed parts and cause torpor by the effluvia of ill-smelling substances. For the uterus does not issue forth like a wild animal from the lair, delighted by fragrant odors and fleeing bad odors; rather it is drawn together because of the stricture caused by the inflammation.

(*Gynecology* III.26 and 29; Temkin 1956: 149, 152, 153)

Aretaeus

Like Soranus and Galen, Aretaeus the Cappadocian, as his epithet suggests, was born in the eastern Empire, and like the two more famous physicians, Aretaeus probably made his name at Rome. We are not sure when he lived, but neither does he mention Galen (which due to Galen's enormous authority any medical writer coming after him was almost obligated to do) nor does Galen mention him, though he mentions by name virtually every earlier medical writer with whose theories he disagrees. It is generally assumed, therefore, that the two were close contemporaries and as such did not refer to each other's work in what seems to have been a convention of the time. This would place Aretaeus in the second century C.E. Aretaeus's extant works focus on specific acute and chronic diseases and the corresponding therapies. In discussing "hysterical suffocation," Aretaeus goes further than any previous medical writer in animating the womb.

In the middle of the flanks of women lies the womb, a female viscus, closely resembling an animal; for it is moved of itself hither and thither in the flanks, also upwards in a direct line to below the cartilage of the thorax, and also obliquely to the right or to the left, either to the liver or spleen; and it likewise is subject to prolapsus downwards, and, in a word, it is altogether erratic. It delights, also, in fragrant smells, and advances towards them; and it has an aversion to fetid smells, and flees from them; and, on the whole, the womb is like an animal within an animal. . . . The affection occurs in young women, but not in old. For in those in whom the age, mode of life, and understanding is more mobile, the uterus also is of a wandering nature; but in those more advanced in life, the age, mode of living, understanding, and the uterus are of a steady character. Wherefore this suffocation from the womb accompanies females alone.

   The uterus in women has membranes extended on both sides at the flanks, and also is subject to the affections of an animal in smelling; for it follows after fragrant things as if for pleasure, and flees from fetid and disagreeable things as if for dislike. If, therefore, anything annoy it from above, it protrudes even beyond the genital organs. But if any of these things be applied to the os, it retreats backwards and upwards. Sometimes it will go to this side or that—to the spleen and liver, while the membranes yield to the distention and contraction like the sails of a ship.
   (*On the Causes and Symptoms of Acute Diseases* II.11 and *Therapeutics of Acute Diseases* II.10; Adams 1972: 285–87 and 449)

Here we can see how ingrained was the belief that female anatomy caused stereotypical irrational female behavior in that a physician who accepted the anatomical discovery of the membranes holding the womb in place still blamed the willful movements of that organ for producing erratic behavior in women.

Galen

The most authoritative individual medical author in antiquity, and into the Renaissance, was Galen, a native of Pergamum who was active in Rome from the mid- to the late second century C.E. He was an extremely prolific writer, but he did not concern himself particularly with gynecological matters, perhaps because he believed that male and female bodies could be viewed as the same for all but reproductive purposes. He went even further than Soranus in assimilating male and female genitalia.

The female is less perfect than the male for one, principal reason—because she is colder; for if among animals the warm one is the more active, a colder animal would be less perfect than a warmer. A second reason is one that appears in dissecting . . .
    All the parts, then, that men have, women have too, the difference between them lying in only one thing, namely, that in women the parts are within [the body] whereas in men they are outside, in the region called the perineum. Consider first whichever ones you please, turn outward the woman's, turn inward, so to speak, and fold double the man's, and you will find them the same in both in every respect. Then think first, please, of the man's turned in and extending inward between the rectum and the bladder. If this should happen, the scrotum would necessarily take the place of the uteri, with the testes lying outside, next to it on either side; the penis of the male would become the neck of the cavity that had been formed; and the skin at the end of the penis, now called the prepuce, would become the female pudendum [vagina] itself. Think, too, please, of the converse, the uterus turned outward and projecting. Would not the "testicles" then necessarily be inside it? Would it not contain them like a scrotum? Would not the neck [the cervix], hitherto concealed inside the perineum but now pendent, be made into the male member? And would not the female pudendum, being a skinlike growth upon this neck, be changed into the part called the prepuce? It is also clear that in consequence the position of the arteries, veins, and spermatic vessels would be changed too. In fact, you could not find a single male part left over that had not simply changed its position; for the parts that are inside in woman are outside in man. You can see something like this in the eyes of the mole, which have vitreous and crystalline humors and the tunics that surround these and grow out from the meninges, as I have said, and they have these just as much as animals do that make use of their eyes. The mole's eyes, however, do not open, nor do they project but are left there imperfect and remain like the eyes of other animals when these are still in the uterus.
    (*On the Usefulness of the Parts of the Body* XIV.6; May 1968: 628–29)

It is clear from the analogy to the mole's eyes that Galen did not mean that the female genitalia were the male's "inside out." The scrotum and the penis had been translated upwards—hence the need to add the injunction to "fold double" the male's to produce the female organs. The reason women's genitalia remained inside their bodies was that they did not have sufficient heat to "perfect" them, that is, cause them to project from her body. In a sense, however, this lack of perfection was a piece of perfect planning on the part of nature, for it was only the position of the uterus that permitted human reproduction.

In the female [Nature] has located the uterus below the stomach, because she found that this place is best for sexual intercourse, for receiving the semen, and also for the growth of the fetus and its birth when it has been perfected. For you would not find any place in the whole body of the animal more suitable for any of these uses I have mentioned; it is best for coitus because it is far removed from the instruments of the face, most opportune for the growth of the fetus because it can be very greatly distended without pain, and most useful for birth because the fetus will emerge more easily if its exit is directed downward and is near the legs.

(*On the Usefulness of the Parts of the Body* XIV.3; May 1968: 622)

Near the beginning and the end of his career Galen wrote treatises on the anatomy of the uterus. He tells us that his earlier effort (which we no longer have, though the later treatise may be a reworked version) was written for midwives, showing that he, like Herophilus and Soranus, expected midwives to be educated, literate, and concerned with more than simply pragmatic knowledge about the female body. In describing the positioning of the womb within the body of the woman, Galen makes clear that he believes the relocation of the womb to any other part of the body is impossible. In fact, his description reads almost as if he is trying to hold a very slippery customer prisoner.

The uterus is fused with some [structures], attached to others, suspended from others; some entwine it, some support it; it is fused with the neck of the bladder and rectum at the vagina, as well as with the "testicles" and the spermatic ducts, but it may be said to be attached to the other parts of the bladder and the rectum, to be attached to and suspended from the sacred bone, but suspended only from the spinal marrow and lumbar muscles; both suspended from, fused with, and entwined with nerves; suspended from, fused with, interwoven, and entwined with arteries and veins.

(*On the Anatomy of the Uterus* 4; Goss 1962: 79)

This description may have been a direct challenge to the mobility attributed to the womb by Aretaeus. However, although Galen had imprisoned the womb so tightly, he still believed women were susceptible to exhibiting "hysterical" symptoms and still blamed it on a deprivation of intercourse, which lack adversely affected a woman's reproductive system.

It is generally agreed upon that this disease [that is, "hysterical suffocation"] mostly affects widows, and particularly those who have previously menstruated regularly, had been pregnant and were eager to have intercourse, but were now deprived of all this. Is there a more likely conclusion from these facts than that in these patients the retention of menstrual flow or of semen causes the so-called uterine condition, by which some women become apnoic, suffocated or spastic? And possibly, this affliction is made worse by the retention of semen. . .

It became evident to me that a badly composed semen has a greater power to inflict damage to the whole body than does menstrual discharge. Consequently, a widow could have her monthly flow but retention of troublesome and damaging semen can still occur.

(*On the Affected Parts* V.5; Seigel 1976: 184–85)

Galen compared the retained semen in a woman's body to spider venom and the saliva of a rabid dog.

Apart from the fact that he considered women imperfect because of their lesser heat, evidenced by their internal reproductive organs, Galen says little about the difference between male and female natures. That he did consider such a natural difference existed, however, is shown by a passage explaining the teleology of body hair.

The hair of the beard not only protects the cheeks but also serves to ornament them; for a man seems more stately, especially as he grows older, if he has everywhere a good covering of hair. . . . On the other hand, for woman, the rest of whose body is always soft and hairless like a child's, the bareness of the face would not be inappropriate, and besides, this animal does not have an august character as the male has and so does not need an august form. For I have already shown many times, indeed throughout the work, that Nature makes for the body a form appropriate to the character of the soul. And the female sex does not need any special covering as protection against the cold, since for the most part women stay within doors, yet they do need long hair on their heads both for protection and ornament, and this need they share with men.

(*On the Usefulness of the Parts of the Body* XI.14; May 1968: 530–31)

Thus, while Galen did not blame the female reproductive parts for causing women to behave erratically, he believed women were naturally inferior, less "august" than men, citing as evidence internal reproductive organs and lack of facial hair. Here biology, while not explaining particular character traits, was used to validate the socially superior role of men. In a sense, this would make it more difficult for women to challenge their social position vis-à-vis men, for while many women could point out that they were no more cowardly, erratic, deceitful, etc., than the average man, they could not produce a beard or penis—signs that were needed to prove they had achieved the "perfect" human nature.

Conclusion

The female body was understood increasingly in the same terms as the male body in the medical writings of antiquity, which may have correlated with women's playing an increasingly more diverse social role; however, it also meant that the archetypical female function of menstruation lost its positive connotations of a natural purge and developed aspects of the Judeo-Christian "curse." Moreover, while fewer specific aspects of "female" behavior were attributed to biology, the concept that women were generally less perfect than men because of their lesser heat became axiomatic and was supported by citing anatomical facts that indisputably separated most men and women.

NOTES

1. From later antiquity we have treatises by Cleopatra and Metrodora, and Aetius of Amida quotes chapters on gynecological matters from a work by a certain Aspasia. Other female medical authorities are referred to by Galen and Pliny.

2. See Figure 5.6 for young girls at vigorous play.

3. "Crisis" was the term given by the Hippocratics to the point in the disease when the diseased material in the body had separated off and was ready to be evacuated. If this was achieved the crisis was complete and the patient recovered. Otherwise the diseased material was reabsorbed and the patient relapsed till the next crisis. If no crisis occurred or none was ever successful, the patient died.

4. Epistaxis (bleeding from the nose) was considered almost as good a sign of recovery as menstruation because the menstrual blood could travel through the passages of a woman's body either downward or upward to be evacuated.

5. This word derives from the Greek word for womb, but it was not a word used by the Hippocratics. Where the womb moved to was significant in treating the disease, and when a generalizing term was used it was usually *pnix* or "suffocation".

6. Aristotle argued against the Hippocratics that no animal could produce two seminal residues.

7. This may have contributed to the association of the apocryphal story of Hagnodice studying with Herophilus (see Chapter 5, "Education and Professions").

TRANSLATIONS

Adams, Francis. 1972. *The Extant Works of Aretaeus the Cappadocian.* Boston. (Originally published 1856)

Barker, Ernest. 1973. *The Politics of Aristotle.* Oxford. (Originally published 1946)

Goss, Charles M. 1962. "On the Anatomy of the Uterus." *Anatomical Record* 144: 77–83.

Hanson, Ann Ellis. 1975. "Hippocrates: *Diseases of Women I.*" *Signs* 1: 567–84.

———. 1992. "Conception and Gestation in the Hippocratic Corpus." *Helios* 19: 31–71.

Jones, W. H. S. 1979–84. *Hippocrates.* Vols. 1–4. Loeb Classical Library. Cambridge, Mass. (Originally published 1923–31).

Lonie, Iain M. 1981. *The Hippocratic Treatises "On Generation"; On the Nature of the Child; "Diseases 4."* Berlin.

May, Margaret T. 1968. *Galen on the Usefulness of the Parts of the Body.* Ithaca, N.Y.

Peck, A. L. 1979. *Aristotle XIII: Generation of Animals.* Loeb Classical Library. Cambridge, Mass. (Originally published 1942)

Seigel, Rudolph E. 1976. *Galen on the Affected Parts.* Basel.

Staden, Heinrich von. 1989. *Herophilus: The Art of Medicine in Early Alexandria.* Cambridge.

Temkin, Oswei. 1956. *Soranus: Gynecology.* Baltimore, Md.

Thompson, D'Arcy W. 1984. *History of Animals.* Books 1–9 in *The Complete Works of Aristotle,* edited by Jonathan Barnes, 1: 774–984. Princeton, N.J.

WORKS CITED

Campese, Silvia, Paula Manuli, and Giulia Sissa. 1983. *Madre Materia.* Turin.

Dean-Jones, Lesley. 1991. "The Cultural Construct of the Female Body in Classical Greek Science." In *Women's History and Ancient History,* edited by Sarah B. Pomeroy, 111–37. Chapel Hill, N.C.

———. 1992. *Women's Bodies in Classical Greek Science.* Oxford.

Gourevitch, Danielle. 1984. *Le Mal d'être femme: La femme et la médecine dans la Rome antique.* Paris.

Joly, Robert. 1978. *Hippocrate.* Vol. 13. Paris.

Hanson, Ann Ellis. 1987. "Diseases of Women in the Epidemics." In *Actes de colloque hippocratique 1984,* edited by Gerhard Baader and Franz Steiner, 29–41. Stuttgart.

———. 1990. "The Medical Writer's Woman." In *Before Sexuality,* edited by David Halperin, John Winkler, and Froma Zeitlin, 309–38. Princeton, N.J.

————. 1991. "Continuity and Change: Three Case Studies in Hippocratic Gynecological Therapy and Theory." In *Women's History and Ancient History*, edited by Sarah B. Pomeroy, 73–110. Chapel Hill, N.C.

King, Helen. 1983. "Bound to Bleed: Artemis and Greek Women." In *Images of Women in Antiquity*, edited by Averil Cameron and Amélie Kuhrt, 109–27. Beckenham.

————. 1986. "Agnodike and the Profession of Medicine." *Proceedings of the Cambridge Philological Society*, n.s. 32: 53–75.

————. 1989. "The Daughter of Leonides: Reading the Hippocratic Corpus." In *History as Text*, edited by Averil Cameron, 13–32. London.

————. Forthcoming. "Once upon a Text: The Hippocratic Origins of Hysteria." In *Hysteria in Western Civilization*, edited by G. S. Rousseau and R. Porter, Berkeley and Los Angeles.

Littré, Emile. 1962. *Oeuvres complètes d'Hippocrate*. 10 vols. Amsterdam. (Originally published Paris, 1839–61)

Lloyd, G. E. R. 1983a. "The critique of traditional ideas in Soranus' gynaecology." In his *Science, Folklore and Ideology*, 168–82. Cambridge.

————. 1983b. "The female sex: Medical treatment and biological theories in the fifth and fourth centuries B.C." In his *Science, Folklore and Ideology*, 58–111. Cambridge.

Saïd, Suzanne. 1983. "Féminin, femme et femelle dans les grands traités biologiques d'Aristote." In *La Femme dans les sociétés antiques. Actes des colloques de Strasbourg (mai 1980 et mars 1981)*, edited by Edmond Lévy, 93–123. Strasbourg.

FURTHER READING

Betz, Hans Dieter. 1986. *The Greek Medical Papyri in Translation, Including the Demotic Texts*. Chicago.

Clark, Stephen R. L. 1982. "Aristotle's Women." *History of Political Thought* 3: 177–91.

Cooper, John M. 1988. "Metaphysics in Aristotle's Embryology." *Proceedings of the Cambridge Philological Society* 214: 14–41.

Dean-Jones, Lesley. 1992. "The Politics of Pleasure: Female Sexual Appetite in the Hippocratics and Aristotle." *Helios* 19: 72–91.

Hanson, Ann Ellis. 1987. "The Eighth Month Child: Obsit Omen." *Bulletin of the History of Medicine*. 61: 589–602.

Horowitz, Maryanne Cline. 1976. "Aristotle and Woman." *Journal of the History of Biology* 9: 183–213.

King, Helen. 1987. "Sacrificial Blood: The Role of the *Amnion* in Ancient Gynecology." *Helios* 13: 117–26.

Lefkowitz, Mary R. 1981. "The Wandering Womb." In her *Heroines and Hysterics*, 12–25. New York.

Morsink, Johannes. 1979. "Was Aristotle's Biology Sexist?" *Journal of the History of Biology* 12: 83–112.

Padel, Ruth. 1983. "Women: Model for Possession by Greek Daemons." In *Images of Women in Antiquity*, edited by Averil Cameron and Amelié Kuhrt, 3–19. Beckenham.

Pomeroy, Sarah B. 1978. "Plato and the Female Physician (*Rep.* 454d2)." *American Journal of Philology* 99: 496–500.

Rousselle, Aline. 1988. *Porneia: On Desire and the Body in Antiquity*. Translated by Felicia Pheasant. Oxford.

Sissa, Giulia. 1990. *Greek Virginity*. Translated by Arthur Goldhammer. Cambridge, Mass.

Staden, Heinrich von. 1992. "Women, Dirt and Exotica in the Hippocratic Corpus." *Helios* 19: 7–30.

II

WOMEN IN
THE ROMAN WORLD

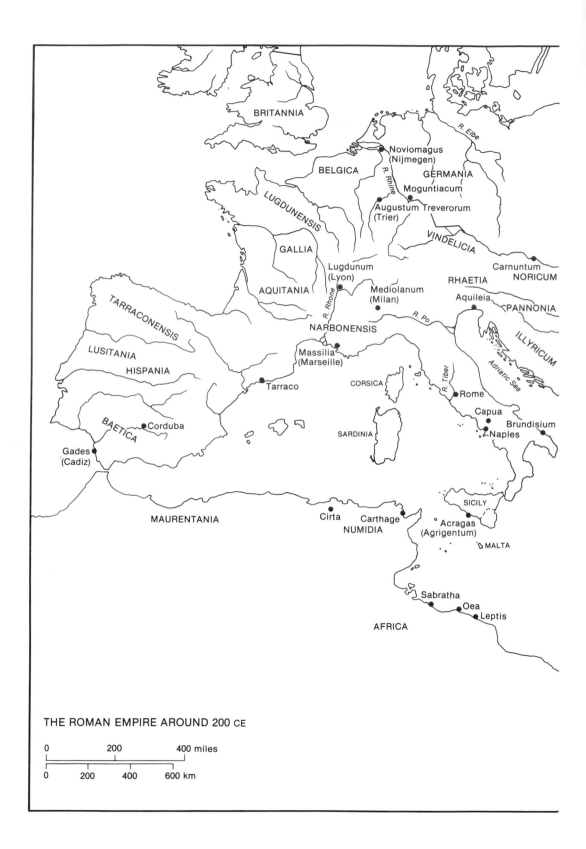

BRITANNIA

BELGICA

GERMANIA

Noviomagus
(Nijmegen)

R. Rhine

Moguntiacum

LUGDUNENSIS

Augustum Treverorum
(Trier)

VINDELICIA

R. Elbe

GALLIA

Lugdunum
(Lyon)

Carnuntum
NORICUM

AQUITANIA

RHAETIA

PANNONIA

TARRACONENSIS

R. Rhone

Mediolanum
(Milan)

Aquileia

NARBONENSIS

R. Po

ILLYRICUM

LUSITANIA

Massilia
(Marseille)

R. Tiber

Adriatic Sea

HISPANIA

CORSICA

Tarraco

Rome

BAETICA

Corduba

Capua

SARDINIA

Brundisium

Gades
(Cadiz)

Naples

MAURENTANIA

Cirta

Carthage

SICILY

Acragas
(Agrigentum)

NUMIDIA

MALTA

Sabratha

Oea

Leptis

AFRICA

THE ROMAN EMPIRE AROUND 200 CE

0   200   400 miles

0   200   400   600 km

Aquincum
(Budapest)

DACIA

Tomis

Black Sea

MOESIA

R. Danube

ARMENIA

Epidamnus

THRACIA

MACEDONIA

Byzantium

BITHYNIA

PONTUS

Aegean Sea

GALATIA

CAPPADOCIA

ASIA

PARTHIA

Corinth

Athens

CILICIA

Antioch

Ionian Sea

ACHAIA

Sparta

SYRIA

R. Tigris

RHODES

R. Euphrates

CYPRUS

CRETE

Caeserea

Jerusalem

Alexandria

CYRENAICA

ARABIA PETRAEA

Oxyrrhynchus

EGYPT

R. Nile

Syene

We have followed the lives of Greek women from the Archaic age to the sophistication of Hellenistic Alexandria. Now, as we turn to the western Mediterranean, we must go back again to the eighth century B.C.E., to the founding of Rome, and the civilizations of her neighbors, the Etruscans of northern Italy, and the Greek colonial cities of Sicily and south Italy. Rome would rise at the cost of the Etruscans and south Italian Greeks, but both cultures have left visual traces of their elegant material cultures. These must at first compensate for the visual poverty of the surviving art and monuments of early and Republican Rome.

The excursus on the women of Etruria illustrates from tomb paintings, sarcophagi and cinerary urns, the participation of women in society, their feasting and sharing in public entertainments. The durability of gold and bronze has preserved women's ornaments—mirrors, makeup chests and exquisite filigree jewelery—that display the intricacy of Etruscan artisanry and their enjoyment of sensuous forms in the representation of myths.

Despite the absence of any Etruscan narrative or poetry, something of these women and their influence emerges when we follow women in the Roman historical tradition from the early legends of Romulus to the more lavish and urban phase of Etruscan domination under the kings of the sixth century. But unlike Archaic Greece and Classical Athens, Rome itself had no narrative record of its society and no preserved literature before the mid-third century. Thus the chapter on Republican Rome paradoxically depends on later sources for the women of the Monarchic and early Republican period (approximately 750–250 B.C.E.) than for the period of the Punic Wars in the second half of the third century B.C.E., when the first Latin poets began to compose narrative historical epics of these wars and playwrights colored their version of Greek comedy with contemporary Roman social detail. The named women of the first five hundred years were types—role models or bad examples—upon whom male writers imposed their prejudices or ideals. Only with the second century did great wealth, power, and leisure come to a section of Roman society, and with them a familiarity with Greek material culture.

It is clear that the politicians and spokesmen of this period were embattled in the face of the temptations of surplus wealth and new life-styles brought back from Hellenistic Greece and Asia Minor. The existence of Greek or other foreign entertainers and courtesans at Rome changed Roman male sexual habits but also taught Roman women a new level of self-assertion, facilitated by the surplus wealth of conquest. At the same time extended overseas campaigns removed the menfolk of both the officer class and the ranks from civilian life for long periods, offering or imposing independence for women of all classes. Marital fidelity was threatened by the availability of slaves and prostitutes of both sexes, and writers claimed that divorce was on the rise.

By about 50 B.C.E. Rome had become a city of about a million persons, comparable perhaps to Alexandria in size, and increasingly like Alexandria in its multicultural population of native Roman citizens, newcomers from Italy, Greek and "barbarian" slaves, and freedmen and freedwomen (freed slaves whom the law defined as standing somewhere between free and unfree). The life of cities has always contained worse extremes of luxury and poverty than that of compact towns with stable populations. Chapter 10 isolates a pattern of female behavior that evolved from affluence and attracted public interest in both life and art. Great ladies and self-reliant noncitizen women without family or status paraded their sexual charms and their relationships before a public both fascinated and prurient. Young men were infatuated and old men voiced disapproval: the civic order had broken down, the writers cried, and a license learned during the disruption of civil war persisted despite the moral revival launched by the new leader, Julius Caesar's heir, Augustus.

The years in which Rome and her empire were controlled by Augustus (27 B.C.E. to 14 C.E.) saw both apparent and genuine changes in the position of women in the family. The chapter on women and the family in the Augustan age focuses on this vital period of stabilization. If legislation of financial and political rewards for marriage and parenthood (and penalties for adultery) affected only the privileged and publicly visible classes, the ideology and attendant social pressure certainly had an impact on the representations of domestic life in the non-elite strata as well. Our account of the Augustan age shows how the example set by the imperial family was promulgated in the monumental art of the period. Other factors converged to turn the energies and care of Romans inward to the family: ethics now focused more on the individual's private obligations, so that from the first generations private letters and public treatises reflect this new awareness of the importance of reciprocal fidelity and affection within marriage and give new attention to the bearing and education of children as well.

By the accident of a natural disaster, one town, Pompeii, was artificially preserved in its condition of 79 C.E., its houses and shops and public buildings a witness to its busy life of trading and small-town politics. Chapter 12 elicits from public inscriptions, graffiti, and domestic architecture the roles performed by the women of Pompeii from the local benefactress to the waitresses and prostitutes.

The civilization of the Roman empire now embraced both the Greek cultures of the world after Alexander—not only Greece but Asia Minor, Syria, and the hinterlands as far as the Euphrates and Tigris—and western Europe including England and southern Scotland. Recent discoveries of wooden writing tablets from the

Roman encampment of Vindolanda adjacent to Hadrian's Wall in Britain (built around 125 C.E.) provide us with the sense of a Roman woman as vivid as the family portraits that confront us from so many stone funerary slabs (Fig. 1). In these portraits, women appear with their husbands and children, they hold purses, fans, and pets, and the inscriptions on many of the monuments give names, ages, relationships, and even affectionate compliments to the deceased. The society of first- and second-century Roman garrison families such as that of Volusia Faustina and her officer-husband who lived at Lincoln (Fig. 1) is brought back to life as well through the letter sent by a woman named Claudia Severa to invite her friend Sulpicia Lepidina to visit her on her birthday.

Claudia Severa to her Lepidina Greetings.
On the 3rd day before the Ides of September, sister, for the day of the celebration of my birthday, I give you a warm invitation to make sure that you come to us, to make the day more enjoyable for me by your arrival, if you come. Give my greetings to your Cerialis. My Aelius and my little son send you [?] their greetings.

[hand of a second person] I shall expect you sister. Farewell sister, my dearest soul, as I hope to prosper, and hail.

[hand of a third person] To Sulpicia Lepidina (wife) of Flavius Cerealis: from Severa.
   (middle to late second century C.E.; Bowman and Thomas 1987: 38)

The modern editors note that whereas the main letter is in "an elegant professional script," the second "somewhat clumsy" hand must be written by Severa herself and is almost certainly "the earliest known example of writing in Latin by a woman."
   Even on the frontier, women celebrated their birthdays together as they did at Rome. A letter by Fronto, the tutor of Marcus Aurelius (ruler from 161–180), tells of his wife's visit to Marcus's mother Domitia Lucilla on *her* birthday:

I have sent my Gratia to keep your mother's birthday with her, and bidden her stay there until I come . . . Meanwhile I have pledged my word that Gratia shall run no risk of starvation. For your mother will share with her protégé the tidbits you sent her. Nor is my Gratia a great eater . . . She will live contentedly enough even on nothing but your mother's kisses.
   (To Marcus Caesar 2.8, mid-second century, C.E.; Haines 1962)

However indulgent and trivializing the male comment, these women clearly enjoyed domestic leisure and a degree of comfort. Even on the drafty northern frontier, officers' wives and women of the local elite might maintain the social niceties of urban life.
   In North Africa too, Rome had fostered wealth and urbanization from Morocco (Mauretania) to Tunisia (Roman "Africa," the home of Fronto, Apuleius, and Augustine) to the Hellenized

Figure 1. Tombstone (possibly second or third century C.E.) of Volusia Faustina, a citizen from Lincoln, in Roman Britain, who had been married to the military officer who appears beside her.

214

cities and native villages of Egypt, whose dry sands have preserved so many fragmented archives with public and private records and letters. Thus, the discussion of the High Empire must include more than two centuries of women both urban and rural, from every civil and social status. Chapter 13 opens with a portrait gallery of elite wives, and an interpretation of the public images of the imperial women fostered by successive emperors from Vespasian to Septimius Severus. Across the empire, in Italy, Africa, and the Greek East, inscriptions honor the daughters, wives, and widows of leading public men for their benefactions and record the statues and titles and priesthoods they received in return. In the second part of this far-flung chapter, we survey the scattered evidence for educated women and women's education, for the roles of women in specialized domestic service, in the working world of trade, as medical attendants, and even as witches. Inscriptions rather than literary texts illuminate how slave women might legally end their servitude and laboriously construct a family life for themselves and their partners and children. Difficult as it is to recover the lives of unlettered hardworking women, the class of ex-slaves had good reason to be proud of its achievements. Because freedmen and freedwomen seem to have been particularly fond of recording their lives on stone in word and image, we have been able to assemble a mosaic of their diversity from the epitaphs and reliefs of these centuries. Their lives have not until recently been part of history, but it is hoped that readers will reach the end of our study with a new sense of interest in and sympathy with these uncelebrated women of the Graeco-Roman world.

WORKS CONSULTED

Bowman, A. K., and J. D. Thomas. 1987. "New Texts from Vindolanda." *Britannia* 18: 125–42.
Haines, C. R., trans. 1962. *Marcus Cornelius Fronto*. Loeb Classical Library. Cambridge, Mass.

7

REPUBLICAN ROME I:
FROM MARRIAGE BY CAPTURE
TO PARTNERSHIP IN WAR—
THE PROUD WOMEN
OF EARLY ROME

This chapter will cover more than five hundred years, from the founding of Rome in 753 B.C.E. to 202 B.C.E, the year of Rome's victory in her life-and-death war to free Italy from the occupying forces of Hannibal of Carthage. This period begins before the accepted date of the Homeric poems and ends a century after the death of Alexander, but it was not until the last decade of the third century that Rome's relatively simple culture of farming, war, and religion attempted any literary record of its history. Thus our knowledge of women's roles during these five hundred years depends on a very few simple inscriptions and a much later historical tradition: even Rome's first historians, Fabius Pictor (late third century) and the elder Cato (234-149 B.C.E.) only survive at second hand, and the would-be historian of these centuries must depend on the idealistic reconstructions of Livy and the Augustan poets.

According to the Romans' own tradition their community began without women. In the days when princes were little more than successful shepherds, Romulus, son of an Alban princess, Ilia, by the god Mars, was exposed with his twin brother Remus, suckled by a wolf and brought up by the shepherd who rescued the babies. Once he discovered his royal birth and restored his grandfather to the kingship of Alba, he left with his shepherd band to found a new community on the Palatine hill by the Tiber crossing. This was the future city of Rome. To increase the number of fighting men, he offered asylum to fugitives from nearby communities. But only enemies ever suggested that Rome should find its women among fugitives and criminals. Roman legendary tradition—first known to us from Ennius (239–169 B.C.E.)—had their founder and his men seize by

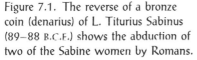

Figure 7.1. The reverse of a bronze coin (denarius) of L. Titurius Sabinus (89–88 B.C.F.) shows the abduction of two of the Sabine women by Romans.

force the virtuous daughters of Rome's reluctant neighbours, the Sabines (Fig. 7.1). It was even said that the thirty virgins that were carried off gave their names to Rome's first local citizen units, the *curiae*. Ideologically the myth of the "Rape of the Sabines" combines the ritual of marriage by capture (as practiced at Sparta: see Chapter 2) with a guarantee of the purity of Rome's first mothers. The Sabines quickly became mothers in the popular version of the story: when the next campaign season came round and their angry parents mobilized the village militias to attack Rome the Sabine wives rushed on to the battlefield with their Roman babies to separate and reconcile the communities. Marriage had made them Roman, and in one of Rome's earliest historical plays these women side with their husbands, and reproach their armed fathers, "when you have stripped the spoils from your sons-in-law, what victory inscription will you set up?" (Ennius, *Sabine Women*; trans. Elaine Fantham)

Two accounts of this "rape of the Sabines" by sophisticated Augustan writers, the patriotic historian Livy and the skeptical love-poet Ovid, show the gamut of attitudes to women, from respect toward the mother of one's children to indulgent mockery of the naive but charming young creatures needing to be fulfilled by masculine lovers. Livy's account dates from just after 30 B.C.E.: Ovid writes a generation later, at the turn of the era.

Romulus accordingly, on the advice of his senators, sent representatives to the various peoples across his borders to negotiate alliances and the right of intermarriage for the newly established state. . . . More often than not his envoys were dismissed with the question whether Rome had thrown open her doors to female, as well as to male, runaways and vagabonds, as that would evidently be a more suitable way for Romans to get wives. . . . Deliberately hiding his resentment, he prepared to celebrate the Consualia, a solemn festival in honor of Neptune, patron of the horse, and sent notice of his intention all over the neighbouring countryside. On the appointed day crowds flocked to Rome, partly, no doubt, out of sheer curiosity to see the new town. . . . All the Sabines were there too with their wives and children. . . . Then the great moment came; the show began, and nobody had eyes or thought for anything else. This was the Romans' opportunity: at a given signal all the able-bodied men burst through the crowd and seized the young women.

. . . The girls' unfortunate parents made good their escape, not without bitter comments on the treachery of their hosts and heartfelt prayers to the God to whose festival they had come in all good faith in the solemnity of the occasion, only to be grossly deceived. The young women were no less indignant, and as full of foreboding for the future.

Romulus, however, reassured them. Going from one to another he declared that their own parents were really to blame, in that they had been too proud to allow intermarriage with their neighbours; neverthless they need not fear; *as married women they would share all the fortunes of Rome, all the privileges of the community, and they would be bound to their husbands by the dearest bond of all: their children.* He urged them to forget their wrath and give their hearts to those to whom chance had given their bodies. . . . The men too played their part: they spoke honied words and vowed that it was passionate love which had prompted their offence. No plea can better touch a woman's heart.

(Livy 1.9, Sélincourt 1960: 43–44, abridged)

> The king gave the sign for which
> They'd so eagerly watched. Project Rape was on. Up they sprang then
>   With a lusty roar, laid hot hands on the girls.
> As timorous doves flee eagles, as a lambkin
>   Runs wild when it sees the hated wolf,
> So this wild charge of men left the girls all panic-stricken
>   Not one had the same color in her cheek as before—
> The same nightmare for all, though terror's features varied:
>   Some tore their hair, some just froze
> Where they sat; some, dismayed, kept silence, others vainly
>   Yelled for Mamma: some wailed; some gaped;
> Some fled, some just stood there. So they were carried off as
>   Marriage bed plunder: even so, many contrived
> To make panic look fetching. Any girl who resisted her pursuer
>   Too vigorously would find herself picked up
> And borne off regardless. "Why spoil those pretty eyes with weeping?"
>   She'd hear, "I'll be all to you
> That your Dad ever was to your Mum"
>   (Ovid, *Art of Love* I.116–31; Green 1982: 169–70)

But against this vote of confidence in Rome's women, we must balance the tale of betrayal reported by Livy in the same narrative. While the Sabines were besieging the Roman citadel on the Capitoline hill, a girl called Tarpeia, who was either daughter of the garrison commander, or a Vestal virgin (see below, under "Vestal Virgins") showed the Sabines a secret way up to the citadel. When she asked as her reward, "what you wear on your left arms" (meaning their gold bracelets) they crushed her to death with the weight of their shields (worn over their left arms) (Fig. 7.2). The story reflects Woman as Other, untrustworthy, so petty that she puts love of finery before love of country.

Both legends are represented on coins of the late Republic (Figs. 7.1 and 7.2), but not for any message they conveyed about women. The name of the moneyer who commissioned the design, Titurius Sabinus, shows that he was advertising his name and Sabine origin, and the women were immediately recognizable signs of the stories about Rome's connection with the virtuous past.

These reverses (the "backs" of the coins) are virtually the only representation of human women among the vast range of Roman Republican coin types. Neither did the early Republic leave behind images of individual mortal women or of their activities, although this can be said as well of mortal men from the same period. Rome's distrust of Etruscan and Greek luxury, including art, combined with its early emphasis on the subordination of the individual to the needs of the fatherland. Thus, as in the early days of the North American colonies, there was little support for the visual arts; only the family death masks (*imagines*) of ancestors who held public office, brought out at public funerals to demonstrate the family's record of service, could attest to the existence of a portrait art. Polybius describes these early public funerals and the carrying of the masks as long since outmoded in his own era, the second century B.C.E. However, we would not expect him to mention masks for women, as they could not hold any public office. By Polybius's day there were wall paintings showing scenes from Roman history, perhaps reliefs with scenes of public ceremonies, and a few portraits of important statesmen and generals, but among these no mortal women appear.

In the early Republic it seems likely that all art was religious or funerary, the preserved monuments of Rome's neighbours in central Italy

Figure 7.2. Reverse of a denarius of L. Titurius Sabinus (89–88 B.C.E.) showing the death of Tarpeia. The woman who showed the secret path to the Roman citadel to the Sabines as they came to avenge the rape of their daughters and sisters, Tarpeia, is shown here crushed by the shields of the Sabines.

include funerary and votive images of men and women such as the fine terra-cotta votive statue from Latium (Fig. 7.3) a monument probably commemorating a third-century young woman offerant or petitioner to the god or goddess. Despite the lack of objects from early Rome, a written record does suggest the existence of statues of some women as well as death masks, statues, and battle paintings with images of men; none of these remains to us today. Several lost statues of named women are reported by the encyclopedist Pliny the Elder (d. 79 C.E.) in his history of art, and by other sources of the first and second centuries C.E:

1. The equestrian statue of Cloelia (fifth century B.C.E.?): "This distinction was actually extended to women with the equestrian statue of Cloelia, as if it were not enough for her to be clad in a toga, although statues were not voted to Lucretia and to Brutus who had driven out the kings, owing to whom Cloelia had been handed over with the others as a hostage." (Pliny the Elder 34.29; Rackham 1968: 149)

2. "A decree was passed to erect a statue to a Vestal Virgin named Taracia, Gaia, or Fufetia 'to be placed where she wished' an addition that was as great a compliment as the fact that a statue was decreed in honor of a woman" (undatable). (Pliny the Elder 34.25; Rackham 1968: 147).

3. The bronze statue of "Gaia Caecilia, consort of one of Tarquin's sons" (late sixth century B.C.E.) recorded by Plutarch as found in the temple of Sancus together with her dedication of sandals and her spindle "as tokens of her love of home and her industry." (Plutarch, *Roman Questions* 30; Babbitt 1972: 53).

4. The Vestal Quinta Claudia, whose statue (second century B.C.E.) in the vestibule of the temple of the Great Mother remained miraculously unburnt in the fire of 22 C.E. (Tacitus *Annals* 4.64, Valerius Maximus 1.8.11)

5. A seated likeness (end of second century B.C.E.) of Cornelia, mother of the Gracchi and daughter of Scipio Africanus "once stood in the colonnade of Metellus, but is now in Octavia's Buildings" (see Chapter 9, p. 265). (Pliny 34.31; Rackham 1968: 147)

These statues, all honorific, include at least one made during the recipient's lifetime (no. 2). She was to have decided where it should be displayed. The statue of Cloelia shown on horseback in a type that had always been associated with military valor, is important in marking a new trend, as is the statue of the Vestal "Taracia." Pliny comments explicitly both on the honor and on the public nature of these images of women of the highest rank in Republican society.

Some Early Heroines

Perhaps the most significant of these examples, at least for early Rome, is the girl Cloelia; Pliny registers predictable masculine indignation be-

Figure 7.3. A terra-cotta statue of a young woman (third-century B.C.E.) from Latium. Distantly related to the korai of late Archaic Greece, the serene facial expression and elaborate hair and ornaments of the figure demonstrate the impact of outside cultural influences on art in Italy during the Roman Republic.

cause Cloelia wears the honorific garment of the male citizen (the toga, which we know was also once worn by women) and is depicted on horseback, like a military commander. It may seem strange that she should be shown mounted, but the pose may have been adapted from the Hellenistic Greek tradition of depicting queens on horseback, or perhaps it implied honor for her deed of masculine heroism. Cloelia had been carried across the Tiber among a group of noble Roman maidens taken hostage by the Etruscans:

One day, with a number of other girls who had consented to follow her, she eluded the guards, swam across the river under a hail of of missiles, and brought her company safe to Rome, where they were all restored to their families.
                                        (Livy. 2.13; Sélincourt 1960: 43–44).

Twice in his early history Livy shows the women acting collectively for the public good: the first instance was the crisis of the early fifth century when the exiled leader Marcius Coriolanus marched against Rome at the head of a Volscian army. When a delegation of the Senate and even priests could not make him relent,

the women of Rome flocked to the house of Coriolanus' mother Veturia and his wife Volumnia. . . . They succeeded in persuading the aged Veturia and Volumnia, accompanied by Marcius' two little sons, to go into the enemy's lines and make their plea for peace.
                                        (Livy 2.40; Sélincourt 1960: 150)

[The Roman mother commanded respect. At the sight of his approaching mother Coriolanus flinched but went to kiss her and received this rebuke.]

I would know before I accept your kiss whether I have come to an enemy or to a son, whether I am here as your mother or as a prisoner of war. Have my long life and unhappy old age brought me to this, that I should see you first an exile, then the enemy of your country? Had you the heart to ravage the earth which bore and bred you? When Rome was before your eyes, did not the thought come to you "within those walls is my home, with the gods that watch over it—and my mother and my wife and my children"?
                                        (Livy 2.40; Sélincourt 1960: 150)

Veturia's authority and her invocation of the metaphor of land as mother decided the course of history. When Coriolanus was shamed and withdrew to ignominious exile, the Senate consecrated a temple to Women's Fortune (Fortuna muliebris) to honor the women's achievement.

The second intervention of the women is more conventional. In 390 when Rome was occupied by a force of marauding Gauls, the invaders demanded a ransom to leave the city. Livy mentions the women's offering only after the event:

When it was found that there was not enough gold in the treasury to pay the Gauls the agreed sum, contributions from the women had been accepted, to avoid touching what was consecrated. The women who had contributed were formally thanked, and were further granted the privilege, hitherto confined to men, of having laudatory orations pronounced at their funerals.

(Livy 5.50; Sélincourt 1960: 396–97)

They may have been honored in other ways. Certainly Virgil shows among the rejoicing after Rome's liberation "the chaste mothers taking the sacred objects through the city in soft carriages" (*Aeneid* 8.665–66; Mandelbaum 1961).

The evidence of a few exceptional artifacts shows that Rome's material culture was surprisingly rich even in the fourth century, and that women were both patrons and users of precious objects. The inscription on the famous bronze container, called the Ficoroni cista, (Fig. 7.4):

NOVIOS PLAUTIOS MADE ME AT ROME:
DINDIA MACOLNIA GAVE ME TO HER DAUGHTER

bears witness that Roman women not only possessed but had the wealth to commission precious works of considerable sophistication. Was this a wedding gift? Certainly the exquisite bronze chest, made in Rome for a Praenestine family, uses Hellenistic techniques for its complex zoomorphic feet, its handle of Dionysus flanked by two satyrs, and its athletic scenes taken from the epic *Argonautica* of Apollonius of Rhodes.

Another of the heroines, Quinta Claudia, won her statue for service to a religious cult. In 204 B.C.E., when the barge carrying the statue of the Great Mother up the Tiber to Rome ran aground, Quinta, after a pious prayer, used her own hair as a barge rope to tow it to its destination near the site of Romulus's original settlement on the Palatine, where Cybele's temple was erected.

Conflicting versions of the myth of Claudia make her either a married woman or a Vestal virgin (see below under "The Vestal Virgins: A Special Civic Cult"). In either case she was suspected of unchastity and vindicated her honor by praying that the goddess would only let her move the barge if she were chaste. Romanticizing legends like this became part of Roman patriotic tradition just because Roman society was so late in producing its own literature; the first known dramatic and epic poets come five hundred years after the legendary founding of the city, almost two hundred years after the great age of Athenian drama. So the legendary traditions about queens and other women of early Rome were shaped by writers of a later age, motivated by the need to represent a Roman past as heroic and virtuous as Athenian legend had made Theseus or the early kings of Attica. In the edifying exemplary tales of Cicero and the idealizing narrative of Virgil, Livy, or Ovid, the early Romans succeeded through moral excellence, and their wives and mothers raised their voices only like Veturia, to remind their menfolk of their duty to the country.

The legends of the monarchy and early Republic introduce women into the public narrative as instruments either of political bonding or political change. Occasionally, women can also be glimpsed in their pri-

Figure 7.4. A large engraved bronze container, the Ficoroni cista, dates to fourth-century B.C.E. Rome but was found in a tomb in Palestrina, a nearby town. It is one of the earliest signed objects from Italy, and bears the name of Novios Plautios. The style, a blend of late Classical Greek and Etruscan elements, demonstrates the degree to which early Roman art was shaped by these two cultural forces.

vate roles as wives concerned with fertility and motherhood, and with worship and sacrifice to women's cults. Only the Vestal virgins, the order of priestesses supposedly introduced to Rome by Romulus's successor Numa, (traditionally dated 715–673 B.C.E.) bridge these categories, serving a public cult on behalf of the state, yet one that is in some sense private, because secluded from men.

Roman noble families in the late Republic and Empire used their daughters' marriages to make alliances with promising young officers or politicians, or to bind competing clans and power groups. So it was natural that in their legends of the past they should invent marriages to explain transfers of power to new dynasties. Just as Virgil gives the Trojan prince Aeneas a legitimate claim to the Latin kingdom of the shadowy King Latinus through marriage to his even more shadowy daughter Lavinia, so Numa and other successors to the monarchy of Rome are given a link to the previous king through marriage. But the women are ciphers until Rome enters the phase of Etruscan domination. Romans saw the relative prominence of women in Etruscan society as a factor in its supposed degeneracy (See Chapter 8). Hence they constructed their legends of the dynasty from Tarquinia to reflect women's power both used and misused. So the beneficent power of Tanaquil, gifted in the interpretation of omens, and king-maker both for her husband Tarquinius Priscus and the Italian "slave" child Servius Tullius, turns in the next generation to the vicious intrigues of Tullia and her husband Tarquin the Proud *(Superbus)*. The military absences of husbands and fathers, increasing as Rome grew powerful and her enemies more distant, is a factor in early legends and will become a major factor in both the sufferings and the evolving autonomy of Roman women (cf. Evans 1991).

The two most famous women in Roman legend, Lucretia and Verginia, are sacrificial figures, like Alcestis and Iphigenia in Greek mythology. But in contrast they earn their fame as much by their role in stimulating male political action as for their undoubted virtue. Ideologically the Roman woman's primary virtue was *pudicitia* (not so much chastity, as sexual fidelity enhanced by fertility). This was the female equivalent to *fides*, a man's loyalty to his friends and his country. So Romans cherished the legends of Lucretia the wife and Verginia the virgin daughter.

Lucretia's domestic tragedy became a public revolution (see Chapter 8). Raped in her husband's absence by King Tarquin's son (himself a kinsman of her husband), Lucretia summoned her father, husband, and maternal uncle, declared herself dishonored and killed herself "rather than be an example of unchastity to other wives." Romans believed that popular outrage at her death provoked the expulsion of the Tarquin dynasty and the creation of the free people's government *(res publica)*. Lucretia's husband, Collatinus, and her uncle, Lucius Junius Brutus, led the revolution and were among the first annual elected magistrates. But gender ideology pointed the moral of the story with contrasting depictions of the bad wives and the good:

Now Ardea was beset by Roman forces
and suffered the slow stalemate of a siege.
While there was time and enemies shunned battle,
the camp relaxed and left its soldiers idle:
Young Tarquin entertained his friends with feasting
and wine in plenty. Then the prince spoke out:
"while Ardea's defiance keeps us fighting
and will not let us take our weapons home
how well do you think our marriages are cherished,
and do our wives have any thought of us?"
Each man proclaims his wife in competition
as tongue and heart grow hot with draughts of wine,
till Collatinus rises and gives answer.
"Words are worth nothing, let us trust in deeds:
The night is young: to horse! Let's ride for Rome."
        The plan's approved, the horses are made ready
and bear their masters home; the royal palace
is their first call: they find the door unguarded.
The royal brides with garlands at their throats
carouse all night with wine jugs by their side.
From there they seek Lucretia. She was spinning
baskets of soft wool set before her couch.
The slave girls spun their portion in the lamplight,
their mistress spoke to them in gentle tones.

"Hasten dear girls, for we must send your master
the cloak that we have woven very shortly.
But what news have you heard? For you hear gossip.
How long now do they say the war will last?
You soon will fall, Ardea, to better men.
O wicked town, to keep our husbands from us.
Only let them be safe! But mine is daring
and rushes into danger with drawn sword.
My heart fails when I think of him in battle,
I faint and icy cold seizes my breast."

She broke off, weeping, dropped the tautened threads
and let her gaze fall sadly in her lap.
This too became her; chaste tears made her lovely,
her beauty matched the goodness of her heart.
        (Ovid, *Fasti* 2.720–58; trans. Elaine Fantham)

Lucretia's work on her husband's cloak evokes the main domestic duty of the Roman wife—wool-working, including carding, spinning, and weaving the heavy cloth of the toga and other garments; a later Roman epitaph claims

"Stranger, I have but a little to say. Stand and read. This is the ugly tomb of a fair woman. Her parents gave her the name Claudia. She loved her husband with her heart and bore two sons. One she has left on earth, the other she has placed beneath it. Her talk was charming and her walk was graceful. She kept her house, and worked the wool. That is all"

(Warmington 1940: I.18)

The tale of the girl Verginia, more complex, allows the maiden no initiative, but brings home to modern readers the importance of women's free status to protect them from sexual abuse. Sixty years after the expulsion of the Tarquins, ten commissioners were appointed to codify the laws of Rome; one of them, Appius Claudius, lusted after Verginia, the well-bred daughter of one gallant soldier absent on military service, and betrothed to another, the tribune Icilius. In order to get possession of her, Appius suborned a man to claim that she was not a freeborn girl but his own slave. In Rome, as in Greece, the masters of slave women had the unrestricted use of their bodies. So when Verginia's father could not prevent the monstrous verdict,

he took Verginia and her nurse over to the shops by the shrine of Cloacina. . . . Then he snatched a knife from a butcher, and crying "there is only one way, my child, to make you free," he stabbed her to the heart.

(Livy 3.48.5; Sélincourt 1960: 236)

Again the demonstration of injustice provokes a popular uprising and the reassertion of liberty. It is significant that each major step in the development of Roman political progress was associated by legend with the defense or vindication of women against abuse by those outside the family. We might see a parallel with the way in which the expansion of Roman Imperial power would be justified by the defense of client-communities against the aggression of foreign states.

Fathers and Husbands: Roman Marriages

While we may contrast the moral initiative of the married Lucretia with the passive innocence of the virgin, both legends reflect the continuing role of the father. In Roman family law the father (*paterfamilias*) was also lord of the descendant family. His control (*patria potestas*) carried the right of life and death over the entire household, which included his children and other slave and freed dependants. In principle he determined the survival or exposure to die of any child born to his wife or in his household, and his wife was powerless to protest the infanticide of a legitimate and healthy child. But given the high child mortality, family pressure might shame a reluctant father into bearing the cost of rearing a third son or second daughter (Rawson 1986).

In the most common form of early Roman marriage a daughter would pass from her father's control into the *manus* (hand) of her husband, losing membership in her own *gens* (family) to enter his. Her position in domestic law would differ little from that of her own daughters. But although she no longer took part in the domestic cults of her own family, it is not clear how much she could share in her husband's family cults. Descriptions of household ceremonies to Vesta and the Lares (goddess of the hearth, and gods of the household supplies), show daughters rather than wives supporting the paterfamilias in the daily rites.

For a complex series of financial and political reasons, the natal family of a woman might not wish to give her away in a *manus* marriage. There was another, looser, form of marriage without *manus*, already attested to in the *Twelve Tables*, Rome's earliest law code, written around 450.

Any woman who does not wish to be subjected in this manner to the hand of her husband should be absent three nights in succession every year, and so interrupt the *usucapio* (prescriptive right) of each year.
(Table VI of the *XII Tables*, Lewis/Reinhold I. 105 1990: 111)

While tradition explicitly denies the existence of divorce in early Rome, there are many signs of mistrust between husband and wife. Inconsistent traditions report that the laws of Romulus authorized a husband, in consultation with his wife's relatives, to put her to death for adultery or for drinking wine (Dionysius of Halicarnassus 2.25), or to repudiate her for poisoning his children or counterfeiting his keys or for adultery. (Plutarch *Romulus* 25). Women were often suspected of poisoning, since they lacked weapons for killing but had access to the preparation of food. On one occasion in the fourth century a great number of Roman wives were given a collective public trial and found guilty of poisoning their husbands (Livy 8.22). Even in the more sophisticated second century the elder Cato (235–149) declared that any woman who committed adultery would also resort to poison—presumably of her husband. What is behind this paranoia? Food poisoning from heat and contamination? Or the ill-effects of love potions *(amatoria)?* When a wife's standing depended on her reproductive capability and her husband was impotent or indifferent she might well turn to untested aphrodisiacs. The "poisoning of children," too, may refer to abortion (or miscarriage) rather than the crimes of a wicked stepmother against children by a previous wife. But Rome was a prudish society; it is often difficult to guess the reality behind veiled euphemisms.

Fertility in Marriage and in Cult

As a community of peasant soldiers, Rome needed sons, and stressed the need by calling the lowest unpropertied class *proletarii*, "producers of manpower." Fertility was precious, and explains the tradition that the first Roman to divorce was Spurius Carvilius Ruga, in or around 231 B.C.E. It is clear from Gellius's text, cited below, that this was not the first divorce in Rome, but a new kind of "no-fault" divorce. Earlier wives may have been divorced for adultery or other serious breaches of conduct without the return of their dowries, but Ruga was divorcing his wife for barrenness, thus setting a legal precedent for returning the dowry when the wife was guilty of no offense (Watson 1967).

Servius Sulpicius in his treatise *On Dowries* declares that legal measures to define wives' property first became necessary when Spurius Carvilius . . . a nobleman, divorced his wife, because there were no children from her body, in the five hundred and twenty-third year of the city. Indeed, Carvilius is said to have greatly loved the wife that he repudiated, and to have held her very dear for her sweet character. But he put the sanctity of his oath before his love and inclination, because he had been required by the censors to declare that he would have his wife "for the sake of begetting citizen children."

(Aulus Gellius 43; trans. Elaine Fantham)

The oath Carvilius had to swear before the quinquennial review of the censors was simply a reiteration of the Roman formula of marriage. It is clear that these magistrates aimed to foster the birthrate by verifying whether citizens were married and pressuring bachelors to marry; but men had many motives for wanting children, especially sons. A father needed an heir not only to inherit the family property and continue its name, but to maintain the cult of ancestors, and to tend the father's tomb after death. Hence he had the right to retain his children after a divorce. It was surely a powerful deterrent to a wife anxious to escape a wretched marriage that she could not do so without losing her children (on divorce, see Treggiari in Rawson 1991).

At Rome's beginnings infertility was not only a family but a national hazard; Ovid describes such a crisis in Romulus's time to explain the cult of Lucina, goddess of childbirth, and the ancient fertility rites of the Lupercalia.

> For once when cruel misfortune kept wives barren
> and women bore few pledges of their love
> Romulus (who was ruling when this happened)
> cried out, "We raped the Sabines to no purpose.
> If our offenses brought us war, not manpower,
> we would have profited to have no brides."
> Beneath the Esquiline a grove untended
> for many years grew in great Juno's honor;
> in supplication there both wives and husbands
> bowed down and prayed for help on bended knees.
> Then suddenly the treetops stirred and murmured
> mysterious words, as if the goddess spoke.
> "The sacred goat must impregnate your women,"
> she said. The crowd was dumb with puzzled fear.
> There was an augur (time has lost his name)
> who came an exile from Etruscan soil;
> he slew the goat and made the women offer
> their backs for beating with the strips of hide.
> So when the moon began its tenth new crescent
> the wives were mothers and their husbands sires.
> Lucina, thanks to you! The grove has named you   [a pun on *lucus*],

or else your role as goddess of the light   [another pun, on *lux*].
Gentle Lucina, pity pregnant women,
and bring to birth the burden of their wombs.
                    (Ovid *Fasti* 2.423–55; trans. Elaine Fantham)

Wives who wished to conceive offered themselves at the Lupercalia to be whipped by the Luperci, young men dressed in goatskins, who raced round the foot of the Palatine, striking with thongs of goathide any woman in their path. Juno, the protectress of marriage, also presided over childbirth, under the name Lucina, with other vaguer spirits to help the woman in labor, whether the baby came head first (helped by Porrima, "the forwarder") or feet first in a breech birth—which needed the aid of Postverta "the turner" (Aulus Gellius 16.16.4).

Roman Religion: Goddesses and Women's Cults

It might be said that Rome had subordinated its goddesses as it subordinated its women. Neighboring cities honored patron goddesses like Diana of Aricia (the goddess whose priest-consort had to fight a challenger each year for his continued privilege), or Juno, represented on coins armed and in goatskin headdress, as warrior patroness of Lanuvium. Unlike the Greek goddess Hera, whose imagery as wife and mother obscures any reference to a military identity, the Juno of Lanuvium seems to draw on the model of Athena, warrior-goddess, as well as on local Italian traditions. The denarius of the mid-first century that shows a girl making a cult offering of food to Juno's sacred serpent (Fig. 7.5) confirms an incidental allusion made by Propertius, writing in the late first century B.C.E. According to Propertius, if the serpent refused food, this proved the girl was not a virgin. This coin is one of very few images of women's cult activities from the Republican centuries.

At Rome, Juno had been merely Jupiter's consort, grouped with his child Minerva in the Etruscan Trinity that occupied the three chambers of the Capitoline Temple. Her public worship was subordinated to that of Jupiter and cult acts in her honor seem to have been confined to women. But it would be oversimplifying to speak generically of "women's cults." Noncitizens were excluded and even citizen-women observed separate cults based on their caste or social standing. Thus a woman born to patrician parents was herself a patrician unless she married a plebeian; then her caste, like her clan, became that of her husband.

This caste division is reflected in two anecdotes, one reflecting the political implications of intermarriage, the other its religious consequences. Once again a male historian presents women as motivators of political change. Livy attributes the final successful agitation of the leading plebeians for access to the highest magistracy—the consulship—to the jealousy felt by one sister, with a plebeian husband, for her sibling, whose patrician husband was consul, and escorted by lictors (Livy

Figure 7.5. Reverse of a denarius of L. Roscius Fabatus (64 B.C.E.) showing the feeding of the goddess Juno's serpent.

6.34). Condescendingly, ("a woman's feelings are affected by little things" (tr Radice)) the historian blames the petty jealousy of the weaker sex, when it is quite clear (but not so good a story) that the women's father and the plebeian husband had agreed to agitate for this political "reform" and had the power to make it happen.

Once the plebeians acquire the right to the consulship, a parallel instance of the "caste problem" generates a religious innovation for women—the new cult of plebeian chastity:

A quarrel . . . broke out among the married women at the shrine of Patrician Chastity . . . Verginia, daughter of Aulus, a patrician married to a plebeian, the consul Lucius Volumnius, had been prevented by the matrons from taking part in the ceremonies on the grounds that she had married outside her patrician rank. A short altercation followed, which when feminine tempers ran high, blazed out into a battle of wills. Verginia proudly insisted and with reason, that she had entered the temple of Patrician Chastity as a patrician and *a chaste woman, who was the wife of one man, to whom she had been given as an unmarried girl* and was ashamed neither of her husband nor of his honours and achievements. Then she confirmed her noble words by a remarkable deed. In the Vicus Longus, where she lived, she shut off part of her great house, large enough to make a shrine of moderate size, set up an altar in it, and then summoned the married plebeian women. After complaining about the insulting behaviour of the patrician ladies, "I dedicate this altar" she said "to Plebeian Chastity, and urge you to ensure that it will be said that it is tended more reverently than the other one, if that is possible, and by women of purer life. Thus just as the men in our state are rivals in valor, our matrons may compete with one another in chastity."

(Livy 10.23; Radice 1982: 319–20)

One phrase here deserves separate comment: "the wife of one man" is not a fancy phrase for monogamy. In Roman thinking the *Univira*, who had slept only with one man, and never remarried after the loss of her husband, was most honored as the sexual ideal; but the ideal was in conflict with both the widow's need for a social protector and society's need for children; there would come a time when it was overridden by legislation (see Chapter 11).

But although the mass of Romans, rich and poor, were plebeians, there was a further division of status marked by both dress and cult. The respectable married matrona was to be identified by her long stola, an overgarment worn over her dress and covering her ankles, and the vittae or headbands covering her hair; this was said by later authors to distinguish her from respectable noncitizens and from the half-world of unmarried women living by their sex. On a statue of a matron (Fig. 7.6) from the time of Augustus (27 B.C.E.–14 C.E.) we can see the stola with its shoulder straps, rarely depicted except apparently to honor ladies of a later era for their old-fashioned virtues. The stola and certainly the vittae seem to have gone out of fashion by the time this statue was made.

In general, noncitizen women were excluded from cult as they were from citizen marriage. But in his poem celebrating the rites of the Roman calendar, Ovid seems to invite married women and freedwomen alike—"Latin mothers and daughters-in-law, and you who lack the long overdress and fillets"—to share in the ritual washing of Venus on April 1. In honor of Fortuna Virilis (Fortune of men) all the women also offered incense and a drink of honeyed milk and poppyseed and bathed together in the men's bath. Ovid explains the ritual as guaranteeing that men would be blinded by the goddess to the bodily defects of their womenfolk (*Fasti* 4.133–60). Although modern scholars have sought to keep respectable and free-living women apart by distinguishing the two rituals, the poet carefully includes all women in each of the different cult acts.

Normally, however, only the religious observances of the matronae are reported. In the crisis of the Hannibalic invasion after 218 B.C.E. religious rites proliferated to reassure the civilian population, and a series of collective women's offerings is recorded; in the first year of the war the matrons gave a bronze statue to Juno the Queen (Livy 21.62). Next

Figure 7.6. Statue of a matron from Rome (ca. 27 B.C.E. to 14 C.E.) wearing a stola over her tunic; long and without sleeves, the garment may have been decorated with stripes to indicate the rank of the woman.

year they offered a formal banquet, with a couch spread to receive her image *(Lectisternium)*. Women of slave origin contributed separately to the cult of Feronia (Livy 22.7). The most interesting sequence of female cult and cooperative action occurred in 207:

[To expiate a prodigy] the priests decreed that three times nine virgins should go through the city in procession singing a hymn. But when they were rehearsing the hymn composed by Livius Andronicus in the temple of Jupiter the Stayer, lightning struck the temple of Juno the Queen on the Aventine.

The soothsayers declared that this portent concerned the married women who must placate the goddess with an offering. All the married women resident in Rome or inside the tenth milestone were summoned by edict of the aediles, and themselves elected twenty-five women to receive contributions from their dowries. From these they made a golden bowl as a gift and carried it up to the Aventine, where a sacrifice was made with due holiness and decency.

(Livy 27.37.7-10; trans. Elaine Fantham)

(The women's contributions were almost certainly gold ornaments from their personal effects melted down to compose the bowl, rather than money realized by sale of property.) As for the virgins' processional hymn, Livy reports in detail the special ritual devised for the occasion.

From the temple of Apollo two white cows were led through the Porta Carmentalis into the city. Behind them were carried two statues of Juno the Queen in cypress wood; then seven and twenty maidens in long robes marched, singing their hymn in honor of Juno the Queen. . . . Behind the company of girls followed the Decemvirs, wearing laurel garlands and purple-bordered togas. From the gate they proceeded along the Vicus Iugarius into the Forum.

In the Forum the procession halted, and passing a rope from hand to hand the maidens advanced, accompanying the sound of their voice by beating time with their feet (timing their song by the rhythm of their steps). Then . . . they made their way to the Clivus Publicius and the temple of Juno the Queen. There the two victims were sacrificed by the Decemvirs and the cypress statues borne into the temple.

(Livy 27.37.11-15; trans. Elaine Fantham)

It was essentially only in religious acts that young maidens would be seen in public; so Virgil describes the only public appearance of the princess Lavinia, accompanying her mother to the temple.

And Queen Amata, too,
with many women, bearing gifts, is carried
into the citadel, Minerva's temple
upon the heights: at her side walks the girl
Lavinia, the cause of all that trouble,
her lovely eyes held low.

(*Aeneid* 11.477–80; Mandelbaum
1971: 290)

The Vestal Virgins: A Special Civic Cult

One group of women was more public than private; the six Vestal virgins, who were chosen before the onset of puberty to live for thirty years in celibacy tending the sacred fire of the round temple of Vesta in the heart of the Forum. A coin (Fig. 7.7) of Clodius Vestalis minted in 41 B.C.E. has an image of his ancestor, the Vestal Quinta Claudia, on the reverse. This image may copy the statue erected in her honor by the

Figure 7.7. Denarius of Clodius Vestalis (41 B.C.E.), the reverse of which
shows the seated figure of Quinta Claudia, the Vestal who had a statue
erected in her honor by the Senate in
Rome.

Senate (see above); in any case, it is the only known likeness of a named
woman found on public coinage of the Republic and dates from the period of the civil wars that ended the Republic.

Roman tradition held that the goddess Vesta had no image in her
oldest shrine in the forum, although a coin of Cassius Longinus seems to
show the goddess with her ritual ladle *(simpuvium)* in a form that suggests the existence of statuary models. According to Pliny the Elder, the
shrine also contained as talismans for the generative survival of the na
tion a sacred phallus *(fascinum)*, the Di Magni (household gods) of
Troy, and a sacred Trojan image of Athena known as the Palladium. It
would have been hard for a man to verify these details, since the shrine
was closed to all men. Certainly the Vestals sacrificed their own years of
fertility to transfer their powers to Rome and the renewal of the generations.

Although the Vestals' relief (Fig. 7.8) from a public monument, perhaps from the time of Tiberius (14–37 C.E.), is far later than the period
covered by this chapter, it shows a scene that may have been common
in the Republic also. The six Vestals were frequently seen at public banquets and games where they received special seats of honor; they had
the right to make their own wills, unlike other women of the time, and
were treated in some ways like men. On the other hand they were bound
by ritual and taboo. If the sacred flame went out, it could not be relit
from an ordinary firebrand, but had to be rekindled by rubbing a boring
stick into a hole. On June 5 each year the Vestals sacrificed a pregnant
heifer, and ritually burned both mother and fetus, cleansing the temple
with these ashes and other special materials; during the days of cleansing from this sacrifice to the Vestalia on June 15 it was ill-omened for
any young woman to marry. The Vestals' unique service to the state

Figure 7.8. Fragment of a marble relief from Rome showing Vestals banqueting (ca. 14–37 C.E.). The relief probably came from a public monument commissioned by the state, although it is no longer possible to know its original location or purpose.

earned special privileges and penalties, described here by Plutarch, writing at the beginning of the second century C.E.

They had power to make a will in the lifetime of their father; they had a free administration of their own affairs without guardian or tutor, . . . when they go abroad they have the *fasces* [a ceremonial bundle of rods and ax that symbolized power over corporal and capital punishment] carried before them; and if in their walks they chance to meet a criminal on his way to execution, it saves his life, upon oath made that the meeting was an accidental one, and not concerted or of set purpose. Any one who presses on the chair on which they are carried is put to death.

    If these Vestals commit any minor fault they are punishable by the high priest only, who scourges the offender, sometimes with her clothes off, in a dark place with a curtain drawn between; but she that has broken her vow is buried alive. . . . A narrow room is constructed underground to which a descent is made by stairs; here they prepare a bed and light a lamp and leave a small quantity of food, such as bread, water, a pail of milk, and some oil; so that a body which has been consecrated and devoted to the most sacred service of religion might not be said to perish by such a death as famine. The culprit herself is put in a litter which they cover over and tie her down with cords on it, so that nothing she utters may be heard. They then take her to the Forum. All people silently go out of the way as she passes. . . . When they come to the place of execution, the officer looses the cords and then the high priest lifting his hands to heaven, pronounces certain prayers to himself before the act and then he brings out the prisoner, being still covered, and placing her upon the steps that lead down to the cell turns away his face with the rest of the priests. The stairs are drawn up after she has gone down, and a quantity of earth is heaped up over the entrance to the cell, so as to prevent it being distinguished from the rest of the mound. That is the punishment of those who break their vow of virginity.

(Plutarch, Numa 10; trans. R. Warner in Fuller 1959: 49–50)

In view of the genuine reverence felt for this cult, it is not surprising that Augustus, when finally elected chief priest in 12 B.C.E., copied the device of the plebeian Verginia and created his own domestic version of the public worship. Augustus took control of the cult of Vesta by incorporating a new shrine of the goddess into his own residence on the Palatine. The emperor thus identified his domestic hearth with the sexual renewal of Rome and her empire; even as chief priest he might not enter the shrine, but he could surely control its attendants (Beard 1980).

Contacts with Other Cultures

How did it affect Roman women when the early phases of Roman society encountered the influence of the Greek cultures of Sicily and south Italy? It used to be thought that access to Greek works of art and mythology at Rome in the years of Etruscan domination was followed by intellectual isolation and cultural impoverishment in the early Republic, until finally in the third century Roman forces in south Italy renewed contact with the richer cultures of Greater Greece *(Magna Graecia)*. More recently excavations in the Forum Boarium, one of the oldest parts of Rome, have revealed fifth-century reliefs with Greek mythological subjects and encouraged the belief that Greek influence returned quickly to Rome, or was never absent.

Although the life of respectable Greek women in southern Italy may have been as circumscribed as in mainland Greece, it is fully represented in art, both sacred and secular, reverent and luxurious. In southern Italy, especially in the city of Locri, the cult of Kore (the Maiden) was associated with that of Aphrodite and honored with votive terra-cottas in various shapes. Besides the figurines of the goddess herself, models of naked kneeling women have been found singly at the feet of female burials, and in mass deposits alongside shrines of Kore (Fig. 7.9), while

Figure 7.9. Mold-made terra-cotta figures of kneeling women from Locri, fifth century B.C.E. Such statuettes came from the deposits associated with shrines of Kore, as well as from women's burials.

the clay tablets of Locri (see Chapter 1) illustrate every phase of preparation for a marriage either of the Maiden to Hades or of a mortal woman like those who served the goddess. (Fig. 7.10).

Although Ceres and Libera (Proserpina) were identified with Demeter and Persephone, their cult, shared with the Italic god Liber (Bacchus), and established at Rome at the beginning of the fifth century, presents a striking contrast with the Greek cult. The cult of Ceres seems to have been a political measure to appease social discontent. Certainly Libera/Proserpina did not have any separate cult, and the worship at the new temple in the Forum Boarium was primarily a cult of Ceres as patroness of Rome's commercial traders in wheat and other imports.

Women's rituals in Sicily and southern Italy are also reflected by the many vases that appear to celebrate marriage, and may have been created as wedding gifts or furnishings. These often depict women holding mirrors or putting on their jewelry, while winged figures of Eros or Nike hover benevolently around them. One elaborately ornate vase-type, the lebes gamikos (Fig. 7.11), combined such scenes with elaborate lids and free-standing figurines of doves or cupids (Trendall 1988). It is clear that women's religious and secular interests were important in the Greek communities of southern Italy. Their chief cult, that of Demeter and Persephone, was wealthy and honored with votive gifts: their weddings,

Figure 7.10. Terra-cotta plaque from fifth-century B.C.E. Locri. A woman picks fruit, here, while on other plaques from the series at the temple of Kore women perform ritual acts, all apparently in preparation for the marriage either of Kore to Hades or of the dedicant of the plaque.

their self-adornment, and their beauty were depicted on vases commissioned or produced for mass retail sale. The sensuality and luxury of such artifacts, produced and used in Greek communities in southern Italy during the third century B.C.E., may lead us to question whether Roman life in this period was dominated by the moral puritanism that later writers like Cicero, Sallust, and Livy claim for the past that they idealized.

In Rome and central Italy almost no representations of women survive before the first century B.C.E.; even in a funerary context they are symbolized only by the plainest female ornament. A pair of sandals, a makeup box or bowl are sometimes shown in relief on simple stone funerary cippi, as markers for the gender of the dead, parallel to the tools

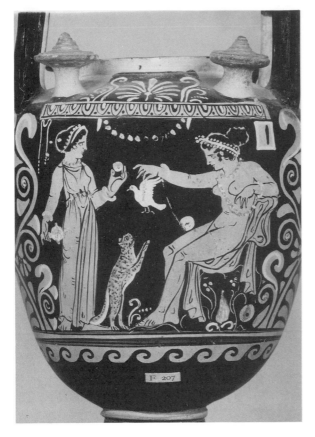

Figure 7.11. Wedding vase (lebes gamikos) from Campania, south of Rome, by the Danaid Painter, showing a scene of women with pets in an interior; dated to the fourth century B.C.E. The female nudity depicted here is in contrast to Athenian vases, where only prostitutes are shown nude.

of various trades found on the cippi of their male counterparts. But the more affluent women's lives may have been more luxurious than the archaeological remains indicate. The cosmetics and trappings not attested to by material remains can be recovered from comic scripts from the end of the third century. The plays were adapted from Greek comedies, but their success implies Roman interest in the frivolous Greek world to the south. A surviving fragment by Naevius (ca.270–204 B.C.E.), Rome's first comic playwright, delights in portraying a flirtatious girl dancer from Tarentum, the chief city of Apulia:

She gives herself to each in turn, and passes from hand to hand like a member of a dance troupe; she nods to one man, winks at another, caresses this man and embraces the other; her hand is busy over here, she stamps her foot over there, she gives her ring for one to admire, and entices another with a pout of her lips. While she sings with one man, she writes messages with her finger to another.

(Naevius, Tarentilla, frag. 2; trans. Elaine Fantham)

The inexpensive colorful statuettes of dancers, acrobats, chatting women and fluttering cupids produced from molds are of a type widespread in Hellenistic Greek culture and bring before us this world of flirtation and play (Fig. 7.12). The terra-cotta figurine (of a dancer) found

Figure 7.12. Terra-cotta figurine from south Italy (third-century B.C.E.) representing a dancing woman in a flowing garment and wreath, her elongated body and small head typical of the Hellenistic terra-cottas found at Tanagra and Myrina; this one comes from Taranto where the type was also extremely popular. See also Chapter 5, Figures 5.5 and 5.6.

in Apulia is a typical product of south Italian Greek culture. The images of a pleasure-loving life and the interest in female beauty offered by so many forms of south Italian art find a match in the representation of women in the art and culture of Rome's other neighbours, the Etruscans to the north. Etruscan culture was older than that of Rome, and continued to flourish long after its brief century of domination in early Rome (617–510 B.C.E.) and the shrinking of Etruscan power within the area enclosed by the Arno and the Tiber. But whereas the life of women in Greek Sicily and southern Italy remained private and separate from that of men, we have seen that Roman women, perhaps as a legacy of Etruscan influence in early Roman society, had a recognized role in public. Even so, both Greek and Roman women might well have envied the luxury and social importance of women in the culture of the great Etruscan cities that will be described in Chapter 8.

TRANSLATIONS

Babbitt, F. C. 1936/1972. *Plutarch: Moralia*. Vol. 4. Loeb Classical Library. Cambridge, Mass.

Green, P. 1982. *Ovid: The Erotic Poems*. Harmondsworth, Middlesex.

Fuller, E. (ed.) 1959. *Plutarch: Lives of the Noble Romans*. R. Warner trans. New York.

Lewis, N. and Reinhold, M. 1990. *Roman Civilization: Selected Readings*, vol. 1. New York.

Mandelbaum, A. 1961. *The Aeneid of Virgil*. New York.

Martin, C. 1979. *The Poems of Catullus*. Baltimore, Md.

Rackham, W. 1952/1968. *Pliny: Natural History*. Loeb Classical Library. Cambridge, Mass.

Radice, B. 1982. *Livy: Rome and Italy*. Books 6-10. Harmondsworth, Middlesex.

Scott-Kilvert, I. 1979. *Polybius: the Rise of the Roman Empire*. Harmondsworth, Middlesex.

Sélincourt, A. de. 1960. *Livy: The Early History of Rome*. Books 1-5. Harmondsworth, Middlesex.

Warmington, E. H. 1940. *Remains of Old Latin*. Vol. 4. Loeb Classical Library. Cambridge, Mass.

WORKS CONSULTED

Beard, M. 1980. "The Sexual Status of Vestal Virgins." *Journal of Roman Studies* 70: 12–27

———, 1989. with J. North and S. F Price, *Pagan Priests*. Cambridge.

Crook, J. A. 1967. *Law and Life of Rome*. Ithaca.

Degrassi A. 1963–65. *Inscriptiones Latinae Liberae Rei Publicae*. Florence.

Evans, J. K. 1991. *War Women and Children in Ancient Rome*. New York.

Gardner, J. F. 1986. *Women in Roman Law and Society*. Bloomington, Ind.

Pomeroy, S. B. 1976. "The Relationship of the Married Woman to Her Blood Relatives at Rome," *Ancient Society* 7: 215-27.

Rawson, B., ed. 1986. *The Family in Ancient Rome: New Perspectives*. Ithaca, N.Y.

Saller, R. 1984. "*Familia, Domus* and the Roman Conception of the Family," *Phoenix* 38: 336–55.

——— 1986. "*Patria Potestas* and the stereotype of the Roman family," *Continuity and Change* 1: 7-22.

Trendall, A. D. 1989. *Red Figure Vases of South Italy and Sicily: A Handbook*. London.

Watson, A. 1967. "The Divorce of Carvilius Ruga" *Tijdschrift voor Rechtsgeshiedenis*. 33: 38–50.

Further Reading.

Gardner, J. F., and T. Wiedemann. 1991. *The Roman Household*. Oxford.

Hallett, J. P. 1982. *Fathers and Daughters in Roman Society: Women and the Elite Family*. Princeton, N.J.

Lewis, N., and M. Reinhold 1980 *Roman Civilization Volume I Selected Readings: The Roman Republic and the Augustan Age*. New York.

Scafuro, A. 1989. "Livy's Comic Narrative of the Bacchanalia" in *Studies on Roman Women* ed., A. Scafuro, Part 2, *Helios* Vol. 16.2, 119–42.

Stehle, E. 1989. "Venus, Cybele and the Sabine Women: The Roman Construction of Female Sexuality" in *Studies on Roman Women* ed., A. Scafuro Part 2: 143-64.

Treggiari, S. 1991. *Roman Marriage: Iusti Coniuges*. Oxford.

Watson, A. 1971. *Roman Private Law around 200 B.C.* Edinburgh.

8

EXCURSUS
ETRUSCAN WOMEN

LARISSA BONFANTE

Around 630 B.C.E. an ambitious Etruscan couple arrived in Rome in a covered wagon. As the man and his highborn wife looked down on the city that was to be their new home, an eagle came down and plucked off the husband's hat and flew back into the sky above the covered wagon; then swooping back down to put the hat back on the man's head, the eagle disappeared into the heavens. The wife, who, like most Etruscans, was skilled at reading omens, joyfully embraced her husband, explaining this event as a sign from the gods that their highest ambitions would be fulfilled. The prophecy came true. Lucius Tarquin became king of Rome and founder of the Tarquin dynasty. His wife was the powerful Etruscan queen, Tanaquil.

Half a century later, another Tarquin became king after killing his royal father-in-law, urged on by his wife, who drove her carriage over her own father's corpse. As the Roman historian Livy tells the story (1.48.5–7),

All agree that she drove into the forum in an open carriage in the most brazen manner, and calling her husband from the Senate House, was the first to hail him as king. Tarquin told her to go home, as the crowd might be dangerous. [On the way the driver] pulled up short in sudden terror and pointed to [her father's corpse] lying mutilated on the road. There followed an act of bestial inhumanity—history preserves the memory of it in the name of the street, the Street of Crime. The story goes that the crazed woman . . . drove the carriage over her father's body. Blood from the corpse stained her clothes and spattered the carriage, so that a grim relic of the murdered man was brought by those gory wheels to the house where she and her husband lived. The guardian gods of that house did not forget; they were to see to it, in their anger at the bad beginning of the reign, that as bad an end should follow.

(Sélincourt 1960)

This last king of Rome, Tarquin the Proud, ruled by fear. His son's rape of the Roman matron Lucretia put an end to the monarchy at Rome. It all started when a drinking party among inactive officers culminated in a contest of wives, for which the men all rode out into the night. They found Lucretia busily directing the women of her household in wool-working. The Etruscan princesses, in contrast, were attending a luxurious dinner party, together with other "beautiful people" of their rank. At the house of Lucretia, Sextus Tarquinius, intrigued and then obsessed by Lucretia's beauty and chastity, returned later to threaten her life and to violate the laws of hospitality as her guest by raping her. The Etruscan tyrants were, as a consequence, driven from Rome, and the Roman Republic was established.

The traditional tales of the Etruscan dynasty at Rome and the events leading up to the rape of Lucretia emphasize the importance of the Tarquins' wives in acquiring the kingship for their husbands, and, along with the stated contrast with the Roman matron Lucretia—who killed herself to preserve her honor and that of her family—dramatically illustrate the different social roles of Etruscan and Roman women. Handed down by tradition and vividly related by Livy, these Roman stories of Etruscan queens seem to reflect elements of local Etruscan customs, many of which agree with what we learn about the Etruscans from the considerable evidence of archaeology. Wall paintings from Tarquinia show luxurious banquets attended by beautifully dressed nobles, men and women together. On a wall painting (Fig. 8.1) from the Tomb of the

Figure 8.1. Drawing of a wall painting showing a couple banqueting on the same couch, from the Tomb of the Painted Vases in Tarquinia (ca. 500 B.C.E.). Her light skin and his dark color, as in Greece, depict gender difference, but here, unlike Greece, where women shown in symposia are prostitutes, the woman is a properly dressed wife: a married couple are shown attending a banquet together.

Painted Vases in Tarquinia, for example, we see a couple served by a small slave, while the husband fondly touches his wife's chin. On the wall hang the lady's necklaces and toilet box *(cista)* along with the usual flower wreaths. Here and elsewhere, women take their places by the men, equal in family lineage. The importance of the married couple, rather than the adult male citizen as in Athens or the paterfamilias in Rome, is clearly shown in the monuments (see Fig. 8.7). This reflects the aristocratic society of the Etruscans, a society in which public and private life were much less differentiated than in contemporary classical societies. All the evidence points to the fact that the lives of upper class Etruscan women, in the Archaic period—especially seventh to fifth centuries—had an element of autonomy and privilege surprising in comparison to that of other women in the ancient Mediterranean world.

Perhaps no feature of Etruscan society differed so much from that of Greece and Rome as the position of women. Recently, much serious study of Etruscan women has been done, stimulated in part by the attention paid to Greek and Roman women. Scholars no longer focus on Bachofen's nineteenth century thesis of an Etruscan matriarchy, nor even on the figure of Tanaquil, recently explained in a historical and religious context. New fields of study include an examination of the religious titles of women, of the types of objects typically found in women's tombs, of women's chariots, of women's jobs. Women's graves of the ninth and eighth centuries B.C.E., for example, contained spinning and weaving equipment, special shapes of tableware, jewelry, belts, and other objects of personal adornment, maybe even including perfume. There were large quantities of amber, prized for its beauty and magic properties: women apparently best knew how to handle the magic powers of amber, just as Tanaquil could read the meaning of bird signs and, in the North, women could read the magic signs of the runes (so the name Gudrun, "good at reading runes"). (Rallo 1989; Bonfante 1985: 287).

In judging this aspect of Etruscan life, as in others, we are limited by the lack of any Etruscan literature. What we have is the accounts of Greek and Roman historians, all of them extremely biased against what they perceived to be Etruscan immorality and self-indulgence. The evidence of inscriptions—some 1300 inscriptions have come down to us—must be interpreted, and so must the monuments. Modern scholars tend to be more comfortable with literary evidence than with the monuments, but the monuments in fact speak to us more directly than does the literature.

For example, the bronze women's mirrors decorated with engraved designs demonstrate that literacy, considerably more widespread in Etruria than elsewhere, and important for religious reasons in all of central Italy, was not confined to men; out of some 3000 mirrors, more than 300 (or 10 percent) are provided with inscriptions, mostly identifying mythological scenes. The example illustrated (Fig. 8.2) shows a loving couple, Turan (Aphrodite) and Atunis (Adonis), a typically Etruscan scene involving an older woman and a younger man. The fringes on the

Figure 8.2. Bronze mirror engraved with a scene of Turan (Aphrodite) and Atunis (Adonis) as lovers. The classical, solemn style is typical of Etruscan art in the second half of the fourth century B.C.E.

shoulders of Turan and her attendant are a sign of divine status or of the high rank of a mortal. The inscription on Athena's shield says that Tite Cale gave the mirror to his mother as a gift. These mirrors, like the richly decorated tombs of women and men, were for the elite; only 2 percent of the tombs at Tarquinia had painted decoration.

Women's tombs were as richly furnished as those of the men; in the early period a few even had chariots buried with them. In the Tomb of the Five Chairs, enthroned male and female ancestors protected the family with their divine status. A tomb painting from Chiusi (Fig. 8.3) shows funeral games and entertainments being performed in honor of a deceased woman, seated, with footstool and parasol—a close parallel to a scene of honors paid to a dead man in the Tomb of the Juggler at Tarquinia. In the tombs the houses of the living were reproduced for the dead, with all the equipment for eating, drinking, and dancing, as well as wall paintings depicting these feasts. Etruscan married couples took part in banquets, in contrast with the men's symposia or drinking parties so popular in Greek life and vase painting; at those Athenian parties only female entertainers and prostitutes were welcome (Fig. 10.1). The rock-cut tombs at Cerveteri reproduce the rooms of an Etruscan house, with doors, windows, chairs, and beds. In the bedrooms the men's and women's beds have different shapes. Jacques Heurgon (1961) pointed out that both types of beds are in fact shaped like normal banquet couches, but that those of the women are encased in house-shaped containers, with pointed "pediments" at the head and foot of the beds. Outside, stone markers showed who was buried in the chamber tombs: phallus-shaped for men, house-shaped for women. Gifts left with dead women consisted of spindle whorls, spools and other wool-working equipment, mirrors and toilet boxes and jewelry, including amber and other "magic" items to ward off the evil eye, and special shapes of jugs and banquet equipment. The splendid dresses in which the women were buried have, of course, been lost to us, but the symbolic and precious nature of their possessions showed their status. Men took with them their armor and their bronze bowls, imported Greek vases and black cups they had used to entertain their numerous guests and show off their status in their lifetime. Later, Hellenistic funerary reliefs show the couple renewing their

Figure 8.3. Painting from the tomb of the Monkey at Chiusi, late sixth century B.C.E., with the deceased woman watching funeral games in her honor.

vows, each spouse followed by attendants. Throughout, the archaeological record seems to express women's high social status along with the distinction in function between them and their men.

Etruscan monuments and the evidence of language and inscriptions thus confirm many of the claims of Greek and Roman authors, though obviously their accounts also contain contemporary clichés concerning barbarians and their luxurious lusty lives, as well as hostility toward an Etruscan way of life that differed so much from their own. Experiencing their difference as a conflict in civilization, Greek and Roman authors expressed it in terms of attitudes to sex and relations between women and men.

The longest ancient literary passage we have about Etruscan customs comes from Theopompus, a Greek historian of the fourth century B.C.E. He was startled by them and drew the worst possible conclusion from what he saw and heard about Etruscan women (the passage is quoted in a work by Athenaeus, a later Greek author).

Among the Etruscans, who were extraordinarily pleasure-loving, Timaeus says . . . that the slave girls wait on the men naked. Theopompos, in the forty-third book of his *Histories*, also says that it is normal for the Etruscans to share their women in common. These women take great care of their bodies and exercise bare, exposing their bodies even before men and among themselves: for it is not shameful for them to appear almost naked. He also says they dine not with their husbands, but with any man who happens to be present; and they toast anyone they want to.

And the Etruscans raise all the children that are born, not knowing who the father is of each one. The children also eventually live like those who brought them up, and have many drinking parties, and they too make love with all the women.

It is no shame for the Etruscans to be seen having sexual experiences . . . for this too is normal: it is the local custom there. And so far are they from considering it shameful that they even say, when the master of the house is making love, and someone asks for him, that he is "involved in such and such," shamelessly calling out the thing by name.

When they come together in parties with their relations, this is what they do: first, when they stop drinking and are ready to go to bed, the servants bring in to them—with the lights left on!—either *hetairai*, party girls, or very beautiful boys, or even their wives.

When they have enjoyed these, they then bring in young boys in bloom, who in turn consort with themselves. And they make love sometimes within sight of each other, but mostly with screens set up around the beds; these screens are made of woven reeds, and they throw blankets over them. And indeed they like to keep company with women: but they enjoy the company of boys and young men even more.

And their own appearance is also very good-looking, because they live luxuriously and smooth their bodies; for all the barbarians living in the West shave their bodies smooth. . . . They have many barber shops.

(Gulick 1927–41: 12.517–18)

Athenaeus also quotes the remark of Aristotle (Gulick 1927–41: vol 1, p. 103) that Etruscans eat with their wives, reclining at table with them under the same blanket; and that Etruscan slaves are very beautiful and dress better than is the custom of slaves.

Theopompus's picture is put together in part from a literary cliché about the luxurious life of the barbarians, in this case the Etruscans; but it is perhaps also based on reports of Greek travelers in Etruria. All the standard charges of luxurious living (Greek, *truphe*) are present: the lust, the nudity, the homosexuality, the parties, the fancy barbers. How much of his account was true? Certainly the extraordinary freedom of the women, emphasized by the implied contrast with Greek women of the time, was more than simply the expression of the author's hostility to a way of life vastly different from his own. So, for example, in a Greek trial in Athens, Ca. 400 B.C.E., the orator Isaeus could prove in defense of his client that a woman was a courtesan who gave herself to anyone, rather than the man's wife, by citing the evidence of neighbors who testified to the quarrels, serenades, and frequent scenes of disorder that took place when the woman was at the man's house. These were proofs that she was a mistress and not a wife. For, he says, "no one, I presume, would dare to serenade a married woman, nor do married women accompany their husbands to banquets or think of feasting in the company of strangers, especially mere chance comers," (Isaeus 3.14; Forster 1983)

A Greek of Theopompus' time felt a deep distaste for the Etruscan custom of the mingling of the sexes at dinner in a respectable context. Seeing husbands and wives so unexpectedly together was such a serious breach of Greek culture and good manners that it must have led Theopompus to imagine that women joined men in another traditionally male place, the gymnasium, where Greek men exercised naked. In fact, Etruscan women did attend games, as we see in paintings and reliefs from Tarquinia from the fifth century, B.C.E. (Fig. 8.4), showing bleachers with spectators, male and female, watching games and contests. But there is no evidence that they were particularly fond of such strenuous physical exercise as Spartan women are said to have practiced—like their husbands, they seem to have preferred spectator sports, though images of women athletes do occur in their art.

Etruscan women may well have raised their own children; here we can only guess at the reality behind Theopompus's statement. Perhaps the ancient custom of infanticide, prevalent in both Greek and Roman societies (but not among the Hebrews and later forbidden by the Christians), was not present among the Etruscans. Their wealth may have made it less necessary, of course, though economic reasons are not necessarily in the foreground in such decisions. Another possible interpretation is that the women were said by Theopompus to raise their own children because legally they could decide what babies were to be brought up and which exposed—unlike Greece and Rome where legally it was the father who "raised up" the baby, acknowledging it as his own and therefore legitimate and a citizen. Etruscan art, in fact, much more than Greek art, and even before the Hellenistic period, focused on scenes of children, often with their mothers or their families.

Much more easily confirmed is Aristotle's remark that the Etruscans eat with their wives, reclining at table with them under the same blanket, and that their house servants, who were very beautiful, dressed better than was the custom of slaves elsewhere in the Classical world. Sarcophagi and tomb paintings often represent deceased couples joined together on their funeral beds as on their banquet couches during their lives. Best known, perhaps, are the terra-cotta sarcophagi from Cerveteri (in Rome and Paris) with figures of husband and wife, with archaic smiles, tenderly embracing (Fig. 8.5): the sarcophagi of "Bride and Groom," as they are usually called in English (they actually represent a married couple, *sposi* in Italian), and the many couples at the happy feasts painted on the walls of tombs at Tarquinia. The blanket mentioned by Aristotle was, like a bridal veil today, long a symbol of the bride as well as of marriage. On the well-known sarcophagus of the Bride and Groom from Cerveteri, now in Rome, the mantle of the husband that covers the legs of the wife is not visible in our illustration. A depiction of a wedding on a relief from Chiusi (Fig. 8.6) shows the bridal pair under a fringed canopy, together with the priest, in a ritual remarkably like a traditional Jewish ceremony in modern America. And the typical gesture of the wife in Etruscan, as in Greek art, shows her holding the veil or mantle away from her face. Two other Etruscan couples are shown in bed together under the same blanket on sarcophagi from a later period. One shows husband and wife, idealized as classically young and beautiful and naked (Fig. 8.7). To have them both naked would have been a most unusual situation in Greece, where nudity was customary for men, but identified women as prostitutes; it is understandable in an Etruscan context, where the women enjoyed great privilege, perhaps even comparable to that of men.

Figure 8.4. Copy of a wall painting from the Tomb of the Chariots (Tomba delle Bighe) at Tarquinia, fifth century B.C.E., with men and women seated together on bleachers, watching games and contests.

Figure 8.5. Terra-cotta sarcophagus of a husband and wife from Cerveteri of the sixth century B.C.E., showing the couple on their couch. The Archaic Ionic style of the figures shows the Etruscans' skillful use of this international style in this influential period of their history, when they provided important models for Roman art, religion, and culture.

Similarly, the Etruscans had commissioned a naked cult statue of a goddess in the sixth century B.C.E. for a sanctuary at Orvieto (Fig. 8.8); the naked statue of the so-called Cannicella Venus was found in a sacred area within the necropolis of Cannicella at Orvieto, the ancient sanctuary of Volsinii. This highly unusual commission had gone to a Greek

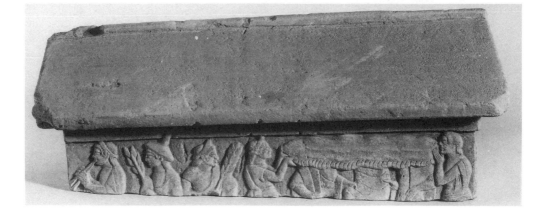

Figure 8.6. Limestone relief from Chiusi, ca. 500 B.C.E., showing a wedding, the couple with a priest under a canopy and musicians playing in celebration. Again, the theme of the married couple shows how important this subject was in aristocratic Etruscan society.

sculptor used to making naked statues of kouroi, male youths, around 530 B.C.E.—the statue was made of island marble and carefully repaired in antiquity. Several centuries earlier than Greek representations of nude goddesses in monumental form, the Etruscan goddess suggests again a different attitude to gender and the body.

Etruscans, even slaves according to Aristotle, dressed luxuriously by Greek and Roman standards. Athenians called certain luxurious ladies' sandals with gold laces "Etruscan." (Ehrenberg 1943: 278, citing Kratinus 131.) The Romans adopted Etruscan rounded mantles as their citizen's normal toga, as well as their purple and bordered garments for triumphal garb, and for children, priests and magistrates. Etruscan women were usually represented with mantles and shoes, indicating that they went outdoors as much as the men—in contrast to the women of Athens, usually shown on vases of the Archaic and Classical periods at home, wearing the chiton (or, if courtesans "on the job" at drinking parties, naked).

The women we have been discussing were, of course, all of them members of the elite, the aristocracy. But the wealth of archaeological evidence from pre-Roman Italy allows us to see something of the religion and beliefs of the more humble. Votive figures from Italian sanctuaries reflect the private cults of the modest and poor. Healing sanctuaries with thousands of votive terra-cotta and bronze figurines have been found, testifying to the devotion of those who came there. In the seventh and sixth centuries, votive offerings consisting of a group of these bronze statuettes—a male figure, often a warrior, a female figure, and an animal statuette—are probably not divinities but a family unit, a household: the married couple accompanied by an animal representing their property. This type of votive offering was popular in north Etruria and was widely exported around Europe. Some sanctuaries, evidently the ancient equivalent of fertility clinics, specializing in women and children,

Figure 8.7. Lid of a limestone sarcophagus of the mid-fourth century B.C.E., from Vulci; a couple recline together as if on their marriage bed. Their nudity and the idealization of the bodies suggests their closeness in the marriage bond.

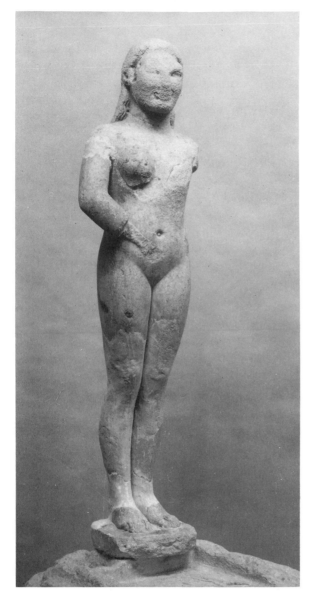

Figure 8.8. The "Cannicella Venus,"
(ca. 530 B.C.E.) cult statue of a nude
goddess, the Etruscan Venus, from the
Cannicella necropolis Orvieto (ancient
Volsinii).

received thousands of votive statuettes from worshipers asking for the
procreation or protection of children or thanking the divinity for favors
received. Many of the faithful gave so-called anatomical ex-votos, tiny
models of uteri or breasts. But the majority of ex-votos consisted of swad-
dled babies or mothers and children, including mothers nursing their babies. This theme of the nursing mother (or kourotrophos) is all but completely absent from Classical art of mainland Greece and the world of
the Greek islands and Asia Minor. This remarkable contrast reflects profound differences between Greek art and thought and that of the Etruscans and other peoples of ancient Italy, since figures of nursing mothers
were popular all over Italy in Etruscan, south Italian, and Sicilian art,

in regions where the concept of mother goddesses ruling over fertility and the birth of children had never ceased to be important.

Images of nursing mothers were particularly frequent in the art of the fourth to the first centuries B.C.E.; they were votive gifts in sanctuaries where different languages were spoken, but geographical proximity, religious customs, and cultural influences formed a common bond among different peoples in central and southern Italy. While the image of the mother (often seated) was adopted from Greek art, the baby was a purely Etruscan addition (Fig. 8.9).

Figure 8.9. Votive terra-cotta figurines of mothers with infants and young children on their laps, a subject rare, almost nonexistent in Greek art but common in the art of Italy from early times. There are numerous examples of these mold-made figures; the ones illustrated here come from the fourth century B.C.E., Satricum.

Was a religious reason enough to account for the importance of the motif of mother and child in the art of ancient Italy, or did the culture include a special affection for children, as was apparently the case in ancient Egyptian society? Historical changes in attitudes and family feelings, as well as family structure, are currently debated by scholars. Certainly affection between husband and wife was shown openly in Etruscan art (we are reminded of Theopompus's shocked description of the servant reporting that the master is in bed, presumably with his wife), much more openly than in Greece or other Mediterranean societies where it is still considered improper to exhibit conjugal love in public, or even to speak of it. Several loving couples are shown in which one of the partners is affectionately chucking the other under the chin (Fig. 8.1), and we could suggest that the nursing-mother images also signify special familial bonds as well as religious symbolism.

At the beginning of this chapter, we saw some formidable Etruscan women at home and abroad, together with their husbands and with their families. There is also tantalizing evidence about Etruscan women's relations with one another. We see women working together at textile production on a seventh-century object decorated in Etruscan style, a bronze axe-shaped pendant from a rich woman's tomb in Bologna (Fig. 8.10); its relief decoration shows women at work carding, spinning, and weaving. Sixth-century wine-jugs of black bucchero, a typically Etruscan pottery fabric, show groups of running naked girls, perhaps reflecting

Figure 8.10 Drawing of the front and back of a seventh-century B.C.E. bronze pendant found in the tomb of a woman in Bologna. The reliefs include important women seated on thronelike chairs working wool in the same demonstration of feminine domesticity seen in Greek and Roman art.

some ritual initiations of young girls into adulthood. Elsewhere, two women are shown traveling together in a carriage on sarcophagus reliefs as well as, apparently, on a sixth-century terra-cotta relief plaque from a building at Murlo, near Siena. Two women are represented enthusiastically (romantically?) embracing in a scene on an engraved mirror.

Like art, language, preserves traces of women's lives and their importance in Etruscan society. Funerary inscriptions give evidence of women's names. Roman women had no names of their own; they were known first as their fathers' daughters and later as their husbands' wives, when they came into the husband's manus, or legal power, as in the legal formula of marriage, *ubi tu Gaius, ego Gaia* (as you are Gaius, I am Gaia). Etruscan women had their own names—Tanaquil, Seianti. They apparently passed their rank to their children; the frequent use of both the father's name and the mother's name in Etruscan inscriptions attests to the mother's importance. The name of Seianti Hanunia Tlesnasa is inscribed on a brightly painted sarcophagus in the British Museum (Fig. 8.11). The dowager herself appears on the cover, mirror in hand, holding out her veil and wearing all her precious jewelry. That she lived to be more than eighty years old is shown by an analysis of

Figure 8.11. Painted terra-cotta sarcophagus (ca. 150 B.C.E.) of a woman named Seianti Hanunia Tlesnasa, showing the richly bejeweled figure of the deceased reclining on the lid as on her banqueting couch. Her gesture, pulling the veil from her face, is common for brides and wives.

her bones, still inside the casket after all these years. Scientists have reconstructed her face, so we can see what one of the last of the great Etruscan ladies looked like. Soon after her death, the sophisticated, luxurious, aristocratic Etruscan culture, in which women enjoyed the kind of status associated elsewhere only with men, disappeared into that of the victorious Romans.

TRANSLATIONS

Cary, E. 1937. *Dionysius of Halicarnassus: Roman Antiquities*. Loeb Classical Library. Cambridge, Mass.

Forster, E. S. 1983. *Isaeus*. Loeb Classical Library. Cambridge, Mass.

Gulick, C. B. 1927–41. *Athenaeus: Deipnosophistae*. Loeb Classical Library. Cambridge, Mass. vol 6 (rev. 1955)

Sélincourt, A. de. 1960. *Livy: The Early History of Rome*. Books 1–5. Harmondsworth, Middlesex.

WORKS CONSULTED

Bachofen, J. J. 1967. *Myth, Religion and Mother Right*. Princeton, N.J. (Originally published 1861 and 1870)

Bartoloni, G. 1989. "Marriage, Sale and Gift. A proposito . . . di alcuni corredi femminili . . ." 35–54 in *Le Donne in Etruria* ed. A. Rallo, Rome.

Bianchi Bandinelli, R. 1982. *L'arte etrusca*. Rome.

Bonfante, L. "Etruscan Couples and their Aristocratic Society." in *Reflections of Women in Antiquity*, edited by Helene P. Foley, 323–43. New York.

Bonfante, L. 1984. "Dedicated Mothers." In his *Visible Religion*, 3: 1–17. Leiden.

————. 1985a. "Amber, Women and Situla Art." Special issue of *Journal of Baltic Studies*, edited by Joan Todd, 16: 276–91.

————. 1985b. "Votive Terracotta Figures of Mothers and Children." In *Italian Iron Age Artefacts in the British Museum*, edited by J. Swaddling, 195–201. Papers of the Sixth British Museum Classical Colloquium. London.

Briguet, M-F. 1988 *Le sarcophage des époux de Cerveteri du Musée du Louvre*. Paris. (Enlarged version, Florence, 1969)

Ehrenberg, V. 1943. *The People of Aristophanes: A Sociology of Old Attic Comedy*. Oxford.

Grottanelli, C. 1987. "Servio Tullio, Fortuna e l'Oriente." *Dialoghi di Archeologia*, 3d ser., 5: 71–110.

Haynes, S. 1989. *"Muliebris certaminis laus."* In *Atti II Congresso Internazionale di Studi Etruschi 1985*, 1385–1405. Rome.

Heurgon, J. 1961. "Valeurs féminines et masculines dans la civilisation étrusque." *Mélanges de l'Ecole française à Rome: Antiquité* 73: 142–43.

————. 1964. *The Daily Life of the Etruscans*. New York.

Kaimio, J. 1975. "The Ousting of Etruscan by Latin in Etruria." In *Studies in the Romanization of Etruria*. Acta Instituti Romani Finlandiae, 5: 85–245. Rome.

Kajanto, I. 1972. "Women's Praenomina Reconsidered." *Arctos* 7: 13–30.

Nielsen, M. 1989. "Women and Family in a Changing Society: A Quantitative Approach to Late Etruscan Burials." *Analecta Romana Instituti Danici* 17–18: 53–98.

————. 1990. "Sacerdotesse e associazioni cultuali femminili in Etruria: testimonianze epigrafiche ed iconografiche." *Analecta Romana Instituti Danici* 19–20: 45–67.

Peruzzi, E. 1970. "Il nome femminile," Tabu onomastici," and "La donna nella società." In *Origini di Roma*, 1: 49–86. Florence.

Pfiffig, A. J. 1975. *Religio Etrusca*. Graz.
Rallo, A., ed. 1989. *Le donne in Etruria*. *Studia Archeologica* 52. Rome.
Torelli, M. 1975. *Elogia Tarquiniensia*. Florence.
Webster, T. B. L. 1972. *Potter and Patron in Classical Athens*. London.

FURTHER READING

Bonfante, L. 1986. *Etruscan Life and Afterlife*. 232–78. Detroit.
————, and G. Bonfante. 1983. *The Etruscan Language: An Introduction*. New York.
————. 1978. *Etruscan Art*. Harmondsworth, Middlesex.
Haynes, S., *The Augur's Daughter* (London 1987).
Macnamara, E. 1973. *Everyday Life of the Etruscans*. London.
————. 1990. *Etruscans*. British Museum Blue Books. London.
Pallotino, M. 1975. *The Etruscans*. Harmondsworth, Middlesex.
Sprenger, M., and G. Bartolini. 1986. *The Etruscans*. New York.
Steingräber, S. 1986. *Etruscan Painting*. New York.

9

REPUBLICAN ROME II: WOMEN IN A WEALTHY SOCIETY—ARISTOCRATIC AND WORKING WOMEN FROM THE SECOND CENTURY B.C.E.

Rome's war in Italy against the invading Carthaginian general Hannibal (218–202 B.C.E.) brought more than religious innovations; it forced major transformations of Roman society. Italy was occupied for more than fifteen years, and the city had to mobilize new armies each year to replace her losses, changing radically the economy of the peninsula and the gender balance of power in the city. Women, either widowed by the heavy casualties or in their husbands' absence, had to take control at least within the home. However, the austerities of the war were followed by a flush of prosperity and money beyond Rome's power of absorption from the easier victories over Macedon and Syria. In 215, taxes had been imposed on the wealth of independent women to raise money for military pay, and a new austerity law, the Lex Oppia, restricted women's finery and withdrew their privilege of riding in carriages; the law, unreported in the urgencies of the military narrative, only arouses the historians' interest in peacetime when a move was made to repeal it (195 B.C.E). The repeal was supported by vigorous women's demonstrations and a surge of masculine anxiety, provoked less by the risks inherent in repeal than by the new mood of the women. The speeches on both sides freely composed by Livy still convey vividly the anxiety of male conservatives, and the arguments that a Roman would use to justify rewarding women with greater luxury (34.3–4).

From Cato, the conservative consul, comes the fantasy of women beyond control:

Just review all the rules for women by which your ancestors controlled their license and through which they subjected women to the husbands; yet you can scarcely control them, even when bound by all these restraints. So if you will let them undermine each element and finally be raised level with men, do you think that they will be tolerable? As soon as they begin to be our equals they will be our masters . . . you give way to them against the interest of yourselves, your estates and your children. As soon as the law no longer imposes a limit on your wife's extravagance you certainly will not be able to impose it.

(Livy 34.3.1–3; trans. Elaine Fantham)

More interesting is Valerius's counterclaim, which reviews for us the occasions from the early Republic when women appeared in public to serve the state:

In the beginning under Romulus, when the Capitol was taken and there was a pitched battle in the forum, did not the women calm the fighting by their intervention between the armies? After the expulsion of the kings when the Volscian legions under Coriolanus had pitched camp at the fifth milestone, did not the wives turn back the enemy force that would otherwise have crushed the city? To leave out past history, when we needed money in the last war, did not the widows' fund help out the treasury, and when the gods were summoned to our aid in desperate times, did not the wives set out in a body to welcome the Great Mother from Ida?

(Livy 34.5.8–10; trans. Elaine Fantham)

For Valerius, display is the woman's glory:

Women cannot claim magistracies or priesthoods or triumphs or military decorations or awards or the spoils of war. Cosmetics and adornment are women's decorations. They delight and boast of them and this is what our ancestors called women's estate

(Livy 34.7.8)

Of course Cato was not alone. We can illustrate popular prejudices about women's "extravagance" from the contemporary diatribe of a bachelor in Plautus's comedy, *The Pot of Gold*. This misogynist imagines rich wives demanding luxuries and boasting of their dowries:

"Well sir, you never had anything like the money I brought you and you know it. Fine clothes and jewelry indeed! And maids and mules and coachmen and footmen and pages and private carriages. As if I hadn't a right to them." *[He continues in his own words]*—wherever you go nowadays you find more wagons in front of a city mansion than you can find around a farmyard. That's a perfectly glorious sight, though, compared with the time when the tradesmen come round for their money. The fuller, the ladies' tailor, the jeweller, the woollen worker, they're all hanging round. And there are dealers in flounces and underclothes and bridal veils, in violet dyes and yellow dyes, or muffs, or balsam scented footgear; and then the lingerie people drop in on you, along with shoemakers and squatting cobblers and slipper and sandal merchants and dealers in mallow dyes; and the belt makers flock around and the girdle makers along with them, And now you may think you've got them all paid off. Then up come weavers and lace makers and cabinet makers—hundreds of them—who plant themselves like jailers in your halls and want you to settle up. You bring them in and square accounts. " 'All paid off now anyway,' you may be thinking" when in march the fellows who do the saffron dyeing—some damned pest or other, anyhow, eternally after something.

(Plautus, *Pot of Gold*, 498–550; trans. Elaine Fantham)

The comic catalog may not be greatly exaggerated. Roman victories brought immense wealth into the hands of the military commanders and their families. An example is the account given by the Greek historian Polybius (writing after 160 B.C.E) about the family settlements of his young patron, Scipio Aemilianus. Scipio passed on his deceased grandmother's possessions to his divorced and impoverished mother. The same passage gives an idea of the huge dowries owed by Scipio's family to his sisters' husbands, dowries required for them to keep his sisters in the style to which they were accustomed (see also Dixon 1985b).

(Aemilia) the sister of Scipio's father . . . left her nephew a large fortune and his handling of this legacy gave the first proof of the nobility of his principles. Whenever Aemilia had left her house to take part in women's processions, it had been her habit to appear in great state, as befitted a women who had shared the life of the great Africanus when he was at the height of his success. Apart from the magnificence of her personal attire and the decoration of her carriage, all the baskets, cups, and sacrificial vessels or utensils were made of gold or silver, and were carried in her train on such ceremonial occasions, while the retinue of maids and men—servants who accompanied her was proportionately large.

(26) Immediately after Aemilia's funeral Scipio handed over all her splendid accoutrements to his mother. She had been separated from her husband for many years, and her means were far from sufficient to keep her in a state which was suitable to her rank. In previous years she had stayed at home on such ceremonial occasions. But now when a solemn sacrifice had to take place, she drove in all the state and splendour which had once belonged to Aemilia. All the women who witnessed the sight were moved with admiration for Scipio's goodness and generosity.

(27) After this there arose the matter of Scipio's obligation to the daughters of the great Africanus. When Scipio came into his inheritance it was his duty to pay each of the daughters half their portion. Their father had arranged to pay each of them fifty talents. Half of this sum had been paid to the husbands of each by their mother at the time of their marriage, but the other half was still owing. . . . Roman law laid it down that this part of their dowry that was still due should normally be paid to them over a period of three years; the first payment, consisting of the personal property, being made within ten months, according to the usual custom. Scipio however instructed his banker to pay each of the daughters within ten months the entire twenty-five talents

(Polybius 31.26–27; Scott-Kilvert 1979)

Polybius's motive is praise of his young patron, but the values of wealthy women appear clearly from the context. While men feared any attempt by young wives to be noticed in public (different noblemen allegedly divorced their wives for being seen with a freedwoman, for attending the games, and even for appearing in public uncovered [Valerius Maximus 6.3.10–12]), wealthy husbands used their older wives as indexes of their affluence—a form of conspicuous consumption noted by Thorstein Veblen in his *Theory of the Leisure Class* (1899).

Religious ceremonies were the women's equivalent of military parades; their luxury, however much a matter of competition between women, also reflected glory on their husbands. Even Virgil, in the pageant of Roman history depicted on Aeneas's great shield, mentions the women of Rome only as they are seen riding to a religious occasion in carriages, (see Chapter 7). Whether the funerary carriages shown on Etruscan funerary urns were the same as those of living women in Rome is unclear (see Chapter 8). That the carriage was a sign of high status and wealth is beyond doubt.

Dowries were known well before the second century, but it is at this time that they developed from a practical transfer of household goods or a plot of land to major economic tools. They feature as a grievance in Cato the elder's invective against the increasing power of women:

To begin with, the woman brought you a big dowry: next she retains a large sum of money which she does not entrust to her husband's control, but she gives it to him as a loan: lastly when she is annoyed with him she orders a "reclaimable slave" to chase him about and pester him for it.

(Cato, quoted by Gellius 17.6.8; Gardner 1986: 72)

It was too easy for the husband to rely on the use or interest from his wife's dowry money, and find himself in difficulties when required to return it on divorce. Lawyers refined the classification of dowry, distinguishing the woman's original paternal gift from any additional wealth that accrued to her. They even devised rules to cover the proportion that the husband could retain in the event of divorce. One-sixth was retained for the support of each surviving child, while deductions for marital faults ranged from one-eighth for minor offenses to one-sixth if the wife were divorced for adultery (Gardner 1986 ch. 6 Dowry, at p 112). These are modest enough deductions when we bear in mind that an adulterous wife could be lawfully killed when caught in the act by her father; if we are to believe Cato's speech *On the Dowry*, her husband had the same right.

When a man has launched a divorce, the arbitrator is like a Censor to the woman. He has the authority to impose what seems good to him, if the woman has acted in any wrong or disgusting fashion. She is fined if she drinks wine; if she has had a dishonorable relationship with another man, she is condemned.
. . . .
If you were to take your wife in the act of adultery, you could freely kill her without a trial; whereas if you were to commit adultery . . . she would not dare to lift a finger against you, nor would it be right

(Gellius 10.23; trans. Fantham)

It was seen as an imbalance in society if any women controlled larger estates than men of the same class. One sign of public anxiety is the Voconian Law of 169 B.C.E. that forbade a man in the top property class from making his daughter heir to more than half of his fortune; behind such legislation is the knowledge that money once left to a daughter passed out of the family.

Despite such indications of women's growing economic power, it seems that the disciplining of women, even for public offenses, was still a family rather than a public concern. Thus in the widespread scandal of the Bacchanalian conspiracy (186 B.C.E.) women found guilty of participating in the alleged orgies were handed over by the magistrates to their kinsmen for punishment. This could mean execution, or simply confinement on a country estate, where they could be kept out of the public eye. But if anecdotal evidence for the father's protection of his daughter's chastity may well belong to this period, there are signs that married women were passing out of their husbands' control. While the military commander was away campaigning for years at a time in Macedonia or Spain his wife would have a household staff to help her manage his affairs; admittedly the law still required women to conduct any legal business through the intermediary of a male tutor, but it became increasingly common for women to appoint their own puppets, freedman, or family clients who would do what they were told (cf. Evans 1991).

The most memorable woman of the Republic stands at the beginning of accelerating political and intellectual change. Cornelia (180?–105? B.C.E.), daughter of Scipio Africanus and wife of Tiberius Sempronius Gracchus, was widowed after she had borne twelve children, only three of whom survived. Her daughter Sempronia married the national hero Scipio Aemilianus, and her sons Tiberius and Gaius Gracchus attempted social reforms that brought immediate violence and prolonged political change. Rome had no royalty yet, but the widowed Cornelia had the status of a princess; she had even refused an offer of marriage from King Ptolemy of Egypt. Instead, she devoted herself to the education of her two sons. She brought Greek philosophers, Blossius from Cumae and Diophanes from Mytilene, to educate the young men, and surely also conversed with the scholars herself.

But there is a conflict in the accounts of Cornelia; we find it natural to assume that she encouraged her sons in their political idealism and attempts to transfer to Rome the practices of Greek democracy. Yet by the end of the Republic, historians could cite verbatim letters written by Cornelia to her younger son Gaius denouncing his revolutionary activities.

I would venture to take a solemn oath that except for the men who killed Tiberius Gracchus no enemy has given me so much trouble and toil as you have done because of these matters. You should rather have borne the care that I should have the least possible anxiety in old age, that whatever you did you thought it sinful to do anything of major importance against my views, especially since so little of my life remains. . . . Will our family ever desist from madness? . . . Will we ever feel shame at throwing the state into turmoil and confusion? But if that really cannot be, seek the tribunate after I am dead.

(Excerpt preserved by Cornelius Nepos "On the Latin Historians;" Horsfall 1989: 43)

It is a pity to challenge the authenticity of the earliest letter surviving from a Roman lady, and in the past these letters have been doubted simply because men questioned her ability to write them. That is not the issue. These letters served too well the propaganda of conservative reaction against the continued attempts at radical reform in the next generation. As a child of Scipio, Cornelia was herself exempt from criticism; so once she was dead it was opportune to "find" letters in which she turned on her sons as Veturia had once denounced Coriolanus.

The marble base survives of the now-lost statue of Cornelia (seated like Whistler's Mother), the first likeness of a secular Roman woman set up by her contemporaries in a public place. Art historians have been able to show that her statue was copied by a Greek sculptor of classicizing taste from the image of the seated Aphrodite by Pheidias. In turn the "Cornelia" became the model for a series of seated Roman ladies, culminating four hundred years later in the portrait said to be of Helena, mother of the emperor Constantine (Fig. 9.1).

This calm Hellenizing likeness of the Roman mother was to be manipulated for political ends. Erected after her death by the next wave of reformers to honor her as mother of the Gracchi, and set in the portico of defeated political enemies, her statue would survive the counterrevolution of Sulla, to be displayed in the renamed portico, now in honor of Octavia, sister of Augustus. But apparently during the conservative reaction against the attempts of later reformers to extend power to the popular assembly, the reference to her famous sons on its base was discreetly filed away and replaced, to put her status as daughter of Africanus before her role as mother (Coarelli 1978). Cornelia may have turned in her grave, but she will not be the only deceased woman commemorated for virtues she neither possessed nor esteemed.

Working Women: Freeborn, Slave, and Freedwomen

Life was very different for the wives of ordinary peasant soldiers. The prolonged absence of husbands must have forced hardship and initiative onto both peasant women and city wives. This description of the upbringing of the best Roman soldiers from an ode of Horace (65–8 B.C.E.) shows how the mother's authority had to replace the absent father:

> They were a hardy generation, good
> farmers and warriors, brought up to turn
> the Sabine furrows with their hoes, chop wood
> and lug the faggots home to please a stern
> mother at evening when the sun relieves
> the tired ox of the yoke . . .
> (Horace, *Odes* 3.6; Michie 1963: 138)

An extreme case of these peasant households occurs in Livy, when the chief centurion Spurius Ligustinus is displayed volunteering for service in Macedonia in 173 B.C.E. No wonder he volunteers, since he is at

Figure 9.1. Statue (early fourth century C.E.) of a woman of the Constantinian court (Helena, mother of Constantine?) that may replicate the seated statue of Cornelia, mother of the Gracchi, the first public statue of a Roman woman who was not a priestess.

the top of his profession, and has won many prizes and decorations. It is worthwhile to use his biography to reconstruct that of his wife:

"My father left me an acre of land and a little hut in which I was born and brought up, and to this day I live there. When I first came of age, my father gave me as wife his brother's daughter, who brought with her nothing but her free birth and her chastity, and with these a fertility which would be enough even for a wealthy home. We have six sons and two daughters, both of whom are now married. Four of our sons have assumed the toga of manhood. Two wear the boy's bordered toga."

(Livy 42.34; trans. Elaine Fantham)

Quite so, and our hero, now fifty, has served twenty-two years away from the little hut and the eight children, with only brief periods at home between campaigns. He may have brought home good prize money, but he has not had to bring them up, or find food to put in their mouths each day. To appreciate this woman's burden of motherhood we should also add to the eight surviving children the miscarriages and still-births so frequent in ancient society. Of course the family (essentially only one set of in-laws!) may have helped her out. But who would plant and harvest their piece of land until the children were old enough to help? Such a woman learned independence with a vengeance.

Our sources are indifferent to the life of the poor in town and country. At the bottom of the heap must be the slave women of the country, though Cato seems to have paid the slave women on his model farm for breeding (and his instructions to his overseer suggest that the overseer's wife has at least a chance of idle gossip); but when Varro's manual on farming recommends providing sturdy women for the shepherds it is clear just how harsh were the conditions under which they would live.

See that the housekeeper perform all her duties. If the master has given her to you as wife, keep yourself only to her. Make her stand in awe of you. Restrain her from extravagance. She must visit the neighbouring and other women very seldom, and not have them either in the house or in her part of it. She must not go out to meals or be a gadabout. She must not engage in religious worship herself or get others to engage in it for her without the orders of the master and mistress . . . she must be neat herself and keep the farmstead neat and clean. She must clean and tidy the hearth every night before she goes to bed (other duties omitted).

(Cato, *On Agriculture* 143; Hooper and Ash 1936: 125)

In the case of those who tend the herds in mountain valleys and wooded lands and keep off the rains not by the roof of the steading but by makeshift huts, many have thought it advisable to send along women to follow the herds, prepare food for the herdsmen, and make them more diligent. Such women should, however, be strong and not ill-looking. In many places they are not inferior to the men at work . . . being able either to tend the herd or carry firewood and cook the food, or to keep things in order in their huts. As to feeding their young, I merely remark that in most cases they suckle them as well as bear them. . . . when you were in Liburnia you saw mothers carrying logs and children at the breast at the same time, sometimes one, sometimes two [not necessarily twins] *showing that our newly delivered women who lie for days under their mosquito nets, are worthless and contemptible.* . . . In Illyricum it often happens that a pregnant woman, when her time has come, steps aside a little way out of her work, bears her child there, and brings it back so soon that you would say she had not borne it but found it.

(Varro, *On Agriculture* 2.10.6–8; Hooper and Ash 1936: 409–411)

The city slave would live in a house, but in cramped quarters, feeding on leftovers, depending for his prospects of freedom and a family upon the master's whim. An educated male slave, or a personal lady's maid, might hope for early freedom, but if the maid had borne children to a slave partner, either he or she would have to pay for their liberty. She might be punished or sold if she offended her mistress—perhaps by pleasing her master too well—as suggested by the lead curse tablet from the Republican period aimed at the destruction of a female slave:

> Danae, the new maidservant
> of Capito. Accept this offering
> and destroy Danae. You have cursed
> Eutychia, the wife of Soterichus.
>   (Degrassi *Inscriptiones Latinae*
>   *Liberae Rei Publicae* II.1145;
>   trans. Elaine Fantham)

Or again she might be sold for failing to gratify her master! The slave woman who was not sold away from her partner or child could be sent away from them to hard labor on the country estate. The death of a master or mistress could free large numbers of slaves by their will, or it could uproot them to be sold away from the only home they knew. In Rome as in Greece slave women who did not earn their freedom before they grew old would become the cheapest and most abused of slaves. The ultimate poverty for the free man was to be reduced to "one old slave woman." The worst fate was to be that unwanted creature.

The skilled slave who earned freedom was in the position of many immigrants in American society; by hard work in a small shop, or Thermipolium (wine bar) or a workshop weaving and dying textiles, the freedman or woman might afford the rent of an apartment and even make savings, to buy and train their own skilled slaves. But either might have to use the first savings to buy a partner's freedom *(contubernalis)* and that of any children they might have had.

The funerary reliefs of the late Republic in Rome, set into the walls of tombs along the roads leading into the city and thus visible to the passing world, occasionally document the kind of freed slave families who had saved a bit of money and now wished to take their place among the free citizens of Rome. The surviving examples of freed persons' tomb reliefs from the first century B.C.E. are few in number (Fig. 9.2), but they offer inscriptions that give names as well as images of couples and kin such as Blaesus, freedman of Caius and Blaesia, freedwoman of Aulus, slaves of the same family. The strangely haunting relief of a mother, father, and child (Fig. 9.3) belongs to the same type so favored by freed slaves from this period into the first century C.E. The woman extends an admonitory hand to touch her husband, as the little boy peeps out from behind them. The inscription with its many names cannot be used to identify the self-absorbed family group set before us, but the woman's gesture is based on a scene from high art, showing the divine couple Venus and Mars; yet the simple and veristic style of the relief seems worlds away from such classical sources. For the freed slaves who commissioned this group of reliefs, upward mobility came from the public self-representation of family, something to which only a free person was entitled, since a slave had no right to her or his own children, or to make

Figure 9.2. Tombstone of a couple who were freed slaves from a burial in Rome, first century B.C.E. Their names appear in inscriptions on the stone that would have been inserted into the front of a tomb enclosure; the stone was to be seen by passersby.

Figure 9.3. Tombstone of a family group, mother, father, and child, from the late first century B.C.E. in Rome.

a legal contract such as marriage. And despite the frequently rough style of many of these images, status was also sought by the use of models based on the tastes of the upper classes; men with grim death-mask faces, women with ever youthful and relatively idealized features, poses based on classical prototypes all contributed to the freed slave's sense of belonging to the legitimate world of free Romans.

Little is known of women's training in crafts, though wool-working was the basic chore of the household slave, to which she would return in any unoccupied hours. There is more evidence for women trained as entertainers. In the funeral epitaph for the child actress Eucharis quoted here, Licinia her patroness is more likely to have been an ex-actress and freedwoman of the Licinii than a member of that noble family.

EUCHARIS, FREEDWOMAN OF LICINIA, A MAIDEN TRAINED AND
ACCOMPLISHED IN ALL THE ARTS: SHE LIVED FOURTEEN YEARS.

Stop, you whose wandering glance lights on this house,
of death: linger and read our epitaph.
Words that a parent's love gave to this child
When her remains had reached their resting place.
Just as my youth was green with budding talent
and growing years promised a hope of fame,
The grim hour of my death came on too soon
Forbidding life and breath beyond this time,

Skilled as a pupil of the Muses' teaching
I who so recently danced to grace the show
Of noble patrons, I who first appeared
before the people in a Greek performance,
See! in this grave the cruel fates have placed
My ashes, unresponsive to my song.
My patroness's love and care and praise
Are silenced by the pyre, and still in death.
The daughter left her father to lament,
The later born preceded him in doom.
Twice seven birthdays lie with me engulfed
In death's abode, and everlasting gloom.
Please as you go pray earth lie soft upon me.
              (*Inscriptiones Latinae Liberae Rei Publicae* II. 803;
                                        trans. Elaine Fantham)

Women who lived by sex might buy girl slaves or raise foundlings to work for them when they had aged, but we should not exclude the training of women in crafts and catering. They had no monopoly on the luxury crafts and trades, but the demand for both men and women increased with Roman prosperity, and is attested to by the named specializations of the slave women whose ashes fill the columbaria (underground group burial chambers) of the early empire.

The Last Phase of the Republic and the Impact of Civil War

The age that celebrated the dead Cornelia saw increased emphasis on individuality, as noblemen composed their autobiographies in Greek or Latin and noblewomen earned the privilege of a public eulogy at their funeral. The practice begun by the conservative Catulus's eulogy of his mother (Cicero, *De Oratore* 2.44), was exploited for self-advertisement by Caesar himself:

> My aunt Julia's family was descended from Kings on her mother's side, and her father's is related to the gods. For the Marcii Reges, whose name her mother bore, descend from Ancus Marcius. The Julii, the clan from which my family comes, descend from Venus herself.
>
> (Suetonius, *Caesar* 6.2; trans. Elaine Fantham)

Cicero himself accepted from Caesar's murderer, M. Junius Brutus, the commission to write a laudatory biography of Brutus's cousin Porcia, modeled on the traditional spoken eulogy (Plutarch, *On the Virtues of Women* 242e). Clearly the politicians saw praise of their womenfolk as a means to their own or their family's distinction, but their own political conflicts soon led to a situation where the women had to share in political as well as public burdens.

Two generations of civil war from 90 to 30 B.C.E. killed and exiled the heads of many noble families and left the initiative to the surviving women; a Valeria Messalina showed her initiative in accosting and winning in marriage the autocrat Sulla; more conventional women used their position for political influence. Caecilia Metella extended her protection to save Cicero's client Roscius from his personal and political enemies, while Sallust could name the now-unidentifiable Praecia, mistress of a disreputable consul Cethegus, as the bestower of office to whom all aspirants should apply. Some women were more interested in money than politics. Cicero's wife Terentia, for example, ran her financial affairs through her steward Philotimus, and seems to have exploited Cicero's enforced absence from 51 to 47 to profit at her husband's expense.

> You write to us that my resources and yours and Terentia's will be available. Yours no doubt, but what resources of mine can there be? As for Terentia, to say nothing of innumerable other incidents, doesn't this cap all? You asked her to change 12,000 Sesterces, that being the balance of the money. She sent me 10,000 with a note that this was the amount outstanding. When she nibbles such a trifle from a trifle, you can see what she will have been doing when a really large amount is involved.
>
> (Cicero, *Letters to Atticus* 11.24.3; Shackleton Bailey 1965–66: 61–63)

When this action on her part led to divorce, Cicero had to raise the funds to return her dowry, while negotiating to retain a fraction for the expensive Athenian education of their twenty-year-old son. This seems to have been in the form of property, but there was difficulty in securing the rentals from another freedman of Terentia. Further troubles arose when Cicero tried to protect the children's rights in his own new will, and ensure that they received the proper share of their mother's fortune. Whatever the ultimate settlement, Terentia's continued wealth enabled her to remarry more than once and she lived to be more than a hundred.

In contrast, Cato's half-sister Servilia had more influence than money. Independence was forced upon her. Servilia's father, mother, and uncle Livius Drusus were killed or died when she was a child and her first husband was murdered by Pompey a decade later. She used her skills to make alliances through the marriage of her daughters with rising politicians from different groups, and even after the death of Caesar, who had once been her lover, one of her sons-in-law, Lepidus, was a privileged Caesarian who could help her secure changes in a senatorial decree on behalf of the "tyrannicides," her son Brutus and her son-in-law Cassius.

Women's Education: Women as Public Speakers

Power like Servilia's surely came from family connections, but she can hardly have achieved so much without an education. It is a pity that there is so little evidence for the education of the daughters of Rome, and certainly not enough to measure improvement. Cornelia, wife of Pompey and daughter of Metellus Scipio, must have been exceptional:

The young woman had many charming qualities apart from her youth and beauty. She had a good knowledge of literature, of playing the lyre, and of geometry, and she was a regular and intelligent listener to lectures on philosophy
(Plutarch, *Pompey* 55; from *Fall of the Republic*; Warner 1972: 216)

This is more like a Greek education than a Roman; music and geometry were not part of the Roman curriculum even for men. Usually girls would receive their early education from attending the instruction of their brothers, and thus might acquire Greek, read Homer and some Latin poetry, and do some elementary exercises in Latin composition; but they would be married by the age that their brother moved on to a tutor in rhetoric. Cicero offers further evidence for women's interest in philosophy, when he reports to Atticus that his friend Caerellia has pirated from Atticus's copyists a prepublication copy of his work *On Ends*.

Caerellia, in her amazing ardor for philosophy no doubt, is copying from your people. She has this very work *On Ends*. Now I assure you (being human, I may be wrong) that she did not get it from my men. It has never been out of my sight.
(Cicero, *Letters to Atticus* 13.21a, (327); Shackleton Bailey 1965–66: 215)

Caerellia also corresponded with Cicero, who in his turn wrote routinely to provincial governors on behalf of her business interests. He had reason to oblige her, since he was literally in her debt (*Letters to Atticus* 12.51; Shackleton Bailey 1965–66).

Surely some of these educated and leisured women wrote poetry? Certainly Cicero in his defence of Caelius (64) makes fun of his enemy Clodia (on whom see Chapter 10) as a composer of dramatic Mimes, but his mocking use of the Greek word for "poetess" is more likely to be a witty metaphor for her intrigues and perjury. Clodia herself did not appear in court, but in this period of anomalies women are reported as speaking in court for the first time. Valerius Maximus reports that Maesia of Sentinum earned the name Androgyne for pleading in her own defense before the praetor. Her case probably belongs to the period of Sulla's return, when Italian communities were stripped of civil rights; this was a period of lawlessness, in which men were on the run and women might have to defend themselves and their property from physical or legal attack (Marshall 1990). Less charitably, Valerius reports:

Afrania, wife of the Senator Licinius Bucco, was addicted to lawsuits and always pleaded her own case before the praetor, not for lack of friends to speak for her but because she was quite shameless. So from her constant harassment of the magistrate's tribunals with this unnatural yapping she became a notorious example of female abuse of court, so much so that the very name of Afrania is used as a charge against women's wicked ways. Her breath lasted out until the second consulship of Caesar with Servilius [46 B.C.E.].

(Valerius Maximus 8.3.2; trans. Elaine Fantham)

It was among the early achievements of the heroine we know as Turia (of whom more will be said in Chapter 11) that she drove bands of brigands away from the family estate and later vindicated her legal claim to it, but it is likely that Turia mobilized the household for defense without actually fighting, and financed and secured legal advocacy without appearing in court.

Women and Civil War: The Last Years of the Republic

The most honored example of a woman speaker also emerges from the upheaval of civil war; Hortensia, daughter of a great orator and widow of the Republican Servilius Caepio, pleaded before the triumvirs in 42 B.C.E. to remove the special taxes imposed on the womenfolk of the proscribed. The historian Appian (second century C.E.) is probably drawing on his invention when he makes Hortensia argue the injustice of this tax on the basis of gender:

Why should we pay taxes when we have no part in the honours, the commands, the statecraft for which you contend against each other with such harmful results? "Because this is a time of war," you say. When have there not been wars, and when have taxes ever been imposed on women, who are exempted by their sex among all mankind?

(Appian, *Civil War* 4.32; White 1979: 197)

Her eloquence and the unprecedented sight of noblewomen brutally driven away from the triumviral tribunal provoked such public indignation that the women won their concessions. Hortensia is admired, whereas Afrania is abused, because Hortensia was appealing in defense of a whole social group, before an irregular magistracy imposing an irregular tax (Snyder 1989, p 126).

But Appian's civil war narrative, despite its gratifying tribute to wifely fidelity, cover a period of unprecedented disturbance, when an outlawed senator might have to hide in a sewer or a roofspace, or disguise himself as a charcoal burner to escape his assassins (cf. *Civil War* 4.13).

In this disturbance one woman herself became a military leader. Fulvia had been wife to the radical tribune Clodius and the Caesarian Curio before she married her last husband Mark Antony. (Cicero, who hated Antony, told him in public that he was doomed because he had at home the fatal monster that had killed Clodius and Curio before him). When Antony was commander in chief in the East, perhaps before his relationship with Cleopatra began, Fulvia combined with Antony's brother Lucius to lead a rebellion of Italian cities against Octavius's land confiscations (Babcock 1969). The story of their propaganda war has been revealed by the insults scratched on the slingshots of either side: "Octavius, you suck!" "Octavius the wide-arsed!" "L. Antonius and Fulvia, open wide your asses!" (Hallett 1977 pp 157–8). In Rome the ultimate insult to a man was "to suffer the woman's lot"; that is, to be penetrated, and most vulgar abuse exploits this.

Yet it was Fulvia who summoned Antony's friends with their armies and rallied the defenders of Perusia. When L. Antonius was defeated and forced to surrender, Fulvia finally slipped away to join Antony in Greece. She fell sick and died at Sicyon. With typical incomprehension Appian offers a hostile and trivializing obituary: "the death of this turbulent woman, who had stirred up so disastrous a war on account of her jealousy of Cleopatra, seemed extremely fortunate to both of the parties who were rid of her" (*Civil War* 4.55; White 1972).

Fulvia's death freed Antony for a new marriage alliance, and Octavian used Octavia, the younger of his two sisters, in a vain attempt to make a lasting tie with his rival. As Plutarch describes her, Octavia was a model wife, reenacting the peacemaking role of the original Sabine brides, bearing her husband children, and even, in the style of the late Republic, securing him military forces.

Octavia had sailed with him from Greece, but at her request he sent her away to her brother when she was pregnant, having already borne him one daughter. She went to meet Caesar on the journey and taking his friends Maecenas and Agrippa with her, she met . . . and begged him not to neglect her, since from being a very happy woman she had become most wretched. For now all men looked to her as the sister of one commander and wife of the other. "If the worst should happen," she said, "and war break out, it is uncertain which of you is fated to win and which to lose, but my role will be wretched in either case."

. . . .

When the agreement was made that Octavian should give Antony two legions for the Parthian war, and Antony should give Caesar a hundred warships, Octavia obtained over and beyond the agreement twenty swift ships from her husband for her brother and a thousand soldiers from her brother for her husband. . . . Antony took with him Octavia and his children by her and Fulvia, and set off for Asia.

(Plutarch, Antony 35; trans. Elaine Fantham)

In Plutarch's last chapter, after Antony and Cleopatra are dead, Octavia is seen supervising the upbringing and marriages of all Antony's children: his son by Fulvia, Iullus Antonius, she married to Marcella, her younger daughter by her first husband. Antony and Cleopatra's daughter, Cleopatra Selene, she married to Juba of Mauretania. In turn she secured the marriage of her own daughters by Antony to Domitius Ahenobarbus, the grandfather of Nero, and to Octavian's stepson Drusus, destined to be ancestor of two emperors, Caligula and again Nero. In his sister, Octavian had the best of models for the ideal of domestic loyalty that he would set before the women of Rome.

Patterns of Domestic Life and Death

It would be fairer to the society of the late Republic to form a picture of the lives of aristocratic women from those living before the civil war. Here we must recognize two patterns of family structure unfamiliar to recent society: first the likelihood of marriages ending in the death of the husband (usually ten years older than his wife) or the young wife, as a consequence of childbirth; second an accepted pattern of divorce and remarriage, leading to a wide age spread between siblings and half-siblings growing up in the same household. Thus, for example, Octavian's half-sister by his father's first wife was ten years older than the younger Octavia, his full sister, while his mother's remarriage to Marcius Philippus seems to have brought him further half-sisters (see Bradley 1991, chapters 6 and 7; analysis of key social factors, p. 171).

Even before the outbreak of civil war in 50, any well-born woman of the period might live through this sequence of remarriages; consider the best-known biography of a private woman—the life of Cicero's daughter Tullia. Born in 76 B.C.E., she was married in her teens to a man in his late thirties, and lost him to a natural death when he was just over forty. After a brief union with the patrician Furius Crassipes, ending in divorce, she and her mother decided on her last disastrous marriage to Cornelius Dolabella during her father's absence as governor of Cilicia, while he was still trying to find for her a husband not submerged in debt. Dolabella's role as a supporter of Caesar may have helped the women after Pompey's defeat but the man himself was useless. After the loss of Tullia's first pregnancy they lived apart, and a year later Cicero seriously debated whether to press for divorce so that the baby she was carrying might be brought up by her family. But his own financial need, which prevented him completing the payment of the dowry, also obstructed the divorce. In 45 B.C.E. Tullia died of postpuerperal complications after bearing a son who probably died within weeks. She was just over thirty. But although Cicero never recovered from her loss and tried to erect a shrine in her memory, his many letters convey no idea of her personality. Was she gentle? Was she witty? Was she cultured? The famous letter of condolence from Servius Sulpicius, then governing a Greece ruined by Roman warfare, balances the little that the future had to offer a woman of her class against the conventional record of Tullia's past satisfactions:

But I suppose you grieve for *her*. How often must you have thought, and how often it has occurred to me, that in this day and age they are not most to be pitied who have been granted a painless exchange of life for death! What was there after all to make life so sweet a prospect for her at this time? What did she have or hope? What comfort for her spirit? The thought perhaps of spending her life wedded to some young man of distinction? Do you suppose it was possible for you to choose from this modern generation a son-in-law suitable to your child? Or the thought of bearing children herself, whose bloom would cheer her eyes, sons who could maintain their patrimony, would seek public office in due course, and act in public affairs and their friends' concerns like free men? Was not all this taken away before it was granted? The loss of children is a calamity, sure enough—except that it is a worse calamity to bear our present lot and endure.

. . . .

Tell yourself that she lived as long as it was well for her to live, and that she and freedom existed together. She saw you, her father, Praetor, Consul and Augur. She was married to young men of distinction. Almost all that life can give, she enjoyed: and she left life when freedom died. How can you or she quarrel with fortune on that account?.

(Cicero, *Letters to his Friends.* 4.5 (248); Shackleton Bailey 1978: 248)

The vicarious achievements of Tullia's past are not peculiar to this generation. Many recur in the moving elegy composed by Propertius for another Cornelia, the stepdaughter of Octavius who would become Augustus Caesar, but Cornelia could add pride in her three children to Tullia's record of virtue and family glory. This is a man's perception of a good woman, and it is men who gave this poem its title as "the queen of elegies," but Cornelia's account of her life is still worthy to be the last quotation, because it best represents the ideals and realities of life for the only women we come to know from the time of the Roman Republic, the women of the privileged and endangered ruling class. Like Hortensia she is depicted as speaking in her own defence—but before the last judgment of Hades:

THE DEAD CORNELIA ADDRESSES HER JUDGES

I was born to this, and when the wreath of marriage
Caught up my hair, and I was a woman grown,
it was your bed, my Paullus, that I came to
and now have left. The carving on the stone
says SHE WED BUT ONCE. O fathers long respected
victors in Africa, be my defense . . .

I asked no favours when Paullus was made censor:
no evil found its way within our walls.
I do not think I have disgraced my fathers:
I set a decent pattern in these halls.
Days had a quiet rhythm: no scandal touched us
from the wedding torch to the torch beside my bier.
A certain integrity is proof of breeding:
the love of virtue should not be born of fear.
Whatever the judge, whatever the lot fate gives me,
no woman needs to blush who sits at my side—
not Cybele's priestess, Claudia, pulling to safety
the boat with the holy image, caught in the tide:
not the Vestal who swore by her robe she would rekindle
the fire they said she had left, and the ash blazed flame:
and most of all not you my mother, Scribonia—
all but the way of my death you would have the same . . .

For my children I wore the mother's robe of honor;
It was no empty house I left behind.
Lepidus, Paullus, still you bring me comfort
you closed my eyes when death had made me blind.
Twice in the curule chair I have seen my brother;
they cheered him as a consul the day before I died.
And you, my daughter, think of your censor-father,
choose one husband and live content at his side.
Our clan will rest on the children that you give it,
Secure in their promise I board the boat and rejoice.
Mine is the final triumph of any woman,
that her spirit earns the praise of a living voice.
    (Propertius *Elegies* 4.11; Carrier 1963: 191–92 excerpted)

If we are too conscious of a public voice, of a censor's wife upholding official virtue; if these claims ring hollow because historians remind us that Cornelia's mother Scribonia was deserted by Augustus the day after she bore him a daughter, who would herself submit to enforced dynastic marriages followed by exile and disgrace; if we follow the careers of Cornelia's sons Lepidus and Paullus, to their consulships in 1 and 6 C.E.—the elder condemned to death for conspiracy, the younger "spared the perils of marrying a princess" (Syme 1939: 422)—this is to let the hazards of closeness to a rising dynasty blind us to the other, personal, values that Cornelia implies. We have deliberately broken off before the most moving and timeless part of her poem, where she turns to bid farewell to her husband and children. The reader may seek this out and read it privately.

TRANSLATIONS

Carrier, C. 1963. *The Poems of Propertius.* Bloomington Ind.
Hooper, W. D. and H. B. Ash. 1936. *Cato and Varro: on Agriculture.* Loeb Classical Library. Cambridge, Mass.

Horsfall, N. 1989. *Cornelius Nepos: A Selection*. Oxford.

Mandelbaum, A. 1961. *The Aeneid of Virgil*. New York.

Martin, C. 1979. *The Poems of Catullus*. Baltimore Md.

Michie, J. 1963. *The Odes of Horace*. New York.

Perrin, B. 1917. *Plutarch: Lives*. Loeb Classical Library. Cambridge, Mass.

Scott-Kilvert, I. 1979. *Polybius: the Rise of the Roman Empire*. Harmondsworth, Middlesex.

Shackleton Bailey, D. R. 1965–66. *Cicero's Letters to Atticus*. Vols. 1–6, Cambridge.

———— 1978. *Cicero's Letters to his Friends*. Vols. 1 and 2. Harmondsworth, Middlesex.

Warner, R. 1958. *Plutarch: the Fall of the Roman Republic* Harmondsworth, Middlesex.

White, H. 1972 *Appian's Roman History* Vol. 3, Loeb Classical Library. Cambridge, Mass.

WORKS CONSULTED

Babcock C. L. 1969. "The Early Career of Fulvia" *American Journal of Philology* 86: 1–32.

Beard, M and M. Crawford, 1985. *Rome in the Late Republic; Problems and Interpretations*. London.

————, 1989 with J. North and S. F. Price, *Pagan Priests*. Cambridge.

Bradley, K. 1991 *Discovering the Roman Family*. Oxford.

Carp, T. 1983 "Two Matrons of the Late Republic." *Women's Studies* VIII 189–200, reprinted from H. P. Foley, ed., (1981) *Reflections of Women in Antiquity*. New York, 343–54.

Coarelli F. 1978. "La Statue de Cornélie, Mère des Gracches et la crise politique à Rome au temps de Saturninus" in *Le Dernier Siècle de la Répulbique Romaine et L'Epoque Augustéenne*. Strasburg 1978: 13–28.

Corbier, M. 1991. "Family Behavior of the Roman Aristocracy: Second Century B.C.-Third Century A.D." *Women's History and Ancient History*, ed. S. B. Pomeroy. Chapel Hill, N.C. 173–95.

Crook, J. A. 1967. *Law and Life of Rome*. Ithaca, N.Y.

Delia, D. 1991. "Fulvia Reconsidered," *Women's History and Ancient History*. (see Corbier) 197–217.

Degrassi A. 1963–65. *Inscriptiones Latinae Liberae Rei Publicae*. Florence.

Dixon, S. 1984. "Family Finances: Tullia and Terentia," *Antichthon* 18, 78–101.

————, 1985a "The Marriage Alliance in the Roman Elite," *Journal of Family History* 358–78.

————, 1985b "Polybius on Roman women and Property," *American Journal of Philology* 106: 147–70.

————, 1989. *The Roman Mother*. Norman, Okla.

Evans, J. K. 1991. *War Women and Children in Ancient Rome* New York.

Gardner, J. F. 1986. *Women in Roman Law and Society* Bloomington, Ind.

Hallett, J. 1977. "*Perusinae Glandes* and the changing Image of Augustus, *American Journal of Ancient History* 2: 151–71.

Kleiner, D. E. E. 1977. *Roman Group Portraiture: The Funerary Reliefs of the Late Republic and Early Empire*. New York.

Marshall, A. J. 1990. "Roman Ladies on Trial: the Case of Maesia of Sentinum" *Phoenix* 44: 46–59.

Phillips, J. E. 1978. "Roman Mothers and the Lives of Their Adult Daughters," *Helios* 6: 69–80.

Pomeroy, S. B. 1976. "The relationship of the married woman to her blood relatives at Rome," *Ancient Society* 7: 215–27.

Rawson, B., ed. 1986. *The Family in Ancient Rome: New Perspectives*. Ithaca, N.Y.

————, ed. 1991 *Marriage, Divorce and Children in Ancient Rome*. Oxford.

Saller, R. 1984. "*Familia, domus* and the Roman conception of the Family." *Phoenix* 38: 336–55.

—— 1986 "*Patria potestas* and the Stereotype of the Roman Family" *Continuity and Change* 1: 7–22.

Scafuro, A., ed. 1989 *The Women of Rome. Helios* I and II

Snyder, J. M., 1989. *The Woman and the Lyre: Women Writers in Classical Greece and Rome.* Carbondale, Ill.

Treggiari, S., 1984. "*Digna condicio;* Betrothals in the Roman Upper Class." in *Studies in Roman Society, Classical Views/Echos du Monde Classique* 3: 419–51.

—— 1991 "Divorce Roman Style: How easy and how frequent was it?" in *Marriage, Divorce and Children.* ed., B. Rawson, 47–68.

FURTHER READING

Corbier, M. 1991. "Divorce and Adoption as Roman Familial Strategies, in *Marriage Divorce and Children in Ancient Rome* ed., B. Rawson. Oxford 47–78.

Dixon, S. 1991. "The Sentimental Ideal of the Roman Family." In *Marriage Divorce and Children* ed., B. Rawson 99–113.

Fantham, E. 1991. "*Stuprum:* Public Attitudes and Penalties for Sexual Offences in Republican Rome," *Classical Views/Echos du Monde Classique* 10: 267–91.

Gardner, J. F. and T. Wiedemann 1991. *The Roman Household.* Oxford.

Hallett, J. P. 1982. *Fathers and Daughters in Roman Society: Women and the elite family* Princeton, N.J.

Treggiari, S. 1981. "*Concubinae,*" *Papers of the British School at Rome* 49: 59–81.

—— 1991. *Roman Marriage: Iusti Coniuges.* Oxford.

Watson, A. 1967. *The Law of Persons in the Later Roman Republic.* Oxford.

—— 1971. *Roman Private Law around 200 B.C.* Edinburgh.

10

EXCURSUS
THE "NEW WOMAN": REPRESENTATION AND REALITY

Chapter 9 has shown how Rome came under the influence of both Etruscan culture in its first three hundred years and was introduced in the second century B.C.E. to the social customs of Greece and the Hellenized lands of Asia minor. Yet, although Rome became increasingly Hellenized during the last century of the Republic, it was still predominantly a society suspicious of sexual pleasure, and remote from any concept of love as a passion bringing joy and sorrow.

The symposium is the only context in Greek society or literature in which men associated with women who lived by their charms and their sexuality, but these women were not equal partners; instead, they were usually hired, either as musicians for collective entertainment or as short-term sexual companions for individual guests (Fig. 10.1). These marginalized women had no other role in society; to be an unprotected foreigner was at times little better than the position of a slave (see Chapter 3).

As in Greece, so in Rome well-born wives were differentiated from the shadowy foreign or freedwomen who lived by their sexual charm. But respectable Roman women had always been accepted at social occasions among their own class; hence there was not the clear dividing line between the "respected" domestic wife and the exploited outsider familiar from Greek society. To judge from our sources in the last years of the republic, the more independent women of good family were now beginning to decide for themselves what kind of social occasion they enjoyed. Both in ostensibly factual texts and in imaginative writing a new kind of women appears precisely at the time of Cicero and Caesar: a woman in high position, who nevertheless claims for herself the indulgence in sexuality of a woman of pleasure. The theme of this chapter is this new pattern of female behavior and its influence on the celebration of love and submission to women in Roman poetry between the time of Catullus

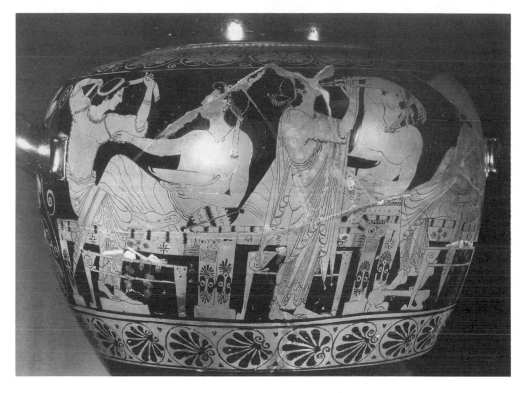

Figure 10.1. Greek red-figure vase made in Athens, late sixth century B.C.E., signed by Smikros; on the body are depicted a flute player and a hetaira amusing the male guests at a symposium.

(85?–54 B.C.E.) and Ovid (43 B.C.E.–17C.E). This period coincides with the rise of Caesar and the first thirty years of Augustus's long principate.

To visualize the world of these "modern" women we must forget the respectable dinner parties described by Cornelius Nepos (writing after 50 B.C.E.):

There are numerous actions decent by our standards which are thought base [by the Greeks]. For what Roman is ashamed to take his wife to a dinner-party? Where does the lady of the house not occupy the place of honor, and receive guests? This is all very different in Greece: she is only invited to dinners of the family and sits only in the inner part of the house, which is called the women's quarters: no one enters unless bound by ties of kinship.

(*Lives of the Foreign Generals*, preface 6–7; Horsfall 1989: 29–30)

Instead, realistic prose reportage and the emerging genre of personal love elegy offer glimpses of glamorous and assertive women, living a life of parties and self-gratification and choosing their own lovers. They are portrayed both inside elite society and in a more shadowy undefined half-world. Two of these women, at least, named by Cicero and Sallust, were historical figures, though male prejudice has surely distorted the record of their lives. Of the women celebrated by love poetry Catullus's beloved has been identified with the historical Clodia, wife of Metellus.

Although she is the only poetic mistress that can be identified with any confidence, Apuleius, writing two centuries after Catullus, provides names "from real life" of the women beloved by each of the poets. This is little more than the predictable search for biography. Women like Tibullus's Delia or Ovid's Corinna are more imaginative creations than real flesh-and-blood lovers; the poets themselves are skillful in omitting any detail that might even define the social status of the women they celebrate. But whatever the basis in society for this new model of woman, the literary figure sets a fashion. Corresponding with this "new woman" is what one might call a "new man," the poet-lover characterized by a voluntary and quite un-Roman subordination to her dominant personality.

First and most famous of these femmes fatales is "Lesbia," the brilliant and faithless lover represented in the poetry of the young Veronese aristocrat Valerius Catullus. Although his poems are not arranged sequentially, to narrate the rise and fall of their relationship, they enable the reader to evoke its nature, and the discrepancy between his idealism and her experience. For Lesbia is a married woman and the relationship begins as a secret.

> Lesbia hurls abuse at me in front of her husband.
>   That fatuous person finds it highly amusing!
>   Nothing gets through to you, jackass, —for silence would signal
>   that she'd been cured of me, but her barking and bitching
> show that not only haven't I been forgotten
>   but that this burns her, and so she rants and rages
>   (Poem 83; Martin 1979: 120)

Their first meeting is arranged through an accommodating friend.

> He gave me access to a field once forbidden
>   he gave me a house and gave me its mistress also,
> and in that place we explored our mutual passion.
>   there my radiant goddess appeared to me, stepping
> lightly, and paused once—to stand with the sole of her sandal
>   on the wellworn threshold and her bright foot crossed it
> as in that time when passionate love for her husband
>   brought Laodamia to the house which Protesilaus
> had built in vain . . .
>   (68.67–75; Martin 1979: 102)

Catullus, who also wrote beautiful poems in celebration of marriage, gives to this clandestine union the symbolism (for example, crossing the threshold) and sanctity of a marriage.

> Darling, we'll both have equal shares in the sweet love you offer
>   and it will endure for ever—you assure me.
> O heaven, see to it that she truly keep this promise,
>   that it came from her heart and was sincerely given,
> so that we may spend the rest of our days in this lifelong
>   union, this undying compact of holy friendship.
>   (109; Martin 1979: 146)

For her he invokes every value of Roman life: the compact between men and nations, friendship itself, and family love. "I didn't regard you just as my mistress then: I cherished you / as a father does his sons or his daughters' husbands" (72.3–4). "An old man cherishes his grandson no more deeply, / watching him nurse in the arms of his only daughter" (68.119–20). As long as his love is reciprocated, Catullus pours out direct addresses to his Lesbia such as were never written by any Greek:

> Lesbia, let us only live for loving
> and let us value at a single penny
> all the loose flap of senile busybodies!
> Suns when they set are capable of rising
> but at the setting of our own brief light
> night is one sleep from which we never waken.
> Give me a thousand kisses, then a hundred . . .
> (5.1–7; Martin 1979: 7)

When she grows tired of him, he knows that he must learn to endure it:

> Yes there were days which shone for you with rare brightness,
> now she no longer wants it. You mustn't want it,
> you've got to stop chasing her now—cut your losses,
> harden your heart and hold out firmly against her.
> Goodbye now, lady: Catullus' heart is hardened,
> he will not look to you nor call against your wishes.
> (8.8–12; Martin 1979: 10)

But he cannot hold out, and the poems of rejection outnumber those of reciprocated love. Their intense pain turns in the end from internalized anguish to graphic abuse of "Lesbia" as one who has become shameless and promiscuous. Witness his message, sent through the intermediaries Furius and Aurelius:

> Back to my girl then, carry her this bitter
> message, these spare words.
> May she have joy and profit from her cocksmen,
> go down embracing hundreds all together,
> never with love, but without interruption,
> wringing their balls dry . . .
> (11.15–22; Martin 1979: 14)

A last poem—or so it seems—does not even have an indirect message for her, but fantasizes his despair at her degradation in terms of the prostitute's tricks and hand-jobs:

> Lesbia, Caelius—yes, our darling,
> yes, Lesbia, the Lesbia Catullus
> once loved uniquely, more than any other!
> —now on street corners and in wretched alleys
> she shucks the offspring of greathearted Remus.
> (58; Martin 1979: 59)

It is predictable for the discarded lover to abuse the woman who rejected him, but students of Catullus's and "Lesbia's" society have seen confir-

mation of his abusive accusations in the account of her way of life offered by another male source, Cicero, who has cause to reinterpret her
relationship with Catullus's successor. For "Lesbia," the name chosen for
his Roman mistress by Catullus, as an admirer of Sappho, is generally
believed to have been the noblewoman Clodia, perhaps ten years Catullus's elder. Clodia was first wife, then widow, of the stuffed-shirt Metellus Celer. After she left Catullus, she went on to an equally intense affair with another brilliant young man from out of town, M. Caelius
Rufus—perhaps the very Caelius addressed in poem 58. Caelius was prosecuted for political violence in 54 B.C.E., and Cicero, as defending coun-
sel, diverted the jury away from Caelius's probable guilt by attributing
the prosecution to Clodia. He portrayed the charges as the malice of a
jilted lover, and depicted her as little more than a high-class harlot. Cicero's version shows us the daughter of one of Rome's noblest families
claiming the sexual freedom of a woman with no social standing to lose,
and making no effort to conceal her behavior—"a woman not just noble
but notorious" (*For Caelius* 32); Caelius's accusers have supposedly reproached him with the "passions, love making, adulteries, visits to
Baiae, beach picnics, parties and revelling, songs, choruses and boat-
trips" of *la dolce vita* (35), and Cicero in turn shames Clodia with the
life-style he claims she has taught Caelius.

Clodia was from a family so noble it could be indifferent to bourgeois public opinion, and her brother, Publius, a maverick demagogue,
was Cicero's most dangerous political enemy. It is into his mouth that
the advocate puts his most damning insults.

Imagine that your young brother is talking to you. "Why are you storming and
raging, sister, why are you crazy? [He breaks into a well-known comic verse.]
Why make a small affair seem great by kicking up a fuss?

You set your eyes on the young next-door neighbour; his health and height
and good looks excited you; you wanted to see more of him; you often got
togther in your gardens. You want to keep this dependent son of a stingy father
tied to you by your purse strings. You can't manage it; he kicks and spits and
drives you off. He doesn't think your presents are worth it. So take yourself off
some place else! You have your gardens by the Tiber carefully located just where
all the young blades come to skinny dip. You can pick up a partner there any
day. Why bother this fellow who rejects you?"

(36; trans. Elaine Fantham)

To win the case, Cicero diverts the jury away from Caelius's political
thuggery and feeds their prejudices with the idea of a woman ready to
finance her lovers; "a widow living loosely, a wanton living promiscu-
ously, a rich woman living extravagantly and a randy woman living like
a harlot" (38; trans. Elaine Fantham).

The historian Sallust (86?–35? B.C.E.) would have us believe that
many married noblewomen of this period found their pleasures outside
marriage. After describing the dissolute young men who joined the failed
coup d'état of Catiline, Sallust constructs a kind of female counterpart
to this revolutionary mob, in this portrait of the wanton wife of a rising politician,

[Sempronia] had often committed many crimes of masculine daring. In birth and beauty, in her husband also and her children, she was abundantly favoured by fortune: well read in the literature of Greece and Rome, able to play the lyre and dance more skilfully than an honest woman should, and having many other accomplishments which minister to voluptuousness. But there was nothing which she held so cheap as modesty and chastity; you could not easily say whether she was less sparing of her money or her honor. Her desires were so ardent that she sought men more often than she was sought by them. Even before the time of the conspiracy she had often broken her word, repudiated her debts, been privy to murder. Poverty and extravagance combined had driven her headlong. Nevertheless she was a woman of no mean endowment; she could write verses, bandy jests and use language which was modest or tender or wanton. In fine she possessed a high degree of wit and charm

(Sallust, *Catiline* 25; Rolfe 1971: 43)

A passage like this, especially in an old-fashioned translation, tells us as much about male imagination (ancient and modern) as about female license, but it should impel us to ask questions about both sexes. Why had these noblewomen suddenly kicked over the traces? And why does a well-brought-up son like Catullus disdain the usual casual fooling around and become infatuated with a bored noblewoman and endow their relationship with all the highest values of Roman public and private life? In Catullus the trigger may have been a unique conjunction of provincial innocence and metropolitan decadence, but the exaltation of extramarital love that is first found in this poetry becomes the dominant principle of a generation of love-poets—poets who found nothing similar in the Greek models of their formal genre.

Propertius and Tibullus, both children of the civil wars, who reached manhood about the time of Octavian's great victory over Antony and Cleopatra (31 B.C.E: their actual dates of birth are unknown), turn the women glorified by their poetry into Lesbias—or Cleopatras. The young lover is a slave, or a squire, subjected by his ruling passion to a brilliant and tyrannical mistress—a Cynthia or Delia, variously represented as living independently, kept by, or married to, another man, or mercenary and victimizing the poet by her pursuit of wealthier men. "Cynthia is not seduced by high office / the only thing that weighs with her / is the weight of a man's purse," cries Propertius (2.16; Warden 1972); Tibullus too laments: "O Delia, reject forthwith that grasping witch's guidance. Must every love give in to bribery? . . . alas! my song is vain. Her door unmoved by words / waits to be knocked by a money-laden hand" (Tibullus 1.5.59–60, 67–68; trans. Elaine Fantham).

Propertius's poetry gives perhaps the fullest picture of the world in which these women lived, though as a poet he freely shapes his invention. In one poem Cynthia speaks as though she were another man's property, locked in and forced to climb out to join him:

> Had you forgotten
> our night games on the Subura
> (nobody slept there), those subterfuges
> that wore a track across my window ledge?

> There I was dangling on a rope
> lowering myself, hand over hand
> into your arms. We used to make love then
> on street corners, twining
> our bodies together, while our cloaks
> took the chill off the sidewalk.
>   (4.7.15–22; Warden 1972: 85)

In another poem she has her own establishment in which Propertius is one client among many:

> No ancient beauty had a house as full of men as yours.
> Not Thais, though the whole of Greece was beating at her doors.
> Or Lais, who from Menander won the title of a play,
> and for the sons of Erichthon became the people's toy.
> What Alexander has destroyed shall be restored by Phryne.
> So many lovers she enjoyed—but you have twice as many.
>   (2.6.1–8; Warden 1972: 85)

The poet-lover protests his enslavement: "he who now lies as dust and ashes / once was the slave of a single love" (2.13.34–35); "No wife nor mistress shall ever seduce me away from you, you shall always be my wife and mistress, both" (2.6.41–42); "You alone are my house, / you, Cynthia, are my parents, you are all the occasions of my joy" (1.11.23–24; trans. Elaine Fantham). Here, in the echo of the orphaned Andromache's words to her husband Hector, is the measure of the seriousness this Roman poet could attribute to his love. More often, however, the portrait of his subjection is mixed with an almost comically vivid presentation of the angry virago whose ugly words contrast with her beauty on his late night visit to her bedside;

> So you've come at last, and only because that other woman
>   has thrown you out and closed the doors against you.
> Where have you spent the night—that night that belonged to me?
>   Look at you creeping back with the dawn, a wreck.
> It'd do you good to have to spend the sort of night
>   you make me spend! You'd learn what cruelty is.
> I sat up over my loom, trying to stave off sleep
>   then tired of that and played the lyre a little.
>   (1.3.35–44; Warden 1972: 9)

But the loom, symbol of the honest wife, and the lyre, symbol of the entertainer, are as incongruous a combination as Propertius's protestations of loyalty and his bouts of wild infidelity.

The most likely place for young men to encounter the women of these affairs, whether hired call girls, professional entertainers like Cytheris, or faithless wives, was again the dinner party. The sixty-year-old Cicero is embarrassed—but perhaps also thrilled—to meet the versatile (and much bedded) actress Cytheris at a party given by her former owner Volumnius:

"I had no idea *she* would be there. But after all, even Aristippus the Socratic did not blush when someone twitted him with keeping Lais as his mistress: Lais is my mistress, he said but I'm my own master. As for me, even when I was young I was never attracted by anything of that sort . . ."

(*Letters to his friends* 9.26 (197); Shackleton Bailey 1978)

Horace, who enjoys imagining a pleasant private dinner with a girl like Cytheris, feeds his moral indignation with the image of a young wife who slips from the dining table to oblige a wealthy guest, apparently condoned by her husband:

> Soon she's pursuing young philanderers
> among her husband's guests. Careless of whom
> she chooses, hugger-mugger she confers
> the illicit pleasure in a half-lit room,
>
> only the husband seeming not to note,
> at any man's command she leaves her place,
> pedlar or captain of some Spanish boat—
> whoever pays the price of her disgrace.
> (Horace, *Odes* 3.6; Michie 1963: 149)

In Latin love poetry the party is a shared pleasure of men and girls; Catullus invites Fabullus to bring his lovely lady—and all the food and wine because the poet is penniless (13). Propertius boasts of his success, "lording it as a guest among the girls" (2.30.16), but marks the end of his affair by imagining the mockery behind his back at all the dinner parties: "I was the latest after dinner joke: everybody had their Propertius story" (3.25.1–2; Warden 1972: 9). Ovid imagines a new seduction at such a party.

> "So your man's going to be present at the dinner party?
>   I hope he drops down dead before the dessert.
> Does this mean no hands, just eyes (any chance guest's privilege)
>   just to look at my darling while he
> lies there with you beside him in licensed embracement
>   and paws your bosom or neck as he feels inclined?" . . .
>
> When he pats the couch, put on your respectable-wife expression
>   and take your place beside him—but nudge my foot
> as you're passing by. Watch out for my nods and eye-talk
>   pick up my stealthy messages, send replies . . .
> (*Amores* 1.4.1–4, 15–18; Green 1982: 89–90)

One poem—the last in which Propertius recalls Cynthia—conveys to the full the range of life in this half-world of Rome's Bohemians. It begins with Cynthia's departure with an effete admirer on an excursion to Lanuvium:

> It's there that Cynthia went, driving a
> team of ponies, elegantly clipped, on a visit
> (so she said) to Juno, though the goddess she was serving
> sounded more like Venus. You saw it, Appian Way, how was it?

That magnificent procession, the pomp
of chariot wheels hurtling across your paving
and she (what a sight) crouched over the pole, swerving
like a demon into every pothole and sump.
As for that smooth-skinned fop, I'd rather not speak
about him, with his fashionable carriage
all draped in silk, the bracelets round the necks
of his Molossian dogs . . .
                    (Propertius 4.8.15–24; Warden 1972: 217–18)

and continues with Propertius's retaliation: a private party.

There's a girl I know called Phyllis, she's a neighbour
of the goddess Diana on the Aventine
not much to recommend her when she's sober
but she's quite charming with a little wine.
Then there's Teia, who lives close to the Tarpeian
gorge—a pretty girl, but when she's in liquor
she isn't satisfied with just one man.
So I asked them over to make the night pass quicker . . .
                    . . on a patch of green
stood a couch well concealed just for the three of us
to lie on. If you wondered, I was in between,
Lygdamus served the wine . . .
                    (4.8.29–36; Warden 1972: 218)

But the party is interrupted by Cynthia's unexpected return "flattening
the doors against the wall, with her hair unkempt but beautiful in the
wildness of her fury: . . . her eyes flashed like thunderbolts; she was savage as a woman could be: the scene as dramatic as the sacking of a city"
(4.8.51–56; Warden 1972: 217 19).

The purpose of the poem is the exaltation of the mistress, represented in heroic terms borrowed from the triumphant return of Odysseus
to reclaim his wife from the suitors: but unlike anything in the *Odyssey*
is the lover's delight in his own abject submission:

so I sued for terms,
desperately throwing my suppliant arms
around the feet she'd hardly let me touch.
                    (4.8.71–72; Warden 1972: 220)

The poet had begun his first book with the image of Love pressing his
victorious foot upon the poet's captive neck. He all but ends with a reiteration of this image. The intensity of Propertius's realization of this
woman and of their emotional relationship surely reflects both a new
attitude to women and a new kind of woman.

What social forces led freeborn women of good family to reject their
protected respectability and claim the sexual license of the outsider?
What changed the values of well-brought-up young men, that they
should openly exalt the kind of affair that had once been transitional

and surreptitious—acceptable only in the interstices between reaching manhood and contracting marriage? For while the poet-lovers still represent themselves as unmarried men, it is also part of their persona that they postpone indefinitely the duty of marriage and reproduction.

It is easier to see why women no longer accepted the demands of respectability. These generations had seen the social order itself repeatedly disrupted. Women were released from surveillance by the absence of their menfolk on campaign, in overseas administration, or during the civil war in flight or exile. While older or more sober women showed their emancipation by taking on responsibility for family finances, political negotiations, or petitions for their husbands' survival, others in less stable marriages might see no reason for fidelity, and daughters married off as a political bond between their father and his allies (or even former enemies) might assert themselves. The age patterns of Roman marriage were designed to avoid any time for the girl's seduction or experimentation before marriage. But if the young wife grew restless, the limited economic control possessed by the husband without legal manus also reduced his power to protest her behavior if it conflicted with the interests of the wife's natal family. In extreme cases, in order to obtain a divorce he still had to pay back five-sixths of her dowry. Unless women had learned chastity as a moral imperative they might claim for themselves the self-indulgence practiced by their husbands.

But why should the men have assigned such life and death importance to these affairs—whether adulterous or merely unsanctioned by society? One reason may have been their own loss of social standing. Propertius and Tibullus both claim to have lost family estates (as did Virgil and Horace) and may not have been sought after as sons-in-law. Another was the more general loss of respect for social structures brought on by the division of the nation into warring camps and the rise of upstarts who now enjoyed the confiscated property of the old upper class. "How could I supply sons to swell my country's triumphs?" says Propertius (2.7.13) in resistance to the idea of marriage. One of his kinsmen had been killed in the civil war, and once Romans were fighting each other, warfare became a nightmare instead of an adventure. Ironically too, Propertius in rejecting a military life invokes as a cautionary example the behavior of Antony, who had brought his own ruin upon him by his obsession with the fatal Cleopatra. Octavian exploited this account of Antony's downfall, adapting the myth of Hercules' submission to the oriental queen Omphale as a reminder of Antony's un-Roman pleasures (Fig. 10.2).

Yet both Hercules and Antony were paradoxically models for the love-poets' own life-style and indifference to "success." Success in public life was now out of men's own control, dependent upon powerful men like Pompey, Caesar, or Octavian. Subordination to a capricious woman was at least an individual choice, and these women may have been easier to satisfy than the military leaders with their incessant political re-

Figure 10.2. Mold for a clay vase (ca. 30 B.C.E.) showing Hercules and Omphale, the Lydian queen with whom Hercules was forced to trade clothing as part of his expiation for murder. The vase, called Arretine because the original center of production for these late Republican and early Imperial relief wares was Arezzo, comes from the workshop of Perennius; this shop seems to have specialized in highly Classicizing images of lovers, mythological and idealized.

alignments and their campaigning on the outer fringe of empire. Society had shown itself unstable and untrustworthy: better to seek a strictly private satisfaction.

We shall never know to what extent women of established family endorsed the life of pleasure described by the elegists, or the degree to which the poets' own actions matched their professions of enslavement to love. As we shall see in Chapter 11, Octavian seems to have been sufficiently alarmed by the decline of marriage and reproductivity among the privileged classes to use legislation to reinforce its appeal; at the same time he made both adultery and the condoning of adultery by an "injured" husband offenses open to criminal prosecution and punishable by expulsion from society. Ordinary anonymous citizens might continue to be chaste or promiscuous unnoticed, but respectability was now enforced on those in the public eye.

This had its impact on both art and life. Ovid, born some fifteen years after Propertius and Tibullus, could build on an elegiac code of love and permute the complexities of a literary love affair as a game with known rules. But he had to be careful in both his "autobiographical" and his prescriptive love poetry. He took care that his tales of Corinna, including her infidelities to himself and to his rivals, could not be reconstructed to suggest a living woman in a defined social milieu; and he took pains—but not quite enough—to direct his teaching of seduction in the *Art of Love* (2 B.C.E.) away from respectable women, ostensibly encouraging young men only in the permitted pursuit of noncitizen "easy" women.

> Aid my enterprise, Venus! Respectable ladies, the kind who
>   wear hairbands and ankle-length skirts,
> are hereby warned off. Safe love, legitimate liaisons
>   will be my theme. This poem breaks no taboos.
>   (*Art of Love* 1.31–34; Green 1982: 89–90)

But at length, when he had exhausted the possibilities of manuals for the men, he turned to instruct the women directly, still claiming to be concerned only with women outside respectability:

> Take lessons from me girls (those of you whom the law,
> And modesty, and your code, will permit): be mindful of
>   creeping
> Old age, don't waste precious time—
> Have fun while you can, in your salad days
>   (*Art of Love* 3.57–61; Green 1982: 89–90)

Had Ovid gone too far? His scandalous advice might still have brought no trouble upon him, if there had been no scandal in high places. But the real-life Clodia and Sempronia found their successors, and it was part of society's vengeance upon Augustus that his only child, Julia, should shame him. As Octavian, he had divorced her mother Scribonia the very day that her female child Julia was born. Yet according to the early fifth-century antiquarian Macrobius, Julia survived neglect and grew up with "a love of literature and much learning, easily accessible in that home," and charmed by her mild courtesy and lack of cruelty (*Saturnalia* 2.5.2). She would dutifully accept an early betrothal by her father to his nephew (who then died), then marriage to his closest friend, the middle-aged Agrippa, by whom she bore five living children, and on Agrippa's death, a final enforced marriage to her father's stepson and Livia's son, Tiberius, who left her and Rome to live at Rhodes. As mother of the two adopted Caesars, Gaius and Lucius, Julia had been publicly honored by her father for her wifely fertility, but even during her "happy" marriage to Agrippa, she boasted of ensuring that she conceived only *his* children by limiting her lovers to the months when she was already pregnant: "I never take on a passenger unless the ship is full" (Macrobius 2.5.9 Richlin 1992: 72). This and other witty retorts quoted by Macrobius, and derived from the Augustan epigrammatist Domitius Marsus, reflect the more sophisticated attitude to women's sexuality of poets like Ovid and of Julia's own circle in Rome. They show Julia herself opposing her conception of what was right for "Caesar's daughter"—luxury, elegance, and sexual autonomy—to the chastity and frugality her father expected of "the daughter of Augustus" (Richlin 1992). But while Julia only claimed the same sexual liberty that her father had himself enjoyed in his youth, (See Suetonius, *Augustus* 63 and 69 and Hallett 1977: 158–60) her behavior violated the model of propriety for royal women cherished by Augustus and presented to the public eye by her stepmother Livia. Once the emperor's wilful ignorance of her sexual adventures was shattered, he denounced and disgraced his daughter with public and uncontrollable rage. It is ultimately from him that we derive the hostile tradition that makes Julia the first *meretrix Augusta* (Imperial whore), a counterpart to the loathed Cleopatra, and one imitated by her own daughter Julia, who would share her mother's fate of exile nine years after her.

The absoluteness of Julia's destruction at Augustus's hands, and the cruel isolation he imposed in exiling her to a barren island, could not put an end to elite adultery, nor could Augustus's sentence of exile on her daughter in 8 C.E., and his equally sadistic relegation of Ovid, Rome's greatest living poet, to a Black Sea garrison outpost in the same year. These imperial acts could and did signal the end of open acknowledgment of adultery, ensuring that men and women in the next generation would not again proclaim their real or imaginary loves in prose or verse. Perhaps caution rather than virtue was all that Augustus restored, but when the circumstances that had undermined family and class stability receded, it is likely that the impetus to glamorize a different kind of partnership receded also. The new woman and the new love poetry were banished, until they returned, first in the heavy disguise of medieval troubadour songs of courtly love, then in the full flush of Romantic and "decadent" nineteenth century poetry and fiction.

TRANSLATIONS

Green, P. 1982. *Ovid: The Erotic Poems*. Harmondsworth, Middlesex.
Horsfall, N. 1989. *Cornelius Nepos: A Selection*. Oxford.
Martin, C. 1979. *The Poems of Catullus*. Baltimore, Md.
Michie, J. 1965. *The Odes of Horace*. New York.
Rolfe, J. C. 1931. *Sallust:* Loeb Classical Library, Cambridge, Mass.
Shackleton Bailey, D. R. 1978. *Cicero's Letters to His Friends*. Vols. 1 and 2. Harmondsworth, Middlesex.
Warden, J. 1972 *The Poems of Propertius*, Indianapolis, Ind.

WORKS CONSULTED

Balsdon, J. P. V. D. 1962. *Roman Women*. London.
Griffin, J. 1985. *Latin Poets and Roman Life*. Oxford.
Hallett, J. 1984a. *Fathers and Daughters in Roman Society*. Princeton, N.J.
———. 1984b. "The Role of Women in Roman Elegy: The Counter-Cultural Sensibility." In *Women in the Ancient World: The Arethusa Papers*, edited by John Peradotto and J. P. Sullivan, 242–62. Albany, N.Y.

Hinds, S. 1988. "Generalizing about Ovid." In *The Imperial Muse*, edited by A. J. Boyle, 4–31. Victoria, Australia.

Mack, S. 1988. *Ovid*. New Haven, Conn.

Richlin, A. 1992. "Julia's Jokes. Galla Placidia and the Roman Use of Women as Political Icons. In *Stereotypes of Women in Power: Historical Perspectives and Revisionist Views*, edited by B. Garlick, S. Dixon, and P. Allen, 65–91. New York.

Snyder, J. 1989. *The Woman and the Lyre: Women Writers in Classical Greece and Rome*. Carbondale, Ill.

Veyne, P. 1988. *Roman Erotic Elegy*. Translated by J. Pellauer. Chicago.

Wyke, M. 1987. "Written Women: Propertius' *Scripta Puella*." *Journal of Roman Studies* 77: 47–61.

———. 1989. "In Pursuit of Love: The Poetic Self and the Process of Reading Augustan Elegy in the 80's." *Journal of Roman Studies* 79: 165–73.

Zanker, P. 1988. "Rival Images: Octavian, Antony and the Struggle for Sole Power" in . In his *The Power of Images in the Age of Augustus*, translated by A. Shapiro, 33–78. Ann Arbor, Mich.

FURTHER READING

Chisholm, K., and J. Ferguson. 1981. *Rome in the Augustan Age*. Oxford. [sourcebook for texts]

Ferrill, A. 1980. "Augustus and His Daughter: A Modern Myth." In *Studies in Latin Literature and Roman History*, edited by C. Deroux, 2: 332–46. Brussels.

Luck, G. 1969. *Latin Love Elegy*. Edinburgh.

Lyne, R. O. A. M. 1980. *The Latin Love Poets*. Oxford.

Thibault, J. C. 1964. *The Mystery of Ovid's Exile*. Berkeley and Los Angeles.

Wilkinson, L. P. 1962. *Ovid Surveyed*. Cambridge.

Wiseman, T. P. 1985. *Catullus and His World*. Cambridge.

Woodman, T., and West, D. 1984. *Poetry and Politics in the Age of Augustus*. Cambridge.

Wyke, M. 1992. "Augustan Cleopatras: Female Power and Poetic Authority." In *Roman Poetry and Propaganda in the Age of Augustus*, 98–140 edited by A. Powell, Bristol.

11

WOMEN, FAMILY, AND SEXUALITY IN THE AGE OF AUGUSTUS AND THE JULIO-CLAUDIANS

In this chapter, we concentrate on the way our sources represent marriage, family, and sexuality in the first eighty years of the Imperial period. The Principate, the period from the accession of Augustus as emperor in 27 B.C.E. to 68 C.E. and the death of Nero, the last of the Julio-Claudian line descended from Augustus and his wife Livia, is extraordinarily rich in wonderful art and literature. Our sources in this chapter include Virgil's *Aeneid*, the elegant and classicizing sculpture of the Ara Pacis Augustae (Altar of Augustan Peace), and the poems of Ovid. In addition, historians such as Suetonius have much to say about the period, legal texts remain with plentiful information about the laws concerning marriage and adultery (although, of course, they leave out much, including information about failed attempts at legislation and a sense of the range of responses to individual laws), and inscriptions provide us with a notion of the ideal standards of conduct for upper-class women. At the same time that this material offers us a sense of the complexities of personal conduct and public ideology in the period, we face the usual problems of trying to write about women from sources made almost exclusively by men; only Sulpicia's poems preserve a woman's voice. And, as ever, the women of the lower classes, slave women, and noncitizen women tend to receive little attention from men whose words and patronage tended to focus primarily on the representation of their own kind. Much was invisible to them since it fell outside the range of their glances.

Marriage

Moral Revival in the Time of Augustus

Captured in stone, the family of the emperor Augustus moves in quiet procession toward the altar at which they will offer a sacrifice in honor of the peace Augustus brings to the Empire (Fig. 11.1). Along with the images of priests and priestesses of the state religion and the members of the Senate, their idealized portraits cover the monumental reliefs on the long sides of the Ara Pacis Augustae, the Altar of Augustan Peace. Made in Rome between 13 and 9 B.C.E., the altar inaugurates a new era both in state relief-sculpture and in Roman political life. Here, apparently for the first time in Roman public art, mortal women and children are represented along with men; members of Augustus's family, his wife Livia, his daughter Julia, her children and the foreign royal children being raised at court, and the Vestal virgins join male officials and priests in a clearly expressed display of the piety of emperor and family.

The presence of the women and children on the altar has multiple meanings, for they speak vividly not only to the totality of Imperial piety but also to the emperor's need to appear as guarantor of peace. Through war and diplomacy he brings peace to the Empire, but, in addition, he offers his family as an assurance that the just-ended civil war can be forgotten and that succession by inheritance can prevent it from ever happening again. The Vestal virgins, keepers of the sacred fire of Rome, guarantee the security of the state as well, and their chastity plays against and casts into sharper relief the alleged fecundity of the Imperial family.

Figure 11.1. The Imperial family in a procession on the Ara Pacis Augustae in Rome (13–9 B.C.E.). The message of dynastic continuity emerges clearly through the presence of women and children in the unusual context of a state monument.

The Augustan emphasis on reproduction that underlies the representation of family on the Ara Pacis, seems to be present in other parts of the altar, too. A panel, its imagery redolent of lush maternal nurturance, shows a woman with two infants surrounded by plants, water birds, and animals. In the panel showing Aeneas about to sacrifice a sow and her suckling young (Fig. 11.2), the imagery of fertility combines with the fulfillment of an oracle's prediction; in Virgil's *Aeneid* (3.390–98 and 8.81–84) this sign tells Aeneas that he has found his new homeland in Italy, where, as in the rich plant life that decorates the lower panels of the altar, rich growth and new life flourish. The altar comes at a time when Augustus was apparently engaged in a multifaceted program of political and moral revitalization of the Roman people; a key part of this campaign was his attempt to police sexual behavior, presumably to raise the rate of legitimate (that is, citizen) births. His new legislation on marriage and adultery (see below) testifies to the emperor's desire to control private behavior, especially what was perceived by some as the sexual irresponsibility of the Roman upper classes.

Figure 11.2. Ara Pacis Augustae panel showing Aeneas and the sow he discovers at the mouth of the Tiber as a sign that his journey from Troy in search of a new homeland has ended in success. The fertility imagery that pervades the altar recurs here to remind Roman viewers that Augustan peace is the guarantee of fertility and a happy future.

The Aeneid and the Image of Marriage

Given Augustus's concern to foster marriage and restore both the stability of family life and the reproductivity of the governing class at Rome, it is useful to look to Augustan literature for a representation of the high official valuation of marriage and women's role as mother. The excerpts from Livy and Ovid cited in chapter 7 show that a woman's honor could be a political issue, and even start a revolution. Augustus himself would quote speeches of old Roman censors that urged reluctant men to marry and reproduce. But if we look to literature for a warmer appreciation of marriage, the picture is strangely disappointing.

The *Odyssey* is built around the sanctity of a good marriage; in a famous passage Odysseus tells the young princess Nausicaa:

> And may the gods accomplish your desire
> a home, a husband, and harmonious
> converse with him—the best thing in the world
> being a strong house held in serenity
> where man and wife agree. Woe to their enemies
> joy to their friends! But all this they know best
> (*Odyssey* 6.180–86; Fitzgerald 1961)

In contrast, Virgil's Aeneas is a man alone, and the women who are or might have been his wives are removed as obstacles to the destiny of Rome, while the princess-bride Lavinia is a simpering cypher whom Aeneas never meets within the compass of the poem. Virgil does show a loving relationship between Aeneas and his Trojan wife Creusa, mother of his heir Ascanius, but when they must escape from Troy, she is left to follow behind the three generations of men and is lost in their panic. Rome's destiny requires her ancestor to be a widower. The ghost of Creusa absolves Aeneas:

> O my sweet husband, is there any use
> in giving way to such fanatic sorrow?
> For this could never come to pass without
> the gods' decree . . . you will reach
> Hesperia, where Lydian Tiber flows
> . . . there days of gladness lie in wait for you:
> a kingdom and a royal bride. Enough
> of tears for loved Creusa. I am not
> to see the haughty homes of Myrmidons
> or of Dolopians or to be a slave
> to Grecian matrons, I, a Dardan woman
> and wife to Venus' son. It is the gods'
> great Mother who keeps me upon these shores.
> And now farewell, and love the son we share.
> (*Aeneid* 2.780–89; Mandelbaum 1961)

Three times he tries to embrace Creusa's ghost, and three times his arms clasp empty air—just as they will when he sees his beloved father's shade in Elysium.

To ensure Aeneas's safe welcome in Carthage, the goddesses of sex and marriage conspire to delude the honorable and generous queen Dido into love for the stranger, whom she takes as consort and sharer of power in her city. Virgil's sympathetic and tragic Dido is perhaps the single best-known woman in all Roman literature: a widow who breaks her oath of celibacy in memory of her murdered husband and devotes herself to Aeneas. But despite the supernatural wedding ritual, Aeneas must obey divine command to leave her, and he answers her reproaches with a stern rebuke:

> I am not furtive. I have never held
> the wedding torches as a husband; I
> have never entered into such agreements.
> If fate had granted me to guide my life
> by my own auspices and to unravel
> my troubles with unhampered will, then I
> should cherish first the town of Troy, the sweet
> remains of my own people.
>   . . . And now the gods'
> own messenger, sent down by Jove himself—
> I call as witness both our lives—has brought
> his orders through the swift air. My own eyes
> have seen the god as he was entering
> our walls—in broad daylight. My ears have drunk
> his words. No longer set yourself and me
> afire. Stop your quarrel. It is not
> my own free will that leads to Italy.
>   (*Aeneid* 4.340–53, abridged; Mandelbaum 1961)

Virgil's own text, for all its sympathy with Dido's suicide, speaks more than once of her guilt *(culpa)* and Roman readers were not likely to see this unofficial and unsanctioned love as having any claim over their hero. Indeed, some readers will have associated Dido, for all her goodness, with that famous contemporary queen, Cleopatra, she who conspired with his weakness to ruin Antony and threaten Rome's integrity. Instead of succumbing to Dido as Antony had to Cleopatra, Aeneas when freshly arrived in Latium will be offered King Latinus's only child, Lavinia, as bride through the proxy of his envoys, and with her the kingdom she symbolizes.

This betrothal provokes the fierce war between Lavinia's former suitor Turnus and Aeneas. The future bride and groom do not meet, but Lavinia appears twice; first we see her among the Latin matrons supplicating Minerva for their city.

>   And Queen Amata too
> with many women, bearing gifts, is carried
> into the citadel, Minerva's temple
> upon the heights: at her side walks the girl Lavinia,
> the cause of all that trouble,
> her lovely eyes held low. The women follow

and they perfume the altars with the smoke
of incense and their voices of lament
pour from the shrine's high threshold.
(*Aeneid* 11.478–83; Mandelbaum 1961)

In the last book she appears again, when her mother speaks of Aeneas as her unwanted son-in-law. "Lavinia's / hot cheeks were bathed in tears; she heard her mother's / words; and her blush, a kindled fire, crossed / her burning face" (*Aeneid* 12.70–72).

Nor do women as mothers receive sympathy against the background of masculine urgency and the nation's fate. Two scenes are particularly revealing. The first occurs in Sicily when Juno, disguised, deceives the tired Trojan women into burning the fleet so that they may settle there, and they are scolded by the child Ascanius: "What is this new madness? Where are you aiming now, alas, poor wretched citizens?[1] You are not burning the Argive foe and enemy camp. These ships are your future hope. See here am I, your Ascanius!" His future and Rome are their reason for existing. One mother alone, for love of her son Euryalus, follows the men to Latium, and she is treated in such way as to provide a bitter contrast between Ascanius's promises and her own reality. To Euryalus, volunteering for a dangerous mission, Ascanius swears that if Euryalus perishes

she shall be a mother to me, lacking
only the name Creusa. No small honor
awaits her now for bearing such a son.
Whatever be the outcome of your deed,
I swear by this my head, as once my father
was used to swear, that all I promised you
in safe and prosperous return belongs
forever to your mother and your house.
(*Aeneid* 9.297–302; Mandelbaum 1961)

When Euryalus's mother hears of his death and wails in mourning, Virgil reports her lament, but the same Ascanius orders her to be taken into custody and confined indoors to stop her upsetting the Trojan fighting men (*Aeneid* 9.500–502). For all Virgil's poetic compassion, he represents the state as a structure in which women must ever serve men's needs or be suppressed.

Adultery and Resistance to Marriage and Reproduction

The disruptions of the civil war years and the changing mores of Roman upper-class life had a profound impact on the behavior of Roman women and men, as the previous chapters have shown. Claims that adultery was rife in Rome weave through the writings of Ovid, as when he has the old "hag" Dipsas say,

Maybe in the days when Tatius ruled, the grubby Sabine women refused to be taken by more than one man; now Mars tries men's souls in far off wars, and

Venus rules in her Aeneas' city. The lovely ladies are at play; the only chaste ones are those no one has courted.

                              (Ovid, *Amores* 1.8.35–44; trans. Natalie Kampen)

He also laughingly claims, at *Amores* 3.4, "A man is really a bumpkin who takes his wife's unfaithfulness seriously; he doesn't know enough about the morals of Rome" (trans. Natalie Kampen). Horace, in *Satire* 1.2, advises men to avoid adultery and matrons as more trouble than they are worth; "It's safer to go second class, I mean go with freedwomen" (trans. Natalie Kampen). With a freedwoman, he never worries

> About her husband just dropping in from the country, the door
> Splitting open, the dog yapping, house in an uproar of crashing
> And pounding on all sides, my girl tumbling head over heels
> Out of bed, as white as a sheet, while her maid (and accomplice)
> Shrieks it's not *her* fault—deathly afraid of her legs
> Being broken as punishment—the wife, thinking now to herself
> "There goes my dowry," while I eye myself sprinting off
> In a panic, my tunic undone, and trying to salvage
> My money, to safeguard my future and save my behind
>   (trans. S. Palmer Bovie)

Clearly, sex with a free married woman could cause a man some terrible problems. However, adultery was defined by law and custom as sex with a married woman other than one's wife; a free man still had sexual access legally to his slaves, to women whose work as prostitutes or barmaids put them outside the law's concern, and to concubines. None of these cases counted as adultery for him, although a married woman was an adulteress if she had sex with anyone but her husband (*Digest* 48.5.1).

An odd footnote to the principle that adultery was extramarital sex by a married woman appears in Seneca's discussion of adultery and lust in a text on legal controversies; the author presents models of disputation that may or may not be based on reality. In one he mentions a case of "the man who caught his wife and another woman in bed and killed them both" (Seneca the Elder, *Controversies* 1.2.23; Winterbottom 1974). That women had sexual relationships with one another is rarely alluded to by male authors, and then usually in so veiled or unclear a way as to make the whole question especially difficult. When Ovid tells the tale of Iphis, a girl brought up as a boy who falls in love with his/ her betrothed, he has the hero(ine) complain bitterly to the gods about the cruelty of her fate; she calls her feelings and her identity "monstrous" and rejects the pleasure of the homoerotic. The gods give her one of the rare happy endings for a woman in the *Metamorphoses* when they turn her into a man on her wedding day (Ovid, *Metamorphoses* 9. 666–791). Martial, writing at the start of the second century, makes explicit reference to the women who behave like men and have sex with girls as well as boys (Martial, *Epigrams* 1.90 and 7.67), and so does the

Greek poet Lucian, whose courtesan won't tell her curious friend exactly *what* two women do in bed (*Dialogues of the Courtesans* 5). The veiled references and insinuations may add up to just one more form of libertine behavior as the writers proceed with their usual castigation of female frivolity.

In a voice of deepest seriousness, the philosopher Seneca, writing to his mother from his exile in Corsica, where he seems to have been sent because of accusations of adultery with Caligula's sister Julia Lucilla, lays out a striking yet typical landscape of sexual irresponsibility:

> Unchastity, the greatest evil of our time, has never classed you with the great majority of women; jewels have not moved you, nor pearls; to your eyes the glitter of riches has not seemed the greatest boon of the human race; you, who were soundly trained in an old-fashioned and strict household, have not been perverted by the imitation of worse women that leads even the virtuous into pitfalls; you have never blushed for the number of your children, as if it taunted you with your years, never have you, in the manner of other women whose only recommendation lies in their beauty, tried to conceal your pregnancy as if an unseemly burden, nor have you ever crushed the hope of children that were being nurtured in your body; you have not defiled your face with paints and cosmetics; never have you fancied the kind of dress that exposed no greater nakedness by being removed.
>
> (Seneca, *Consolation to his Mother* 16.3–5; Basore 1964/1979)

Not only adultery and makeup, shameless dress and conduct were deemed scandalous; the open refusal to bear children brought women much criticism. A poem by Propertius to his Cynthia, written before 23 B.C.E. (see Chapter 10) suggests some resistance by men as well as women; "Why should I beget children for national victories? / There will be no soldier of my blood! / . . . You alone give me joy, Cynthia; let me alone please you. / Our love will mean far more than fatherhood" (Propertius, *Elegy* 2.7; trans. Natalie Kampen). His concern may be with an early version of the Augustan marriage laws that might have separated his beloved from him, perhaps forcing him to marry a "respectable" bride, but the poem suggests that the law was withdrawn or abrogated and the lovers thus were saved.

The possible loss of his mistress to an abortion prompted Ovid to write,

> She who first began the practice of tearing out her tender progeny deserved to die in her own warfare. Can it be that, to be free of the flaw of stretchmarks, you have to scatter the tragic sands of carnage? Why will you subject your womb to the weapons of abortion and give dread poisons to the unborn? The tigress lurking in Armenia does no such thing, nor does the lioness dare destroy her young. Yet tender girls do so—though not with impunity; often she who kills what is in her womb dies herself.
>
> (Ovid *Amores* 2.14.5–9, 27–28, 35–38; trans. Natalie Kampen)

A more even tone on the subject of abortion, less concerned with castigating women for immorality or vanity or with fear for the life of the beloved, comes through the writings of the doctor Soranus who practiced medicine in Rome in the later first century, C.E. He discusses contraception and abortion, giving preferred methods for both; he indicates that opinion was divided in the medical community about the permissibility of abortion:

For one party banishes abortives, citing the testimony of Hippocrates who says: "I will give to no one an abortive"; moreover, because it is the specific task of medicine to guard and preserve what has been engendered by nature. The other party prescribes abortives, but with discrimination, that is, they do not prescribe them when a person wishes to destroy the embryo because of adultery or out of consideration for youthful beauty; but only to prevent subsequent danger in parturition if the uterus is small and not capable of accommodating the complete development, or if the uterus at its orifice has knobbly swellings and fissures, or if some similar difficulty is involved. And they say the same about contraceptives as well, and we too agree with them.

(Soranus, *Gynecology* 1.19.60; Temkin 1956)

Soranus's position as a professional doctor meant that he saw as his patients wealthy women and their valued slaves rather than those whose poverty might have motivated their desire to limit the number of children they had; similarly, he considered legitimate the medical rather than social or emotional reasons for a woman to require an abortion or to use contraception. It does not follow that contraception and abortion were inaccessible to poor women through midwives, or that upper-class women avoided such practices except for medical reasons. Essentially, both in the medical world and in the world of the poet, sexuality, male and female, was under scrutiny and the subject of some disagreement, predictable in a time of social and political transformation.

Legal Definitions and Prescriptions on Marriage and Adultery

It is in this context of changing sexual standards that Augustus's new legislation on marriage and adultery was written and the Ara Pacis carved. They came on the heels of changes in custom that had gradually removed the vaunted absolute power of the father of a family over all his male and female dependents; by the late Republic, for example, few marriages followed the old pattern in which a father passed his daughter and her property into the absolute control of her husband and his family. Paternal power over life and death, power to force a son or daughter to divorce, and family judgment and punishment of the civil crimes of its dependent members all became less common than the texts suggest they were in the early Republic (Rawson 1986: 1–57 and 121–44).

The Augustan laws, designed to penalize those citizens who remained unmarried or childless (women between twenty and fifty and men after the age of twenty-five (see below) and those who committed adultery or married women or men of the "wrong" social rank or status (see below), had as their ostensible goals the moral revitalization of the upper classes, the raising of the birth rate among citizens, and the policing of sexual behavior in the attempt to reintroduce conservative social values and control the social conduct of an upper class seen as more interested in pleasure and autonomy than in duty and community. The laws may, however, really have been attempts to reconfigure social and property relationships; the years of changing customs, of loosened paternal power and of social chaos in the time of the civil wars of the first century, B.C.E., may have set laws out of tune with contemporary practices to such an extent that they were seen as ineffectual in representing reality. Augustus, addressing changed circumstances in a language of conservative values and moral revival, proposed legislation that would make the state and its courts the arbiters of private conduct. The laws, first issued probably in 18 B.C.E. and amended by supplementary legislation more than twenty-five years later in 9 C.E. as the Lex Papia Poppaea, are today known mainly in fragmentary and sometimes distorted form in the writings of later jurists and historians who cite them.

Issues of marriage and reproduction that once had been mainly under the control of families now became, at least on paper, public and the purview of the community as a whole. The laws penalized people who did not marry or have children by attacking their eligibility to inherit wealth.

Unmarried persons, who are disabled by the Lex Julia from taking inheritances and legacies, were formerly deemed capable of taking the benefit of a trust. And childless persons, who forfeit by the Lex Papia, on account of not having children, half their inheritances and legacies, were formerly deemed capable of taking in full as beneficiaries of a trust.

(Gaius, *Institutiones* 2.286; Poste 1890)

And both the Lex Julia on marriage and its revision in the Lex Papia Poppaea rewarded women for having larger families. Normally, as Ulpianus (third century, C.E.) says, "Guardians are appointed for males as well as for females, but only for males under puberty, on account of their infirmity of age; for females, however, both under and over puberty, on account of the weakness of their sex as well as their ignorance of business matters" (Ulpianus, *Rules*, 11.1; trans. S. P. Scott in Leftkowitz and Fant #195).

Guardianship terminates for a freeborn woman by title of maternity of three children, for a freedwoman under statutory guardianship by maternity of four children: those who have other kinds of guardians . . . , are released from wardship by title of three children.

(Gaius, *Institutiones* 1.194, Poste 1890)

Accordingly, when a brother and sister have a testamentary guardian, on attaining the age of puberty the brother ceases to be a ward, but the sister continues, for it is only under the Lex Julia and Papia Poppaea and by title of maternity that women are emancipated from tutelage; except in the case of Vestal Virgins, for these, even in our ancestors' opinion, are entitled by their sacerdotal function to be free from control.

(Gaius, *Institutiones* 1.145; Poste 1890)

Thus, women benefited by the new legislation through having larger numbers of children. Upper-class women and men also sometimes gained by these laws since the emperor could confer the exemption of three children on those who, like the empress Livia and Pliny the Younger, did not in fact *have* three living children of their own.

Augustus may have hoped by legislating privileges for the fathers and mothers of three or more children to ensure an increased birth rate, but we have far more evidence for low reproductivity than for happy fertility among the members of the upper class. Augustus's daughter Julia might give her husband five healthy children, and in turn Julia's daughter Agrippina gave birth to nine, but he himself only produced one child by any of his wives, and since this child was a daughter we may be sure that he and Livia did what they could to produce a son—and failed. Our evidence for infertility, miscarriage, and death in childbirth is so random that we need to include samples from both the previous generation (Cicero's daughter died in childbirth after her second child; neither child survived) and the next century. We know, for example, that Ovid, Seneca, and Pliny the Younger each married three times, and that only Ovid saw a child, one daughter, grow up. Pliny's young wife miscarried and her early death may have been connected with the complications of pregnancy. Another example of combined infertility and death in childbirth leading to the extinction of a blood line is that of Augustus's own adoptive father Julius Caesar, whose daughter Julia, married to Pompey, miscarried and died soon after in childbirth. The implications for women's expectation of life are clear here: to conceive was not guaranteed, to miscarry was all too frequent, to die in childbirth was a high probability, and the survival of infants with or without their mothers was a cause for real rejoicing. It is not surprising that in the generation before Augustus, Catullus had used as a simile for the preciousness of his love for Lesbia the preciousness of the single small grandson born to an aging grandfather by his daughter and only child (Catullus 68.119–24).

Freedwomen also benefitted from the new laws as Dio Cassius, writing in the third century C.E., explains: "since, among the freeborn there were far more males than females [of reproductive age?], he (Augustus) allowed all who wished, except the senators, to marry freedwomen, and ordered that their offspring should be held legitimate." (Dio Cassius 54.16.1–2; Cary 1980). Further, freedwomen could also benefit from the law by attaining a degree of autonomy in the making of their wills; normally, a freedwoman or freedman owed a certain amount of work or share of profits to her or his former owner and remained in a position of legal dependency on the owner whose permission was needed for financial and legal transactions and who inherited the majority of the freedwoman/man's property (Gardner 1986: 194–96).

The Lex Papia Poppaea afterwards exempted freedwomen from the tutelage of patrons, by prerogative of four children, and having established the rule that they could henceforth make testaments without the patron's authorization, it provided that a proportionate share of the freedwoman's property should be due to the patron, dependent on the number of her surviving children.

(Ulpianus, *Epitome* 29.3–6; Abdy and Walker 1876)

Underlying much of this legislation, and embedded in the notion of moral restructuring of social life, was a concern with revitalizing and purifying the family life of the citizens of Rome. It may well have been intended in part to use that purified family life to remind Romans of the moral and social structures that had once, at least theoretically, united a homogeneous community. Thus, part of the law tried to prevent marriage with people of immoral character.

By the Lex Julia senators and their descendants are forbidden to marry freedwomen, or women who have themselves followed the profession of the stage, or whose father or mother has done so; other freeborn persons are forbidden to marry a common prostitute, or a procuress, or a woman manumitted by a procurer or procuress, or a woman caught in adultery, or one condemned in a public action, or one who has followed the profession of the stage.

(Ulpianus, *Epitome* 13–14; Abdy and Walker 1876)

What may be indicated in these laws is a relaxation of paternal control over marriages among the citizens of Rome. Such control was exercised by the emperor in his arrangements for his daughter Julia, although she clearly managed to circumvent other forms of control for a while.

Julia was betrothed first to Mark Antony's son and then to Cotiso, King of the Getans, whose daughter Augustus himself proposed to marry in exchange; or so Antony writes. But Julia's first husband was Marcellus, his sister Octavia's son, then hardly more than a child; and, when he died, Augustus persuaded Octavia to let her become Marcus Agrippa's wife—though Agrippa was now married to one of Marcellus's two sisters, and had fathered children on her.[2] At Agrippa's death, Augustus cast about for a new son-in-law, even if he were only a knight, eventually choosing Tiberius, his step-son; this meant, however, that Tiberius must divorce his wife, who had already given him an heir.

(Suetonius, *Augustus* 63–65; Graves 1957)

Being a political pawn was certainly the fate of men and women of the Imperial house, but arranged marriages were usual, as well, for the young sons and daughters of the propertied classes, as Ovid tells us in his autobiographical poem (*Tristia* 4.10), "When I was but a boy, I was made to marry an unworthy wife— / not for long!" (trans. J. Ferguson in Chisholm and Ferguson 1981: 272). Roman law in this period permitted either party to sue for divorce with relatively little fuss, and the sources suggest that arranged marriages might be susceptible to that end for all sorts of reasons, not only political ones.

Conduct within marriage was also to be controlled by the state, as was sexual behavior outside of wedlock. The *Lex Julia de adulteriis* of 18 B.C.E., a part of the larger *Lex Julia*, includes sections on adultery, homosexuality, and seduction.

... the *Lex Iulia* for the suppression of adultery punishes with death not only those who dishonour the marriage-bed of another [man] but also those [men] who indulge their ineffable lust with males. The same *Lex Iulia* also punishes the offence of seduction when a [male] person, without the use of force, de-flowers a virgin or seduces a respectable widow. The penalty invoked by the statute against offenders is confiscation of half their estate if they be of respect-able standing, corporal punishment and relegation in the case of baser persons.

(Justinian, *Institutes* 4.18.2–3; Thomas 1975)

The law permitted women to bring third-party accusations against adul-terous husbands but granted only to men the right to accuse a spouse of adultery and to divorce or to kill an adulterous wife (or to kill an adul-terous daughter) found *in flagrante* (under certain circumstances). Thus, the new laws were not intended to bring equality to men and women but rather (ostensibly) to regulate sexuality, to bring it into line with the standards of an idealized righteous past. These laws also must have made clear to the senatorial aristocracy that a new age was begin-ning, one in which the state would increasingly intervene in family af-fairs in an attempt to enforce what it characterized as a return to old social values.

It is unclear how the Augustan laws actually affected women's lives since the love poetry and satire of the period do not explicitly mention these laws and the first references to them by historians come only in the late first century C.E. Suetonius, writing in his life of Augustus at the end of the first century C.E., tells us that the emperor "was unable to carry it (the *Lex Julia*) out because of an open revolt against its provis-ions, until he had abolished or mitigated a part of the penalties, besides increasing the rewards [for more children] and allowing a three years' exemption from the obligation to marry after the death of a husband or wife" (Suetonius, *Augustus* 34.1; Rolfe 1970).

Other sources indicate that the *Lex Papia Poppaea*, to which this passage of Suetonius refers, stipulated that two years was the maximum allowable delay for remarriage:

The Lex Julia allows women a respite from its requirements for one year after the death of a husband, and for six months after a divorce: but the Lex Papia allows a respite for two years after the death of a husband and for a year and six months after a divorce."

(Ulpianus, *Epitome* 14; Abdy and Walker 1876)

Although it seems impossible to assess the actual impact of the laws on individuals, their broader message to men and women of the upper classes was that the state would now play an ever-increasing role in their private lives and that role would symbolize the growing control by the emperor over their public lives as well.

Women of the Court

Imperial Women and Dynastic Ideology

That sexuality functioned symbolically in this period seems clear from such stories as that of Suetonius on Augustus's response to the demands of the members of the equestrian class[3] for repeal of the marriage laws.

When the knights . . . persistently called for its repeal at a public show, he [Augustus] sent for the children of Germanicus and exhibited them, some in his own lap and some in their father's, intimating by his gestures and expression that they should not refuse to follow that young man's example.

(Suetonius, *Augustus* 34.2; Rolfe 1970)

Using his family as an ideologically motivated tableau vivant, Augustus provided a living example of the same messages contained in the Ara Pacis sculpture (Zanker 1988: 157–58). Ceremonies would have used the Imperial women in a comparable way, as when Horace describes Livia and Octavia welcoming Augustus back from Spain: "Rejoicing in her peerless husband, let his consort, after offering sacrifices to the righteous gods, now advance, and the sister of our famous chief, and, with the suppliant fillet decked, mothers of maids and sons just saved" (*Ode* 3.14.5–10; Bennett 1978).

The public display of sculptured portraits of the women and children of the court made similar statements, since many were apparently set up as family groups. The examples of the elegant and classicizing marble busts (Fig. 11.3) of the Imperial family from the amphitheater of Arsinoë-Crocodilopolis (Medinet el Fayyum in Egypt) (4–14 c.e., or of the large bronze statues of the family from Veleia in Italy both include Livia. Her portraits, many showing her simply dressed in the long, heavy garments of the matron, her hair often covered by a mantle, build on Hellenistic traditions; virtually no Roman female portraits remain from the Republican period as models for the imagery of Imperial women, but Hellenistic queens such as Berenice or Cleopatra did offer an important prototype that blended ideal beauty, recognizable facial features, and royal identity.

Even when statues of the Imperial women of the period come to us without the archaeological evidence of placement in family groups, they often contain their own stylistic and iconographic codes to communicate the values being promulgated by Augustus. These draw on the Hellenistic models just mentioned, as well as on the imagery of divinities. The portrait of Livia (Fig. 11.4) wearing the diadem of the fertility goddess Ceres (Greek Demeter), dated to the time of Tiberius, conflates empress and goddess to emphasize Livia's maternal role. Similarly, the statue probably of Livia (Fig. 11.5) with a cornucopia, sign of plenty associated with goddesses and personifications such as Fortuna or Salus, Well-being (dated after 41 c.e.), merges fertility, the maternal, and the Imperial in such way as to reinforce the ideas most important to the dynasty: a re-

Figure 11.3. Portrait bust of the empress Livia from Egypt, ca. 4–14 C.E. The simple hairstyle and crisply idealized features are typical of the portraits made while Augustus was still alive.

vived world born of the peace and security brought by Augustus. With the portraiture of Livia, the Roman artists of the court created an appropriate imagery of the empress-matron, an imagery that could represent an important individual, perhaps the most important woman in the Roman world, while at the same time communicating concepts of royalty, family, and gender ideology.

Dynastic Concerns and the Autonomy of Women of the Court

Here it is important to stop and note that the image of Imperial harmony, of the submission of the Imperial family to dynastic needs, is by no means the whole picture. The Imperial women, as we know from literary and archaeological remains, used their positions to construct roles that permitted some of them a degree of autonomy, influence and even opposition to the dominant Imperial ideologies of the period.

Livia and Agrippina the Younger can provide us with examples. Livia's relative autonomy emerges in stories about her meetings with ambassadors and envoys while Augustus was otherwise occupied; her importance to Augustus can be seen in the episode in which we learn that the emperor took notes on Livia's advice and studied them later; and her influence, expressed by writers who clearly worried about it,

Figure 11.4. Portrait bust of Livia from Rome, after 14 C.E., the year Augustus died. The more elaborate hairstyle and the diadem signal her status as Iulia Augusta, adopted into Augustus's own house and sharing in his status; the diadem may also connect Livia with Ceres, the fertility goddess, a connection made useful politically by the fact that in the year 14 her son Tiberius inherited the throne.

Figure 11.5. Portrait statue probably of Livia as a goddess, from Rome but found in Pozzuoli on the Bay of Naples. In the year 41, with the ascent to the throne of her grandson Claudius, who made Livia a goddess, such images become appropriate.

comes through in the stories about her role in advancing favored members of the court (Suetonius, *Augustus* 84.2 and *Claudius* 4.1).

With Agrippina the Younger, we have an imperial woman who used her mother's imagery to foster her own political interests (Wood 1988). Before she fell from favor with her son Nero who sent her into exile, Agrippina the Younger is said to have wanted the power to rule as his regent; she used the imagery of her mother to support her claims. Agrippina the Elder, wife of Germanicus and mother of Caligula and his sister Agrippina, was a central figure in the dynastic sequence, as we have already seen, both because of her connection with Augustus and because, persecuted by Tiberius, she distanced Caligula from his much-loathed predecessor and functioned as an image of the noble martyr.

The Gemma Claudia (Fig. 11.6), with its paired busts of Claudius with his bride Agrippina the Younger facing her deceased parents Agrippina the Elder and Germanicus, was probably made at the expense of a rich citizen as a gift for the marriage that took place in 49 C.E. (Wood 1988, 422). The parallel images of mother and daughter clearly served the men of the dynasty in connecting them to Augustus and legitimating their own claims to power; just beneath that surface, however, rest the claims of Agrippina the Younger herself (Wood, 1988). That she was conscious of these claims seems possible from the reports by Tacitus that he consulted "memoirs of the younger Agrippina, the mother of the emperor Nero, who commemorated for posterity the story of her life and of the misfortunes of her family" (Tacitus, *Annals* 4.53; trans. Natalie Kampen). There, he tells us, he read the story of Tiberius's refusal to allow Agrippina the Elder to remarry after Germanicus's death, as a sign of his fear of her potential strength; there too was the story of her protest to Tiberius for intimidating her allies, including her cousin Pulchra. She

Figure 11.6. The Gemma Claudia, a carved gemstone from Rome, made about 48–49 C.E., and probably representing Claudius, with his wife (also his niece) Agrippina the Younger, facing Germanicus and the elder Agrippina, his wife; Germanicus and Agrippina are the parents of Agrippina the Younger, and Germanicus is the brother of Claudius.

is quoted as saying, "Pulchra is a mere pretext; the only reason for her destruction is that, utterly foolishly, she chose Agrippina for her admiration." The emperor responded by reminding Agrippina that "just because she was not a ruler, it did not mean she had been wronged" (Tacitus, *Annals* 4.52; trans. Natalie Kampen). The stories of the life of Agrippina the Younger preserved in Tacitus's *Annals* speak of a woman whose desire for power was characterized as "masculine despotism" (12.7), who set up a colony of veterans in Germany (12.26), and who sat beside Claudius and received with him the homage of the family of the conquered ruler of Britain. "It was really a novelty, utterly beyond ancient ways, for a woman to sit before the Roman standards. In fact, Agrippina bragged that she was actually a partner in the empire which her ancestors had won." (*Annals* 12.37)

Less dramatic than the stories of empresses as power-hungry and adept at manipulation, but equally significant in marking the dynamic relationship between individual authority and dynastic teamwork, the inscriptions that appeared on the statue bases of Imperial women are explicit in naming the ties of kinship. In these examples from Thasos in the Greek-speaking East, the relation of individual and dynasty is clear: "The people [of Thasos set up a statue of] Livia Drusilla, wife of Augustus Caesar, divine benefactress," and "The people [of Thasos set up a statue] of Julia, daughter of Augustus Caesar, our benefactress, following the tradition of her family" (*Inscriptionae Latinae Selectae* 8784; trans. K. Chisholm in Chisholm and Ferguson 1981: 168). Similarly, "Livia dedicated a magnificent temple to Concord, / and gave it to her husband." (Ovid, *Fasti* 6.637–38; trans. J. Ferguson in Chisholm and Ferguson 1981: Elg(b) p. 204). The empress's patronage of a temple dedicated to the spirit of harmony, both civil and marital harmony, reinforces the messages about the imperial dynastic and moral programs (Flory 1984); these practices of patronage and representation also set the pattern for the relationship of women to state art throughout the next two centuries.

Even in the domestic environment, representations of the Imperial programs of dynastic harmony and well-being could be seen, as Ovid tells in a poem written from exile in Asia. Clearly meant to demonstrate to all readers (including those connected to the emperor whom the poet hoped to convince) that he continued utterly loyal to Augustus despite his sufferings, Ovid writes:

nor is my piety unknown: a strange land sees a shrine to Caesar in my house. Beside him [Augustus] stand the pious son [Tiberius] and priestess wife [Livia], deities not less important than himself now that he has become a god. To make the household group complete, both of the grandsons [Germanicus and Drusus] are there, one by the side of his grandmother, the other by that of his father
(*Ex Ponto* 4.9.105–10; Wheeler 1975)

The reign of Augustus established several crucial patterns that would remain in effect to varying degrees for several hundred years.

First, the Imperial family *was* a family and its continuity under a dignified and protective father and a noble and fertile mother guaranteed the health and happiness of the Roman people, its children. Second, this notion of the model family was disseminated throughout the empire on works of art, coins, and domestic shrines, in the patronage of buildings and the inscriptions that marked them, and in the ceremonies and choreographed public appearances of members of the court. Representation and political program were consciously and effectively joined, and women played a major role in both.

Although moral revival seems less an issue than dynastic propaganda to the emperors of the Julio-Claudian line, all continue to represent the Imperial women and children as symbols of legitimacy and the security of a peaceful future. The great court cameos of the period, the Grand Camée de France (Fig. 11.7), on which Livia sits beside Tiberius and the divine Augustus floats overhead, like the Gemma Claudia (Fig. 11.6), all use family relations symbolized through women as well as sons to document the ruler's right to rule and his provision of a safe future. As we have just seen, these images can also function to document the power of women, whether as conduits for dynastic claims or for their own ends. Coins do so as well, although the mint in Rome was for a long time more reticent about showing the women and children of the court than were the mints of the eastern provinces. In the east, where the Imperial cult included worship of Livia during her lifetime, even though such would have been unacceptable in Rome, coins from Asia Minor show her as Demeter the mother-goddess with Gaius and Lucius, Augustus's heirs at the time, or with Augustus and Tiberius (Fig. 11.8). (See Chapter 6, "Hellenistic Ruler Cult.") Later, however, the women and children of the court begin to appear on the coins of Rome and the west as when Caligula represented Agrippina the Elder in order to demonstrate his relationship to Augustus and the Julian house (Fig. 11.9). A coin of the time of Claudius from Caesarea shows his third wife Messalina (Agrippina the Younger was his fourth wife) on the obverse and his mother Antonia and son Britannicus on the reverse (Fig. 11.10); the coin stresses the emperor's legitimacy through his mother's relationship to Augustus (she was his niece), and uses Messalina as mother of the new era to underline the security of succession. Women thus reinforce the emperor's claims to rule.

What we have been considering is not the sexuality of real Roman women, if such could ever be recuperated, nor the "real" personalities of Livia and her kinswomen, but rather the ideological construction of that sexuality by elite men in their capacities as rulers and as writers. They paint a picture of a society debating the political and moral character of sexuality, a sexuality that threatens the new social order and must be contained within the framework of marriage and reproduction, a sexuality particular to the elite of Rome.

Figure 11.7. The Grand Camée de France, a large carved gemstone made in Rome, perhaps about 20 C.E. At the center Livia sits beside her son Tiberius as other family members look on under the benevolent gaze of the now divine Augustus; the barbarian families in the lowest register play against the Imperial family to express the triumphant nature of Roman peace.

Social Ideology and Sexuality

The Virtues of Women

All women's lives were affected profoundly in various ways by the social ideology being articulated in laws and dynastic imagery by the emperor.

Figure 11.8. Bronze coin from Asia Minor showing Lucius and Gaius, the sons of Augustus's daughter Julia and the intended heirs of Augustus; they both died before they could take the throne.

From the "best" of women to the "worst," the terms were set and debated within the frame of family and reproduction even when women's lives at every social level frequently moved out of the frame. What should a woman be, then, and in whose opinion?

At one pole stands Julia, the daughter of the emperor. To the public she must have seemed Livia's opposite, the "Other" to Augustan matronly morality. Since we can know Julia only through the scabrous jokes Romans told about her and through the court gossip that constructed her as the farthest pole of promiscuity, what we see is a dreadful warning to all those fast-living women whose conduct Augustan policy aimed to transform. It should be noted that no such warning applied to the emperor himself; Suetonius recounts Augustus's taste for extramarital affairs and tells how in his old age Livia even procured women for him (*Augustus* 71.1). And Seneca writes:

The deified Augustus banished his daughter, who was shameless beyond the indictment of shamelessness, and made public the scandals of the imperial house—that she had been accessible to scores of paramours, that in nocturnal revels she had roamed about the city, that the very forum and the rostrum, from which her father had proposed a law against adultery, had been chosen by the daughter for her debaucheries, that she had daily resorted to the statue of Marsyas [a famous spot for prostitutes], and, laying aside the role of adultress, there sold her favors, and sought the right of every indulgence with even an unknown paramour.

(*De Beneficiis* 6.32.1; Basore 1964/1979)

At the opposite pole are such matrons as Scribonia, the mother of Julia who joined her daughter in exile even though Augustus had left her to marry Livia and, as a Roman father, had exercised the right to

A

Figure 11.9. (A) Gold coin (aureus) of Caligula (37–38 C.E.) from Lyon on the reverse of which (B) is a portrait of Agrippina the Elder, his mother, daughter of Julia and granddaughter of Augustus; the purpose of the portrait honoring emperor and mother is as much to connect Caligula with Augustus as it is to honor Agrippina.

B

A

Figure 11.10. Coin of Claudius, dated about 46 C.E. and minted in Caesarea. On the obverse **(A)** is Messalina, his wife at the time; on the reverse **(B)** are his mother Antonia and his son Britannicus. The Imperial family romance thus continues to frame the dual messages of connection to Augustus and to a secure future for the dynasty and so for Rome.

B

control his daughter's marriages and her fate. Scribonia, like the courageous, self-sacrificing matrons who set examples to the community through their willingness to urge their husbands and sons to dignified suicide, demonstrates both the ideal of family loyalty and the spiritual authority of mature wives and mothers.

The funeral eulogies for two upper-class matrons, Murdia and Turia, who lived in the time of Augustus indicate the virtues their male kin found worthy of commemoration. Murdia (*Corpus Inscriptionum Latinarum* 6.10230) had been married twice and had children by both marriages; no blame attaches to the two marriages even though many funeral inscriptions praise men and women alike for being married to one partner for a lifetime. The rarity of a single marriage received note in an age when elite women married very young (probably in their midteens rather than their late teens as seems to have been the case with women outside the aristocracy) to men who were often considerably older than they; hence these women sometimes outlived their husbands rather than divorcing them. How common divorce actually was, as opposed to the frequency with which it was mentioned as a castigation of the moral standards of the age, we do not know, but remarriage appears to have been no rarity. Murdia's son by her first marriage, having commented on the fairness of her will, goes on to say that she was motivated to dispose of her goods as she did because

Consistent in her nature, she preserved by her obedience and good sense the two marriages to worthy men that her parents had made for her; as a married woman she became yet more agreeable because of her merits, and her loyalty made her dearer just as her judgement [concerning her will] left her more honored. After her death, the citizens agreed in praising her. The way she divided her estate in her will displays a grateful and loyal spirit toward her husbands, fairness to her children, and justice in her rectitude.

The funeral tribute of all good women should be simple and similar because their natural goodness, over which they keep guard, does not require variations in language. Further, it is enough that all of them have done the same things that gain them a good reputation; in lives tossed by smaller storms there is less room for original ways to praise a woman. For all these reasons, it seems right to focus on conventional virtues in order not to lose anything of the best and thereby debase what remains.

In this sense, then, my dearest mother won the greatest praise of all, because she was like other good women in her modesty, decency, chastity, obedience, wool-work, zeal and loyalty; at the same time, she was at least the equal to any in her virtue, labor, wisdom and the dangers she faced.

(trans. Natalie Kampen, adapted from Horsfall 29–31
and Lefkowitz and Fant 1982: 139)

For Turia (this conventional name masks the fact that her real identity is still uncertain), her husband delivered a eulogy about 10–9 B.C.E., which, although naming the same virtues celebrated in the *Eulogy for Murdia*, adds public dimensions that resulted from the chaos of the civil war years. Turia and her sister avenged the murders of their parents;

Turia herself raised and found dowries for female kin, protected her husband's interests when he was in exile and helped to bring him back, and secured the punishment of those responsible for his misfortunes. These splendid and courageous actions are recalled, along with her virtues, by the proud and affectionate husband.

"Why . . . recall your inestimable qualities, your modesty, deference, affability, your amiable disposition, your faithful attendance to the household duties, your enlightened religion, your unassuming elegance, the modest simplicity and refinement of your manners? Need I speak of your attachment to your kindred, your affection for your family—when you respected my mother as you did your own parents and cared for her tomb as you did for that of your own mother and father—you who share countless other virtues with Roman ladies most jealous of their fair name? These qualities which I claim for you are your own, equalled or excelled by but few; for the experience of men teaches us how rare they are.
. . . In our day, marriages of such long duration, not dissolved by divorce but terminated by death alone, are indeed rare. For our union was prolonged in unclouded happiness for forty-one years."
(*Corpus Inscriptionum Latinarum* 6.1527; trans. Lefkowitz and Fant #207)

The only shadow across the face of the marriage was the couple's inability to have children, an inability for which Turia took responsibility.

"Disconsolate to see me without children . . . you wished to put an end to my chagrin by proposing to me a divorce, offering to yield the place to another spouse more fertile, with the only intention of searching for and providing for me a spouse worthy of our mutual affection, whose children you assured me you would have treated as your own."

(Ibid.)

He, horrified, refused and says, "I could not comprehend how you could conceive of any reason why you, still living, should not be my wife, you who during my exile had always remained most faithful and loyal" (Ibid.)

In these two eulogies, women's virtues include modesty, propriety, fidelity, industry, and honor. Care in the management of property joins the list as evidence of the prosperity of the two women. However, we do not see here the kind of romantic love and physical passion that Propertius, Ovid, or Sulpicia (see below) describe in their poems; the evidence seems to suggest that Romans associated these intense emotions with affairs rather than with upper-class marriage.

The language of praise for women of the lower strata keeps to the same set of attributes (without the discussion of property, however) and focuses on the same list of virtues. Thus, from first-century Rome comes the tombstone of the freedman butcher Lucius Aurelius Hermia and his wife, "chaste in body, my one and only, a loving woman who possessed my heart, she lived as a faithful wife to a faithful husband with affection equal to my own, since she never let avarice keep her from her duty." She, Aurelia Philematium, tells us, "I was chaste and modest; I did not know the crowd; I was faithful to my husband," The inscription shows that he was her fellow freedman, and she lived with him from the time she was seven (although not explicitly as his wife) until her death at forty. (*Corpus Inscriptionum Latinarum* 6.9499; trans. Lefkowitz and Fant #137). In a relief, the couple stand between the two inscriptions, he togate and she veiled and drawing his right hand to her lips (Fig. 11.11). Such affectionate images are rare for any level of Roman society in this period, but the traditional gesture associated with marriage, the clasping of right hands, appears in several reliefs of freed slave couples throughout the period; a funerary altar from the Vatican dated to the time of Claudius commemorates T. Claudius Dionysius and was set up by his wife and freedwoman Claudia Prepontis who joins hands with him on the relief (Fig. 11.12).

Marital fidelity and harmony, then, are the expressed virtues of women both at the top and in the lower reaches of Roman society in this period; from Livia to Turia to Claudia Prepontis, the public image of the Roman woman is dominated by private imagery. Among the elite, marriages were arranged in the early Empire for economic and political alliances, but the ideology of marriage as we see it here presumes the growth of mutual respect, affection, and loyalty; most desirable for women are a single husband and children and lives that bring honor not

Figure 11.11. Tombstone from early first-century C.E. Rome, made for Lucius Aurelius Hermia and his wife Aurelia Philematium. He wears the citizen's toga and she, her head modestly covered, lovingly and humbly kisses his hand.

Figure 11.12. The funerary altar of T. Claudius Dionysius and Claudia Prepontis, made in Rome about 40–50 C.E. and depicting the couple clasping right hands in the marital gesture (dextrarum iunctio) that signaled the legitimacy of marriage.

only on themselves and their offspring but on their ancestors as well. Similar values appear in the epitaphs of the lower classes in spite of the lack of ancestors or wealth to be honorably used and passed on. The representations of marital affection in word and image have, for freed slaves, the additional function of underlining their freedom itself. Marriage was, after all, the prerogative of the free, and no slave could claim possession of her or his offspring; an iconography of marriage and family asserted social status for this part of the Roman populace (Zanker 1979).

Sex Outside the Ideal

One pole of female sexuality is thus defined by marriage and reproduction, but, as we have already seen from Ovid and Horace, there were other kinds of behavior, other discourses of sexuality, present in the period. The mass-produced lamps, bowls (Fig. 11.13), and other clay objects stamped with images of heterosexual intercourse, images that catalogue more positions than Ovid himself could recommend, are paralleled in the erotic paintings of the brothels and houses of Pompeii (see Chapter 12); they suggest a significant clientele for low-cost as well as expensive images of sex and a distinct taste for an erotic "art" in which ideal-

Figure 11.13. Arretine bowl from Rome, made in the late first century B.C.E. or early first century C.E. Like the Pompeian paintings of lovers from the brothel (Fig. 12.7), the couple appear alone, attentive, and gentle with one another.

ized young couples cavort in cozily domesticated interiors. Despite the frequent use of garlands as interior decoration, the viewer would hardly associate these couples with newlyweds, especially since they seem to be drawn from a Hellenistic tradition of books (said to be by prostitutes; hence, pornography: the writings of prostitutes) that catalogued sexual positions (Brendel 1970: 63–68 and Richlin 1992: *passim*). Rather, the uniformly bronzed young men and their "milky white" partners belong to the world of love poetry, a world outside of marriage.

An affair of sexual passion with a mistress of one's own class or a lower class was the focus of much love poetry by the men of the later Republic and the Imperial period; the poems tell of men's desire and their attitudes to love and sex, and they sometimes construct personalities (though seldom voices) for the mistresses. No woman's perspective is available to counter what Ovid tells us in the *Art of Love*:

> It's all right to use force—force of that sort goes down well with
>   The girls: what in fact they love to yield
> They'd often rather have stolen. Rough seduction
>   delights them, the audacity of near-rape
> Is a compliment—so the girl who *could* have been forced, yet somehow
>   Got away unscathed, may feign delight, but in fact
> Feels sadly let down. Hilaira and Phoebe, both ravished
>   Both fell for their ravishers.[4]
>
>   (*Art of Love* I.673–80; Green 1982)

Similarly, no woman answers Soranus's notion about the pleasure felt even by a woman who has been raped. The physician argues that "the emotion of sexual appetite existed in [her] too, but was obscured by mental resolve" (Soranus *Gynaecology* 1.37; Temkin 1956).

No woman defends Corinna against Ovid's charges of unfaithfulness, or even accuses him of being, perhaps, such an egotist that he has driven his mistress away! Only Propertius allows his Cynthia to speak in her own defense, as when, having told the reader often of his mistress's infidelities, he goes to her house early to see if she is alone. She scolds him: "What are you doing at this hour, spying on your mistress!? Do you think my ways resemble the likes of you? I'm not so easy: to know a single lover like you is enough for me, or maybe a truer one" (Propertius *Elegies* 2.29a.31–35; trans. Natalie Kampen). But here, as in the long poem (IV.7) when Cynthia speaks to him from the grave of the wrongs he did her and of the day when they will be reunited in the underworld, the poet remains always in control of his Cynthia's words; they are always his, as are the words of Tarpeia about her treachery during the Sabine war (*Elegies* 4.4) and those of Cornelia (4.11) who speaks, like Cynthia, from beyond the grave (see Chapter 10 for the Cornelia Elegy).

Sulpicia

Only one female poet speaks in her own voice, and of her we know little. Preserved among the works of Ovid's contemporary, Tibullus, a few poems by Sulpicia remain. Although there are modern critics who argue that Sulpicia is a fiction invented by a male poet (see Chapter 13: Pliny the Younger on the man whose wife is said to have written well), many accept the poems as the work of a woman. In the pieces quoted here, the poet speaks in the voice of a young and unmarried woman from an upper-class background of the Augustan period; her guardian still has some control over her, but she is able, nonetheless, to conduct a passionate love affair with a man whom she calls Cerinthus.

This first excerpt is addressed to M. Valerius Messala Corvinus, her guardian, an aristocratic writer, scholar, and politician and a patron of Tibullus. In it the poet argues against having to spend her birthday in the country. In the second piece she tells Cerinthus that the plan has changed and she will be allowed to stay in town.

> My hateful birthday is at hand, which I must celebrate
>   without Cerinthus in the irksome countryside.
> What can be sweeter than the City? Or is a country villa
>   fit for a girl, or the chilly river in the fields at Arezzo?
> Take a rest, Messalla, don't pay so much attention to me;
>   journeys, my dear relative, are often untimely.
> When I'm taken away, I leave my mind and feelings here,
>   since force keeps me from acting as my own master.
>   ([Tibullus] 3.14; Snyder 1989 131–32)

> Do you know of the dreary journey just lifted off your girl's mind?
>   Now she gets to be in Rome on her birthday!
> Let's all celebrate that day of birth,
>   which has come to you by chance when you least expected it.
>   ([Tibullus] 3.15; Snyder 1989 132)

In the following three fragments, all addressed to Cerinthus, the poet speaks of love and desire; the language she uses, like the pseudonym, reflects the same poetic practices used by her male contemporaries. Just how autobiographical the poems are remains as unclear as the degree to which the writer speaks in a particularly "feminine" style (Santirocco 1979).

> Finally a love has come which would cause me more shame
>   were Rumor to conceal it rather than lay it bare for all.
> Won over by my Muses, the Cytherean goddess brought me
>   him, and placed him in my bosom.
> Venus has discharged her promise; if anyone is said
>   to have had no joys of his own, let him tell of mine.
> I would not wish to entrust anything to sealed tablets,
>   lest anyone read my words before my lover does.
> But I delight in my wayward ways and loathe to dissemble
>   for fear of Rumor. Let me be told of:
> I am a worthy woman who has been together
>   with a worthy man.
>   ([Tibullus] 3.13; Snyder 1989: 130)

It is pleasing—the fact that in your carefree way you allow
  yourself so much on my behalf, lest I suddenly take a bad fall.
So you care more for a skirt—a wench loaded down with
  her wool-basket—than for Sulpicia, daughter of Servius.
There are people concerned about me, and they especially worry
  that I might give way to that lowly mistress of yours.

([Tibullus] 3.16; Snyder 1989: 133)

Light of my life, let me not be so burning a concern to you
  as I seemed to have been a few days ago,
If in my whole youth I in my folly have ever done anything
  which I admit to have been more sorry for
Than last night, when I left you alone,
  wanting to hide my passion.

([Tibullus] 3.18; Snyder 1989: 134)

The picture of a proud young woman in love and vacillating between arrogance and vulnerability, self-protection and desire, may be
unrepresentative of anything but Sulpicia herself; no other poems of the
period by women remain to be compared with hers. Her poems convey a
definite personality even as they follow some of the conventions of love
poetry. The wish to shout one's love from the heights, the anger at being
taken for granted, the adoring apologies and the admissions of passion
are all standard as is the silence of the voice of the beloved. What is
missing is the characterization of the beloved as venal, duplicitous or
trivial; neither is the poet a suppliant figure starving for a kind word or
gesture. Sulpicia's gender and her class seem to play a role in shaping
these few fragments and their projection of her personality; further, they
give us our only hints about how a woman might articulate her own
desire and point of view about love.

No information remains either about the likelihood of a young girl
from the upper classes carrying on a love affair in which loss of virginity
was involved; such girls seem to have married so early that there may
not have been much time or opportunity for premarital experiments.
Further, we know nothing about the language of affection used by
women nor about whether same-sex eroticism ever occurred among girls
(as opposed to adult lesbian sexual activity hinted at in some texts either as castigation of wealthy women or as entertainment for male voy-
eurs by prostitutes or female slaves). Even such information as when
women had their first children or when they went through menopause is
minimal and always contested by scholars; they use data compiled from
the thousands of inscriptions on funerary monuments from all over the
Roman empire to assess numbers of children, mortality rates, and differing valuations of family members according to geographical location,
social class, and time period (Shaw 1987). Despite the difficulties of using such material, scattered, inconsistent, and never scientifically quan-
tifiable, and in spite of the problems of interpretation that come from
inscriptions' formulaic and selective quality, it is possible to suggest a
few things about women's reproductive and family lives. Lower-class
people married later than those from the upper classes, death in child-

birth and infant mortality rates rose as economic and social level fell, and the expressed valuation of daughters rose over time until the number of mentions of daughters on late antique tombstones matched sons (Saller and Shaw 1984). But what sexual and emotional life felt like to women remains obscure because of the way the sources silence their voices.

Chastity and Community

Let your women keep silence in the churches: for it is not permitted unto them to speak; but they are commanded to be under obedience, as also saith the law. And if they will learn any thing, let them ask their husbands at home: for it is a shame for women to speak in the church.

(1 Cor: 14.34–35)

Writing toward the end of the Julio-Claudian period (died ca. 67 C.E.), St. Paul admonishes men to assert their authority over their women and to silence their public voices. What his motivation was for this famous statement remains open to debate, but in it one can read the tensions that were palpable in so many communities in the first centuries B.C.E. and C.E., over the proper roles of women and over what many men perceived as the dangerous incursions of women into public spheres. Both sexuality and voice are thus manifestations of personal autonomy, and both become the textual signs that reveal the underlying social tensions felt in this period about women's proper roles.

St. Paul's attitudes toward sexuality are often seen as characteristic of an early Christian combination of asceticism and misogyny, but however they might be interpreted, some of his opinions are shared by others in this period in the Roman world. When he recommends celibacy, it is to men and women alike and in the interests of focusing the minds of the faithful exclusively on the things of the spirit (7.34); in the same passage, however, he advises those who would marry rather than burn (7.8–9) to treat one another with equal care.

It is good for a man not to touch a woman. Nevertheless, to avoid fornication, let every man have his own wife, and let every woman have her own husband. Let the husband render unto the wife due benevolence: and likewise also the wife unto the husband. The wife hath not power of her own body, but the husband: and likewise also the husband hath not power of his own body, but the wife."

(1 Cor: 7.1–4).

Seneca's comments on equality of chastity in marriage sound rather similar:

You know that a man does wrong in requiring chastity of his wife while he himself is intriguing with the wives of other men; you know that, as your wife should have no dealings with a lover, neither should you yourself with a mistress.

(*Epistle* 94.26; Gummere 1971)

And Musonius Rufus calls on young couples (frag. 14) to make love "to build a wall for the city," through their marital harmony and their progeny. Sexuality thus becomes a discourse on social values and functions. To Paul, celibacy and concentration on the end of the old order ("But this I say, brethren, the time is short: it remaineth, that both they that have wives be as though they had none" [7.29]) are supremely important. Marital harmony as a positive value expressed through women's submission and through equal affection is both secondary and a kind of stopgap necessary to maintain social order within the community before the end of time. To Seneca, equal chastity in marriage signals an investment in the Stoic order and concern for self-control, and for Musonius Rufus, most explicitly, marital sexuality is a part of the maintenance of the community both in harmony and in posterity. At no level are these points of view about equality for women and men on a broader social level (Paul 11.3 and 8–9) or about an autonomous and asocial realm of sexual desire; sexuality for men and women is part of the social fabric here just as in the Augustan laws and works of art.

What we have seen in this chapter is the extent to which women's roles especially in relation to voice, desire, and sexuality were contested and under debate in the Augustan and Julio-Claudian period. The debates were not always in fact *about* women or sexuality, but they frequently focused on women as the locus for the expression of concerns about a broad range of social tensions from class relationships to the political structure and so on. We began with the construction of socially responsible sexuality in the Augustan laws and public art and moved from there to notions of marital affection expressed in private art and epitaphs. Philosophical texts as well as the literature of resistance, the satires of Horace and elegiac poems of Ovid and Propertius, and even the exhortations of St. Paul frame the social and psychic struggles of the period in terms of sex, marriage, and reproduction; women were the signs—although not the voices—that remain to tell us about those struggles.

NOTES

1. This is the only time the women's citizenship is acknowledged.
2. Plutarch suggests that this was all Octavia's idea (*Life of Antony* 87.2)
3. This was the class whose wealth and status were slightly below that of the senatorial families.
4. Typically these rapists were heroes and future divinities, Castor and Pollux the sons of Zeus. Ovid's next role model for rape is the hero Achilles, whose mother was divine.

TRANSLATIONS

Abdy, J. T., and B. Walker. 1876. *The Commentaries of Gaius and the Rules of Ulpian*. Cambridge.

Bovie, S. P. 1959. Horace: Odes and Satires. Chicago.

Basore, J. 1964 / 1979. *Seneca: Moral Essays*. Loeb Classical Library. Cambridge, Mass.

Bennett, C. E. 1978. *Horace: Odes and Epodes*. Loeb Classical Library. Cambridge, Mass.

Cary, E. 1980. *Dio Cassius: Roman History*. Loeb Classical Library. Cambridge, Mass.

Chisholm, K., and J. Ferguson. 1981. *Rome: The Augustan Age: A Source Book*. Oxford.

Fitzgerald, Robert. 1961. *The Odyssey*. Atlanta, Ga.

Graves, Robert. 1957. *Suetonius: Lives of the Caesars*. Harmondsworth, Middlesex.

Green, P. 1982. *Ovid: The Erotic Poems*. Harmondsworth, Middlesex.

Gummere, R. L. 1971. *Seneca: Epistulae Morales*. Loeb Classical Library. Cambridge, Mass.

Horsfall, N. 1982. "Allia Potestas and Murdia: Two Roman Women." *Ancient Society* 12, no. 2: 27–33.

Lefkowitz, M., and M. Fant. 1982. *Women's Life in Greece and Rome* Baltimore, Md.

MacLeod, M. D. 1961. *The Works of Lucian*. Loeb Classical Library. Cambridge, Mass.

Mandelbaum, A. 1961. *The Aeneid of Virgil*. New York.

Poste, E. 1890. *Gaii Institutionum iuris civilis*. 3d ed. Oxford.

Rolfe, J. C. 1970. *Suetonius*. Loeb Classical Library. Cambridge, Mass.

Temkin, O. 1956. *Soranus: Gynaecology*. Baltimore, Md.

Thomas, J. A. C. 1975. *Justinian, Institutes*. Cape Town.

Wheeler, A. L. 1975. *Ovid: Tristia and Ex Ponto*. Loeb Classical Library. Cambridge, Mass.

Winterbottom, M. 1974. *The Elder Seneca*. Vol. 1, *Controversiae*. Loeb Classical Library. Cambridge, Mass.

WORKS CONSULTED

Brendel, Otto J. 1970. "The Scope and Temperament of Erotic Art in the Greco-Roman World." In *Studies in Erotic Art*, edited by Theodore Bowie and Cornelia Christenson, 3–69. New York.

Flory, Marleen B. 1984. "*Sic Exempla Parantur*: Livia's Shrine of Concordia and the Porticus Liviae." *Historia* 33, no. 3: 309–30.

Gardner, Jane. 1986. *Women in Roman Law and Society*. London.

Horsfall, Nicholas. 1982. "Allia Potestas and Murdia: Two Roman Women." *Ancient Society* 12, no. 2: 27–33.

Lefkowitz, M., and Maureen B. Fant. 1982. *Women's Life in Greece and Rome: A Source Book in Translation*. Baltimore, Md.

Rawson, Beryl, ed. 1986. *The Family in Ancient Rome*. Ithaca, N.Y.

Richlin, Amy, ed. 1992. *Pornography and Representation in Greece and Rome*. New York.

Saller, Richard, and Brent Shaw. 1984. "Tombstones and Roman Family Relations in the Principate: Civilians, Soldiers and Slaves." *Journal of Roman Studies*. 74: 124–56.

Santirocco, Matthew. 1979. "Sulpicia Reconsidered." *Classical Journal* 74, no. 3: 229–39.

Shaw, Brent. 1987. "The Age of Roman Girls at Marriage: Some Reconsiderations." *Journal of Roman Studies* 77: 30–46.

Snyder, Jane. 1989. *The Woman and the Lyre: Women Writers in Classical Greece and Rome*. Carbondale, Ill.

Wistrand, Erik. 1976. "The So-called Laudatio Turiae." *Acta Universitatis Gothoburgensis* Göteborg.

Wood, Susan. 1988. "Memoriae Agrippinae: Agrippina the Elder in Julio-Claudian Art and Propaganda." *American Journal of Archaeology* 92, no. 3: 409–26.

Zanker, Paul. 1979. "Grabreliefs römischer Freigelassener." *Jahrbuch des deutschen Archaeologischen Instituts* 90: 267–315.

———. 1988. *The Power of Images in the Age of Augustus*. trans. A. Shapiro Ann Arbor, Mich.

FURTHER READING

Dixon, Suzanne. 1988. *The Roman Mother*. London.

Gardner, Jane F., and Thomas Wiedemann. 1990. *The Roman Household: A Sourcebook*. London.

Garnsey, Peter, and Richard Saller. 1987. *The Roman Empire*. Berkeley and Los Angeles.

Phillips, Jane. 1978. "Roman Mothers and the Lives of Their Adult Daughters." *Helios* 6: 69–80.

Pomeroy, Sarah B. 1975. *Goddesses, Whores, Wives, and Slaves: Women in Classical Antiquity*. New York.

Purcell, Nicholas. 1986. "Livia and the Womanhood of Rome." *Proceedings of the Cambridge Philological Society* 32: 78–105.

Richlin, Amy. 1981. "Approaches to the Sources on Adultery at Rome." In *Reflections of Women in Antiquity*, edited by Helene P. Foley, 379–404. New York.

Stehle, Eva. 1989. "Venus, Cybele, and the Sabine Women: The Roman Construction of Female Sexuality." *Helios* 16, no. 2: 143–64.

Treggiari, Susan. 1973. "Domestic Staff at Rome in the Julio-Claudian Period, 27 B.C. to A.D. 68." *Histoire Sociale: Revue Canadienne* 6: 41–55.

———. 1991. *Roman Marriage*. Oxford.

Wallace-Hadrill, Andrew. 1981. "Family and Inheritance in the Augustan Marriage Laws." *Proceedings of the Cambridge Philological Society* 27: 58–80.

Wiedemann, Thomas. 1989. *Adults and Children in the Roman Empire*. London.

12

EXCURSUS
THE WOMEN OF POMPEII

In a grand house on the Bay of Naples, with servants tumbling over one another, luxury dripping from every wall, table, and couch, a banquet is being conducted among the extremely *nouveaux riches*. The lady of the house, Fortunata, the wife of the freed slave Trimalchio, is not eating: "not even a drop of water does she put into her mouth until she's arranged the silver and divided the left-overs among the slaves" (Petronius, *Satiricon* 67.2; Arrowsmith 1959) Despite her domesticity, she draws less than universal admiration to herself; as someone at the banquet tells his neighbor:

. . . that's Fortunata, Trimalchio's wife. And the name couldn't suit her better. She counts her cash by the cartload. And you know what she used to be? Well, begging your honor's pardon, but you wouldn't have taken bread from her hand. Now god knows how or why, she's sitting pretty: has Trimalchio eating out of her hand. If she told him at noon it was night, he'd crawl into bed. As for him, he's so loaded he doesn't know how much he has. But that bitch has her finger in everything—where you'd least expect it too. A regular tightwad, never drinks, and sharp as they come. But she's got a nasty tongue; get her gossiping on a couch and she'll chatter like a parrot.''

(*Satiricon* 37.2–7; Arrowsmith 1959)

Rich, vulgar, yet practical, Fortunata comes into focus both through Petronius's words, written about the time of Nero (ca. 65 C.E.) and through the preserved marvels of Pompeii, Herculaneum, and the other towns of the Bay of Naples that were suffocated by ash and lava in the great eruption of Mount Vesuvius in 79 C.E. (Fig. 12.1).

The excavation of these towns since the eighteenth century has permitted a clearer view of the lives of Roman women of every social stratum. Rather than dealing primarily with the texts of great authors, a discussion of women at Pompeii draws on inscriptions, architecture, painting, and the bits and pieces of daily life. At Pompeii and Herculaneum, not only can one see the food in bowls still on the table, find the

Figure 12.1. General view of the city of Pompeii.

jewelry women wore, study the decorations for their houses; one can even hear some of their stories.

Women of Property

At the opposite end of the social ladder from Fortunata were such wealthy and aristocratic women as Nero's wife, Poppaea Sabina, who had inherited property at Pompeii; like other aristocratic women with great villas around the Bay of Naples, she owned this property in her own right. Inscriptions on lead plumbing pipes like those found in the sea off nearby Puteoli testify to the ownership of villas by rich women; the sisters Marcia and Rufina Metilia (*Corpus Inscriptionum Latinarum* X.1905) are a case in point. Their villas, like the well-preserved one that may have belonged to the empress Poppaea at Oplontis, just outside of Pompeii, had great gardens, extensive and richly decorated rooms of all sizes, even pools (Fig. 12.2). Although no evidence remains to indicate the empress's personal involvement in the arrangements and furnishings of the villa, Oplontis gives a splendid indication of the style to which people such as she were accustomed (De Franciscis 1975). Their villas

Figure 12.2. View of the villa (possibly belonging to Poppaea, wife of Nero) at Oplontis, outside of Pompeii. Dating to the middle of the first century C.E., the luxurious villa had long colonnades that gave onto gardens, as well as large numbers of richly painted interior spaces.

and houses, with wall paintings, mosaic floors, statuary and bibelots, resemble those of the rich hellenistic merchants of Delos (see earlier) more than the modest houses of Classical Athens; the parallel to the way the female owners themselves differed from Athenian women, perhaps now comparable to Hellenistic queens, is striking.

In the upper stratum of local Pompeian society, perhaps a step below that of the great ladies of the aristocracy, were other women who chose to use their wealth for the public good as well as for their own purposes. One of the most famous of these is Eumachia who, in the years before the earthquake of 64 C.E., paid for the construction of a huge public building in the most important spot in Pompeii, the Forum (Fig. 12.3). Around it were the markets, law courts, and temples of the town, and there the gathered populace might read on the building the inscription: "Eumachia, the public priestess (of Venus), daughter of Lucius, had the vestibule, the covered gallery and the porticoes made with her own money and dedicated in her own name and in the name of her son Marcus Numistrius Fronto, in honor of the goddesses Concord and Augustan

Figure 12.3. View through the main entrance into the building underwritten by the Pompeian priestess, Eumachia, in the middle of the first century C.E., in the Forum of the city. The entrance is marked by a delicately carved acanthus scroll in marble against the brick of the facade.

Piety" (*Corpus Inscriptionum Latinarum* X.810, mid first century c.e.; trans. Natalie Kampen). A statue showing her in the usual pose and costume of a respectable matron (Fig. 12.4) stood in the building as a result of the generous gratitude of the cloth-cleaners; their inscription reads, "To Eumachia, the daughter of Lucius, the public priestess, from the fullers" (*Corpus Inscriptionum Latinarum* X.811; trans. Natalie Kampen). Argument continues about the uses to which the building was put, textile warehouse, auction house, cloth-merchants' guildhouse, or even public meetinghouse; only Eumachia's role as sole patron is beyond dispute, as the inscription indicates (Moeller 1972: 323–27).

Eumachia was not only a rich woman, a holder of an extremely important public priesthood, she was also politically involved. The building's commission seems to have come at just the moment when her son was running for public office, and his mother's generosity would have served him well. She commanded far greater power and wealth than many other women in Pompeii, but that did not prevent some of the others from involving themselves in financial and political affairs. A large property with a colonnaded garden belonged to Julia Felix, who rented it out. A graffito dated between 64 and 79 c.e. (*Corpus Inscriptionum Latinarum* IV.1136; trans. Natalie Kampen), tells us that

> On the estate of Julia Felix, the daughter of
> Spurius Felix, the following are for rent: an
> elegant bath suitable for the best people, shops,
> rooms above them, and second story apartments,
> from the Ides of August until the Ides of August
> five years hence, after which the lease may
> be renewed by simple agreement.

Women and Work

Julia Felix was hardly alone in involving herself in financial affairs, since at every social level below the aristocracy, women in Pompeii seem to have handled money. Women are known from the wood and wax tablets that record money paid to sellers of goods by buyers through the agency of the banker Jucundus (Andreau 1974). Fourteen women are scattered through the more than 150 documents; they normally represent themselves in these transactions although they seem never to have acted as witnesses for the transactions of other people. In November and December of the year 56 c.e., Umbricia Januaria and Umbricia Antiochis, who may have been freed slaves of the fish-sauce merchant Umbricius Scaurus, received money for sales they had made. Umbricia Januaria's document tells us that:

Umbricia Januaria hereby attests that she received from L. Caecilius Jucundus 11,039 sestertii, less a percentage [1–2 percent] as his commission, for the auc-

Figure 12.4. The statue of Eumachia, patron of the building in Figure 12.3. The statue was found in the building, having been given in honor of Eumachia by the corporation of fullers.

tion of goods on her behalf. This action took place at Pompeii on December 12 [56 C.E.], L. Duvius Clodius being the consul at the time.

(Corpus Inscriptionum Latinarum IV, supplement 1, pp. 308–10;
trans. Natalie Kampen)

A few years later, in a tavern in Pompeii, one perhaps similar to the setting for the four small paintings of gamblers and drinkers with their waitress at an inn (Fig. 12.5), a graffito on the wall says, "On the fifth of February, Vettia accepted from Faustilla fifteen denarii with eight asses (the *as* was a small denomination) in interest" (*Corpus Inscriptionum Latinarum* IV.8203, probably after 64 C.E.; trans. Natalie Kampen), and Faustilla reappears, again lending money at interest, on the wall of the house of Granius Romanus (*Corpus Inscriptionum Latinarum* IV.8204). That women lent as well as borrowed and engaged in business as well as philanthropy suggests their relative autonomy at certain social levels.

The world of taverns and cheap food shops saw other women at work as well. Asellina may have owned this tavern after 64 C.E. when

Figure 12.5. A waitress serves customers in a tavern at Pompeii in the mid-first century C.E. This is part of a set of wall paintings that include men playing dice and, perhaps as a consequence of the wine and the dice, getting into a fight.

earthquake damage necessitated so many repairs to buildings (Fig. 12.6), and its walls repeat her name as well as those of Zmyrina, Maria, and Aegle, who may have been waitresses; their single and somewhat exotic names as well as the content of the graffiti suggest that they were slaves, but they nonetheless engaged in the public world of politics as well as of work (*Corpus Inscriptionum Latinarum* IV.7862–64, 7866, and 7873). The graffiti all use the word *rogat* and tell us that a candidate for office is being proposed for the consideration of the passerby. Men and women of the lower classes seem to have favored these public declarations as did respectable matrons such as Taedia Secunda, the grandmother of a candidate of the mid-first century C.E. (*Corpus Inscriptionum Latinarum* IV.7469), even though it is clear that neither women nor slaves of either sex could vote (Franklin 1980; Bernstein 1988). At Asellina's tavern, one of the waitresses speaks to her customers in her own voice in a highly idiomatic Latin: "The lovely Idone greets those who will read this. Idone says that here you may drink for nine *dupondii*," and she tells us prices for better wines as well (*Corpus Inscriptionum Latinarum* IV.1679; trans. Natalie Kampen).

Figure 12.6. View of the interior of the tavern of Asellina, a Pompeian woman known to have employed several other women as waitresses.

Love and Money

The graffiti on Pompeian walls (they date mostly from the mid-first century C.E.) speak of waitresses and other working people as well. In one (*Corpus Inscriptionum Latinarum* IV.8259; trans. Natalie Kampen), Severus the weaver writes that his coworker Successus "loves the tavern maid whose name is Iris, but she really doesn't care about him; even so, he begs and tries to get her to pity him. His rival writes this. Farewell." The badly damaged frescoes from the workshop of the dyer Verecundus showing a woman selling articles at a table and the dyers at work let us know that men and women slaves and perhaps free workers might often have labored together and developed their friendships at work.

Words of love and admiration slid easily into obscenity with the aid of wine as some of the tavern walls tell us: "I fucked the bar girl" (*Corpus Inscriptionum Latinarum* IV.8442; trans. Natalie Kampen) or "Here Euplia laid strong men and laid 'em out" (*Corpus Inscriptionum Latinarum* IV.2310b; trans. Natalie Kampen). A similar story appears on the walls of brothels in Pompeii, although the pictures use a romanticized language unlike these raw words. Above the cubicles (Fig. 12.7) in which undernourished and unglamorous slave prostitutes worked for equally unglamorous men, beautiful boys and girls frolicked in wall paintings. The pictures show clean and lovely young people in comfortable settings with bed linen and pictures on the walls; their varied poses as well as the idealization of the imagery tells the customers the lies they want to hear as they contemplate a few minutes escape (Brendel 1970: 61–66).

Occupying Public Space: Alive or Dead

Whether prostitutes or saleswomen, shoppers in the marketplace or high-ranking priestesses, Pompeian women moved freely through the town. In its public spaces they saw buildings constructed with women's money, statues to women, women at work, and women commemorated even in death. The publicly displayed tombs and tombstones so typical of the outskirts of Roman towns and cities all over the empire bring us still more evidence of women. Here were funerary monuments set up by women for their husbands (Fig. 12.8): on the grave monument (first century C.E.), of C. Munatius Faustus erected in his memory by his wife Naevoleia Tyche, were a portrait of Tyche and a relief of a funeral ceremony (*Corpus Inscriptionum Latinarum* X.1030; trans. Natalie Kampen). On the facade the inscription reads,

Naevoleia Tyche, freedwoman of Lucius, for herself and Caius Munatius Faustus, member of the Augustal priesthood and country-man to whom the decurions, with the consent of the people, granted a *bisellium* (an honorific seat) for his merits. When she was alive, Naevoleia Tyche had this monument built also for her freedmen and those of Caius Munatius Faustus.

Figure 12.7. Interior of one of the several brothels in Pompeii; dated to the last years of the city, the brothel had small frescoes of heterosexual love-making painted above the entrances to the cubicles where the prostitutes worked. Whether these pictures tell us anything about actual sexual practices or are instead as "optimistic" as any advertizing is unclear.

A travertine altar-shaped tomb (ca. 20 C.E.) erected by the Ceres priestess Alleia Decimilla commemorated her husband and son, both community officeholders (*Corpus Inscriptionum Latinarum* X.1036), and a large tomb for Agrestinus Equitius Pulcher in the Porta Nocera cemetery was paid for by his wife Veia Barchilla (D'Avino 1967: 108). Eumachia's tomb stands nearby as does the tomb of M. Octavius and his freedwoman wife Vertia Philumene (Etienne 1977: 333). Upper- and middle-class tombs thus testify both to Pompeian women's use and even control of money and to the family relationships their social standing permitted them. Being honored by a funeral paid for with public money, as were the priestess Mamia and others, was the final testimony to their importance in the community.

Upper-class women lived with husbands, children, slaves, freed slaves, and assorted kin, in grand houses. How they used the space is by no means clear, however; nothing in the spatial arrangements or decorations reveals especially gendered places in the house. A few things are clear though: because ladies had slaves to do the domestic work, the

Figure 12.8. The first-century C.E., tomb monument of C. Munatius Faustus and Naevoleia Tyche in the cemetery of Porto Ercolano at Pompeii. The form recalls an altar, and many of the tombs at Pompeii incorporate reliefs with portraits or scenes of the occupations of the deceased.

kitchen was not the feminine preserve it became in modern times. Neither is there evidence for women's use of separate sitting rooms or dining rooms. Only when an area was given over to production work is women's presence attested to; thus the house of M. Terentius Eudoxus had a peristyle that was used as a weaving workshop. Graffiti in the porticus name men and women as textores (weavers) and netrices (netmakers) (*Corpus Inscriptionum Latinarum* IV.1507). Such use of space in a private house for production probably involved household slaves, and the finds of loom-weights in gardens and peristyles in other houses in Pompeii suggest that men and women slaves worked generating income for families all over town.

Houses for families of modest means were more the rule in some districts in Pompeii than the great mansions; with their smaller rooms and more limited spaces, these two-story houses dominated residential areas such as the Via dell'Abbondanza. The main streets of these neighborhoods had shops to which women and their slaves could walk, and they could easily have walked to public baths like the Stabian and Forum Baths that had sections for women from the second century, B.C.E. on. The women's baths are discreetly tucked away in corners of the much larger men's bathing and exercise areas, an arrangement comparable to what one can still see today in old towns in the Middle East. In some middle- and lower-class districts of the first century C.E., houses contained small workshops for production by families, and one can even find one-room shops with what seem to be living quarters in small mezzanines that speak of meager earnings. Relatively few domestic articles remained for archaeologists in these modest houses, but beds, marble tables, and bronze lamps can be seen along with pottery for daily use and storage. As is the case in the houses of the rich, space use and use of many objects are not clearly gendered, nor can one tell from the way things look whether women or men had a greater role in decorating and furnishing the house.

Women did decorate themselves at Pompeii as elsewhere in the Roman world; both sculpture and paintings reveal norms for women's appearance, and cosmetic jars and jewelry, earrings, pins, and golden hairnets, provide specific evidence. A painting of a young couple, she with gold jewelry and holding a stylus and tablet, presents three important ideas: the representation of the couple, a woman's attractiveness, and female literacy (Fig. 12.9). Such an image locates a woman in a world that combines the very old traditions—marriage and female beauty as natural and necessary—with the notion of female competence; this last is hardly surprising as a motif in the Pompeii we have been exploring, a place where women own property, do business, pay for construction, hold honorific and cultic office, and go about in public.

The Limits of Archaeology

Images unfortunately cannot answer all the important questions about women in Pompeii; archaeological evidence fails to tell us just how much women could and did enter into public life and to what extent their physical mobility was limited by their sense of propriety and duty or by the intervention of fathers and husbands. Surely many of the aristocratic women of Rome felt little need to ask permission to move as they pleased or to enter into political negotiation and intrigue, but the same situation is harder to imagine for the wealthy and middle-class local families of Pompeii. Little information remains even to tell us about the involvement of such women in religious cult, although Mamia, a public priestess who erected a temple (early first century C.E.) "to the spirit of Augustus by herself and with her own money" (*Corpus Inscriptionum Latinarum* X.816; trans. Natalie Kampen), and Eumachia,

Figure 12.9. Wall painting of a couple from a house in first-century C.E. Pompeii; she holds a writing implement and tablets and he a scroll to testify to their learning and thus their status.

priestess of Ceres, indicate the importance of wealthy women as benefactors. Paintings in temples and houses document the presence of religious groups, such as that of Isis, that were especially popular among women (Fig. 12.10). A number of images of the Egyptian goddess and her rituals appear (see ch. 6 above), for example, at the estate of Julia Felix, but

Figure 12.10. Wall painting from first-century C.E. Pompeii; it depicts a ritual at the temple of Isis and includes the white-clad priests, priestesses, and followers of this Egyptian goddess whose cult had attracted women since the Hellenistic period.

there is no way to know if the owner had a special interest in Isis. And finally, the evidence fails to tell us enough about relationships among women, between workers like the waitresses who call on us to vote for their favorite candidate, between free women and their slaves, between businesswomen like the moneylender Faustilla and the women in debt to her.

The eruption of Mount Vesuvius in 79 C.E. covered the towns of Pompeii and Herculaneum and the villas and farms around them. In one sense the eruption was one of the greatest tragedies of all time; in another sense, it did a great favor to archaeology in preserving, as nowhere else, traces of daily life for women and men in every social stratum.

Although the difficulties of interpreting this material are enormous, the reader of Chapter 13 will be keenly aware of the extent to which other periods in Roman history lack comparable minutiae about how people lived, ate, dressed, worked, and played.

TRANSLATIONS

Arrowsmith, W. 1959. *Petronius: The Satyricon.* New York.

WORKS CONSULTED

Andreau, Jean. 1974. *Les Affaires de Monsieur Jucundus.* Rome.

Bernstein, Frances. 1988. "Pompeian Women and the *Programmata.*" In *Studia Pompeiana et Classica in honor of Wilhelmina F. Jashemski,* edited by R. I. Curtis, 1: 1–18. New Rochelle, N.Y.

Brendel, Otto J. 1970. "Scope and Temperament of Erotic Art in the Greco-Roman World." In *Studies in Erotic Art,* edited by Theodore Bowie and C. V. Christenson, 3–97. New York.

Castren, Paavo. 1975. *Ordo Populusque Pompeianus: Polity and Society in Roman Pompeii.* Rome.

D'Avino, Michele. 1967. *Women of Pompeii.* Naples.

De Franciscis, A. 1975. *The Pompeian Wall Paintings in the Roman Villa of Oplontis.* Recklinghausen.

Digest of Justinian 1985. Translated by Alan Watson. Philadelphia.

Etienne, Robert. 1977. *La Vie Quotidienne à Pompéi.* 2d ed. Paris.

Franklin, James, Jr. 1980. *Pompeii: The Electoral Programmata Campaigns and Politics, A.D. 71–79.* Papers and Monographs of the American Academy in Rome 28. Rome.

La Rocca, E., M. de Vos, and E. de Vos. 1976. *Guida Archeologica di Pompei.* Milan.

Moeller, Walter. 1972. "The Building of Eumachia: A Reconsideration." *American Journal of Archaeology* 76, no. 3: 323–27.

FURTHER READING

D'Arms, John. 1970. *Romans on the Bay of Naples.* Cambridge, Mass.

Grant, Michael, et al. 1975. *Erotic Art in Pompeii.* London.

Heyob, Sharon K. 1975. *The Cult of Isis among Women in the Graeco-Roman World.* Leiden.

Jashemsky, Wilhelmina. 1979. *The Gardens of Pompeii, Herculaneum and the Villas destroyed by Vesuvius.* New York.

Packer, James. 1975. "Middle and Lower Class Housing in Pompeii and Herculaneum." In *Neue Forschungen in Pompeii,* edited by Bernard Andreae and Helmut Kyrieleis, 133–47. Recklinghausen.

Richardson, Lawrence, Jr. 1988. *Pompeii: An Architectural History.* Baltimore, Md.

Ward Perkins, John B., and Amanda Claridge. 1978. *Pompeii A.D. 79.* New York.

Will, Elizabeth Lyding. 1979. "Women in Pompeii." *Archaeology* 32, no. 5: 34–43.

13

WOMEN OF THE HIGH
AND LATER EMPIRE:
CONFORMITY AND DIVERSITY

The world of the high and late Empire kept the conservative ideal of
Roman womanhood it had inherited from the Republic. At the same
time, the discrepancy between the gender values of the period and lived
reality was as great as it had always been; women's lives were far more
variable than the ideal indicated, and there were often more extreme
differences in the circumstances of women of different social strata than
there were in the lives of men and women of the same social stratum.
This pattern we have seen as pervasive in all our discussions of Roman
women.

In this chapter, we confront a new issue: geography. How are we to
assess the lives of women across a gigantic and complex empire, one
whose greatest expanse in the second century C.E., included southern
Scotland and the Sahara, the Atlantic coast and inland Turkey? Here
were women of the frontiers to whom the Romans referred as "barbarians" and women of Athens whose cultivation and nobility were irre-
proachable. Not only was the Empire larger and more diverse than ever,
it also played an ever-larger part in the consciousness of the city of Rome
and the emperor. Rulers and their wives now came from the provinces
or from provincial ancestry. Soldiers and merchants came from everywhere and carried the ideas and customs of their own lands to every
corner of the Empire at the same moment that they contributed to the
dissemination of Roman ideas. And finally, in 212 C.E., the emperor Caracalla issued an edict making every freeman and woman who lived in
the Roman provinces a full Roman citizen. Ultimately, the period we
are examining, from the middle of the first century to the end of the
third, saw the creation of a new culture, one in which local ways remained visible while Romanization was taking place and in which Romanization itself gradually changed from being clearly Italian as it ab-

sorbed elements of the local cultures of province and periphery and became increasingly hybrid.

To understand this complicated world is no easy task. Not only do we deal with an expanded geographic field, but the temporal field in this chapter encompasses two and a half centuries, from the death of Nero in 68 to the legalization of Christianity under Constantine in 311–12. This period was full of changes in politics and culture, yet its history has always been difficult to write because the evidence is so scattered and ambiguous. Unlike the Augustan period, the later Empire is represented by few surviving literary texts, especially after the mid-second century, when the interpretive work of an analytic historian like Tacitus is replaced by the anonymous and often self-contradictory biographies of the compendium called the *Historia Augusta*, the history of the rulers. Large-scale public monuments are still constructed until the early third century, then become rare until the end of the century. Private monuments are common everywhere but, like many of the inscriptions of the period, they are often difficult to date; and the abundant archaeological material is unevenly distributed both temporally and geographically. For all these reasons, to write a chronological history of women, never an easy task in any period, becomes almost impossible.

What guides our arrangement and discussion of material in this chapter, then, is a grid with multiple and variable lines on it. Time appears most regularly where place is less visible—in our section on the women of the court. Here, because of the chronology imposed by the rulers themselves, the women of their families can be seen in time, although patterns of historical change in their lives are almost as hard to make out as they are in the lives of "ordinary" women. For them, whoever these "ordinary" women might be, place and social status make more of a difference to the way they live than time seems to, although this is probably as much a result of missing evidence as of enduring or conservative gender roles. Our scattered and varied evidence of women in the high and later Empire, presented according to their social locations, suggests that the conservative Republican gender ideals of the elite men in the city of Rome remained normative and defined "tradition" for many within the Empire. Those in other parts of the Empire who shared the social standing or the social aspirations of that conservative elite drew on this tradition, and they used the gender ideal as a way to speak of *belonging*, whether to a social stratum, a place, or a moral vision. It helped to define them as ROMAN. For the rest, the ideal was unknown, out of reach, or perhaps we simply have no evidence of them and their motives at all. They are, nonetheless, a crucial part of the richness of this cosmopolitan imperial environment, called by the Romans *orbis terrarum*, the entire world.

Figure 13.1. Gold coin of Plotina from Rome, ca. 112–115 C.E., with her portrait on the obverse (A). and Vesta seated on the reverse (B).

A

B

347

Empresses and Women of the Upper Classes

The wife of Agricola, Domitia Decidiana, was a woman of Roman traditional virtue: the marriage, says her son-in-law Tacitus, writing toward
the end of the first century C.E., was characterized by concord and praiseworthy kindness between the partners: "they lived in rare accord, maintained by mutual affection and unselfishness; but in such a partnership
the good wife deserves more than half the praise, just as a bad one deserves more than half the blame" (*Agricola* 6.1; Mattingly 1948). The
Panegyric, which Pliny the Younger, governor of Bithynia under Trajan,
wrote in 100 C.E. to praise the emperor, compliments Trajan on his
choice of partner and lets the world know that the empress Plotina's
traditional goodness (Fig. 13.1: Coin of Plotina associated with goddess
Vesta), like Domitia's, reflected credit on her husband and his public
life:

your own wife contributes to your honour and glory, as a supreme model of the
ancient virtues; the chief pontiff himself, has he to take a wife, would choose
her or one like her—if one exists. From your position she claims nothing for
herself but the pleasure it gives her, unswerving in her devotion not to your
power but to yourself. . . . How modest she is in her attire, how moderate the
number of her attendants, how unassuming when she walks abroad! This is the
work of a husband who has fashioned and formed her habits: there is glory
enough for a wife in obedience. When she sees her husband unaccompanied by
pomp and intimidation, she goes about in silence herself, and so far as her sex
permits, she follows his example of walking on foot.

(*Panegyric* 83; Radice 1975)

Compare this with an inscription of late fourth century C.E., Rome,
set up by a member of the non-Christian elite in honor of his wife Paulina, whom he calls "chaste, faithful, pure in mind and body." Paulina
speaks in her own voice on the back of the statue base:

The glory of my own parents gave me no greater gift than that I have seemed
worthy of my husband; but all fame and honor is in my husband's name . . .
Because of you (husband Agorius), all hail me as blessed and holy, because you
yourself proclaim me throughout the world as a good woman; I am known to
all, even those who do not know me. Why should I not be pleasing, with a
husband such as you?

(*Corpus Inscriptionum Latinarum* 6.1779 / *Inscriptiones Latinae Liberae Rei
Publicae* 1259; Gardner and Wiedemann 1991: 66–67)

Traditional Ideals of Womanhood

Through much of the Imperial period, the *ideal* of Roman womanhood
remained remarkably consistent. The ideal, rooted in the social conditions of the city of Rome, the capital of the great Empire, was articulated by Roman writers, largely men of the elite (upper-class or intellec-

tual), and it drew heavily on the language of the conservative gender ideology of the Republican and Augustan periods, not least because these men, like Agorius, never stopped reading "whatever was composed in Latin or Greek, whether the thought of wise men for whom the gate of heaven stands open, or the verses which skilled powers have composed, or prose writings" (*Corpus Inscriptionum Latinarum* CIL 6.1779; Gardner and Wiedemann 1991: 67). Embedded in law, literature, and art, and supported in the East by comparable Greek traditions of literature (see below, Plutarch's "Advice to Bride and Groom") and social life, the ideal spread to the most Romanized and Hellenized parts of the Empire, often appropriated first by the local upper classes as a part of the process of assimilation and political mobility.

The Roman ideal appears most clearly in those passages in speeches to emperors, letters to mothers, and epitaphs that intend to compliment women. There the ideal was constantly reiterated in language that changed surprisingly little over the course of six hundred years. However, in other genres, it seldom finds pure and disinterested expression. We locate it in poems, histories, letters to friends, entangled in a web of political gossip, spoken in the same breath as castigation, enmeshed in and complicated by practices that seem to modern eyes to be in direct conflict with it. Two examples of upper-class Roman women of Italy mentioned in the letters of Pliny the Younger (compiled between 97 and 112 C.E.) may make the problem visible, if not clear.

[Pompeius Saturninus] has recently read me some letters which he said were written by his wife, but sounded to me like Plautus or Terence being read in prose. Whether they are really his wife's, as he says, or his own (which he denies) one can only admire him either for what he writes, or the way he has cultivated and refined the taste of the girl he married.

(*Letters* 1.16.6; Radice 1975)

The letters cannot be by the wife, according to Pliny, but if they are, the credit must go to her husband for the education he has given her. Again we hear the language of Agorius's wife Paulina, who credits all her fame and honor to her husband, and of Pliny's discussion of Plotina, whose wonderful behavior he says is the work of the husband who formed her.

When credit does go to a woman, Ummidia, it is hardly unproblematically rendered.

Ummidia Quadratilla is dead, having almost attained the age of seventy-nine and kept her powers unimpaired up to her last illness, along with a sound constitution and sturdy physique which are rare in a woman. She died leaving an excellent will: the grandson inherits two-thirds of the estate, and her granddaughter the remaining third. . . . He lived in his grandmother's house but managed to combine personal austerity with deference to her sybaritic tastes. She kept a troupe of pantomime actors whom she treated with an indulgence unsuitable in a lady of her high position, but Quadratus never watched their performances either in the theatre or at home, nor did she insist on it. Once when she was asking me to supervise her grandson's education she told me that as a woman, with all a woman's idle hours to fill, she was in the habit of amusing herself playing draughts or watching her mimes, but before she did she always told Quadratus to go away and work: which I thought showed respect for his youth as much as her affection.

(Pliny the Younger, *Letters* 7.24.1–5, abridged; Radice 1975)

Ummidia's wealth allows her trivial and morally ambiguous pastimes, but she raises her grandson responsibly, keeps him out of the way of her games and her mime troupe, and then leaves all her wealth to her proper heir. Pliny does not mention another proper use of her money, but we can learn it from inscriptions; Ummidia was as generous a patron to her community as Pliny was to his, and she is on record as giving to her hometown, Casinum, a temple, an amphitheater and a stage (Raepsaet-Charlier 1986: 649, no. 829; *Corpus Inscriptionum Latinarum* VI.28526; *Corpus Inscriptionum Latinarum* X.5183 = *Inscriptiones Latinae Liberae Rei Publicae* 5628).

What emerges from these two letters is a sense that female virtue in the old Republican version is no longer the only form (was it ever?) for upper-class womanhood. Education and wealth may be both problematic and respectable at the same time. The writing wife, framed as her husband's creature, is nevertheless part of the game, part of a literate, writing, world; the rich old lady, freed from male control and able to do as she likes, nevertheless, like the men of her class, acts responsibly to her grandson and generously to her community. In neither case is virtue clearly expressed since the women involved are crossing some essential boundaries: both letters reflect the responses of a judgmental and conservative, though not unsophisticated, man, to these complex gender practices. Throughout this chapter we will continue to see representations of women behaving around, against, and near the ideal; however, only when compliments are paid to a mother, wife, or empress are women pictured as fully exemplifying this ideal.

Empresses

Pliny the Younger's *Panegyric*, delivered in 100 C.E. emphasized virtues of modesty and restraint in speaking of Trajan's wife Plotina and the emperor's sister Marciana; the two women lived harmoniously in his household, united without envy or quarrels in their loyalty to the ruler (*Panegyric*, 83; see above, under "Traditional Ideals of Womanhood"). The ideal takes the usual form: self-effacing wives and mothers, dutiful and modest, placing family before everything except perhaps Rome itself. When Hadrian gave his funeral orations for Plotina (in 121 or 123?) and for his mother-in-law Matidia, the niece of Trajan (in 119), he stressed these same virtues once more. After speaking of his personal grief at the death of Matidia, Hadrian went on to describe her fidelity to her husband's memory.

[She mourned him] during a long widowhood in the flower of her life, a woman of the greatest beauty and chastity, [very obed]ient to her mother, herself a mother most indulgent and a most devoted kinswoman, helping all. A burden to no man nor disagreeable to any man, and in her relations with me of extraordinary [goodness], with such modesty that she never asked anything from me [for herself and often] did not ask what I would rather have been asked by the women of my family. She in her good will prayed with many extended vows for such [good fortune] to befall me, and preferred to rejoice in my good fortune rather than benefit from it.

(*Corpus Inscriptionum Latinarum* 14.3579; Smallwood 1966: 56 n. 114)

Despite the laudable harmony of Trajan's household, fourteen years elapsed after he became emperor in 98 before any of the women of his family were depicted on coins, including his wife Plotina, his sister Marciana (whose death in 112 may have provided the impetus for the coinage) and her daughter Matidia. Restraint in providing public honors to the women of the court characterized the reign of Trajan, as it had also the time of Augustus (at least in Rome and the West). The types the Trajanic coins use for these women include association with Vesta, Fides, and Pietas, all about traditional virtues of home, hearth, religion, and children (with Matidia) (Fig. 13.1). As far as we know, none of the Imperial women is represented on the historical reliefs of the period, but Plotina and Marciana did receive the honorific Imperial title of Augusta soon after 100, when Pliny commended them for their modesty in declining the Senate's first offer of the title (*Panegyric* 84). Marciana and her daughter Matidia were the first Imperial women to receive the title without being either wife or mother of an emperor; other honors, however, came to them and Plotina only after Trajan's death. His successor Hadrian, who was married to Sabina, daughter of Matidia and thus grandniece of Trajan, saw his association with these Imperial women as a guarantee of his own authority, for this reason, he declared Plotina Augusta in 128, and had both women deified on their deaths, starting with Matidia in 119 C.E.: "he bestowed special honors upon his mother-in-law with gladiatorial games and other ceremonies" (*Historia Augusta*, Hadrian 9, Magie 1967–68). Along with the funeral oration, he honored her with coins with the label DIVA AUGUSTA MATIDIA (British Museum Collection III: p. 281, nos. 328–32), and erected to her a temple whose remains have been identified in the Campus Martius in Rome. And, making his motives ever clearer, he issued a significant coin on the obverse of which Trajan's portrait appears with the label Divus Traianus, while the reverse shows Diva Plotina (Fig. 13.2); his claims to the throne are thus doubly secured by his wife's lineage and by his own adoption, and he merits the throne as well by the pious honors he offers to his adoptive ancestors (Boatwright 1991a, and Temporini 1978).

In his lifetime, Hadrian's adopted son and successor Antoninus Pius had honored his deceased wife Faustina (d. 141) with a temple in the Roman Forum, had instituted charitable donations to worthy girl chil-

A

B

Figure 13.2. Gold coin of Hadrian, minted after 122 in Rome. On the obverse (A) is the divinized Trajan; on the reverse (B) Diva Plotina. Hadrian uses these images to construct his new divine family.

dren from the Italian countryside (*puellae Faustinianae* [*Historia Augusta, Antoninus* 8]), and had named her *diva* on coins. The emperors who follow become ever more encrusted with honors, ever more clearly godlike, and their wives participate in the process. As these honors escalate in number and hyperbole, the tension increases between traditional womanly reticence and self-effacement on the one hand, and honors, funeral orations, coins, portraits, benefactions, and titles on the other (Faustina the Younger's honors: Dio 72.5, *Historia Augusta, Marcus* 26.8, *Corpus Inscriptionum Latinarum* 14.40, and *BMC* IV, nos. 700–705). By the time of Septimius Severus's reign (197–211), the empress Julia Domna will be addressed as Mater Senatus (mother of the Senate: *BMC* V, clxxvi and cxcv ff.) and Mater Castrorum (mother of the military camps: *Corpus Inscriptionum Latinarum* 8.26598, a title first used apparently for Faustina the Younger when she accompanied her husband Marcus Aurelius to his campaigns in the eastern part of the Empire in 175, as in Dio 72.5, *Historia Augusta, Marcus* 26.8). Automatically granted the title of Augusta, she represents the trend away from the earlier tradition of emperor and empress as first among equals; yet at the same time, her many titles and honors retain their connection to motherhood and the primacy of family.

Only rarely does our evidence provide information about the occupations and interests of individual empresses, about their social and political influence, or about their daily lives. Whether they had public prominence or were seen as essentially modest and retiring, the empresses do seem to have exercised private influence; the evidence is, however, very spotty. Julia Titi, the daughter of the emperor Titus, nominated the consul for 84 C.E., according to the later historian Dio (67.4.2), and Vitellius's wife, Galeria, about whom we also know relatively little, saved the consul Galerius Trachalus from execution in 68 (Tacitus, *Histories* 2.60.2).

Plotina, self-effacing as she may have been, is said to have given advice in domestic matters just as Livia and the other empresses had.

Thus we hear that Trajan betrothed his grandniece Vibia Sabina to Hadrian, "Plotina being in favor of the match, while (he himself), according to Marius Maximus, was not greatly enthusiastic." (*Historia Augusta Hadrian* 2.10). Another abridged collection of Imperial lives (*Epitome de Caesaribus* 42.21; trans. Elaine Fantham) reports that when Trajan let his officials extort from the provincials, Plotina "reproached him for neglecting his own good name . . . and as a result she made him detest unjust exactions." This comment is interesting both for Plotina's role as moral arbiter and for her concern with the world outside of the city of Rome.

The empress' clear awareness of public matters in the provinces can be seen in a letter she wrote to Hadrian after Trajan's death (117 C.E). Inscriptions in colloquial Greek record her formal request to the emperor on behalf of Popillius (head of the Epicurean school at Athens) as well as her letter to Popillius. In the damaged Greek inscription we can see her adherence to Epicurean doctrine as she speaks of the principles of "our school." The letter to the emperor reads,

How much I am interested in the sect of Epicurus you know very well, Master. Your help is needed in the matter of its succession; for in view of the ineligibility of all but Roman citizens as successors, the range of choice is very narrow. I ask therefore in the name of Popillius Theotimus, the present successor at Athens, to allow him to write in Greek that part of his disposition which deals with regulating the succession and grant him the power of filling his place by a successor of peregrine status,[1] should personal considerations make it advisable; and let the future successors of the sect of Epicurus henceforth enjoy the same right as you grant to Theotimus; all the more since the practice is that each time the testator has made a mistake in the choice of successor the disciples of the above sect after a general deliberation put in his place the best man, a result that will be more easily attained if he is selected from a larger group.

(*Inscriptiones Latinae Liberae Rei Pablicae* II. 7784.4–17; Alexander 1938: 161)

The interest of empresses in philosophical matters reappears in information about Julia Domna's patronage of Philostratus and the suggestion that she was even called Julia the philosopher (Bowersock 1969: 103). Julia Domna, Dio says, also took care of petitions and letters for Caracalla when he was emperor, from 211 to 217, (Dio 78.18.2–3 and 79.4.2–3) and held public receptions for the most prominent men, just as did the emperor (Dio 79.4.2–3).

The empresses traveled extensively with their husbands, as we gather from reports (some much later and of questionable reliability) of Plotina's being with Trajan at his death on campaign (*Historia Augusta, Hadrian* 5.9–10) and of Faustina's having accompanied Marcus Aurelius (Dio 72.5). Sabina traveled with Hadrian to Egypt (ca. 130 C.E.) where her friend Julia Balbilla commemorated the visit and her own poetic skill in Greek epigrams on the thigh of the Colossus of Memnon. Despite her Roman name, Balbilla was a Greek noblewoman and her epigrams adopt the dialect and language of Sappho (who lived almost a thousand years before her!) In part of a poem to honor Sabina and the trip to Egypt, Balbilla also proudly identifies herself:

Memnon, son of Dawn and revered Tithonus, sitting before the Theban city of Zeus or Amenoth, Egyptian king, as the priests who know the ancient tales relate, Hail! and may you be keen to welcome by your cry the august wife too of the Lord Hadrian . . .
I do not judge that this statue of yours can perish, and I perceive within me that your soul shall be immortal. For pious were my parents and grandparents. Balbillus the wise and Antiochus the king, father of my father. From their line do I draw my noble blood and these are the writings of Balbilla the pious.

(Bowie 1990: 63)

Like many wives of Imperial governors, and like some of the Julio-Claudian women as well,[2] the women of the later courts traveled into worlds far beyond the imaginings of the writers of the Twelve Tables whose laws placed such clear constraints on the mobility and autonomy of Roman women.

Pliny's evocation of Plotina as a retiring and rather dull matron becomes more colorful when we see the evidence of the travel, the cultivated interests, and the interventions behind the throne of the empress; if she, the least flamboyant of her century, had such a cosmopolitan life, we must see Sabina, Faustina, and the others as at least comparable. This hardly means, however, that these were women who exercised the influence of Augustus's empress Livia. Their lives were apparently more private, more involved with other Imperial women, with family and property, and with literary interests (Boatwright 1991a). The orator Fronto, teacher of the Imperial heir Marcus Aurelius, thought it appropriate to write the following cloyingly conventional birthday greeting to Marcus's mother Domitia Lucilla using the Greek language. However, he was sufficiently in awe of her standards (or her standing) that he first asked his pupil Marcus to check the correctness of the letter (mid-second century, and see the earlier letter about women's birthday celebrations in the introduction).

To the Mother of Marcus
Willingly by heaven, yes, with the greatest pleasure possible have I sent my Gratia (his wife) to keep your birthday with you, and would have come myself had it been lawful. But for myself . . . this consulship is a clog around my feet . . .

The right thing, it seems, would have been that all women from all quarters should have gathered for this day and celebrated your birth-feast, first of all the women that love their husbands and love their children and are virtuous, and secondly all that are genuine and truthful, and the third company to keep the feast should have been the kind-hearted and the affable and the accessible and the humble-minded; and many other ranks of women would be there to share in some part of your praise and virtue, seeing that you possess and are mother of all virtues and accomplishments befitting a woman, just as Athena possesses and is mistress of every art.

(Fronto, *Correspondence* 2.7; Haines 1962)

Although the empresses seem to have had a voice in discussions about the succession in the second century, that voice was far quieter than those of the Severan Julias. Kin of Julia Domna, the three Julias (Julia Maesa, Domna's sister, and Maesa's two daughters, Julia Soaemias and Julia Mamaea) determined the succession and removal of emperors. Soaemias's son Elagabalus became emperor through the intervention of mother and grandmother, and was replaced by his cousin Alexander Severus, son of Mamaea, by the manipulations of *his* mother and grandmother; Julia Maesa remained at the center of the politics of the period from 211 until her death in 226: "When he [Elagabalus] went to the camp or the Senate-house, he took with him his grandmother [Julia Maesa] . . . in order that through her prestige he might get greater respect—for by himself he got none." (*Historia Augusta Elagabalus* 12.2–3; Magie 1967–68)[3]

The intervention or "interference" of the Imperial women in state affairs was always seen as problematic by Roman writers. These men always see such involvements as inappropriate and dangerous, for the women are crossing gender boundaries that are meant to keep social order. Perhaps this is why they constantly elide political and sexual transgressions, for both create *disorder*. No matter how self-effacing the women of the court may have been, no matter what the official claims of their virtue, there seem always to have been rumors of incompatibility or scurrilous tales in circulation about Imperial sexual adventures. Hadrian's wife Sabina may have been chaste, but like Plotina she was childless and "he would have dismissed his wife . . . for being moody and difficult, if he had been a private citizen, as he himself used to say" (*Historia Augusta Hadrian.* 11; trans. Elaine Fantham). Marcus Aurelius's empress Faustina, daughter of his predecessor Antoninus Pius and mother of his many children "allegedly had once seen gladiators pass by and was inflamed with passion for one of them. While troubled by a long illness she confessed to her husband about her passion." The same author goes on to intimate that Faustina's son Commodus was actually fathered by a gladiator:

[H]er son Commodus was actually begotten in adultery, since it is reasonably well-known that Faustina chose both sailors and gladiators as paramours for herself at Caieta. When [the emperor] was told about her so that he might divorce her—if not execute her—he is reported to have said, "if we send our wife away, we must give back her dowry too"—and what dowry did she have but the empire, which he had received from his father-in-law when adopted by him at Hadrian's wish

(*Antoninus.* 19; Birley 1976)

The political goal of this kind of gossip is obvious: the writer damages the reputation of the emperor in an environment where his inability to control his wife speaks worlds of his other inadequacies. A passage about Marcus Aurelius giving Imperial posts to his wife's lovers is just such a piece of scandal (*Historia Augusta. Antoninus* 29) exploiting the spicy combination of sexual transgression and political interference. Unquestionably late, unreliable, and often profoundly silly, *Historia Augusta* (late third and fourth century) reveals the persistence of this standardized gossip about female transgression.

In contrast with such scandalous rumors, the representations of the wives of Hadrian, Antoninus Pius, and Marcus Aurelius in state art and inscriptions provide us with a view of court women that more closely resembles the praise literature of speeches. Stressing marital loyalty (even a kind of affection) and dynastic duty, these monuments erase both the scandalous and the cosmopolitan elements of the lives of the empresses. The Column Base of Antoninus Pius, dated to 161 in Rome, shows the emperor and Faustina I ascending together to the heavens on the back of a strange youthful figure, a psychopomp or being who bears the soul away (Fig. 13.3). Just as the deceased Sabina is borne aloft on the back of an eagle on a relief (after 136–37) in which Hadrian sits watching, the apotheosis of Antoninus and Faustina suggests the marital harmony so important to the public self-representation of the Imperial

Figure 13.3. Base of the Column of Antoninus Pius from Rome, erected around the time of his death, ca. 161 C.E. On the front is the apotheosis of Antoninus and Faustina, his wife, watched by the goddess Roma and the personification of the Campus Martius, the place where the funeral pyres of the emperors and their families burned.

family *as* family. Similarly, in the coins of Imperial couples that present husband and wife clasping right hands in a gesture (the *dextrarum iunctio*) associated with the concord of treaties and of marriage, the visual imagery of the state puts on parade a dutiful and harmonious couple. In fact, the public ideology of concord reached into the private realm (if we can even separate them by this modern polarization) when the senate decreed, on the death of Faustina II (175?), that "silver images of Marcus and Faustina should be set up in the temple of Venus and Roma and that an altar should be erected whereon all the maidens married in the city and their bridegrooms should offer sacrifice." (Dio 72.31.1); they may be shown, on a coin, at the altar below the larger figures of the emperor and empress who join hands as Concordia brings them together (Reekmans 1957; Davies 1985).

The imagery of the good wife persisted, despite the scandal-mongering, in the state-sponsored public images for Faustina's daughter, wife of their adopted son Marcus Aurelius. The coins associate Faustina the Younger with Marcus and their son Commodus (161–75 C.E.) and put her face on the obverse of coins whose reverses often show Felicitas (fruitfulness / good fortune), Felix Temporum (the prosperity of the era), Fecunditas (fertility) or Juno Lucina (protector of women in child-birth) with large numbers of children; the numbers and ages of the children seem to change with the births and deaths of the Imperial offspring (Fig. 13.4). The emperor and his wife thus emerge as the model not just of a dutiful but of a harmonious and fertile marriage: their domestication becomes the pattern of Roman marital harmony, as the state's ideology penetrated the private once more (Fittschen 1982). This aristocratic image of marital concord has earlier models (see Chapter 12), but the Antonine dynasty appears to make the first broad public use of it. This may spring from the urge to win a more intimate loyalty from the empire's people to their rulers as quasi-kinfolk; it may also indicate a state policy of reinforcing traditional (if reformulated) Roman concerns with domestic morality and reproductive responsibility. And as always, such visual ideology serves more powerfully than any speech or decree to remind people of the peace attending civil and dynastic stability.

The most interesting and latest case of the construction of the harmonious Imperial family with its virtuous wife is also the most obvious in its political motives. Septimius Severus, the Roman general from North Africa who overcame other contenders for the Imperial throne after the civil wars at the end of the second century, married Julia Domna, a Syrian aristocrat whom the third century texts describe variously as dramatically beautiful, intellectual, long-suffering, adulterous, powerful, and dangerous (for example, Dio 78.18, Herodian 4.3.8–9, or *Historia Augusta, Severus* 21.6–8). They are frequently represented together with their two sons Geta and Caracalla (or in various combinations) from the early childhood of Geta until Septimius Severus's death in 211. Gold coins show Julia, her heavy looped and braided hair identifying her immediately, with her two boys. The nearly adult sons appear

Figure 13.4. Coin of Faustina the Younger from Rome, ca. 161–176 C.E. The reverse (shown) carries the label Felix temporum, the happy future guaranteed by the woman and her six children, presumably the same number the empress had at the time the coin was minted.

with their parents (riding in their father's carriage, watching their mother make a sacrifice, Caracalla shaking hands with his father as Geta stands between them and Julia Domna looks on approvingly) (Fig. 13.5) on the family arch set up in 206–9 to commemorate their visit to Septimius's birthplace, Leptis Magna (in Libya). And finally, as adults, the sons joined their parents and Caracalla's wife and father-in-law on the Arch set up by the moneychangers in Rome. The vast public imagery of the family was reinforced by the many statue-groups that graced town squares and temple precincts in all parts of the empire; a great series is preserved at Perge, the town from which at least one other major Imperial family group, Hadrianic in date, remains to indicate the way the Imperial family image structured the cityscape.

    Only when we notice the frequent erasure or destruction of the head of Geta is the fiction of the happy family exposed: Geta was murdered by his brother Caracalla when their father died in 211, and Caracalla then decreed that Geta's image be removed from all monuments (a practice called *damnatio memoriae*, erasure of memory.) The blank space where Geta's head had been (now replaced by a modern one) on the

Figure 13.5. Relief with Septimius Severus clasping the hand of his son Caracalla as his second son Geta and his wife Julia Domna (second from the left) look on. The relief dates to about 206 C.E. and comes from the Severan family arch at Leptis Magna in modern Libya.

handshake scene of the Leptis Arch, like the empty place on the arch in Rome, reveals the importance of the family myth—and its fragility. Official representation used Julia Domna as a linchpin to create a family, and thus gave an empress a central place in dynastic iconography in order to insist on a legitimate past and secure future for the people of the Roman empire (Kampen 1991).

What we have been seeing is, first, the discrepancy between texts and visual images that results from their differing traditions and functions and so projects conflicting impressions of the empress. Second, despite changes over time in the way the empresses were depicted and honored, there remained a core of imagery tied to the traditional gendered virtues of the Roman elite; this they preserved and disseminated to the world at large. The women of the court, regardless of how sophisticated and complex they might have been, always are praised in terms of conservative domestic behavior. Finally, all our evidence points to the existence of a long-standing public discourse, going back to the time of Livia and Augustus, about the empress's sexuality. When she is represented for state purposes, it is often because her image acts as an indication of the stable and happy future assured by her reproductive contribution to the dynasty. When she is reproached or slandered, it is through the use of her political interference as it is associated with murderous or adulterous desires and acts: sexuality and power go wrong together, and each is a sign for the other, for each is about the transgression of social boundaries essential to preserving the Roman order. This order in turn depends on an ideal womanhood, defined both by the praise of the empress as a norm and the condemnation of transgressions attributed to her. As the Roman world expanded, the empress's image remained of value for social reproduction on a vast scale.

Women of Wealth

Like the women of the court, rich women throughout the Roman Empire appear to us through the veils of ideology, genre, and chance. Not only do we know them only as far as we have surviving evidence, evidence shaped by the conventions of each genre from praise literature and public art to gossip, but we also read them as texts written by a small number of people who construct them according to their own interests, and these are not always the interests of the women themselves. Adding to these complexities the expanse of the Empire compounds the problems we met in the discussion of the empresses, since now local traditions may intervene. Thus, regional ideals may modify the ideal of womanhood diffused throughout the Empire in part by the image of the empress; how much diversity there was remains difficult to assess because of the uneven and scattered evidence.

The same problems are generated by the random and probably unrepresentative evidence of the conduct of wealthy women. Thus, for example, Pliny the Younger's letters (late first to early second century) tell us a good deal about the vocal and influential upper-class women of Italy who brought lawsuits to preserve their own interests (as when the embarrassed writer had to act on behalf of his mother's old friend Corellia Hispulla in her suit against a very important man [Letter 4.17], or when he represented a mother who brought a criminal case against two freedmen she accused of poisoning her son and forging a will to make themselves his heirs [Letter 7.6]). In addition to being implicated in their fathers' and husbands' legal affairs (for example, Letter 3.9), Pliny tells us that women were called as witnesses in political cases and exerted pressure themselves (Letters 3.11 and 9.13).

By comparison with these and other cases Pliny recounts about his years in Rome, the mention of cases in which women were involved under the writer's governorship in Bithynia (110–12 c.e.) are few; two concern men's petitions that involve women and one is a request for the emperor's permission to let the governor's wife travel for family reasons (10.59, 10.106 and 10.120). Clearly the disputes that needed the emperor's opinion were rarely initiated by women during Pliny's governorship; these letters to Trajan over the course of approximately twelve months are all that Pliny has to tell us about the women in his Eastern province.

More useful than the novel of Apuleius, *Metamorphoses,* for information about the lives of women in his own homeland of North Africa, is the second-century author's account in the autobiographical *Apologia* of the circumstances of his marriage to the mature widow Pudentilla. This stylized defense speech throws light on the differing attitudes and motives of a moneyed woman's male relatives to the question of her remarriage. Prevented from marrying again by the greed of her father-in-law, who feared that her money would pass away from his grandchildren (her sons), the widow finally fell sick "injured by the prolonged inactivity of her sexual organs, and because the lining of her womb was inflamed she often came near to death with her pains. Doctors and midwives agreed that the illness had been brought on by deprivation of married life. . . . while she was still in her prime she should heal her condition by marriage" (*Apologia* 69; trans. Elaine Fantham). So Pontianus, her elder son, encouraged his friend Apuleius to marry her, but once Pontianus himself married, his new father-in-law pushed him to prosecute Apuleius as a fortune hunter who had seduced Pudentilla by witchcraft. Pudentilla herself does not appear in court. Instead, the prosecution argues from one of her letters (written in Greek) "Apuleius is a wizard: I have been bewitched by him into infatuation: come and rescue me, while I am still able to control myself" (*Apologia* 82; trans. Elaine Fantham). Apuleius in turn shows that the letter has been distorted by selective quotation, and restores the context to reinterpret the widow's purpose: "now, as our vicious accusers would persuade you, Apuleius is a wizard and I have been bewitched." Quoting her explicit affirmation of sanity and acceptance of marriage, Apuleius constructs his defense (83, 84). We see a shrewd and mature widow whose personal life has been first sacrificed to the greed of her own father-in-law, then threatened by the greed of a new male interloper—her son's father-in-law. Such family disputes in which the woman is merely an acompaniment of the coveted money and property, and her marriage a matter of men's self-interested manipulation, cannot always have been so lurid as the case Apuleius sets before us, but they persisted as a social injustice into the nineteenth century c.e. Here in second-century Africa the educated and articulate Pudentilla does not appear as a witness to confirm her intentions, but must depend on her new husband to represent her in the courts.

Far more widely distributed evidence about women of wealth and influence comes from the inscriptions of the Roman Empire. All over the Empire and in diverse communities women functioned as benefactors and participants in the public world and used their money to enhance their own and their families' prestige and to fulfill social and religious responsibilities (Nicols 1989). Among the most interesting samples are inscriptions on public buildings and statue bases that tell of the patronage given and honors received by women in many parts of the Empire. For example, from a synagogue in Asia Minor comes a third-century inscription in Greek for Tation who helped finance the construction and decoration of the building:

Tation, daughter of Straton, son of Empedon, having built with her own money this hall and the court enclosure, made a gift of it to the Jews. The Jewish community honored Tation . . . with a wreath and the right of precedence.

(*Corpus Inscriptionum Judaicarum* 2.738; trans. Natalie Kampen)

These inscriptions, naming women of prominent families, including women of the court, also provide an important source of information about gender ideals and practices among the elite of the municipalities and provinces for which no literary evidence survives. Since they are meant to honor the benefactor as much as the recipients, their emphasis is on the social aspects of good character and family and on public material contributions rather than on domestic virtues.

Women of important families gave donations and patronage to the districts where their estates were located, to their birthplaces, and to regions where their own religious responsibilities or their husbands' political duties took them, as indicated by the following inscription (abbreviations expanded from the inscription are indicated by lower-case letters):

TO CASSIA

CORNELIA

PRISCA Daughter of Caius, Most distinguished Lady

WIFE OF AUFIDIUS FRONTO Consul, Pontifex,

PROConsul of ASIA, PATRON OF THE COLONY

PRIESTESS OF AUGUSTA

AND OUR FATHERLAND.

THE PEOPLE OF FORMIAE

gave this base PUBLICLY IN RETURN FOR THE BRILLIANCE

OF HER GENEROUS BENEFACTION.

This late second-century inscription on a statue base from Formiae on the coast south of Rome honors a lady of the senatorial class in terms of her own gift, but it defines her identity by her husband's Imperial magistracy and local patronage before mentioning her own religious office. Other evidence shows that she was in fact the granddaughter of Cornelius Fronto, tutor of Marcus Aurelius (see above). Her priesthood serves Augusta, the empress Julia Domna, and *Patria* "the native land," not an Italian title or local to Formiae but almost certainly conferred on her by a Greek civic community in Asia while her husband was governor, the most prestigious senatorial office he could hold. Italian and Greek, public and private, personal and marital honors are combined in this inscription (*Année Epigraphique* 1971: 34; trans. Elaine Fantham), one of many that could be cited.

Inscriptions permit reconstruction of the long-standing traditions of public benefactions and patronage of wealthy women; both civic and religious honors were granted them in the eastern and western provinces (Nicols 1989, and Forbis 1990). From Utica in North Africa an inscription of the late second or early third century associates the wife and young daughters of the Proconsul Accius Julianus with him as patrons of the community, no doubt in order to guarantee continuity of patronage when the women outlived the middle-aged consul. The women share the senatorial honorific of their husband and father:

> TO L. ACCIUS IULIANUS ASCLEPIANUS, MOST DISTINGUISHED MAN,[4] CONSUL AND
> CURATOR OF THE COMMUNITY OF UTICA
> AND TO GALLONIA OCTAVIA MARCELLA, MOST DISTINGUISHED LADY, HIS WIFE
> AND TO ACCIA HEURESIS VENANTIA, MOST DISTINGUISHED YOUNG WOMAN
> AND TO ACCIA ASCLEPIANILLA CASTOREA, MOST DISTINGUISHED YOUNG WOMAN
> THEIR DAUGHTERS. THE COLONY IULIA AELIA HADRIANA AUGUSTA OF UTICA
> MADE THIS DEDICATION TO THEIR PERPETUAL PATRONS.
>
> (*Corpus Inscriptionum Latinarum* 8.1811;
> trans. Elaine Fantham)

In Africa and central Italy women received the extraordinary status of civic patrons, and in Egypt a woman was named "father of the city" in a move that demonstrates the extent to which the occupation of a public role could confuse gender titulature (Sijpestein 1987: 141–42). The extent to which these honors carried any rights to membership in town councils or to the holding of other public offices remains unclear; the third-century jurist Paulus says that women may not hold civil offices (*Digest* 5.1.12.2), but contemporary inscriptions from Roman Greece and Asia Minor mention women officeholders, including magistrates (Pleket 1969). This is the well-documented case with Plancia Magna of Perge, on the coast of Asia Minor, around 120 C.E. (Boatwright 1991b). The daughter of a senator who had given the City Games and had been rewarded with the title of city founder, Plancia held several important public positions such as *demiourgos*, the magistrate whose name was used to identify the year; she also held a major religious position, as the inscription on the base of a statue erected by the community tells us:

> PLANCIA MAGNA
> DAUGHTER OF MARCUS PLANCIUS VARUS
> AND DAUGHTER OF THE CITY
> PRIESTESS OF ARTEMIS
> AND BOTH FIRST AND SOLE PUBLIC PRIESTESS
> OF THE MOTHER OF THE GODS
> FOR THE DURATION OF HER LIFE
> PIOUS AND PATRIOTIC.
>
> (*Année Epigraphique* 1965, no. 209; trans. Elaine Fantham)

Plancia Magna gave to the city a monumental entrance-gate, parts of which still survive as do a number of its inscriptions and the graceful draped statue of Plancia (Fig. 13.6) that was one of many to decorate the gate. Included among the statues and Greek and Latin inscriptions were the deified Nerva, the deified Trajan and Marciana, the still-living

Figure 13.6. Portrait of the municipal priestess and patron Plancia Magna of Perge, Asia Minor, dated to about 120 C.E.

Plotina and Hadrian, and also Plancia's father and other members of her family and the community of Perge. Paying homage to the Imperial family as well as to her own blood and community family, Plancia used a traditional iconography of cult and kinship to foster the continuing success of her family (Boatwright 1991b).

Women like Plancia Magna or Cassia Cornelia Prisca (both second century C.E.) clearly controlled a substantial private fortune and shared in the ideology of public service for public glory that seems to have motivated generations of Roman men. Even in the Republican period before women had legal power to give away money, the provincials of Greece and Asia had honored governors' wives with statues most probably in thanks for intercession with the governor in local issues. Now the practice was extended to the wives of local magnates as a routine response to benefactions and incentive to their continuation. There is no reliable way of estimating how many women of the Empire received honors from communities in the form of statues and inscribed bases, nor how many gave and on what scale, but the evidence points to a clear connection between honors and the importance of a woman's family (Van Bremen 1983). Women who were chosen as priestesses may not have exercised power in any political sense, but they resembled benefactors in the sense that their public functions did bring them a certain prestige and authority. It was usual in the upper classes for women to be chosen as priestesses; their offices might be little more than a political compliment, as was the case for Cassia Cornelia Prisca, or they could mean a long-term renunciation of domestic life. The Vestals continued throughout the Imperial period to have social and religious importance, and their portrait statues, ranging in date from the second to the fourth century, can still be seen not only in the museums of Rome but also near the house of the Vestals in the ruins of the Roman Forum.

In the Greek part of the Roman Empire, women of "good" family might combine their secular lives with honorific services as priestesses, like Plutarch's friend Clea, priestess of Delphic Apollo. From Plutarch's dedications to Clea of his essays, "On the Bravery of Women" (see below) and "On Isis and Osiris" (late first or early second century), it is clear that she was a learned and revered lady, more like a city councillor or committeewoman than the inspired prophetesses whom we associate with Delphi.[5] Oracles of Apollo, especially in Roman Asia Minor, did have power in that they often determined which women became priestesses. Even priestesses of Athena might be appointed by an oracular decision of Apollo. These priestesses were celibate, but an inscribed oracle from Miletus (late second to early third century C.E.) appoints a widow, Satorneila, the mother of two grown sons:

> Late, O townsmen, concerning a priestess of Athena
> have you come to hear the divine inspired voice—
> . . . .
> for it was necessary that the honor of the priesthood of the self-appearing maiden
> be received by a woman with the blood of noble ancestors
> but after she had previously obtained her share of the gifts of Aphrodite,
> for the Cyprian goddess vies with virgin Athena,
> since the one is uninitiated in love and the bride chamber,
> but the other rejoices in marriage and melodious bridal songs.
> Accordingly, in obedience to the fates and and to Pallas,
> appoint chaste Satorneila as holy priestess.
>
> (Drew-Bear and Lebek 1973)

Priestly offices may, then, have been a way to honor and reward a benefactress, or they may have provided income for needy women or past priestesses in a community (Gordon 1990).

The picture of women's political participation through honors, patronage, and officeholding comes to us from the inscriptions and the odd literary passage as a positive, praiseworthy phenomenon. Fathers, husbands, and sons may be named (they usually are) or unmentioned, but what we see is an indication of the public functioning of wealthy upper-class women. This is true as well for freedwomen with money who were to be found in Italy as patrons for local craftsmen's guilds; these patrons are often named *mater*, as for example Claudia, the wife of a freedman from Faleri Piceni, who is called "mother of the brotherhood of fullers" (*Corpus Inscriptionum Latinarum* 9.5450, undated; trans. Natalie Kampen). These inscriptions suggest the blurring of lines between public and private; for example, a third-century freeborn woman from Sentinum, Memmia Victoria, whose son was a local officeholder *(decurio)*, was named *mater* of an artisans' group (*Corpus Inscriptionum Latinarum* 11.5748).

Women play public roles through private wealth, they enter public consciousness although they are private citizens unable to vote or (apparently) hold office in government, and they influence public events through acts of generosity that keep the men of their families in the public eye as potential officeholders. At every level in the upper classes, from Julia Domna's patronage of the rebuilding of the temple of Vesta in the Roman Forum to the financing by Ummidia Quadratilla of Casinum's temple and amphitheatre, women demonstrate the ambiguity of the terms "public" and "private" for the Roman world. And the inscriptions demonstrate as well the possible differences that social status and region can make to women's lives even as they cling to the traditional list of feminine virtues.

Autonomy and Ambivalence

By comparison with the evidence from inscriptions, the comments of male authors on the (relative) autonomy of women seem striking in their ambivalence. The discussions about the education of wives that appear in the writings of Juvenal, Pliny, and Plutarch, all writing around 100 C.E. offer a picture of what in women's lives and character most irritated, enraged, and provoked laughter among Roman (and Greek) men of a certain class and what they envisioned as the solution.

> Yet a musical wife's not so bad as some presumptuous
> flat-chested busybody who rushes around the town
> gate-crashing all male greetings, talking back straight-faced
> to a uniformed general—and in her husband's presence.
> She knows all the news of the world
> (Juvenal, *Satires* 6.398–403; Green 1967)

> if she's so determined to prove herself eloquent, learned,
> she should hoist up her skirts and gird them above the knee
> scrub off in the penny baths.[6] So avoid a dinner partner
> with an argumentative style, who hurls well rounded

syllogisms like slingshots, who has all history pat:
choose someone rather who doesn't understand all she reads.
I hate these authority citers, . . . who with antiquarian zeal
quote poets I've never heard of. Such matters are men's
concern
(Juvenal *Satires* 6.445–52; Green 1967)

The classical solution to such autonomous behavior is suggested by the Roman Pliny and his Greek contemporary Plutarch, since both wrote of women's education in ways designed to overcome the undesirable characteristics Juvenal so gleefully skewers. Pliny writes (early second century) of his joy in his sweet young wife's love for his work;

Because of her love for me, she has even gone so far as to take an interest in literature; she possesses copies of my writings, reads them repeatedly, and even memorizes them. . . . When I recite from my works, she will sit nearby, behind a curtain, eager to share the praise I receive. She has even set some of my poems to music, and chants them to the accompaniment of a lyre, untaught by any music-teacher, but rather by the best of teachers, love.
(Pliny, *Letters* 4.19.2 and 4; Radice 1975)

Plutarch, even as he mentions casually in his *Advice to Bride and Groom* (late first to early second century) that his wife Timoxena composed an essay for a friend against the use of cosmetics, advises his friend Pollianus, to whom his own essay is addressed, to educate his wife by oral instruction:

As for your wife, you must collect useful material from every source, like the bees, and carrying it in your own self share it with her and discuss it with her, making the best of these doctrines dear and familiar to her. For to her

Thou art her father and lady mother
yes, and a brother too [quoting *Iliad* 6.429]

This kind of study . . . diverts women from absurd conduct; for a woman studying geometry will be ashamed to dance, and she will not swallow any beliefs in magic spells while she is under the spell of Plato's or Xenophon's arguments.
(Plutarch, *Advice to Bride and Groom* 145c–d; trans. Elaine Fantham)[7]

Looking back over our evidence about the roles played by women of the privileged classes and about the reaction of our various sources to women's public activities, there is a constant tension throughout this period of more than two hundred years between female autonomy and achievement and male response. Often the discomfort of Roman writers in the face of public and political roles for women is palpable. Both within the court (as in the stories of Plotina's intervention to ensure that Hadrian was made Trajan's successor: *Historia Augusta, Hadrian* 4.4 and 4.10) and outside (as when governors' wives are portrayed as seeking power), power is condemned as inappropriate precisely because it is political. Yet throughout the Empire, inscriptions congratulate women for their generous use of private and family money for the public good, and the political implications for gaining authority and power for women seem to pose no problem. From the evidence we may draw two conclusions: (1) female political interference, like sexual misconduct, transgressed socially acceptable boundaries for upper-class life, no matter how common it was; and (2) there were alternative, socially acceptable frameworks for elite female autonomy, varying throughout the Empire but consistent in valuing public benefaction and religious service. In the end it is the contradictory and uneven nature of the evidence itself that poses the greatest problem for us in understanding the lives of elite women in the last centuries of the Roman Empire.

The Women of the Lower Strata

Gender and Social Position: Problems of Definition

The lives of women outside the world of grand families, social authority, or large-scale patronage are known to us through evidence that is even more scattered and inconsistent than what remains about elite women. Even the way we speak of this group is plagued by uncertainties. Should these women be called "lower class?" Is there such a thing as a homogeneous "middle class" of freeborn and freed slave artisans, businesspeople, minor priestesses, and professionals? Does it cross geographical boundaries and look the same in city and country, in east and west?

Where, for example, should we place an exceptional figure like Pamphila of Epidaurus in Greece? Our sources tell us that she came from Egypt and was the daughter of one scholar, Soteridas, and the wife of another with whom she lived at Epidaurus about the time of Nero (mid-first century C.E.); she composed some thirty-three books of historical materials *(Hypomnemata Historika)*, which a certain Dionysius and other male scholars characteristically ascribed either to her father or her husband. She also composed epitomes of Ctesias's histories (more than five hundred years old by that time) and treatises "On Disputation," "On Sexual Desire," and other topics. Luckily the bare notice in *Suda*, the tenth-century encyclopaedia, can be amplified by Pamphila's own introduction to her work as reported by the Byzantine anthologist Photius (ninth century):

She says that after thirteen years of living with her husband since she was a child, she began to put together these historical materials and recorded what she had learned from her husband during those thirteen years, living with him constantly and leaving him neither night nor day, and whatever she happened to hear from anyone else visiting him (for there were many visitors with a reputation for learning). And she added to this what she had read in books. She separated all this material that seemed to her worthy of report and record into miscellaneous collections, not distinguished according to the content of individual extracts, but at random, as she came to record each item, since as she says, it is not difficult to classify extracts, but she thought a miscellany would be more enjoyable and attractive.

(Photius 175 S 119b; trans. Elaine Fantham)

Photius adds condescendingly that her style, shown in the prefaces and other comments, was "simple, being the work of a woman," like her thought itself. Yet this extensive work was still used and quoted with respect by antiquarians a century or more after her death. Noble in her learning, child, wife, and friend of scholars, is Pamphila noble in social standing or would we today consider her to be a member of the cosmopolitan middle-class intelligentsia, those who might live in several parts of the Empire during the course of their lives? Is there anything particularly Greek (or Egyptian) about her life? To have been part of a world of learned visitors, with a library at hand, suggests a degree of prosperity that may or may not accompany noble birth or official standing in Greece of the first century C.E.

Once we leave behind the society of the court, and the great landowners with inherited wealth and power, we must imagine the communities of the Empire as mosaics of all kinds of people ranged along continua determined by ethnic, linguistic, financial, legal, and occupational variables, not all of which have analogies in the modern world. To this must be added once again the fact of geographical diversity. Although women of the highest social classes in all parts of the Empire probably shared a rather cosmopolitan life, just as they seem to have been equally subject to conservative norms of gender, this was not necessarily always the case for other women. Not only affected by regional differences, these women will have experienced the world differently inside each region according to their status, income, and the degree of Romanization prevailing in their area.

Tombstones, Social Ideals, Social Realities

The ideal of Roman womanhood, as we have seen it in the context of depictions of upper-class women, certainly played a role in shaping representations of women elsewhere, but there are clear differences in the way this worked. For example, the sexual division of labor—domesticity for women, outside occupations for men—seems to have determined the roles and character attributes that most lower-class families commemorated in women's funerary monuments all over the Empire; the deceased are represented with their families and described in the vocabulary of traditional domestic and feminine virtues: one wife is mourned as "the best and most beautiful, a wool-worker,[8] pious, modest, thrifty, pure and home-loving" (*Corpus Inscriptionum Latinarum* 6.11602 [undated]; trans. Natalie Kampen). This kind of representation is usually found on funerary reliefs, the modesty of whose form and content indicates recipients outside the wealthy classes. The majority of these stelai give only names and ages, but a good many offer other information as well.

To the spirits of the dead. T. Aelius Dionysius the freedman *[auc. lib.?]* made this while he was alive both for Aelia Callitycena, his most blessed wife with whom he lived for thirty years with never a quarrel, an incomparable woman, and also for Aelius Perseus, his fellow freedman, and for their freedmen and those who come after them.

(*Corpus Inscriptionum Latinarum* 6.10676 [from Rome undated, but possibly second century, C.E.]; trans. Natalie Kampen)

Thus, mixed in with formulaic statements of respect and affection such as "she is worthy of commemoration *[bene merenti]*" or that she lived with a husband without quarrels *[sine ulla querella]*, we learn a bit about relationships and demographics. An interesting case of rich detail comes from Rome and tells about Valeria Verecunda, the first important doctor in her neighborhood, who lived thirty-four years, nine months and twenty-eight days; her daughter Valeria Vitalis made the monument for "her sweetest mother" (*Corpus Inscriptionum Latinarum* 6.9477 [3–4th c, C.E.]). The deceased may be honored not only by her immediate family but also by fellow slaves, an owner or patron, or fellow freedmen and women. All this conforms to our understanding of *familia* in the Roman world as conceptually broader than the modern nuclear family. Slaves and freedpeople often constructed family for themselves both from the families of their owners and from each other as a parallel to the ties of duty and affection in free families, and the use of such terms as *collibertae*, "fellow freedwomen," or *contubernales*, "companions in slavery" marks these relationships (Lattimore 1942).

Themes of affection and of praise for much-loved mothers, for sweet-natured and well-educated little girls, and for chaste and unquarrelsome wives are common all over the Empire. The inscriptions from Rome and large provincial towns parallel in words the repeated images on tombstones from such far-flung regions as Phrygia in Asia Minor. There, and to a lesser extent in Italy too, combs, cosmetic jars, hairpins, and sandals stand next to wool baskets, spindles, distaffs, and needles, and to keys and lockplates, to evoke the combination of personal beauty and domestic duty, wool-work and protection of the house and its contents (Fig. 13.7). Some of the Phrygian stones pair husbands' symbols with those of the wife to show the sexual division of labor in visual form: his objects may be scrolls and tablets, sheep and oxen, metal tools or construction materials. In other words, his imagery is more varied and concerned either with literacy as a mark of status or officeholding, or, through the use of attributes, with a money-earning occupation (Waelkens 1977). Beauty and domestic labor for women; culture and occupational identity for men.

The iconography of virtue among those prosperous enough for tomb-portraits indicates a similar tradition of gender differentiation. Women's funerary portrait statues, and this is true in reliefs and sometimes too in the choice of myths for sarcophagi, show a clear preference for Venus (love and beauty) (Fig. 13.8), Ceres or Salus (fertility), Diana (Virginity and Courage) and Hygeia (Health), whereas men prefer Mars (war), Hercules (strength), and Mercury (money-making). The message is conveyed through the use of the odd, very Roman combination of identifi-

Figure 13.7. Tombstone from Dorylaion in Phrygia, an inland section of Asia Minor. Dated to the late second or early third century C.E., it places the objects associated with men's and women's lives into twin doors, perhaps doors to the next world or to the house of the deceased.

able portrait heads with contemporary hairstyles and bodies copied from famous Greek statues of the gods. These funerary portraits, mimicking the use by the Imperial family of portraits in the guise of deities, were popular in the tombs of the later first, second, and early third centuries of our era; the evidence suggests that their patrons were mostly wealthy freed slaves and that the practice tended to be localized in Rome. To have a large-scale portrait statue that uses the formal typology of the grand Greek tradition was certainly to have pretensions to wealth and culture! (Wrede 1981).

Pretensions to culture can also be seen in the sarcophagi that become popular in Italy and the East after about 130 C.E. Sometimes the deceased or her family chose a design and had it made to order, or bought a partially completed piece and had inscriptions and portraits added; in either case women's and men's virtues are represented (though differently) through the use of divine and mythological imagery. A good example is the sarcophagus of Metilia Acte from the late second century C.E. in Ostia (Fig. 13.9). She was a priestess of Magna Mater, her husband a priest; the sarcophagus shows them as Alcestis and Admetus, she who volunteered to die instead of her husband and whose virtue was rewarded by her return to the living. Here both loving devotion and hopes for victory over death appear, and Metilia receives a heroizing

Figure 13.8. Tomb statue of a woman following the model of an earlier Greek statue of Aphrodite, perhaps one such as the "Venus de Milo." This portrait from Rome of the later first or early second century C.E. uses the artistic connections to assert noble virtues of the deceased, who is presented as Venus.

Figure 13.9. Sarcophagus of Metilia Acte and her husband Junius Euhodus, from Rome in the third quarter of the second century C.E. The centralized composition focuses the viewer's eye on the dead woman, reclining on her couch; the narrative elements on either side explain the death of Alcestis in her husband's place (on the left) and her virtue rewarded by her return from the dead (on the right).

commemoration through the appropriation of myth (Wood 1978). Similarly ostentatious monuments to the dead, like the sarcophagi of Asia Minor, in the third century C.E., show men as philosophers, women as muses, and both as readers—cultured people. We thus see the virtues that were considered most appropriate for women and men and the way these reinforced and expressed social expectations that were rooted in a gendered division of labor.

Most funerary images for nonaristocratic women were much simpler and less expensive, resembling the majority of commemorative inscriptions in that they choose to display family rather than gods or myths. In almost every part of the northern and western provinces and Italy, and some parts of the east as well, we find reliefs, ash urns, and altars with husbands and wives, children and parents, facing the viewer as if caught by a nineteenth-century photographer in all their stiff dignity. A family group on a stele made for residents of Dacia (modern Romania) (Fig. 13.10) resembles those of soldiers from Britain, although style and frame differ; in Aquileia in northern Italy another family looks out as silently as one from a painted stele in Thessaloniki in northern Greece. The traditions for such family images go back to the funerary stelai of Classical Athens as well as to Republican Rome, and remain alive as a favored setting for women of the "lower classes" in the Imperial period.

Some tombstones in the provinces that show women with families

Figure 13.10. Stele of a family from Roman Sarmizegetusa in Dacia, a province along the Danube, dated to the second or third century C.E.

provide a sense of regional differences as well as similarities. Although few offer visions of worlds outside the context of family and domestic labor, there are bits of evidence for variation in the degree to which women assimilated into Roman ways. The tombstones show interesting distinctions between the eastern and western provinces through artistic traditions and the use of Greek names and language rather than the Latin of the West. But in addition, the tombstones of some more remote areas, away from coasts, cities, or trade routes, indicate that a number of women may have kept indigenous names, costumes, and customs even after men of their social stratum had taken on Roman ways. The evidence does not permit any statistical conclusions here since the tombstones that remain with both inscriptions and images are few and limited to those people who were prosperous enough to have tombstones and Romanized enough to want them with Roman words and decoration. Umma, a first-century woman from Noricum (modern Austria), wears a splendid local-style felt hat (Fig. 13.11) that goes with her non-Roman name, and other women in the northern and western provinces sometimes wear local brooches or carry local baskets or purses. Local taste is also evident in the large funerary monuments of wealthy merchants near Trier in Germany; many show family portraits and men hunting, but they include panels with the deceased in his place of business while his wife, seated in a local wicker chair on another part of the monument, is prepared for the day by her hairdresser and other attendants (Fig. 13.12). These late second- and third-century tombstones of a richer and more assimilated group nonetheless show their sexual division of labor (*her* inactivity brings *him* status) in localized forms.

The little we know about women in the provinces comes mainly from these many kinds of tombstones, from their rare petitions reported in the codes of Imperial law, from the odd references to a local issue in need of a governor's attention, and from the broad context of changes in the empire. These changes came not only from conquest but from the entrance of soldiers and merchants into new areas (especially the non-Hellenized northern provinces). Intermarriage is hard to track and harder still to quantify, but two laws will certainly have accounted for a growth in the marriages of Roman citizens from all over the Empire with local women. One was Septimius Severus's permission for soldiers who served twenty-five years to marry (Herodian 3.8.4 [first half of the third century]); this regularized some relationships between local women and the troops stationed on the frontiers of Empire. The second, and by far the more important law, was Caracalla's edict of 212 that made all free residents of the Empire full citizens with the right to contract legal marriages. How much these new laws changed women's lives in the provinces remains uncertain because the evidence has to be extrapolated from names and biographical data on tombstones such as we have described, but the impact on their sons, now eligible to serve in the army, and their daughters, now able to marry soldiers, would have meant some changes in patterns of mobility and Romanization. Nevertheless, inscriptions, reliefs, literature, and other testimonia for provincial women both before and after 212 remain firmly rooted in a gendered ideology and division of labor, and the tombstones continue to represent women with families and the signs of traditional domestic labor and virtue.

Only a minority of nonelite Roman women were represented in other forms by inscriptions and visual images, and these differ from one another according to region as well as class: though small in numbers, they raise fascinating questions about the social constraints and possibilities of gender and class in this period. There are a number of inscriptions and a far smaller number of reliefs or paintings that characterize women

Figure 13.11. Tombstone of a woman named Umma, who lived in first-century c.e., Noricum (modern Austria). Her magnificent fur hat, like her name, testifies to the continuing presence of local customs, even after the process of Romanization had begun.

Figure 13.19. Funerary monument from third-century C.E., Neumagen, near Trier; like so many of the tomb markers in this area of Gallia Belgica, the "Elternpaarpfeiler" made for a merchant and his wife took the form of a tall structure decorated with portraits and scenes of everyday life. This detail shows the matron attended by her servants.

by work outside the house (Kampen 1981). Dating most of this material presents enormous problems to scholars, since so few of the inscriptions vary from formula and so many have no archaeological provenance that could add to the information deducible from spelling and letter forms; for this reason, we give almost no dates for the inscriptions we discuss here.

Among the inscriptions we find references to net-makers, including one who made gold nets, perhaps for women's hair: "Viccentia, sweetest daughter, maker of gold nets, who lived for nine years and nine months" (*Corpus Inscriptionum Latinarum* 6.9213 [undated]; trans. Natalie Kampen). We also see fabric and clothing workers (such as Lysis the mender or *sarcinatrix* from Rome who was described as being eighteen years old, thrifty and modest: *Corpus Inscriptionum Latinarum* 6.9882), dye-makers and perfumers, and vendors of fruit and vegetables. Many of these inscriptions name the women's kin, age, status, and sometimes even the locations of their shops:

To the Spirits of the Dead. For Abudia Megiste the freedwoman who was most pious, M. Abudius Luminaris her patron and husband made [this monument]. She was most worthy *[bene merenti]*. She dealt in grain and beans at the Middle Stairs [wherever they were]. Her husband made this monument for himself and his freedmen and freedwomen and heirs and for M. Abudius Saturninus his son who belonged to the senior Esquiline tribe [a sign of social status] and who lived eight years.

(*Corpus Inscriptionum Latinarum* 6.9683 [from Rome, undated];
trans. Natalie Kampen)

The woman on a small relief, probably from the second century C.E., from Ostia (Fig. 13.13), Rome's port city, appears surrounded by the produce and game she sold; even though we know nothing about her identity beyond her occupation, the specificity of the objects lets us know what the patrons of the relief felt was most important. For the working women of our inscriptions and images, as for the people whose lives take symbolic form from the tools and attributes of their lives on Phrygian tombstones, the naming and the representing of *things*, beans and chickens, wool baskets and mirrors, become a way to identity.

Little information remains about the qualifications and training of workers, although two categories of material are helpful here. The first comes from manuals such as those written about medical practice. In the *Gynecology* of Soranus,[9] written in Greek in the second half of the first century C.E., one can find instructions for midwives and information about their qualifications; Soranus says the best are trained in theory as well as in all branches of therapy, can diagnose and prescribe, and are free of superstition (Soranus, *Gynecology* 1.2.4; Temkin 1956). Soranus also gives information about the qualifications of wet nurses. His de-

Figure 13.13. Small marble shop relief of a saleswoman from Ostia, dated to the mid-second century C.E. Cages of chickens and rabbits form the counter on which are a basket for live snails and two monkeys for the entertainment of customers and passersby.

scription of the ideal wet nurse, that she be in her prime and have given birth two or three times, insists on the need for experience with children as well as specific physical qualifications (Bradley 1986). He lists emotional characteristics such as self-control and sympathy:

Not ill-tempered: since by nature the nursling becomes similar to the nurse and accordingly grows sullen if the nurse is ill-tempered, but of mild disposition if she is even-tempered. Besides, angry women are like maniacs and sometimes when the newborn cries from fear and they are unable to restrain it, they let it drop from their hands or overturn it dangerously. For the same reason the wet-nurse should not be superstitious and prone to ecstatic states so that she may not expose the infant to danger when led astray by fallacious reasoning, sometimes even trembling like mad. . . . And she should be a Greek so that the infant nursed by her may become accustomed to the best speech.
(Soranus 2.12.19; Temkin 1956).

The second category of material about the qualifications of workers, papyrus documents from Roman Egypt, provide us with apprenticeship contracts, as in this example from the second century C.E. Oxyrrhynchus, in which a woman (with her brother as guardian) contracts a slave to a weaver to learn the trade over the course of four years

during which time the woman is to feed and clothe the slave and bring her to her instructor every day from sunrise to sunset so that the girl can perform all the duties assigned to her by him that are relevant to the aforesaid trade; her pay for the first year to be eight drachmas a month, for the second similarly twelve, for the third sixteen, for the fourth twenty. The girl is to have each year eighteen days off for festivals, but if she does no work or is sick for some days, she is to remain with her instructor for an equal number of days at the end of her time of service. The instructor is to pay for trade taxes and expenses.
(*Papyri Oxyrrhynchi* 1647; Lefkowitz and Fant 1982: no. 222)

The occupations of rural slave women may have differed from those of working women, free and enslaved, in urban areas; Columella, who wrote a book on agricultural life around the end of the Julio-Claudian period (ca. 60), describes life on a prosperous estate both for the wife of the estate manager (the couple are often slaves or freed) and for female slaves:

[A]t one moment she will have to visit the loom and impart any superior knowledge which she possesses, or, failing this, learn from one who understands the matter better than she does; at another moment she will have to look after those who are preparing the food for the family. Then too she will have to see that the kitchen and the cowsheds and also the mangers are cleaned, and she will have to open the sick wards [for the slave population] from time to time, even if they contain no patients, and keep them free from dirt, so that, when necessary, the sick may find them in an orderly and healthy condition.
(Columella, *De Re Rustica* 12.3.8; Forster and Heffner 1968)

The female slave is said to "have recourse to wool-work on rainy days or when, owing to cold or frost, a woman cannot be busy with field work" (Columella, *De Re Rustica* 12.1.6). The extent to which regional differences and variations in the scale of the farm or estate would have influenced work patterns is unclear from Columella's work and may emerge instead from the archaeology of rural areas.

From legal texts or graffiti we hear of women whose reputations were often badly compromised by the nature of their work in public with men and alcohol. Those who managed stores (*institrices*) and worked as tavernkeepers, cooks, barmaids, and waitresses are referred to in the legal texts about *tabernariae* as quasi-prostitutes. The term may characterize only tavernworkers or apply more broadly to all workers in *tabernae*, defined in this case as shops:

If any woman should commit adultery, it must be inquired whether she was the mistress of a tavern or a servant girl . . . if she should be mistress of the tavern, she shall not be exempt from the bonds of the law. But if she should give service to those who drink, in consideration of the mean status of the woman who is brought to trial, the accusation shall be excluded and the men who are accused shall go free, since chastity is required only of those women who are held by the bonds of the law, but those who because of their mean status in life are not deemed worthy of the consideration of the laws shall be immune from judicial severity.

(*Theodosian Code* 9.7.1 [late fourth century]; Pharr 1952) [10]

Being of "mean status in life" to Roman law meant more than simply being poor or close to origins in slavery; it also meant that one was subject to different treatment by the law. The text here claims that these lowly women are not subject to the severity of the law, but the reason is that they are beneath contempt, outside the requirements of consideration given and responsibility expected of "decent" women. Whereas people of high status could expect to be taken seriously in the courts, the lowly (in the later empire they were even referred to as *humiliores*, humble people, in contrast with *honestiores*, "gentlemen and ladies") could be subjected to torture to extract information from them, could expect capital punishment rather than exile for certain serious crimes, and could routinely expect less protection from the law than others. So being unworthy of consideration of the law put women who worked in certain public contexts automatically into the same legal realm as prostitutes.

Certainly there were prostitutes and madams everywhere in the Empire, although sex workers seldom name their jobs on tombstones. A rare example is Vibia Calybeni "the freedwoman madam. She made her money without defrauding others" (*Corpus Inscriptionum Latinarum* 9.2029 [undated]; trans. Natalie Kampen). More common are the obscene scribbles on barroom walls that brag about sex with the innkeeper or the waitress (these come from many periods and places in the Empire).

The other occupations we have been discussing apparently granted women at a certain level of society a bit of prestige as well as income, just as they did routinely for lower-class working men; both sexes may name their jobs on tombstones (in addition to age and kinship), but this is recorded far more often for men than for women and is more common in Italy and the western provinces than in the east. Nevertheless, both slaves and free women were commemorated with occupation names that suggest less distance between them than the legal texts might indicate.

This lack of a clear differentiation between slave and free working women is consistent in many inscriptions and also in the few visual images that remain. These present vendors, serving women, nurses, and midwives in such a way that one cannot tell whether the subjects were slaves, freedwomen, or freeborn workers. The midwife shown delivering a baby in a small and inexpensive second-century C.E. terra-cotta relief that decorated a tomb from Ostia's cemetery has no attributes that indicate her legal status; the focus of the scene is the activity itself. The image is interesting not only for its representation of a birthing chair and the information it provides about contemporary practices but also because it was accompanied by another terra-cotta showing a male doctor and male patient and because an inscription on the front of the tomb specified that the patron was a woman (Fig. 13.14).[11] These reliefs and paintings, like the inscriptions that mention the occupations women practiced outside the household, come from very scattered sites in Italy,

Figure 13.14. Terra-cotta painted relief of a midwife delivering a baby from a tomb in the Isola Sacra Necropolis of Ostia, mid-second century C.E.

Gaul, North Africa, and the eastern provinces. Whether we should interpret the small numbers and scattered locations as evidence for the rarity of women's nondomestic work or as an indication that it seldom added enough to a woman's status to merit inclusion on a tombstone (or perhaps even lowered status in comparison with traditional domestic occupations) is unclear. The existence of these bits of information does suggest that economic forces as well as personal inclination may have drawn some women into nondomestic work settings. But the preponderance of occupations associated with clothing and fabrics, food, and the care and health of infants and women indicates that many of these jobs were only one step outside the home and so did little to rearrange the gendered division of labor among working women, both free and slave.

Far more clearly honorific for women we might consider middle class (freed slaves as well as members of the business, tradesman, or artisan strata) were the positions they held in cults all over the Roman Empire. The popular cult of Isis was much favored by women of all classes in Italy and the western provinces, as we learn from the description in Apuleius's novel, *Metamorphoses*, (third quarter of the second century) of a procession:

At the head [of the procession] walked women crowned with flowers, who pulled more flowers out of the folds of their beautiful white dresses and scattered them along the road; their joy in the Saviouress appeared in every gesture. Next came women with polished mirrors tied to the backs of their heads, which gave all who followed the illusion of coming to meet the Goddess, rather than marching before her. Next, a party of women with ivory combs in their hands who made a pantomime of combing the Goddess' royal hair, and another party with bottles of perfume who sprinkled the road with balsam and other precious perfumes; and behind these a mixed company of women and men who addressed the Goddess as "Daughter of the Stars" and propitiated her by carrying every sort of light—lamps, torches, wax candles and so forth. . . . Then followed a great crowd of the Goddess' initiates, *men and women of all classes and every age*, their pure white linen clothes shining brightly. The women wore their hair tied up in glossy coils under gauze head-dresses; the men's heads were completely shaven, representing the Goddess' bright earthly stars, and they carried rattles of brass, silver and even gold, which kept up a shrill and ceaseless tinkling.

(Apuleius 18; Graves 1951; emphasis added by Natalie Kampen)

Some female devotees of Isis are proudly depicted with their ritual implements on their funerary altars; such a woman appears with her *sistrum* or ritual rattle on an altar from Rome that was dedicated by Valeria, a woman who held the cult rank of *mater*: "To the Spirits of the Dead. For Flavia Taeleta and Flavia Faustilla, Valeria Prima Mater (dedicated this)" (Later first or second century C.E., Doria Pamphili; *Corpus Inscriptionum Latinarum* 6.18442; trans. Elaine Fantham and Natalie Kampen). Inscriptions record Jewish women such as Caelia Paterna called "mother of the synagogue of the people of Brescia" (*Corpus Inscriptionum Latinarum* 5.4411 [undated]; trans. Natalie Kampen), who held offices, although not priesthoods, in synagogues throughout the Empire. Like many of their non-Jewish sisters, they gained in prestige and social standing in their communities through this honorific service and through their active patronage of buildings and institutions.

Christian women in Rome and the provinces were the only ones who differed from the model we have articulated for pagan and Jewish women; in the period before Constantine made Christianity a fully legal religion in his Edict of Toleration (311–12 C.E.), these women sometimes lost position and even families and lives through their involvement with their church. Whether because of overt persecution or simply through the loathing of Christianity that came from stories about cannibalism and incest, only the lowliest or the most privileged in Roman society could openly and with impunity admit to being a Christian. Of martyrdoms and persecutions we have many reports, including the famous narrative supposedly by St. Perpetua who tells her own story of captivity in third-century Carthage. Not only does she recount the attempts of her father to persuade her to recant, the visions she has, and the bravery of those around her, she also gives a picture of days spent in prison:

I was terrified, as I had never before been in such a dark hole. What a difficult time it was! With the crowd the heat was stifling; then there was the extortion of the soldiers; and to crown all, I was tortured with worry for my baby there.
(*Acts of the Christian Martyrs* 8; trans. H. Musurillo in Lefkowitz and Fant 1982: no. 266)

No less miserable was the situation of those questioned by Pliny the Younger when he was governor of the province of Bithynia and trying to extirpate the growing Christian presence in his area. He writes to Trajan (ca. 110) that he sought the truth "by torture from two slave-women, whom they call deaconesses, I found nothing but a degenerate sort of cult carried to extravagant lengths" (Pliny, *Letter* 10.96.8; Radice 1975). These deaconesses may have been the closest equivalent to the office-holders of the contemporary synagogue, but they were by no means priestesses. Permitted, briefly, to serve the orthodox church by assisting the priest in ministering to the sick and needy, counseling women, and even occasionally giving sermons, these women must have held positions of significant authority in the years before the Edict of Toleration. For the deaconesses, as for ordinary Christian women of the second and third centuries, little information remains, both because of persecution and because many of the church fathers who wrote in those years had little interest in women except as martyrs or objects of theological debate (on deaconesses, see Romans 16.1).

At the other end of the moral scale from religious service but overlapping with it were the less reputable rituals of magic in its many guises from folk medicine and fortune-telling to magic and witchcraft. Many of the women recorded by Roman writers as engaged with magic were from the lower classes and especially from certain parts of the east such as Thessaly and Syria, although elite Greek and Roman women were casti-

gated for hiring such women to teach them the art of poisoning or for
doing the dirty work themselves (for example, Tacitus, *Annals* 3.23,
4.8–11, or 13.1). Urban male fantasies are reflected in the tales of witchcraft in Ovid's *Metamorphoses*, in Lucan's Thessalian witch Erichtho,
who raises corpses from the dead for prophecy (*Civil War*, book 6), and
in Apuleius's witch Pamphile, who is also from Thessaly, which many
ancient writers conceived as the wildest part of Greece. They transform
what they do not understand, at one and the same time turning the
peasant women working as midwives or gathering herbs and remedies for
sick villagers into alien and dangerous forces and castigating lustful
women by charging them with the casting of spells and the mixing of
potions. Priestesses and witches alike are, in a sense, public women,
serving officially or unofficially those outside their own families. Two
sides of the same coin, they reflect the same permeability of the line
between public and private that we saw among the women of the court
and the wealthy benefactors of towns, workers' organizations, and religious cults. At the same time, they create a picture of the lives of women
outside the elite and outside of Rome that includes both the misunder-
standings and prejudices of elite men and the variations around and beyond the norms of domestic virtue that can be seen as well in the pride
taken in work as well as in family.

Gender and the Bottom of the Social Hierarchy

Before we end this discussion of women outside the aristocracy, we need
to underscore the complex status distinctions within the "lower classes."
We have, after all, been talking about women who were freeborn, who
were freed slaves and who were slaves, yet whose economic level within
each group could be as different as the conditions under which they lived
socially and geographically. Understanding the distinctions is hard in
part because of the nature of the evidence (for example, the legal texts'
concern with distinctions between free, freed and slave); the laws have
little concern with the potential economic similarities between categories. Again, the indifference of upper-class writers to distinctions between the freed and freeborn poor may mask distinctions that once mat-
tered to lower-class people. And the way that people outside the upper
classes thought about status, what it meant to them and where gender
and degree of Romanization fit into those conceptions, remain clouded
both by the upper-class literary and legal sources and by the conventional, even formulaic nature of the things people said about the dead.
Yet our evidence suggests that there may well have been similarities in
wealth and culture between some freeborn and freedwomen and that
large numbers of freeborn and freed slave women looked nothing like
Petronius's ostentatious and grasping Fortunata or Apuleius's lustful
Thessalian witches. Instead, they were of modest means and took care
to commemorate their familial and domestic lives; only a few of the
women who worked outside the home could also afford to record such

work on tombstones. And, perhaps most important in the context of a discussion of the tension between gender ideals and practices, most women of the prosperous lower classes, those who could be commemorated, clung to the traditional ideals of Roman womanhood as these were interpreted in their own part of the Empire.

At the bottom of the Roman social hierarchy, came slaves, nonpersons in a legal sense, whose bodies and labor belonged to their owners. The occupations of enslaved women and men may often have resembled those of freed and free people, but there was a central difference; the slave served *all* of her or his owner's needs and desires, and these included not only the agricultural, artisanal, and domestic labor already mentioned, but sexual services as well. This took three directions: reproduction of slaves, serving the sexual desires of male family members, and prostitution for the owner's profit. In each case a woman's body served another's interests[12]

Corresponding to the low status of slave women and their lack of control over their bodies are a set of representations of them as immoral and venal. Ignorant or drunken slave nurses, maids who act as go-betweens for adulterous lovers and demand bribes for illicit services are clichés in Roman comedy (Plautus, *Menaechmi* and *Truculentus*) and elegy (Ovid, *Amores* 2.7 amd 8) long before the conservative Messala's complaint in Tacitus (later first to early second century):

Now the newborn child is handed over to some little Greek skivvy, along with one or other of the male slaves, usually the most worthless . . . and the boy's green and fresh years are steeped in their ignorant stories and ideas.

(Tacitus, *Dialogue on Orators* 29; trans. Elaine Fantham)

How much the low and sexualized status of slaves was a result not just of upper-class Roman attitudes to slavery, but also of Roman ideas on ethnic hierarchies is unclear, but it appears that some foreign women, especially those from Syria and the East in general became associated with hypersexuality as well as with witchcraft. Although Apuleius's Pamphile (third quarter of the second century), the wife of a wealthy miser in Thessaly, is both Greek and free, she is characterized as a lust-maddened witch:

She is believed to be the foremost mistress of magic and of all the spells of the grave. By breathing certain words and charms over sticks and stones and other trivial objects, she can cast all the light of the starry firmament into the depths of hell and reduce them again to original chaos. For as soon as she has caught a glimpse of any good-looking young man, she is overwhelmed with desire and sets both her eye and her soul on him. She makes wheedling endearments, takes possession of his spirit, entangles him with endless snares of immeasurable love. Then if any resist her filthy passion, she despises them . . . and turns them instantly into stones and sheep and any other animal she wants, and others she kills outright.

(2.5; trans. Elaine Fantham and Natalie Kampen)

The issue here is not Roman racial prejudice but rather the way status, gender, and ethnicity coincide. The woman of low status, like the woman of Thessaly or Syria, is open to charges of hypersexuality, of witchcraft, of criminality; she becomes Other.

The ultimate Other is the "barbarian," the man or woman from outside the frontier, subject to conquest and enslavement as well as to Romanization. These are the figurations of the separation between inside and outside, between civilization and its opposite; they were used not for ethnography or the folklorist's interests but as a way to describe Roman victory and, by opposition, Roman civilization. Whereas the funerary portraits of prosperous women from Palmyra or Roman Egypt (Fig. 13.15) preserve local materials and style elements such as the figures in traditional Pharaonic style, and may well have looked fairly exotic to Italian or Greek viewers, they do speak for the local population and its values and concerns. By comparison, the representation of "barbarian" women in Roman historical texts and images tells us less about "barbarians" than about the Romans themselves. The most familiar visual type is the mourning "barbarian" woman on coins and reliefs. She may stand with a chained "barbarian" man beside a military trophy, or sit head in hands, desolate at its foot, or drag along in a triumphal process as she does in the Severan arch at Leptis Magna (ca. 206). She recurs as the emblem of defeat in narrative settings as well, taken prisoner, or in flight, or even being killed, as on the Column of Marcus Aurelius in Rome (ca. 180) (Fig. 13.16).

Until the emperor reaches out to raise her up and transform her into the personification of a happy province (Fig. 13.17) as is the case with Hadrian and Africa, the "barbarian" woman remains the Roman sign of conquest and the marker of that which is *not* Roman, outside of civilization.

Stories of "barbarian" women differ from visual images in telling us different things and with different motivation. Tales of "barbarian" queens leading troops against Rome, from Boudicca in Britain (first century C.E.) (Tacitus, *Agricola* 16.1; Mattingly 1948) to Zenobia in the East (third century C.E.), grant a certain misguided heroism to the Amazon-like women even as they go down in defeat. Writing about the queen of Palmyra who invaded Rome's eastern territories and perhaps Egypt, Trebellius Pollio constructs for Zenobia a personality vivid in its gender mixing:

[A]rrayed in the robes of Dido and even assuming the diadem, she held the imperial power in the name of her sons Herennianus and Timolaus, ruling longer than could be endured from one of the female sex. . . . She lived in regal pomp. It was rather in the manner of the Persians that she received worship and in the manner of the Persian kings that she banqueted; but it was in the manner of a Roman emperor that she came forth to public assemblies, wearing a helmet and girt with a purple fillet, which had gems hanging from the lower edge, while its center was fastened with the jewel called cochlis, used instead of the brooch worn by women, and her arms were frequently bare. Her face was dark

Figure 13.15. Painted linen mummy covering with the portrait of a woman named Ta-sheret-wedja-hor, who was married to a priest of Serapis; the portrait comes from Roman Egypt and dates to around 225 C.E. The combination of Pharaonic imagery and Severan hairstyle and portrait elements suggests the complexity of social and cultural relations in Egypt from the Ptolemaic period on.

Figure 13.16. Detail from the Column of Marcus Aurelius in Rome, later second century C.E. The Romans have taken a section of German enemy territory and are threatening and killing some of the women.

Figure 13.17. Gold coin of Hadrian helping to raise up a kneeling woman identified by the label as Africa; Rome, after 130 C.E. Hadrian and Antoninus Pius both used female figures on coins and relief sculpture to personify the various provinces of Rome's Empire.

and of a swarthy hue, her eyes were black and powerful beyond the usual wont, her spirit divinely great, and her beauty incredible . . . her voice was clear and like that of a man. Her sternness, when necessity demanded, was that of a tyrant, her clemency, when her sense of right called for it, that of a good emperor.

(*Scriptores Historiae Augustae: Thirty Pretenders* 30.2–3, 13–18; Magie 1967–68)

The fact that Zenobia had managed to fight and defeat Roman forces until she was taken by Aurelian and brought to Rome a prisoner meant that the author had to establish her credentials as a worthy opponent with characteristics a Roman could respect. In fact, he even quotes a letter supposedly from Aurelian to the Senate in which the emperor justifies taking a woman in triumph against accusations that it was an unmanly deed *(non virile munus)* saying "those very persons who find fault with me now would accord me praise in abundance, did they but know what manner of woman she is, how wise in counsels, how steadfast in plans, how firm toward the soldiers, how generous when necessity calls, and how stern when discipline demands" (30.5). Manly in certain respects, feminized through the same terms that are used for descriptions of eastern despots (the emphasis on luxury and jewels, for example), dazzlingly beautiful, nonetheless Zenobia is included in this text, says Trebellius Pollio, "that I might make a mock of Gallienus, a greater monster than whom the Roman state has never endured" (31.7). Composed between 298 and 303, Zenobia's ennobling portrait is a means to political ends, designed to condemn the ruler who could not stop her and praise the successor who did.

Tacitus's *Germania*, written some two hundred years earlier, also presents non-Roman women, on one level at least, as strong and righteous:

The men take their wounds to their mothers and wives, and the latter are not afraid of counting and examining the blows, and bring food and encouragement to the fighting men.

It stands on record that armies wavering on the point of collapse have been restored by the women. They plead heroically with their men, baring their bosoms before them and forcing them to realize the imminent prospect of their enslavement—a fate which they fear more desperately for their women than for themselves.[13] It is even found that you can secure a surer hold on a state if you demand among the hostages girls of noble family. More than this they believe that there resides in women an element of holiness or prophecy, and so they do not scorn to ask their advice or lightly disregard their replies.

(*Germania* 7–8; Mattingly 1948)

The underlying program of the *Germania* helps to explain the positive elements here, since they clearly imply both contrast with the vaunted decadence and self-indulgence of women and men in Rome and a desire to unify the latter around their difference from the barbarous Germans. Nonetheless, toward the end of the *Germania*, Tacitus notes with contempt a group so degenerate that they are ruled by women:

"woman is the ruling sex. That is the measure of their decline, I will not say below freedom but even below decent slavery" (*Germania*, 45). Clearly the message in both texts and visual images focuses on Roman moral and political concerns and functions as much for exhortation as for descriptive purposes. Neither slaves nor barbarians nor even conquered queens were in a position to leave much behind that would speak to their own perceptions of their status and way of life and of the many differences within each category that reveal the categories themselves as products of Roman imagination and power.

Conclusion

Plutarch's dedication of his "Brave Deeds of Women" (the text dates probably between 90 and 120) to his good friend Clea, a Greek woman of the upper classes, gives us a sense of the way time, place, class, and gender interweave in the thought and life of the later Roman Empire:

Regarding the virtus of women, Clea, I do not hold the same opinion as Thucydides. For he declares that the best woman is she about whom there is the least talk among persons outside regarding either censure or commendation, feeling that the name of the good woman, like her person, ought to be shut up indoors and never go out. But to my mind Gorgias appears to display better taste in advising that not the form but the fame of a woman should be known to many. Best for all seems the Roman custom, which publicly renders to women, as to men, a fitting commemoration after the end of life.
(Plutarch, "On the Bravery of Women," 242e–243e; Babbitt 1968)

Referring to the Greek authors of the past and to the normative Athenian tradition of keeping women secluded and their names unmentioned in public as a sign of their respectability, Plutarch places himself in the camp of modern Roman life; still Greek, he claims that respectable women should remain unseen, but their fame and good deeds should be commemorated publicly. In this passage, the relation between Greek and Roman, between elite and working women, between past and Roman present crystallizes as the author prepares to recount the brave and wondrous deeds of the women of the past.

Some of the women Plutarch discusses—Semiramis, Tanaquil, Porcia—have featured in earlier chapters in our book, but their world is far from either the pomp of the Imperial court or the daily occupations and domestic concerns of the freeborn and freedwomen of Italy and the provinces. We have chosen and considered here material from an enormous and disparate number of possibilities in order to show the tension between Roman upper-class gender traditions and ideals, the dominant ideologies, and the social and economic forces that permitted women some degree of autonomy or even authority. Just as these elements are always in complex and unstable relations with one another both historically and geographically, so also is there a tension between apparently opposed notions of public and private, Roman and outsiders, "upper" and "lower" class, that demonstrates how these categories blur and shift, often merging into continua through their own complexity or through the social and political needs of empire or period.

By the end of this period, new forces are shaping gender relations. The discussion of family and sexuality in Chapter 11 already articulated some of the positions that appear in the arguments over the nature of sexuality and of gender in late antiquity. The changing shape of the Empire and its shifts in population as new groups entered or took power had an impact on women and on gender ideology just as did new religious doctrines and new social attitudes. The writing and art of late antiquity, beginning with the age of Constantine, are beyond the scope of this book, but it is important to stress that much new research on the family, on ideas about the body and sexuality and on attitudes toward masculinity and femininity within a spiritualized religious framework is adding to our fund of knowledge about the positions of women and ideologies of gender in the beginning of the Middle Ages (see Further Reading for more information) Theological shifts of emphasis to the celibate body and to chastity equally for women and men or to the family in Christ rather than the secular family, may have had only a minimal impact on the daily lives of the large number of women in the late Empire; nevertheless, such evidence as that from tombstones showing an increased valuation on burials of children and women in Christian communities (Shaw 1984), suggest that there may have been changes not only in social ideology but in social practice as well—enough eventually to change some parts of women's lives and expectations as the map of the great Empire itself changed its shape.

NOTES

1. "Peregrine status" is used to indicate that the candidate might lack Roman citizenship.

2. For example, Tacitus, *Annals* 3.34, where Drusus defends husbands who take their wives with them to Imperial posts [21 C.E.].

3. The author tells us at 1.2 and at 12.3–4 with equal conviction that Elagabalus's mother and his grandmother were each first to attend the Senate "like a man" and witness the drafting of legislation. Confirmation from other sources is lacking.

4. The use of "most distinguished" or *clarissimus* for a man and *clarissima* for a woman is typical of later Roman inscriptions, especially from the mid-third century onward.

5. These did not in fact function as priestesses but were local women chosen as mouthpieces for divine inspiration.

6. Like a tunic-wearing, Diogenes—careless male intellectual?

7. For this text the old Loeb edition with translation by Babbitt is quite misleading, because it mentions reading in books, where Plutarch speaks only of his wife "hearing about" geometry, ethics, and astronomy from her husband—and that in a carefully predigested form.

8. *Lanifica* here is a standard Roman compliment that probably indicates that she was attentive to her domestic duties rather than that she was a wage- or pieceworker.

9. See p. 196, and note that he was born in Asia Minor, trained in Alexandria and practiced in Rome.

10. This is a very late source but there are comparable rulings from the first and second centuries as well: Paul, *Sententiae* 26.11 and *Digest* 23.2.44.

11. The patron was buried in the tomb with her mother and her husband, but it is not clear whether the midwife represents the mother or the daughter.

12. This is true as well of young male slaves, as Martial's epigram 12.46 indicates: "it's they [the slave boys] who give [your husband] what you as a wife don't want to give" (Ker 1968).

13. Besides this centurion's assault on a foreign queen in Livy 38.24 and the rape of Boudicca's daughters (Tacitus, *Annals* 14.31), there is little written evidence for Roman soldiers raping their female captives, but neither is there any parallel in the texts to the slaying of the female " barbarian" on the Column of Marcus Aurelius.

TRANSLATIONS

Alexander, Paul. 1938. "Speeches and Letters of the Emperor Hadrian." *Harvard Studies in Classical Philology* 49: 141–78.

Babbitt, F. C. 1968. *Plutarch.* Loeb Classical Library. Cambridge, Mass.

Birley, A. 1976. *Lives of the Later Caesars.* Harmondsworth, Middlesex.

Bowie, E. L. 1990. "Greek Poetry in the Antonine Age." In *Antonine Literature*, edited by D. A. Russell, 53–90. Oxford.

Church, A. J., and W. J. Brodribb. 1942. *Complete Works of Tacitus.* New York.

Drew-Bear, H., and W. D. Lebek. 1973. "An Oracle of Apollo at Miletus." *Greek, Roman and Byzantine Studies* 14: 65–75.

Forster, E. S., and E. Heffner. 1968. *Columella: De Re Rustica.* Loeb Classical Library. Cambridge, Mass.

Gardner, J. F., and T. Wiedemann. 1991. *The Roman Household: A Sourcebook.* New York.

Graves, R. 1951. *Apuleius: Transformations of Lucius.* New York.

Green, P. 1967. *Juvenal: The Sixteen Satires.* Harmondsworth, Middlesex.

Haines, C. R. 1962. *Marcus Cornelius Fronto.* Loeb Classical Library. Cambridge, Mass.

Ker, W. C. A. 1968. *Martial.* Loeb Classical Library. Cambridge, Mass.

Lefkowitz, M., and Fant, M. 1982. *Women's Life in Greece and Rome.* Baltimore, Md.

Lewis, N., and M. Reinhold. 1966. *Roman Civilization: Sourcebook II: The Empire.* New York.

Magie, D. 1967–68. *Scriptores Historiae Augustae.* Loeb Classical Library. Cambridge, Mass.

Mattingly, H. 1948. *Tacitus on Britain and Germany.* Harmondsworth, Middlesex.

Pharr, C. 1952. *The Theodosian Code and Novels.* Princeton, N.J.

Radice, B. 1975. *Pliny: Letters and Panegyrics.* Loeb Classical Library. Cambridge, Mass.

Smallwood, E. M. 1966. *Documents illustrating the principates of Nerva, Trajan and Hadrian.* Cambridge.

Temkin, O. 1956. *Soranus: Gynecology.* Baltimore, Md.

WORKS CONSULTED

Boatwright, Mary Taliaferro. 1991a. "Imperial Women of the Early Second Century." *American Journal of Philology* 112: 513–40.

———. 1999b. "Plancia Magna of Perge: Women's Roles and Status in Roman Asia Minor." In *Women's History and Ancient History*, edited by Sarah B. Pomeroy, 249–72. Chapel Hill, N.C.

Bowersock, Glenn W. 1969. *Greek Sophists in the Roman Empire*. Oxford.

Bradley, Keith. 1986. "Wet Nursing at Rome: A Study in Social Relations." In *The Family in Ancient Rome: New Perspectives*, edited by Berly Rawson, 201–29. Ithaca, N.Y.

Davies, Glenys. 1985. "The Significance of the Handshake Motif in Classical Funerary Art." *American Journal of Archaeology* 89, no. 4: 627–40.

Fittschen, Klaus. 1982. *Die Bildnistypen der Faustina minor und die Fecunditas Augustae*. Göttingen.

Forbis, Elizabeth P. 1990. "Women's Public Image in Italian Honorary Inscriptions." *American Journal of Philology* 111: 493–512.

Gordon, R. L. 1990. "The Veil of Power, Emperors, Sacrifices and Benefactors." In *Pagan Priests*, edited by Mary Beard and John North, 201–34. London.

Kampen, Natalie Boymel. 1981. *Image and Status: Representations of Working Women in Ostia*. Berlin.

———. 1991. "Between Public and Private: Women as Historical Subjects in Roman Art." In *Women's History and Ancient History*, edited by Sarah B. Pomeroy, 218–48. Chapel Hill, N.C.

Lattimore, Richmond. 1942. *Themes in Greek and Latin Epitaphs*. Urbana, Ill.

Lewis, N., and M. Reinhold. 1966. *Roman Civilization: Sourcebook II: The Empire*. New York.

Marshall, A. 1989. "Ladies at Law: The Role of Women in the Roman Civil Courts." In *Studies in Latin Literature and Roman History*, edited by Carl Deroux, 35–54. Collection Latomus 206. Brussels.

Mattingly, Harold. 1936. *Coins of the Roman Empire in the British Museum*. Vol. 3, *Nerva to Hadrian*. London.

Nicols, John. 1989. "Patrona civitatis: Gender and Civic Patronage." In *Studies in Latin Literature and Roman History*, edited by Carl Deroux, 117–42. Collection Latomus 206. Brussels.

Pleket, H. W. 1969. "The Social Position of Women in the Greco-Roman World." In *Epigraphica*. Vol. 2, *Texts on the Social History of the Greek World*, 10–41. Leiden.

Raepsaet-Charlier, Marie-Therese. 1986. *Prosopographie des Femmes de l'Ordre Senatorial*. Brussels.

Reekmans, Louis. 1957. "La *dextrarum iunctio* dans l'iconographie romaine et paléochretienne." *Bulletin de l'Institut Historique Belge à Rome* 31: 23–95.

Richlin, A. 1984. "Invective against Women in Roman Satire." *Arethusa* 17: 67–80.

Shaw, Brent D. 1984. "Latin Funerary Epigraphy and Family Life in the Later Roman Empire." *Historia* 33: 457–97.

———. 1991. "The Cultural Meaning of Death: Age and Gender in the Roman Family." in *The Family in Italy from Antiquity to the Present*, ed. David I. Kertzer and Richard P. Saller, 66–90. New Haven,

Sijpestein, P. J. 1987. "A Female Bouleutes." *Bulletin of the American Society of Papyrologists* 24: 141–42.

Smallwood, E. Mary. 1966. *Documents Illustrating the Principates of Nerva, Trajan, and Hadrian*. Cambridge.

Temporini, Hildegard. 1978. *Die Frauen am Hofe Trajans*. Berlin.

Van Bremen, Riet. 1983. "Women and Wealth." In *Images of Women in Antiquity*, edited by Averil Cameron and Amelie Kuhrt, 223–42. Detroit, Mich.

Waelkens, Marc. 1977. "Phrygian Votive and Tombstones as Sources of the Social and Economic Life in Roman Antiquity." *Ancient Society* 8: 277–315.

Wood, Susan. 1978. "Alcestis on Roman Sarcophagi." *American Journal of Archaeology* 82: 499–510.

Wrede, Henning. 1981. *Consecratio in Formam Deorum*. Mainz.

FURTHER READING

Brown, Peter. 1988. *The Body and Society: Men, Women and Sexual Renunciation in Early Christianity*. New York.

Dixon, Suzanne. 1988. *The Roman Mother*. London.

Gardner, Jane F. 1986. *Women in Roman Law and Society*. London.

Garnsey, Peter, and Richard Saller. 1987. *The Roman Empire: Economy, Society, and Culture*. Berkeley and Los Angeles.

Gourevitch, Danielle. 1984. *Le Mal d'être femme: La femme et la médecine à Rome*. Paris.

Hallett, Judith. 1984. *Fathers and Daughters in Roman Society*. Princeton, N.J.

Heyob, Sharon. 1975. *The Cult of Isis among Women in the Graeco-Roman World*. Leiden.

Hopkins, Keith. 1965a. "Age of Roman Girls at Marriage." *Population Studies* 18, no. 3: 309–27.

———. 1965b. "Contraception in the Roman Empire." *Comparative Studies in Society and History* 8, no. 1: 124–51.

Kleiner, Diana E. E. 1987. "Women and Family Life on Roman Imperial Altars." *Latomus* 46: 545–54.

Kraemer, Ross. 1983. "Women in the Religions of the Greco-Roman World." *Religious Studies Review* 9: 127–39.

Lifshitz, Baruch. 1967. *Donateurs et fondateurs dans les synagogues juives*. Paris.

MacMullen, Ramsey. 1980. "Women in Public in the Roman Empire." *Historia* 29: 208–18.

———. 1986. "Women's Power in the Principate." *Klio* 68: 434–43.

Marshall, Anthony J. 1975. "Roman Women and the Provinces." *Ancient Society* 6: 110–19.

Rawson, Beryl, ed. 1986. *The Family in Ancient Rome*. Ithaca, N.Y.

Rousselle, Aline. 1988. *Porneia: On Desire and the Body in Antiquity*. London.

Saller, Richard. 1984. "*Familia, Domus*, and the Roman Conception of the Family." *Phoenix* 38: 336–55.

———, and Brent Shaw. 1984. "Tombstones and Roman Family Relations in the Principate: Civilians, Soldiers and Slaves." *Journal of Roman Studies* 74: 124–56.

Shaw, Brent. 1987. "The Family in Late Antiquity: The Experience of Augustine." *Past and Present* 115: 3–51.

Treggiari, Susan. 1976. "Jobs for Women." *American Journal of Ancient History* 1: 76–104.

———. 1979. "Lower-Class Women in the Roman Economy." *Florilegium* 1: 65–86.

———. 1991. *Roman Marriage*. Oxford.

Wiedemann, Thomas E. J. 1989. *Adults and Children in the Roman Empire*. London.

CHRONOLOGY

Major events from the Greek and Roman world 776 B.C.E.–313 C.E., with events and persons from this text.

	Greece and the Greek world	Italy and the Roman world
776	First Olympiad	Etruscans in northern Italy
753		Romulus founds Rome (traditional date)
	Homeric poems: Hesiod	
733	Syracuse founded as first Greek colony in Sicily. Greek colonies founded in southern Italy and Campania.	
716		Numa king at Rome
675	Lycurgan reform at Sparta	
673		Tullus Hostilius king
ca. 660–570	Age of tyrants	
642		Ancus Martius king
625	Poetry of Sappho and Alcaeus	
616		Tarquinius Priscus founds Etruscan dynasty
594	Solon archon at Athens	
582–573	Pythian, Nemean, Isthmian Games established	
579		Servius Tullius king
566	Reorganization of Panathenaic festival	
546	Pisistratus tyrant at Athens	
534		Tarquinius Superbus king
509		Expulsion of Tarquins; establishment of Roman Republic

	Greece and the Greek world	Italy and the Roman world
508	Cleisthenes sets up democracy at Athens	
490	Defeat of Persians at Marathon.	
484	First victory of Aeschylus (drama competition—first recorded tragedy by Aeschylus)	
483		Coriolanus turned back from Rome
480	Defeat of Persians at Salamis	
470	Pindar's first Olympian	
468	First victory of Sophocles	
455	First production of Euripides	
451	Periclean citizenship law	Decemvirate at Rome
447	Parthenon begun	
444	Euripides' *Alcestis*	
443		Lex Canuleia permits patrician-plebian intermarriage
ca. 440	Hippocratic school of medicine found on Cos	
431	Peloponnesian War breaks out. Euripides' *Medea*	
425	Aristophanes' *Acharnians*	
421	Peace of Nicias between Athens and Sparta	
415	Euripides' *Trojan Women*	
411	Aristophanes' *Lysistrata*	
406	Deaths of Euripides and Sophocles	
404	Defeat of Athens	
399	Trial of Socrates	
392	Aristophanes' *Ecclesiazusae*	
390	Xenophon writing	Gauls capture Rome
387	Plato founds Academy	
386	Spartan hegemony in Greece	
366		Plebians admitted to consulship
361	Sparta defeated by Thebes	
359	Philip becomes king of Macedonia	
338	Philip defeats Athens at Chaeronea; dominates mainland Greek city-states	Rome controls Latium and Campania

	Greece and the Greek world	Italy and the Roman world
336	Alexander becomes king and builds empire in Asia	
335	Aristotle founds Lyceum at Athens	
331	Founding of Alexandria	
323	Death of Alexander	
300	Ptolemy I founds Museum of Alexandria	
	Nossis of Locri writes poetry	Wealth of Greeks in southern Italy
280		War between Rome and Pyrrhus of Epirus in southern Italy
276	Ptolemy II marries Arsinoë II	
273	Birth of Berenice II	
272		Rome captures Tarentum
264		Rome fights Carthage in Sicily
247	Ptolemy III marries Berenice II. Callimachus's "Lock."	
240		Rome defeats Carthage. First plays at Rome.
239	Birth of Ennius	
234	Birth of Cato	
218		Rome declares war on Carthage. Hannibal crosses Alps and occupies southern Italy.
216		Defeat of Rome at Cannae
215		Lex Oppia
214–206	First war between Philip of Macedonia and Rome	
212		Rome establishes games of Apollo
207		Victory at Metaurus. Hymn to Juno.
204		Great Mother brought from Pergamum. Ennius and Plautus writing. Scipio invades Africa.
202		Rome defeats Carthage
200–197	Philip of Macedonia fights second war with Rome	
197	Rome defeats Macedonia at Cynoscephalae	
196	Flamininus proclaimed the freedom of Greece at the Isthmian Games	
195		Cato the Elder consul. Repeal of Lex Oppia.

	Greece and the Greek world	*Italy and the Roman world*
192–188	War between Antiochus of Syria and Rome. Antiochus occupies Greece.	
188	Rome defeats Antiochus; annexes Sicily with Treaty of Apamea	
186		Bacchanalian conspiracy suppressed by Senate
167	Rome defeats Perseus of Macedonia at Pydna Polybius brought to Rome	End of Macedonian monarchy
166–160		Plays of Terence
149	Third war between Rome and Carthage	Death of Cato the Elder
148	Rome fights against Macedonia and defeats Achaean league	
146	Rome destroys Corinth and Carthage	
	All mainland Greece incorporated in Roman Empire	
133	Tiberius Gracchus's popular reforms. Rome inherits Pergamum.	
123–121	Tribunates of Gaius Gracchus; attempt to enfranchise Italians	
112–106	Rome fights Jugartha of Numidia. 107 Marius consul.	
104–101	Marius repeatedly consul. 104 Defeats Teutones. 102 Defeats Cimbri.	
100	Marius consul sixth time. Birth of Caesar.	
91	Italian allies demand citizenship. Social war.	
88	Sulla consul; marches on Rome, then campaigns against Mithridates in Greece	
86	Sulla captures Athens	
82	Sulla returns, with civil war; made dictator.	
70	Cicero becomes famous with speeches against Verres	
63	Cicero consul. Pompey conquers Mithridates and east.	
59	Julius Caesar consul; alliance with Pompey and Crassus. Poetry of Catullus and Lucretius.	
49	Civil war between Caesar and Pompey. Caesar meets Cleopatra VII.	
48	Caesar dictator in absolute power at Rome	
44	Caesar assassinated. Renewed civil war.	
43	Octavian consul. Antony shares power in east.	
42	Octavian and Antony defeat republicans Brutus and Cassius at Philippi	
41	Antony goes to Egypt. Fulvia leads resistance in Italy.	
40	Antony marries Octavia. Pact with Octavian at Brundisium. Virgil writing *Eclogues*. Horace writing *Satires* and *Epodes*.	

Roman Empire
including Greek world

39	Octavian has daughter Julia by Scribonia. Divorces her. Marries Livia, mother of Tiberius and Drusus.
31	Antony and Cleopatra defeated at Actium by Octavian
30	Octavian annexes Egypt. Cornelius Gallus first governor.
29	Livy begins history of Rome
27	Octavian "restores" Republic; named Augustus. Propertius and Tibullus writing love elegies.
25	Ovid begins his *Amores*
23	Horace's *Odes* 1–3 published
19	Deaths of Virgil and Tibullus
18	Augustan laws on marriage between classes, against adultery
17	Secular games. Horace composes secular hymn.
9	Dedication of Altar of Peace
2	Augustus saluted as father of his country *(pater patriae)*. Julia banished. Ovid's *Art of Love*.

C.E.

8	Younger Julia banished. Ovid exiled.
9	Lex Papia Poppaea
14	Death of Augustus. Tiberius emperor. Livia becomes Augusta.
37	Death of Tiberius. Caligula emperor.
41	Assassination of Caligula. Claudius emperor; exiles Seneca.
49	Agrippina empress; recalls Seneca as Nero's tutor
54	Death of Claudius. Nero emperor. Seneca's moral essays, poetry of Lucan and Persius, Petronius's *Satyricon*.
65	Nero orders death of Seneca, Lucan, Petronius
68	Year of four emperors. Civil war ends with accession of Vespasian.
79	Titus becomes emperor. Vesuvius destroys Pompeii and Herculaneum.
81	Domitian becomes emperor
90–95	Quintilian's *Education of the Orator*
96	Domitian assassinated. Pliny the Younger begins to publish *Letters*. Plutarch writing *Moral Essays* and *Lives*.
98	Trajan declared emperor
100	Trajan comes to Rome
101–6	Trajan conquers Dacia
110–11	Pliny governs Bithynia. Tacitus writing *Histories*.
114–17	Trajan's Parthian Campaign. Jewish revolt.

Roman Empire
including Greek world

117	Hadrian succeeds Trajan. The age of great Imperial ladies: the dowager empress Plotina, Marciana, Gratidias, the empress Sabina. Tacitus writing *Annals*. Juvenal writing *Satires*.
ca. 125	Death of Plutarch
130	Hadrian in Egypt. Julia Balbilla inscribes Memnon colossus. Soranus writing on gynecology.
138	Death of Hadrian. Antoninus Pius emperor.
155	Apuleius's *Apology*; self-defense on charge of witchcraft
161	Death of Antoninus. Marcus Aurelius emperor. Apuleius writing *Golden Ass* (as late as 180?)
	Galen writing on medicine
180	Death of Marcus Aurelius. Commodus emperor.
193	Death of Commodus. Septimius Severus founds new dynasty. Influence of Empress Julia Domna.
212	Caracalla emperor. Declares universal citizenship for free inhabitants of Empire, thus enabling them to be taxed.
218–22	Elagabalus emperor
222–35	Death of Elagabalus. Rule of Alexander Severus.
235–84	Succession of short-lived military rulers. Economic and cultural decline. (Because of the dearth of contemporary writing, sources are public and private inscriptions.)
284	Diocletian reestablishes control of Empire through tetrarchy: separate government of eastern and western halves of Empire. Restores economic stability.
306	Diocletian dies. Succeeded by Constantine.
312	Constantine defeats Heraclius at battle of Mulvian Bridge
313	Edict of Milan legitimates Christianity

ART CREDITS

Maps

Page 2–3: The Greek World Around 300 B.C.E. After Map 9 in J. Boardman et al., *Oxford History of the Classical World*, 1986. © Oxford University Press 1986. Reprinted by permission of Oxford University Press.

Page 206–207: The Roman Empire Around 200 C.E. After Map 10 in J. Boardman et al., *Oxford History of the Classical World*, 1986. © Oxford University Press 1986. Reprinted by permission of Oxford University Press.

Figures

Part I

1   Marble stele of Mnesarete (early 4th century B.C.E.). Munich, Glyptothek Gl.491. Photo: C. Kopperman.

1.1   Archaic vase (ca. 550–540 B.C.E.) from Clazomenai. London, British Museum B121. Photo: Museum, courtesy of Trustees.

1.2   Red-figure Athenian vase (ca. 460 B.C.E.). Rome, Museo Nazionale Etrusco di Villa Giulia. Photo: Soprintendenza Archeologica di Etruria Meridionale.

1.3   Kore from the Acropolis (dedicated in the 480s). Athens, Acropolis Museum 686. Photo: TAP Service.

1.4   Kore of Phrasicleia (ca. 530 B.C.E.). Athens, National Archaeological Museum. From *Athens Annals of Archaeology*, V, 1972, p. 312, fig. 14.

1.5   Funerary relief (540–530 B.C.E.) from Attica. New York, Metropolitan Museum of Art 11.185. Hewitt Fund, 1911; Munsey Fund, 1936, 1938, and Anonymous Gift, 1951. Photo: Museum.

1.6   Plan of the sanctuary at Eleusis. From G. Mylonas, *The Hymn to Demeter and Her Sanctuary at Eleusis*, Washington University Studies, 1942, fig. 2.

1.7 Black-figure Attic vase (ca. 520 B.C.E.). Wuerzburg, Martin von Wagner Museum L308. Photo: Museum.

1.8 Fragment of a fifth-century B.C.E. relief. Naples, Museo Nazionale Archeologico. Photo: Soprintendenza Archeologica delle Province di Napoli e Caserta Napoli.

1.9 Seventh-century B.C.E. ivory statuette. Izmir, Archaeological Museum. From E. Akurgal, *Griechische und Römische Kunst in der Türkei*, pl. 69a.

1.10 Monumental Greek stone statue (ca. 650 B.C.E.). Athens, National Archaeological Museum 1. Photo: TAP Service.

1.11 Mirror (ca. 480 B.C.E.). Brauron, Archaeological Museum. Photo: Second Ephoria of Classical Antiquities.

1.12 Early Attic funerary vase (760 B.C.E.). Athens, National Archaeological Museum 804. Photo: TAP Service.

1.13 Funeral plaque (ca. 500 B.C.E.). Paris, Museé du Louvre. Photo: Museum.

1.14 Funeral plaque (ca. 540–530 B.C.E.). Berlin, Antikensammlung, Staatliche Museen F1813. Photo: Museum.

1.15 Vase from the end of the sixth century B.C.E. Athens, Cerameikos Museum 691. Photo: German Archaeological Institute, Athens.

1.16 Loutrophoros (ca. 490–480 B.C.E.). Paris, Museé du Louvre. Photo: Museum.

2.1 Statuette of female athlete. London, British Museum 208. Photo: Museum, courtesy of Trustees.

3.1 Tombstone of Aristylla (ca. 430–425 B.C.E.). Athens, National Archaeological Museum 766. Photo: TAP Service.

3.2 Tombstone of Pausimache (ca. 390–380 B.C.E.). Athens, National Archaeological Museum 3964. Photo: TAP Service.

3.3 Detail of the east frieze of the Parthenon (ca. 440–432 B.C.E.). London, British Museum. Photo: Museum, courtesy of Trustees.

3.4 Vase fragment (ca. 430 B.C.E.). Basel, Private Collection of Dr. Herbert A. Cahn. Photo: D. Widmer.

3.5 East frieze of the Parthenon (ca. 440–432 B.C.E.). Paris, Museé du Louvre. Photo: Museum.

3.6 Dionysiac vase (ca. 450 B.C.E.). San Antonio Museum of Art 86.134.64. Gift of Gilbert M. Denman, Jr. Photo: Museum.

3.7 Vase (ca. 440 B.C.E.). Tarquinia, Museo Nazionale Archeologico. Photo: Soprintendenza Archeologica di Etruria Meridionale.

3.8 Interior of an Attic white-ground cup (ca. 480 B.C.E.). Munich, Staatliche Antikensammlungen und Glyptothek 2645. Photo: Museum.

3.9 Perfume vase (ca. 380 B.C.E.). Karlsruhe, Badisches Landesmuseum B39. Photo: Museum.

3.10 Black-figure vase (ca. 550–540 B.C.E.). Berlin, Antikensammlung, Staatliche Museen F1686. Photo: Bildarchiv Preussischer Kulturbesitz.

3.11 White-ground lekythos (ca. 440 B.C.E.). Athens, National Archaeological Museum 1935. Photo: TAP Service.

3.12 White-ground lekythos (ca. 430 B.C.E.). Munich, Staatliche Antikensammlungen und Glyptothek 6254. Photo: Museum.

3.13
3.14 Pyxis for cosmetics (ca. 440–430 B.C.E.). London, British Museum 1920.12–21.1. Photo: Museum, courtesy of Trustees.

3.15 Epinetron (ca. 420 B.C.E.). Athens, National Archaeological Museum 1629. Photo: TAP Service.

3.16 Loutrophoros (ca. 430 B.C.E.). Boston, Museum of Fine Arts 03.802. Francis Bartlett Collection. Photo: Museum.

3.17 Plan of a house (fifth century B.C.E.). After S. Walker, "Women and Housing in Classical Greece: The Archaeological Evidence" in A. Cameron and A. Kuhrt, editors, *Images of Women in Antiquity*, Routledge & Kegan Paul, 1983, p. 87, figs. 6.2a–6.2b.

3.18 Interior of a cup (ca. 470 B.C.E.). Berlin, Antikensammlung, Staatliche Museen F2289. Photo: Museum.

3.19 Vase (ca. 450 B.C.E.). London, British Museum E219. Photo: Museum, courtesy of Trustees.

3.20 Grave stele of Plangon (325–320 B.C.E.). Munich, Staatliche Antikensammlungen und Glyptothek G1.199. Photo: Museum.

3.21 Vase (ca. 450 B.C.E.). London, British Museum E190. Photo: Museum, courtesy of Trustees.

3.22 Water-jar (ca. 520 B.C.E.) from Athens. Toledo Museum of Art 1961.23. Gift of Edward Drummond Libbey. Photo: Museum.

3.23 Vase (ca. 460 B.C.E.). New York, Metropolitan Museum of Art 07.286.74. Rogers Fund, 1907. Photo: Museum.

3.24 Vase (ca. 460 B.C.E.). Bernisches Historisches Museum 12227. Photo: Museum.

3.25 Symposium vase (490–480 B.C.E.). New York, Metropolitan Museum of Art 20.246. Rogers Fund, 1920. Photo: Museum.

3.26 Drinking cup (520–510 B.C.E.). Madrid, Museo Arqueológico Nacional 11.267. Photo: Museum.

3.27   Detail of a symposium vase (ca. 500 B.C.E.). Malibu, California, J. Paul Getty Museum 80.AE.31. (Artist: Phintias; Title: Attic Red-figure Kylix; Medium: Terracotta; Size: H. 12.6 cm, W. 39.1 cm, Diameter 30.8 cm). Photo: Museum.

4.1   Black-figure vase (ca. 520–500 B.C.E.). Munich, Staatliche Antikensammlungen und Glyptothek 1711. Photo: Museum.

4.2   Outside of a cup (ca. 510 B.C.E.). Oxford, Ashmolean Museum 1927.4065. Photo: Museum.

4.3   Attic vase (ca. 440–430 B.C.E.). Jerusalem, Israel Museum 75.15.18. Photo: Museum.

4.4   Shield of Athena Parthenos (mid-fifth century B.C.E.). From E. Harrison, *American Journal of Archaeology*, 85 (1981), p. 297, fig. 4.

5.1   Marble bust of Cleopatra. Berlin, Antikensammlung, Staatliche Museen 1976.10. Photo: Museum.

5.2   Silver tetradrachm of Cleopatra (39–37 B.C.E.). New York, American Numismatic Society. Photo: ANS.

5.3   Silver tetradrachm of Cleopatra (37 B.C.E.). New York, American Numismatic Society. Photo: ANS.

5.4   The Ptolemies. From R. Bianchi et al., *Cleopatra's Egypt: Age of the Ptolemies*, p. 10. © Brooklyn Museum 1988. Courtesy of the Brooklyn Museum.

5.5   Terra-cotta figurine from Benghazi (330–300 B.C.E.). London, British Museum C718. Photo: Museum, courtesy of Trustees.

5.6   Terra-cotta figurine from Tanagra (ca. first half of third century B.C.E.). Paris, Museé du Louvre. Photo: Museum.

5.7   Silver tetradrachm (246–221 B.C.E.) of Queen Berenice II. New York, American Numismatic Society. Photo: ANS.

5.8   Portrait bust (second half of the third century B.C.E.) of Queen Berenice II. Munich, Staatliche Antikensammlungen und Glyptothek 543. Photo: Museum.

5.9   Faience jug from Alexandria (ca. 240 B.C.E.). Antalya, Archaeological District Museum. Photo: Museum.

5.10   Portrait (ca. 270–246 B.C.E.) of Ptolemaic queen Arsinoë II. New York, Metropolitan Museum of Art 20.2.21. Rogers Fund, 1920. Photo: Museum.

5.11   Marble votive relief (late second century B.C.E.). Munich, Staatliche Antikensammlungen und Glyptothek 206. Photo: Museum.

5.12   Statue in black granite (Ptolemaic period). Munich, Staatlichen Sammlung Ägyptischer Kunst GL.WAF 26b. Photo: Museum.

5.13   Tombstone (second century B.C.E.) from Izmir. London, British Museum 1947.7–14.2. Photo: Museum, courtesy of Trustees.

5.14   Tombstone from late fourth or third century B.C.E. Cambridge, Arthur M. Sackler Museum 1905.8, Harvard University Art Museums. Gift of Edward W. Forbes in Trust to the University. Photo: Museum.

5.15   Athenian vase (ca. 500 B.C.E.). From A. Furtwängler and K. Reichhold, *Griechische Vasenmalerei*, Vol. I, Bruckmann, 1900, pl. 34.

5.16   Statue of Aphrodite (ca. 350 B.C.E.). Vatican Museum 812. Photo: Museum.

5.17   Statue of the crouching Aphrodite. Rome, Museo Nazionale delle Terme. Photo: Soprintendenza Archeologica di Roma.

5.18   Terra-cotta statuette from Naucratis (first century B.C.E. to first century C.E.). London, British Museum C574. Photo: Museum, courtesy of Trustees.

5.19   Terra-cotta statuette from Tanagra (ca. 350–325 B.C.E.). London, British Museum C243. Photo: Museum, courtesy of Trustees.

5.20   Statue (third century B.C.E.). Munich, Staatliche Antikensammlungen und Glyptothek 437. Photo: Museum.

Part II

1   Tombstone (possibly second or third century C.E.). London, British Museum. Photo: Museum, courtesy of Trustees.

7.1   Reverse of a denarius of L. Titurius Sabinus (89–88 B.C.E.). London, British Museum BMC 2322. Photo: Museum, courtesy of Trustees.

7.2   Reverse of a denarius of L. Titurius Sabinus (89–88 B.C.E.). London, British Museum BMC 2328. Photo: Museum, courtesy of Trustees.

7.3   Terra-cotta statue of a young woman (third century B.C.E.). New York, Metropolitan Museum of Art 16.141. Rogers Fund, 1916. Photo: Museum.

7.4   Ficoroni cista (fourth century B.C.E.). Rome, Museo Nazionale Etrusco di Villa Giulia. Photo: German Archaeological Institute, Rome.

7.5   Reverse of a denarius of L. Roscius Fabatus (64 B.C.E.). Photo: Hirmer Verlag.

7.6   Statue of a matron from Rome (ca. 27 B.C.E. to 14 C.E.). Parma, Museo Nazionale. Photo: German Archaeological Institute, Rome.

7.7   Reverse of denarius of Clodius Vestalis (41 B.C.E.). London, British Museum BMC 4196. Photo: Museum, courtesy of Trustees.

7.8   Fragment of a marble relief (ca. 14–37 C.E.). Rome, Museo Conservatori. Photo: German Archaeological Institute, Rome.

7.9   Mold-made terra-cotta figurine (fifth century B.C.E.). Reggio Calabria, Museo Nazionale. Photo: Soprintendenza Archeologica della Calabria.

7.10   Terra-cotta plaque from fifth century B.C.E. Reggio Calabria, Museo Nazionale. Photo: Soprintendenza Archeologica della Calabria.

7.11   Lebes gamikos from Campania (fourth century B.C.E.). London, British Museum F207. Photo: Museum, courtesy of Trustees.

7.12   Terra-cotta figurine from south Italy (third century B.C.E.). New York, Metropolitan Museum of Art 11.212.20. Photo: Museum.

8.1   Drawing of a wall painting from the Tomb of the Painted Vases in Tarquinia (ca. 500 B.C.E.). Photo: German Archaeological Institute, Rome.

8.2   Engraved bronze mirror (second half of the fourth century B.C.E.). From Gerhard, *Etruskische Spiegel*, p. 112.

8.3   Painting from the tomb of the Monkey at Chiusi (late sixth century B.C.E.). Photo: German Archaeological Institute, Rome.

8.4   Copy of a wall painting from the Tomb of the Chariots (fifth century B.C.E.). Tarquinia, Museo Nazionale Archeologico. Photo: German Archaeological Institute, Rome.

8.5   Terra-cotta sarcophagus (sixth century B.C.E.). Paris, Museé du Louvre. Photo: Museum.

8.6   Limestone relief from Chiusi (ca. 500 B.C.E.). Chiusi, Museo Civico. Photo: Soprintendenza Archeologica di Firenze.

8.7   Lid of a limestone sarcophagus (mid-fourth century B.C.E.). Boston, Museum of Fine Arts 86.145. Gift of Mrs. Gardner Brewer. Photo: Museum.

8.8   Cannicella Venus (ca. 530 B.C.E.). Orvieto, Museo Civico. Photo: German Archaeological Institute, Rome.

8.9 Votive terra-cotta figurines (fourth century B.C.E.). Florence, Museo Archeologico. Photo: Soprintendenza Archeologica di Etruria Meridionale.

8.10 Seventh-century B.C.E. bronze pendant. Bologna, Museo Civico Archeologica. Photo: Museum.

8.11 Painted terra-cotta sarcophagus (ca. 150 B.C.E.). London, British Museum D786. Photo: Museum, courtesy of Trustees.

9.1 Statue of a woman (early fourth century C.E.). Volterra, Museo Guarnacci. Photo: German Archaeological Institute, Rome.

9.2 Tombstone of a couple (first century B.C.E.). Rome, Museo Nuovo. Photo: German Archaeological Institute, Rome.

9.3 Tombstone of a family group (late first century B.C.E.). Vatican Museum 10490. Photo: Museum.

10.1 Greek red-figure vase (late sixth century B.C.E.). Brussels, Musées Royaux d'Art et d'Histoire A717. Photo: ACL.

10.2 Mold for a clay vase (ca. 30 B.C.E.). New York, Metropolitan Museum of Art 19.192.21. Rogers Fund, 1919. Photo: Museum.

11.1 The Imperial family in a procession on the Ara Pacis Augustae in Rome (13–9 B.C.E.). Photo: Fototeca Unione Presso Accademia Americana.

11.2 Ara Pacis Augustae panel. Photo: German Archaeological Institute, Rome.

11.3 Portrait bust of the Empress Livia from Egypt (ca. 4–14 C.E.). Copenhagen, Ny Carlsberg Glyptotek 615. Photo: Museum.

11.4 Portrait bust of Livia from Rome (after 14 C.E.). Bochum, Ruhr-Universität. Photo: I. Berndt.

11.5 Portrait statue of Livia. Copenhagen, Ny Carlsberg Glyptotek 531. Photo: Museum.

11.6 The Gemma Claudia (ca. 48–49 C.E.). Vienna, Kunsthistorisches Museum. Photo: German Archaeological Institute, Rome.

11.7 The Grand Camée de France. Paris, Bibliothèque Nationale. Photo: Library.

11.8 Bronze coin from Asia Minor. London, British Museum BMC 44. Photo: Museum, courtesy of Trustees.

11.9 Aureus from Lyon (37–38 C.E.). London, British Museum BMC 7. Photo: Museum, courtesy of Trustees.

11.10 Coin of Claudius, dated about 46 C.E. London, British Museum BMC 242. Photo: Museum, courtesy of Trustees.

11.11   Tombstone from early first-century C.E. Rome. London, British Museum 2274. Photo: Museum, courtesy of Trustees.

11.12   Funerary altar (40–50 C.E.). Vatican Museum XXXI.14.70. Photo: Museum.

11.13   Arretine bowl, made in the late first century B.C.E. or early first century C.E. Boston, Museum of Fine Arts 13.109. Gift of E. P. Warren. Photo: Museum.

12.1   General view of Pompeii. Photo: Alinari/Art Resource.

12.2   View of the villa (ca. middle of the first century C.E.) at Oplontis. Photo: German Archaeological Institute, Rome.

12.3   View through the main entrance into the building underwritten by the Pompeian priestess, Eumachia. Photo: German Archaeological Institute, Rome.

12.4   Statue of Eumachia. Naples, Museo Nazionale Archeologico. Photo: Alinari/Art Resource.

12.5   Wall painting from Pompeii (mid-first century C.E.). Naples, Museo Nazionale Archeologico. Photo: German Archaeological Institute, Rome.

12.6   View of the interior of the tavern of Asellina. Photo: Alinari/ Art Resource.

12.7   Interior of brothel in Pompeii, dated to the last years of the city. Photo: Alinari/Art Resource.

12.8   Tomb monument (first century C.E.), Pompeii. Photo: German Archaeological Institute, Rome.

12.9   Wall painting from a house in first-century C.E. Pompeii. Naples, Museo Nazionale Archeologico. Photo: Alinari/Art Resource.

12.10   Wall painting from first-century C.E. Pompeii. Naples, Museo Nazionale Archeologico. Photo: Soprintendenza Archeologica delle Province di Napoli e Caserta Napoli.

13.1   Gold coin of Plotina (ca. 112–115 C.E.). London, British Museum BMC 525. Photo: Museum, courtesy of Trustees.

13.2   Gold coin of Hadrian, minted after 122 C.E. Vienna, Kunsthistorisches Museum. Photo: H. Tscherni.

13.3   Base of the Column of Antoninus Pius from Rome (ca. 161 C.E.). Photo: Alinari/Art Resource.

13.4   Coin of Faustina the Younger (ca. 161–176 C.E.). London, British Museum BMC 953. Photo: Museum, courtesy of Trustees.

13.5   Relief (ca. 206 C.E.) from the Severan family arch at Leptis

Magna in modern Libya. Photo: German Archaeological Institute, Rome.

13.6   Portrait of Plancia Magna. Antalya, Archaeological District Museum. Photo: German Archaeological Institute, Rome.

13.7   Tombstone from Dorylaion, dated to the late second or early third century C.E. Photo: German Archaeological Institute, Athens.

13.8   Tomb statue from the late first or early second century C.E. Vatican Museum. Photo: German Archaeological Institute, Rome.

13.9   Sarcophagus of Metilia Acte (third quarter of the second century C.E.). Vatican, Museo Chiaramonti. Photo: German Archaeological Institute, Rome.

13.10   Stele of a family (second or third century C.E.). Deva Museum. Photo: German Archaeological Institute, Rome.

13.11   Tombstone of Umma (first century C.E.). Altenburg, Archäologischer Park Carnuntum 10809. Photo: Archäologischer Park.

13.12   Funerary monument from the third century C.E. Trier, Rheinisches Landesmuseum. Photo: Museum.

13.13   Small marble relief (mid-second century C.E.). Ostia, Museo Ostiense. Photo: German Archaeological Institute, Rome.

13.14   Terra-cotta painted relief (mid-second century C.E.). Ostia, Museo Ostiense. Photo: German Archaeological Institute, Rome.

13.15   Painted linen mummy covering (ca. 225 C.E.). Boston, Museum of Fine Arts 54.993. Gift of Mrs. Arthur Deven's Class. Photo: Museum.

13.16   Detail from the Column of Marcus Aurelius in Rome (late second century C.E.). Photo: German Archaeological Institute, Rome.

13.17   Gold coin of Hadrian. London, British Museum BMC 870. Photo: Museum, courtesy of Trustees.

INDEX

Names that appear in full capitals are names of Greek and Roman women. Page numbers followed by the letters "f" and "n" denote illustrations and notes, respectively.

imperial ideology on virtuous women, 315;
marriages of, 305
JULIA DOMNA (wife of Septimus Severus),
352-353, 362, 366; images of, 357-358, 359f;
myth of happy family life of, 358-359;
patronage of, 366
JULIA MAESA (sister of Julia Domna), 355
JULIA TITI (daughter of Titus), 352
Julio-Claudian Rome, 294; influence of
Augustus' reign on, 313, 314f; and tensions
over proper role of women, 326-327
JUNO (goddess), 230, 231f, 299; cult of, 230,
232-234; statue of, and women's offerings
during Hannibalic invasion, 232-233
Justin, 144, 145
Justinian, *Institutes*, 306
Juvenal, *Satires*, 366-367

Kalathos, 109
Kanephoroi, at Panathenaic procession in
honor of Athena, 86
Korai: of Archaic period, 19, 20f, 21f, 22, 173;
clothing of, compared with costumes of
Spartan women, 59, 60f; functions of, 22;
funerary relief from Attica, 23f; original
contexts of, 12
KORE (PERSEPHONE, LIBERA) cult of, 36, 37f,
237, 238f
Kottabos (Athenian party game), 116

LAIA OF CYZICUS (Hellenistic artist), 168
LALA. *See* LAIA OF CYZICUS
Land ownership, by Spartan women, Aristotle's
criticisms of, 65-66
Lares, 228
LASTHENIA OF MANTINEIA (student at
Plato's Academy), 167
Latium, statue of young woman from, 220, 221f
LAVINIA, 234; in Virgil's *Aeneid*, 297, 298-299
Law-court cases: and Athenian women, 75-76,
80, 111-115; of Caelius, 284; initiated by
Roman women, 272, 360; and marriage
contracts in Hellenistic period, 159; as source
of information on women, 74, 360-361; of
women accused of poisoning husbands in
early Roman Republic, 228; women of late
Roman Republic speaking during, 273. *See
also* Legal petitions
Laws: and Athenian women, 70, 74-76, 111-113,
114; funerary, 76; in Plato's *Republic*, 118-
119; regulating women mourners in Archaic
period, 46-48; *Theodosian Code*, on
tavernworkers or servants accused of
adultery, 380. *See also* Augustan laws; Law-
court cases
Lebes gamikos (vases from Greek Italy), 258,
259f
Legal petitions, as source on lower strata
women in Roman provinces, 375-376
Legal texts: on distinctions between free, freed,
and slave, 384; as source of information on

women in Augustan Rome, 294; on tavern
workers as quasi-prostitutes, 380
Legitimacy of children: and confinement of
women in Classical Athens, 103; court cases
on, 80
Lenaia festival of Dionysus, 87, 88f, 89f
Lepidus (son of Cornelia), 272, 277
"LESBIA," in Catullus's poetry, 282-284, 304
Lesbianism. *See* Love, female homoerotic
Letters: about women, 212-213, 271, 272, 276,
287, 349-350, 360-361, 367; written by women,
213, 264, 349, 353, 354
LIBERA, cult of, 238
Libya, Amazon men in, 134
Ligustinus, Spurius, 265-267
Literacy: of Hellenistic period women, 141,
142f; of Roman women, 212, 342, 368, 370,
373; of Spartan women, 60; of women in
Classical Athens, 106, 107f; of women of
Pompeii, 341, 342f
Literary sources: on Amazons, 129; on Archaic
period women, 10, 12; on "barbarian" women
of Roman Empire, 386, 389; on Dionysiac
rites, 90-91; on early Roman Republic, 211,
216, 240; Etruscan, absence of, 211; on
funerary behavior, 76-77; on Hellenistic
period women, 141, 169-171, 179-180; on later
Roman Empire, 346; on marriage in Augustan
Rome, 297-299; on nonaristocratic women of
Archaic period, 50, 53, *see also* Homer; and
praise for Berenice II, 146; on rape of the
Sabines, 217-219; on women in Augustan
Rome, 294
LIVIA (AUGUSTA) (wife of Augustus), 291,
295, 304, 354, 359; on Grand Camée de
France, 314f; and ideal of virtuous women in
Imperial Rome, 292, 315, 320; inscriptions to,
312; portraiture, 308f-310f, 313; relative
autonomy of, 308, 310
Livy, 222-223, 228, 297; on Cato's attitude
toward uncontrolled women, 260-261; on cult
of plebeian chastity, 231-232; on Etruscans,
222, 244; on heroines of early Roman
Republic, 222-223; on intermarriage between
plebeians and patricians, 230-231; on absent
fathers, 266; and moral puritanism of early
Rome, 239; on rape of the Sabines, 217-219;
on Tanaquil, 243; on Verginia, 227; on
women's cults in early Roman Republic, 231-
234
Locri Epizephyrii (Greek city in Southern
Italy), 32; clay tablets of, 238, 239f;
sanctuary of Persephone at, 36-37
Loutrophoroi: 51f; and women mourners, 49
Love, female homoerotic, 165, 325; and
Augustan adultery laws, 300-301; in Sparta,
58
Love, heterosexual: female susceptibility to,
and Hellenistic writers, 169-171; in
Hellenistic period, 169-173; and ideal of
virtuousness of women of Augustan Rome,

Love, heterosexual (*continued*)
319; and "New Woman" in last century of
Roman Republic, 280–281: romantic and
idealized notion of in Classical Athens, 101
Love poetry: of Augustan Rome, 323; of
Catullus, 281-284; on dinner parties, 287; of
last century of Roman Republic, *see* "New
Woman"; of Ovid, 290-291; of Propertius, 285-
286; of Sulpicia, 324-325
Love potions, and poisonings, 228
Lower strata women of Roman Empire, 368-390;
and "barbarians," 386, 388f; Christian
women, 383; and concept of *familia*, 370; and
concepts of virtue, 370-371, 373; in cults, 382-
383; definitional problems, 368-369; and ideal
of Roman womanhood, 369-370; inscriptional
evidence on tombstones as source on, 369-
378; intermarriage with Roman citizens, 375-
376; non-Roman, *see* "Barbarian" women; in
provinces; legal petitions as source on, 375-
376; qualifications for working, 378-379; and
rituals of magic, 383-384; and Roman social
hierarchy, 390-394; rural-urban differences,
379-380; status distinctions between, 384-
390.*See also* Freedwomen; Slave women
Lucan, *Civil War*, 384
Lucian, *Dialogues of the Courtesans*, 301
LUCILLA, DOMITIA, 354
LUCINA (goddess of childbirth), 229-230
Lucius (Mark Antony's brother), 274, 315f
LUCRETIA, 225-227, 244
Lupercalia (Roman fertility ritual), 229-230
Luxury: Etruscan, 247-249, 252; Roman, 261-
262. *See also* Wealthy women
Lycurgan constitution: legends associated with,
66; Plutarch on, 64; and Sparta as utopia, 63
Lycurgus, 61; constitution of Sparta and,
Plutarch on, 57; laws at Sparta attributed to,
74. *See also* Lycurgan constitution
Lycurgus, *Against Leocrates*, 79-80
Lysias, 74, 79, 95, 111-112, 113-114; *Funeral
Oration*, 128
LYSIMACHE (priestess of Athena), 93
LYSISTRATA. *See* Lysimache
LYSISTRATE (priestess of Demeter and
Persephone in Archaic period), 38-39

Macedonian kings, and imposition of Greek
culture on Egypt, 9
Macrobius, *Saturnalia*, 291
Maenads (followers of Dionysus), 87, 91f
MAESA, JULIA, 355
MAESIA OF SENTINIUM, 273
Magic. *See* Witchcraft; Witches
Magistracies, awarded to Hellenistic period
women, 155-156
Maidens: of Archaic period, initiation into
adulthood, 12-18; of Classical Athens,
initiation into adulthood, 70, 80-81; in early
Roman Republic, public appearances of, 234;

participation in religious rituals in Classical
Athens, 83, 84f, 85f, 86f
Maids, in Roman Republic, 267-268; in Roman
Empire, 385
Makeup, in Augustan Rome, 301
Male genitals, images of: at Haloa festival, 92,
93; at Thesmophoria festival, 87
MAMIA (priestess), 339, 341
Mantles. *See* Blankets
Manus, marriage with and without, 227-228
Maps: of Greek world around 300 b.c.e, 2-3; of
Roman Empire around 200 c.e., 206-207
MARCIANA (sister of Trajan), 350-351, 363
Mare women, in Semonides' poem, 42-43
Marital fault, in Roman law: and abortion,
228; and adultery, 228; and appearance in
public, 262; and poisoning, 228
Marriage: and absence of military fathers, 265-
266; arranged by mothers, 275; in Augustan
Rome, 294-306, 320f; and availability of
slaves and prostitutes in Roman Empire, 211;
by capture, and rape of the Sabines, 217;
caste intermarriage, 230-231; and chastity in
Augustan and Julio-Claudian Rome, 327;
citizen-noncitizen intermarriage, 375; and
Civil War, 289; in Classical Athens, 68-73, 75,
83, 101; depiction of Amazons as hostile to,
131-134; earliest extant Greek contract, 158-
159; in early Roman Republic, 227-228, 230-
232, 233f; and education of girls in late
Roman Republic, 272; Etruscan, 245, 248-250,
251f, 253f; in Hellenistic period, 166, 171-173;
Hesiod's recommendations on, 39-40; in
Homeric epics, 11; ideal in Archaic period,
26-27; and ideal of virtuous woman in
Augustan Rome, 320-321; in late Roman
Republic, 225, 272, 289-290; and laws on
dowry and in Roman Republic, 263; in New
Comedy, 162; to one man only (univira),
232, 276; and political alliances, 225;
prohibited for slaves in late Roman Republic,
268, 270; Roman ideal of harmony in, 327,
357, 369-370; and Roman soldiers, 213, 265-
266, 375; in Sappho's poems, 15-16; and
Spartan women, 61, 62-63; transition from
maidenhood to, 22, 24-25, 26-27, 70; of
widows in Roman Empire, 361
Married Women. *See* Wives
Martial, *Epigrams*, 300
MATIDIA (niece of Trajan), 350-351
"Matriarchy, myth of," and Amazon myth, 132-
133
Matrilineal naming, in Hellenistic period, 165
Matrona (married women in Rome), status of,
218, 232. *See also* Wives
Mature women. *See* Older women
MEDEA, 68-70, 73; Hellenistic versions of, 169
Medical writings: on Amazons, 134; Aristotle's,
190-194; of Herophilus, 194-196; Hippocratic
Corpus, 184-190; on women, 183-204. *See also*
Gynecological writings, Greco-Roman

Medicine: Hellenistic period women and, 168; Roman women practitioners, 215, 370, 378-379

MEGALOSTRATA (Spartan poet), 60

MEGISTE, ABUDIA (vendor), 378

MELANIPPE (in Euripides' *The Captive Melanippe*), 95-96

MELANTHO (in Homer's *Odyssey*), 52

MELISSA, 26

MELOSA, 81

MEMMIA VICTORIA (*mater* of artisans' group), 366

Men: military absences of, and legends of early Roman Republic, 225; as mourners in Archaic period, 46-48; role in Homer's *Iliad*, 34. *See also* Fathers

Menelaus: in Euripides' *Andromache*, 72; in Homer's *Odyssey*, 50

Menstruation: Aristotle on, 191-192; Galen on, 202; Herophilus on, 195; in Hippocratic Corpus, 186-188; Pliny on, 198; Soranus on, 197-198

Mentors, for maidens in Archaic societies, 12-13

MESSALINA, VALERIA, 271, 313; portrait on coin, 317f

METILIA ACTE (priestess of Magna Mater–Cybele), 351, 353; tombstone of, 371, 373f

METILIA, MARCIA, 331

METILIA, RUFINA, 331

Midwives: Athenian women in role of, 109; in Roman Empire, 378, 381f; Soranus on, 196

Mirrors: Etruscan, 245-247, 246f, 257; as religious dedications by aristocratic women during Archaic period in, 36; on tombstones of unmarried women in classical Athens, 83; in vase paintings in classical Athens, 98, 109

Miscarriages, in Roman Republic, 229

Misogyny: in Archaic period, 39-44; and New Comedy, 162

MNESARETE, 97; stele of, 5, 6f, 7-8

Modesty: of Archaic period women, 22; and confinement to women's quarters, 79-80; and virtuous women of Augustan Rome, 318, 319; and women of Roman Empire, 351, 369

MOERO, 163

Money lending, by women of Pompeii, 336

Monuments. *See* Funerary monuments; Steles

Morality: and Augustan marriage laws, 302-306; in Augustan Rome, 294-296; and Hellenistic writers, 169-173; in imperial Rome, and ideal of virtuous women, 314-315, 318-321

Motherhood: authority of, and absence of fathers, 265; and daughters' transition from maidenhood to marriage, 27-33; in Etruscan art, 255-256; in Virgil's *Aeneid*, 299; and women of Roman Republic, 220, 223, 225, 261, 264-265, 291-292, 299, 313. *See also* Childrearing

Mourners. *See* Men, as mourners in Archaic period; Women mourners

MURDIA, eulogy of, 318

Musicians. *See* Entertainers

MYRRHINA (Amazon queen): tomb of, 129

MYRRHINE, on vase painting of funerary scene in Archaic period, 49, 50f

Mysteries of Thesmophoria, 87. *See also* Demeter, mysteries of; Eleusinian mysteries

Mythological imagery, on tombstones of women of Roman Empire, 371, 373f

Naevius, *Tarentilla*, 240

Naming of women, 151-154; avoidance of, 79, 183, 184; in classical Athens, 81-83; and Etruscans, 257f, 258; and mythological names for women at Athenian weddings, 98; in *Partheneia* of Alcman, 60

NAUSICA, 297

NAUSICAA (in Homer's *Odyssey*), 22, 24-25, 26-27

NEAERA, 112, 114-115

NEMESIS (goddess), 36

NEOBOULE (in Archaic period poem), 25-26

Nepos, Cornelius, *Lives of the Foreign Generals*, 281

Nero, 275, 294, 330, 346

Nerva, 363

New Comedy: on females, 169; as source on Hellenistic period women, 162-163; standard plot of, 162-163

"New Woman" of late Roman Republic, vii; Augustus's daughter Julia as, 291-292; compared with Hellenistic period women, 110; at dinner parties, 286-287; love poetry as source on, 281-284, 285-286; number of, 290; and Octavian's legislation, 290; and Ovid's writings, 290-291; sexual behavior of, 284-285; and sexuality and love, 280-281; social forces influencing, 288-292; sources on, 281-282

Nicaea, 159

NICANDRE: kore dedicated to Artemis, 19, 36, 37f

Nonaristocratic women: of Archaic period, 50, 52-53; of Augustan Rome, and ideal of virtue, 319-320; Etruscan, 252, 254-255; in Pompeii, homes of, 340-341; Spartan, 61. *See also* Concubines; Freedwomen; Lower strata women of Roman Empire; Slaves

North Africa, Roman, 215; women of, 361, 363

NOSSIS OF LOCRI (Hellenistic poetess), 165-166, 173

Nudity: and Archaic period korai, 23f; in Athenian vase paintings, 106, 116, 117f, 118f; in Etruscan art, 250, 251-252, 253f, 254f; in Greek art, changes in Hellenistic period, 173-174, 175f, 176-177, 178f; and Italian Greek votive statues, 237; of racing girls at rites of Artemis at Brauron, 85f; and representations of Etruscan married couples, 253f; of Spartan women participating in athletics, 59, 60f, 62

Numa, 225

Nurses: in Archaic period, 29, 52; in Classical Athens, 109

PHRYNE (Praxiteles' mistress), 174
Pietas, 351
Pig women, in Semonides' poem, 42
Pinakes: depicting Persephone and Demeter, 32, 33f; funerary iconography and, 48
PLANCIA MAGNA (priestess, benefactress), 363, 364f
PLANGON, 104, 106f
Plato: on intellectual culture of Spartan women, 60; *Laws*, on Scythian women warriors, 134; *Republic*, 59, 63, 66, 118-121; women students at Academy of, 167
Plautus: *Menaechmi*, 385; *Pot of Gold, The*, 261; *Truculentus*, 385
Plays. *See* Comedies; Drama
Plebeians, and patricians, in early Roman Republic, 230-232
Pliny the Elder, 93; *Natural History*, 168; on power of menstrual blood, 198; on Roman statues of women, 220; on shrine of Vesta, 235; on statue of Cloelia, 220, 222
Pliny the Younger, 304, 354; *Letters*, 349-350, 360-361, 367, 383; *Panegyric*, 348, 350; on Plotina, 354; quoted, 348, 349, 360, 367, 383; on women writers, 324, 349
PLOTINA (wife of Trajan), 349, 350, 352-353, 354, 364, 367; letters to Hadrian, 353; portrait on coins, 346, 347f, 348, 351, 352f; and title of Augusta, 351; travels with Trajan, 353
Plutarch: *Advice to Bride and Groom*, 367; *Antony*, 136, 274-275; on Clea, 365; *Cleomenes*, 150; description of Cleopatra, 136; on education of women, 367; interest in status of women, 74; *Life of Lycurgus*, 58, 62-63; on Lycurgan constitution, 64; *Numa*, 236-237; on Octavia, 274-275; *On the Bravery of Women*, 365, 390-391; *On Isis and Osiris*, 365; *On the Virtues of Women*, 271; *Pericles*, 78; *Pompey*, 272; quotations purported to be words of Spartan women, 63-64; on religious role of women, 95; *Roman Questions*, 220; *Romulus*, 28; *Sayings of Spartan Women*, 63-64; as source on Hellenistic period women, 144; as source on Spartan women, 57; on Sparta's decline in fourth century, 64-65; *Theseus*, 129; on Vestal Virgins, 236-237; on women mourning for Adonis, 77-78
Poetry: as source on Archaic period women, 10, 11, 12; as source on Classical period women, 69-74; as source on Spartan women, 56-57; as source on Hellenistic period women, 140; as source on "New Woman," 280-281. *See also* Love poetry; Poets
Poets: Hellenistic, as source of information on Hellenistic women, 141-144; Hellenistic women, 163-167; Spartan women, 60
Poisoning: Roman women accused of, 228; teachers of art of, 384
Political role: of empresses, 352-353; of Roman women, 230-232, 272-273; of wealthy women, 363, 368; of women of Pompeii, 337

Polybius, 150, 219; on wealth of Roman women, 262
Pompeii: (ch. 12), 330-344; erotic paintings in brothels and houses of, 322; general view of, 331f; preservation of, as source of information on Roman women, 212-213, 330-331. *See also* Women of Pompeii
Pompey, 272, 275
POPPAEA SABINA (wife of Nero), 331
PORCIA, 271, 390
PORRIMA (goddess), 230
Poseidippus, *Hermaphroditus*, 162
POSTVERTA, 230
"Pouting girl, the" (Kore), 19, 20f
PRAECIA, 271
Praise and blame themes: in Archaic period art and literature, 10-11, 26-27; in Homeric poems, 39; and ideal of virtuous women in Augustan Rome, 315-321; and Lucretia myth, 225-227; and named women of Roman Empire, 211; and nonaristocratic women, 50, 52-53; and Spartan women, 56, 63
PRAXILLA, 163
PRAXINOA (in Theocritus's *Odes*), 142-144
Praxiteles, statue of Aphrodite at Cnidos, 173-174, 175f, 176
Pregnancy, in Hippocratic Corpus, 186. *See also* Childbirth
PREPONTIS, CLAUDIA, 320, 321f
Priestesses, 215, 334, 341, 371, 382, 384; of Classical Athenian cults, 93-96; in Roman Empire, 362-363, 365; in Hellenistic period, 151; naming of, in Classical Athens, 81; statuette from Ephesus, 34, 35f; taking of "professional" names by, 95. *See also* Vestal Virgins
PROCNE (in Sophocles' *Tereus*), 70
Professional women, in Hellenistic period, 140
Prometheus (god), 39, 40
Promiscuity: of Amazons, 133-134; of Julia, 315. *See also* "New Woman"
Propertius, 230, 285; on childbearing, 301; *Elegies*, 276-277, 301, 323; love poetry of, 285-286, 287-288, 323; rejection of military life, 289; resistance to marriage, 289
Prophets, women as, 95
PROSERPINA. *See* LIBERA
Prostitutes: in Classical Athens, types of, 116, 280, 281f; in Classical Athens, vase paintings of, 116, 117f, 118f, 173; and nudity, 23f; in Pompeii, 338, 339f; prohibitions against marrying in Augustan laws, 305; quasi-, in Roman law, 380; in Roman Empire, impact on marriage and divorce, 211, 259, 280, 300, 305, 380; in Roman Republic, 232, 270
Provinces, Roman. *See* Africa, Asia Minor, Bithynia, Britain, Dacia, Egypt, Germany, Greece, Phrygia, Syria
Prudery: in early Roman Republic, 228, 239; of Greek and Roman historians, and attitudes toward Etruscan women, 245